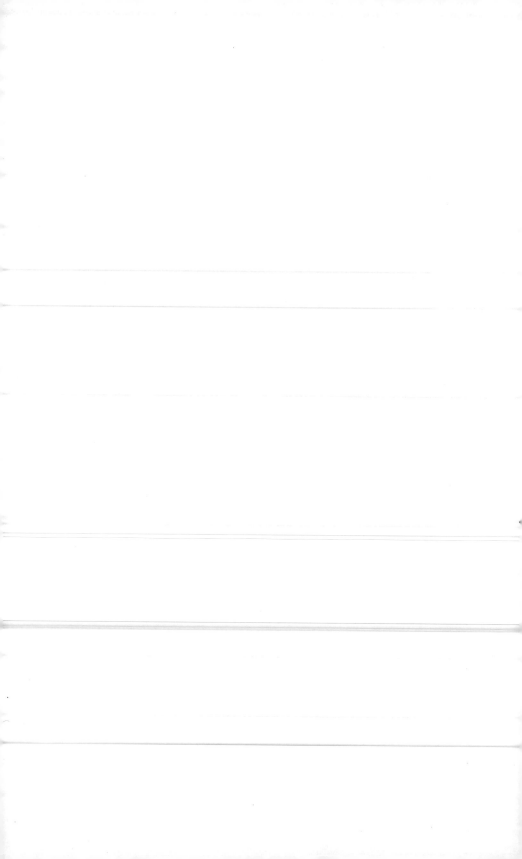

Maestros in America

Conductors in the 21st Century

Roderick L. Sharpe
Jeanne Koekkoek Stierman

THE SCARECROW PRESS, INC.
Lanham, Maryland • Toronto • Plymouth, UK
2008

SCARECROW PRESS, INC.

Published in the United States of America by Scarecrow Press, Inc.
A wholly owned subsidary of
The Rowman & Littlefield Publishing Group, Inc.
4501 Forbes Boulevard, Suite 200, Lanham, Maryland 20706
www.scarecrowpress.com

Estover Road
Plymouth PL6 7PY
United Kingdom

British Library Cataloguing in Publication Information Available

Library of Congress Cataloging-in-Publication Data

Sharpe, Roderick L., 1945–
    Maestros in America : conductors in the 21st century / Roderick L. Sharpe, Jeanne Koekkoek Stierman.
        p. cm.
    Includes bibliographical references, discographies, and index.
    Adams, John—Alsop, Marin—Amado, David—Ansbacher, Charles—Baker, Robert Hart—Barenboim, Daniel—Barra, Donald—Bay, Peter—Beck, Crafton—Ben-Dor, Gisèle—Bjaland, Leif—Blomstedt, Herbert—Bond, Victoria—Botstein, Leon—Brott, Boris—Brown, Justin—Bychkov, Semyon—Christie, Michael—Conlon, James—Cooper, Grant—Cumming, Edward—Davies, Dennis Russell—Davis, Andrew—Deal, Karen Lynne—Delfs, Andreas—DePreist, James—Diemecke, Enrique Arturo—Dohnanyi, Christoph von—Eschenbach, Christoph—Falletta, JoAnn—Farberman, Harold—Figueroa, Guillermo—Foster, Lawrence—Freeman, Paul—Gilbert, Alan—Gittleman, Neal—Graf, Hans—Hanson, George—Harth-Bedoya, Miguel—Hege, Daniel—Ioannides, Sarah—Itkin, David—Jackson, Isaiah—Jansons, Mariss—Järvi, Kristjan—Järvi, Neeme—Järvi, Paavo—Jean, Kenneth—Kahane, Jeffrey—Kalmar, Carlos—Kreizberg, Yakov—Lane, Louis—Levine, James—Levine, Joel—Ling, Jahja—Litton, Andrew—Llewellyn, Grant—Lockhart, Keith—Lockington, David—Loebel, David—
    ISBN-13: 978-0-8108-6022-3 (hardcover : alk. paper)
    ISBN-10: 0-8108-6022-8 (hardcover : alk. paper)
    1. Conductors (Music)—United States—Biography. I. Stierman, Jeanne Koekkoek. II. Title.
ML402.S405 2008
784.2092'273—dc22   [B]   2007049738

Contents

Preface

Orchestral conductors occupy a broad swath of music history. The modern concept of the conductor dates from around the turn of the nineteenth century, and any book claiming to be a comprehensive history would need to be either very long or very concise. In conductor documentation, one approach has been to focus on the towering few while largely ignoring the majority of worthy individuals practicing their craft. On the other hand, a comprehensive directory-style volume of biographical facts would be a useful reference tool but not make for very stimulating reading. Our approach has been to provide short biographical and critical essays and to impose certain parameters to make our work both manageable and meaningful. We have limited inclusion to three categories: people born in the U.S., naturalized U.S. citizens, and foreign conductors holding a permanent appointment in the U.S. Limiting the book to only the first two categories would have presented a distorted picture of professional orchestral activity in the U.S. due to the high proportion of noncitizens occupying the podiums of orchestras, especially at the higher levels. In addition, all individuals included had to have been active as conductors at the start of the new millennium. Thus, we claim that this book is about American conductors and conductors in America in the twenty-first century. If such a date smacks of gimmickry, it serves as well as any other to impose realistic limits on our endeavors. Indeed, the millennial marker (01/01/2001) also acts as a buffer between what has been and what may likely come to be in the orchestral and operatic fields in the new century. At that date, certain individuals were coming to the end of long and distinguished careers with roots in an even earlier age, while others were just setting out. In providing a collection of sketches of individuals currently or recently practicing the conductor's art, we hope to provide insight into the state of orchestral music-making in the U.S. as it is, has been, and may become.

We included all the music directors of the top three tiers, based on each orchestra's budget, of member institutions published by the American

Symphony Orchestra League (which changed its name to The League of American Orchestras in January of 2008) in the January 2006 issue of *Symphony* magazine—please see appendix B for a list of these orchestras and their tiers. Most internationally known American conductors not holding permanent appointments in the U.S. at that date were also included, as were distinguished foreign conductors who had held and then relinquished music directorships with American orchestras between 2001 and 2006. In addition, we included a few conductors from less wealthy orchestras whom we felt demonstrated special merit (e.g., Benjamin Zander) and several upcoming female conductors to provide a fairer gender balance.

Each entry is a biographical essay containing the essential facts of the conductor's birth, education, and career. In addition, we have included assessment and commentary gleaned from articles, interviews, reviews, and, in some cases, personal observation. It was our intention to present as rounded and fair-minded a portrait of each artist as possible. We tried to allow for the fact that critics can be biased and conductors can be caught on a night when either they or their orchestras are in less than top form. The length of essay varies with the eminence of the conductors, which is more or less determined by their reputation and the standing of the orchestras with which they work. Another factor is that much more information about top-level artists is available. Thus, a conductor of one of the so-called Big Five orchestras (an oft-disputed designation that refers to the New York PO, Boston SO, Chicago SO, Cleveland O, and Philadelphia O) gets much more space than the music director of a third-tier regional orchestra. As we discuss more fully in the introduction, all the artists included in this book are remarkable and highly gifted individuals.

We have adopted a number of conventions throughout the book. Names appearing in bold are cross-references to a separate entry for that person. Institutions mentioned frequently are always abbreviated, thus *The Met* for *The Metropolitan Opera*, *Harvard* for *Harvard University*, and *Juilliard* for *The Juilliard School of Music*. We have used the abbreviations U.S. for United States, SO for Symphony Orchestra, PO for Philharmonic Orchestra, CO for Chamber Orchestra, YO for Youth Orchestra, YSO for Youth Symphony Orchestra, and so on. Within each entry, we refer to, say, the Buffalo PO at its initial appearance and the BPO subsequently.

The annotations appended to each entry consist of *Further Reading* and *Selected Recordings*. In the latter category, we have limited choices to five or fewer. In terms of conductors who have made many hundreds of recordings, this is unfortunately a rather inadequate sampling. What we have tried to do is provide a representative selection that relates to the previous text. Thus, they are *selected* as opposed to *recommended* recordings, although they are in-tended to show the practitioner in the most favorable light. The recordings are mostly in CD format, but occasionally video recordings (DVDs) were se-lected as being particularly apropos. We have tried to provide recordings and videos that are currently obtainable via the Web. The citations for *Further Reading* are almost all in English. The exceptions are marked as such and were included as being particularly relevant and without an English equivalent.

In compiling this book, we are greatly indebted to the resources provided by Western Illinois University Libraries and the following student assistants: Liz Hornbaker, Becky Parmer, and Stacy Ervin. We reserve special thanks for Chrissy Wainwright, who helped set up the project and worked on the ini-tial research. Our thanks also extend to Alan Blyth and John Canarina for providing valuable insight, suggestions, and encouragement. We also express our deep appreciation for the patience, understanding, and assistance of Dan and Krista, our respective spouses.

Introduction

Conductors exhibit a unique set of skills and abilities, some of which can be developed and others of which seem to be innate.[1] The biographical sketches that follow document some of these highly talented individuals, whose necessary qualities include acute hearing, vivid musical imagination, phenomenal memory, charisma, and effective communication skills. The act of conducting requires its practitioners to anticipate and signal what is about to happen through gesture and body language, while at the same time monitor what they are actually hearing. Conductors take inspiration from what they conceive to be the composer's intentions, gleaned, usually, from the printed score, but influenced by a familiarity with performance practice and their own musical experience.[2] They seek to realize their conception in private study and propagate their vision during the rehearsal process, leading to a performance, or series of performances, which will be faithful, inspirational, and moving to players and listeners alike—or else preserve in archival form (recording) the most intense thoughts of which they are capable at that particular time. Great conductors have the ability to grasp the architectural span of a piece of music as a whole, in which individually crafted musical gestures combine to form an integral whole. When conductors achieve the status of music director, they may be responsible for planning not only individual programs but also entire seasons, consulting with administrators and agents about which soloists and guest conductors to invite, often several years in advance.[3] In addition, they are increasingly expected to be cultural icons, social schmoozers, and fundraisers for their constituencies, roles some relish and others do not.[4]

Unlike their instrumental and vocal colleagues, novice conductors get little opportunity to practice their art. In Europe the traditional route to the podium has been to progress through the ranks of provincial opera houses, starting out as a *repetiteur* coaching singers and becoming intimately acquainted with the standard operatic repertoire through daily hands-on experience. In the U.S., conductors have tended to be the product of academia, gaining as much experience as they can through student, youth, and community orchestras. The enterprising ones will form their own groups, often focusing on contemporary music. Others have emerged from the ranks of orchestral musicians, observing many conductors at work and appraising their strengths and weaknesses. The next step is to secure a position as an assistant conductor to some orchestra, hoping to impress through the opportunities to conduct pops, educational, and family concerts, with the possibility that, should the maestro one day be "indisposed," he or she can step up at short notice and make a big impression.[5]

Competitions are another vehicle that traditionally has been a step-up in the profession. Many of the individuals featured in this book, both native and foreign, have been successful contestants, and winning has bolstered their careers.[6] It is also true, though, that some winners of these same events are rarely heard of again. Conducting competitions wax and wane: the two most famous, the Mitropoulos and the Stokowski, both based in New York City, petered out, and the ill-fated Maazel/Vilar barely established itself before its unseemly demise. Realizing the transient nature of even the most famous of these, attempts to provide training opportunities of a more substantial nature have been made. Most prominent of these was the Exxon/Arts Endowment program, which apprenticed young conductors to leading orchestras such as the Pittsburgh and National SOs, giving them exposure and mentoring over several years. Similar opportunities have been supplied by Michael Tilson **Thomas**'s New World Symphony, the American Symphony Orchestra League's Conductors Guild and Conducting Fellows Program, the Los Angeles Philharmonic Institute, Leonard **Slatkin**'s National Conducting Institute, the Aspen Music Festival's American Academy of Conducting, and, of course, many years of summer school programs for conductors at Tanglewood.

However, exposure and success too soon may have drawbacks for promising conductors faced with inflated expectations and lacking sufficient basic experience or knowledge of the repertoire. Novices are obliged to take on heavy schedules involving a good deal of rushing about in order to seize every available opportunity, which may result in premature burnout. Add to this the fickleness of a public seeking out the next sensational wunderkind, and it is hardly surprising that some fall by the wayside or fail to live up to their initial promise. The difficulty of bridging the gap between the conservatory and professional life is one of the factors that discourage the promotion of native-born talent. Another is simply bias. Orchestra boards, promoters, and the public view a (sometimes inferior) foreigner—especially one with an exotic name—as more of a box office draw than an equally talented or superior American. Marin **Alsop**, who has had to contend with the additional gender bias, states, "It doesn't appear that America strives to nurture and promote its own talent."[7] One can only marvel that conductors with ordinary-sounding names like John **Nelson** or David **Robertson** have done so well!

The increase in the number and quality of American orchestras, thanks to the wealth of talented instrumentalists being produced by music schools and universities over recent decades, has provided increasing opportunities for the aspiring American conductor. Many have achieved distinction among the second- and third-tier orchestras (whose performance standards often rival those of the so-called top tier). Writing in 1982, Roger Dettmer identified fifty or so American conductors employed by leading regional orchestras, most prominently, then, **Previn** in Pittsburgh, **Slatkin** in St. Louis, and **Zinman** in Rochester.[8] In a 1990 piece, Donal Henahan argued that boards should be duty bound to choose native conductors even if it resulted in a temporary lowering of standards, in the belief that sooner or later a crop of Leonard Bernsteins would surely emerge.[9] The success of Michael Tilson **Thomas**, Andrew **Litton**, Steven **Sloane**, David **Robertson**, and Marin **Alsop** would tend to support that forecast. Writing about **Thomas**'s success in San Francisco, Anthony Tommasini suggested that in view of the myriad extracurricular activities the music director is required to perform, "American orchestras would do better having energetic musicians (ideally Americans) in charge day to day and to bring in the eminent masters, Europeans or otherwise, as invaluable guests."[10] However, there is still a tendency for boards and management at lower levels to opt for foreign talent, thereby perpetuating a long-standing anti-U.S. bias. Music director search committees, even when they include representation from the players and audience, are usually dominated by managers and administrators whose approach is based on their business experience and who find it hard to make decisions based purely on artistic merit and potential. At the time of writing (2006), a survey of the country's top forty orchestras found that fourteen (35%) conductors qualified as "Americans" (including Lorin **Maazel**, who was actually born in Paris, and Paavo **Järvi**, an Estonian-born, naturalized U.S. citizen).[11] Of the rest, six orchestras were led by Germans, five by Britons, two each by Austrians and Finns, and one each by an Argentinian/Israeli, a Swiss, a Brazilian, a Mexican, a Peruvian, and an Indonesian. Of the traditionally labeled "Big Five" orchestras (Boston, Chicago, Cleveland, New York, Philadelphia), two were led by Americans (Lorin **Maazel** and James **Levine**), the highest percentage ever. A recent preconcert survey of Baltimore SO patrons during the orchestra's director search revealed a very low preference for leadership by an

American conductor. In the event, the poorly handled appointment of Marin **Alsop** in 2005 was a momentous and controversial snafu in which bias, both national and gender, played a role. Cultural snobbery and a harking back to a golden age of the maestro, epitomized by the likes of Toscanini, Szell, Reiner, Stokowski, and Walter, with only Bernstein rivaling foreign dominance, has resulted in a mindset that only foreigners can really be any good. Indeed, despite Bernstein's breakthrough at the New York PO, the hope that this precedent would open up top orchestral posts to native talent went largely unfulfilled; what may have been anticipated as a flood proved to be no more than a trickle.

Bernstein also did the lion's share of mentoring. After abandoning his role as musical evangelist to the American man-and-woman in the street, he devoted his considerable pedagogical prowess to nurturing young talent. The roster of his protégés includes a number of the individuals featured in this book, among them Michael Tilson **Thomas**, Marin **Alsop**, Eiji **Oue**, Justin **Brown**, Uri **Segal**, and Michael **Stern**. One must also acknowledge the contributions of teacher/conductors the likes of Pierre Monteux, Max Rudolf, Harold **Farberman**, Gunther Schuller, and Jorge **Mester**. In academia the names of Jean Morel, Otto-Werner Mueller, Sixten Ehrling, and Gustav Meier frequently occur in the résumés of the artists contained in this book.

There is a natural rhythm to the stages of a music director appointment: selection of a shortlist of candidates, tryouts, appointment, honeymoon period, maturation with satisfaction or disillusionment, resignation/retirement—and the cycle begins over again.[12] The mystique surrounding the hiring has been likened to a mating ritual in which conductors and orchestras sniff each other out, so to speak. The process may take, on average, two to three years, or even as long as five in some instances.[13] As Bernard Holland observed: "Symphonic matrimony is rarely for life and not always for love."[14] Or, to hear some tell it, the whole process is fixed by shadowy agents and managers manipulating the interested parties like pawns in a glorified chess game.[15] The pundits have engaged in much soul-searching speculation as to what constitutes a good fit. There is still a sense that the constituency involved in the selection process (one hopes reflecting the views of the players, the management, the artists' agents, and the audience) tends to play it safe, valuing caution and tradition over challenge and innovation. In weighing risk vs. no-risk, the conservative faction can point to a number of instances when a bolder choice back-fired.[16] In general, the feeling is that it is better to opt for the tried and tested for music director (what Norman Lebrecht, in typically acerbic fashion, characterized as those who are "punctual, polite, and infinitely practical—which explains the deadly tedium at the heart of concert life"[17]) and invite the firebrand as a guest. Not wanting to offend or alarm the existing, albeit aging and diminishing, audience is an important consideration at a time when orchestras are more than ever dependent on box-office receipts because the revenue stream from recording contracts has dried up, the draw of superstar conductors has diminished, and the economic and political climate has led to a reduction of sponsorship and subsidy. On the other hand, progressive or struggling management teams see the need for innovation and rejuvenation of the kind that a gifted young conductor with good communication skills can bring in order to attract a potential clientele.[18] Another factor in selection is the tendency to appoint a successor with an opposite temperament or outlook to the most recent incumbent: **Zinman** succeeded by **Termirkanov** in Baltimore, **Slatkin** by **Vonk** in Saint Louis, and de Waart by **Oue** in Minnesota are obvious examples.

The early years of the new millennium saw a remarkable opportunity to evaluate the selection process due to an unprecedented spate of vacancies on podiums in the U.S. and around the world. This unusual coincidence generated a plethora of metaphors such as "seismic shift," "changing of the guard," "baton revolution," and "domino effect." The departures of **Ozawa** (Boston), von **Dohnanyi** (Cleveland), **Masur** (New York), and **Sawallisch** (Philadelphia) indicated a major generational shift. Rather than heralding an era of unadulterated innovation, the dozen or more vacancies that arose and were filled in North America resulted in an interesting mix of conservative and progressive choices. The wealthier and more venerable institutions tended to take a more cautious approach: **Maazel**[19] to New York, **Eschenbach** to Philadelphia, and **Levine** to Boston. In the mildly controversial choice of **Welser-Möst** to lead in Cleveland, the orchestra adhered to a belief, still prevalent especially among older players, that Austro-German conductors represent the authority and tradition that safeguards the core repertory. The leading second-tier orchestras made more adventurous choices, even providing opportunity to a couple of the younger generation of indigenous talent: **Spano** in Atlanta and **Robertson** in Saint Louis. For the rest, the move of Paavo **Järvi** to Cincinnati, Mario **Venzago** to Indianapolis, and Osmo **Vänskä** to Minnesota ushered in a new and exciting generation of Europeans. The orchestras of Houston and Milwaukee were perhaps looking for a happy medium by appointing two relatively young Europeans: Hans **Graf**, an Austrian, and Andreas **Delfs**, a German, respectively.

Personalities aside, the approach and attitude of conductors are constantly evolving. The tyrannical maestro epitomized by Toscanini, Szell, and Reiner would not be tolerated by today's musicians. Nor would the following generation's maestro mystique, typified by Bernstein, Solti, and Karajan, who, as figureheads of their respective record companies, enjoyed iconic status. The jet-setting superstar ensconced on his pedestal is human, and exceptional prowess in a field such as conducting does not necessarily make for a well-rounded or even appealing personality. In mythology, the hero is often fatally flawed; this is true of conductors too, as Norman Lebrecht showed in his book *The Maestro Myth* by exposing the soft underbellies of some of the twentieth century's major figures.[20] Addressing the Conductors Guild in 1993, Kurt **Masur**, the recently appointed music director of the New York PO, spoke about orchestral music-making as "a creative partnership between conductor and orchestra."[21] This *primus inter pares* model is one frequently espoused in the biographical portraits that follow. Players and conductors are frequently on first name terms, and, with mutual respect established, there is less of the blind deference shown to conductors than was the norm thirty years ago. For their part, conductors are more willing to allow players' ideas to shape and mold performances.

Managing a professional symphony orchestra is highly complex and expensive to boot. The inherent fiduciary dilemma of orchestras and arts organizations in general was identified as long ago as 1966 by two Princeton professors.[22] Their main thesis, Baumol's Cost Disease as it came to be known, claims orchestras will always be chasing their tails because their output can never keep up with costs that persistently rise at a rate higher than inflation. And if their "product" becomes less appealing to the market (audiences, charitable foundations, local and national government funding agencies, etc.)—which seems to have been the case over recent decades—this has to be offset by aggressive marketing, innovation, and high ticket prices. This economic "flaw" affects labor relations and repertoire choices, among other factors. Just as the orchestral world saw extensive changes in leadership in the early years of the twenty-first century, so also was there a marked increase in the number of orchestras in financial straits and/or involved in acrimonious labor disputes with their musicians. The dysfunctional collective bargaining process led to a number of strikes/lockouts,[23] and the increasing financial pressures due to economic and political factors in the environment at large resulted in many orchestras amassing sizeable deficits and, inevitably, a number of bankruptcies.

The latter half of the twentieth century saw a rapid expansion in the number of orchestras because there was a large pool of talented instrumentalists in the post–World War II boom.[24] As recovery continued, many communities beyond the Northeast and the West Coast were eager to present themselves to the world as cultured and sophisticated. The acquisition of a symphony orchestra served as a marker. Horowitz quotes a study from 1939 which claims that the number of orchestras had grown from 17, pre–World War I, to 270.[25] Dettmer's 1982 article identifies 72 first- and second-tier orchestras compared with 15 in 1943.[26] Describing the increase in opportunity that orchestras of the second and third tiers should be providing to young American conductors, a 1989 *Newsweek* article states that there were 161 such then in existence compared with 63 twenty years earlier (an increase of 155 percent).[27] Clearly, the twentieth century witnessed exponential growth in the number of concerts given by orchestras across the U.S. In the peak year of 2000 they attracted audiences totaling 32 million, generating revenue of $1.27 billion. At the same time, orchestras nationwide were experiencing financial strains. Between 1980 and 2000 at least six orchestras went bankrupt, although four of these were later resuscitated. ASOL (The American Symphony Orchestra League) claims a membership of around 1,800 orchestras currently operating in the U.S. (2006), broken down into eight categories by budget. They range from full-time salaried, to part-time professional pay-per-service, collegiate, community, and youth orchestras.

Conductors operate upon the broader canvas of live orchestral concertizing. It is hardly necessary to point out that they don't produce any sound of their own. The health of the musical environment in which they operate is vital to their artistic survival and prosperity. It may just be coincidence, but the turn of the new millennium precipitated one of classical music's periodic crises, and an apparently serious one. Unforeseen events, notably those of September 11, 2001, and the dot-com bust, seemed to combine with cultural trends to deliver a severe body blow. The deteriorating economy in the early years of the new century affected the principal pillars of financial support on which orchestras had increasingly come to depend: grants and contributions from corporations and wealthy donors. But other more endemic problems seem to lie within the classical music business itself. These problems include the aging and diminishing of audiences, further marginalization of the genre in the culture at large, reduction of music curriculum in public schools, and a string of orchestras in financial crisis leading to labor unrest between players and management. Add to these difficulties rapacious agents and the growing discrepancy between what star conductors and rank-and-file musicians get paid, spiraling ticket prices, the failure to endear audiences to the product of contemporary composers, and an increasing sense of classical music as a museum art mired in ritualistic and archaic conventions. These are generalizations, of course, and there are many notable instances of individuals and orchestras introducing innovation and outreach to stem the decline. The following essays reveal many conductors who are deeply concerned about the future of classical music and how to assure its survival.

The cellist Julian Lloyd Webber, writing in 2002, claimed that classical music as a profession had changed more in the recent four or five years than in all the previous thirty.[28] He added: "musicians—and everyone else involved in classical music—have been forced to step outside their comfort zones and discover reality." In adapting, orchestras face a dilemma, it seems. They can either maintain an archival role as custodians of the great orchestral masterpieces or they can metamorphose into what Pierre Boulez has labeled "ensembles of possibilities" that incorporate the flexibility of cross-cultural, cross-media presentations exploiting more fragmented formats, often in nontraditional venues. At the risk of "falling between two stools," they can try to do both. One of the most wholeheartedly innovative approaches in the U.S. has been Houston's Orchestra X, founded in 1997, the brainchild of dynamic, if eccentric, conductor John Axelrod, who attempted to present classical music (Beethoven, indeed!) in an "interactive, multicultural, multi-disciplinary, almost confrontational environment that still preserves the integrity of the music." Similar efforts have been conducted by Jonathan **Sheffer**, first with the Eos Orchestra (1995–2004) and then, since 2001, with Red {an orchestra}. But whichever route orchestras choose, they run the risk of alienating their existing (if diminishing) audience and/or failing to attract a new one, which could likely spell doom in the short term. Too often, repertoire choices are driven with an eye to the bottom line. Most believe that if orchestras do not present a substantial menu of the traditional and familiar, audiences will quickly dissipate.

This dilemma is being addressed in a variety of ways. One is the effort didactically inclined conductors are making to increase the audience's comfort zone through preconcert, or preperformance explications.[29] Musical educators such as conductor/composer Rob Kapilow continue to evangelize for classical music with presentations that seek to shatter any mystique and make the listening experience meaningful to diverse audiences. Reevaluating cultural relevancy within communities is another priority. Recently, Esa-Pekka **Salonen** was praised for helping make the Los Angeles PO "the hippest, hottest cultural ticket in town." Themed concerts or even entire seasons have become a very common approach. Adapting to twenty-first century lifestyles is another requirement. Concerts have become more casual, with flexible scheduling to include such concepts as early evening "commuter concerts." To attract audiences from a wider demographic, orchestras must divest themselves of the aura of snobbism and reduce ticket prices to realistic levels. As the provision of music education in the public schools has declined, orchestras have stepped in to fill the void with alliances, workshops, and special performances. It seems that the ears of younger generations are somewhat more attuned to moderately atonal contemporary music familiar to them from film soundtracks and other media than to the standard classical repertory. Orchestras are beginning to exploit modern technology to enhance not only concert promotion but the actual listening experience. Some have installed "Big Screens" for interactive presentations and close-ups of performers, in effect combining the live and TV concert experience. A couple of California geeks devised the Concert Companion, a hand-held electronic device that provides a real-time commentary as the music is performed. Michael **Christie** has devised something similar that he calls *Keeping Score*. Orchestras have also seized on technology to provide opportunities for downloading their performances. The classical music world was heartened to learn that 1.37 million people had taken advantage of a free download of all nine Beethoven symphonies offered by the BBC. Classical music downloads continue to grow significantly, accounting for 12 percent of the market in 2006 compared with 3–4 percent of sales in stores. Most encouraging was the agreement, signed in August 2006, between forty-eight classical music institutions and the American Federation of Musicians to implement a new fee payment structure that allows recording and distribution of live performances. Orchestras are seeking out viable niches for themselves within the cultural environment. Smaller regional orchestras, for example, are looking to find an identity and programming that is not in direct competition with more prestigious orchestras in the same region. Such schemes as Composer in Residence and dedicated series such as the Chicago SO's MusicNOW and the Pacific SO's American Composers Festival are attempting to attract audiences for contemporary music.

Perhaps the greatest challenge that classical music faces is the listening experience itself. Very few people in the U.S. have cause to listen to music in a more than superficial way. The music that they ubiquitously hear in stores, restaurants, elevators, and the like is nothing but sound wallpaper filling an aural void. When people go to live rock concerts the atmosphere is charged with spectacle and euphoria, and the required aural attention span is rarely stretched to more than a few minutes at a time. The intense kind of concentrated, disciplined, and prolonged listening that has become the tradition at orchestra concerts is quite alien to most people. It wasn't always so, of course. Eighteenth- and nineteenth-century concerts and soirees were not the pious and well-mannered affairs that they are today. Although a class of listeners that C. P. E. Bach described as "connoisseurs and amateurs" has always existed, it wasn't until well into the nineteenth century that the hallowed reverence and expectations of at least reasonable listening behavior from audiences became the norm. Why? The perception of music changed.

People understood that music, by its very nature, was complex and could be perceived and understood on a number of levels. One of the principal elements for its complexity is the dichotomy between its Apollonian (head/intellect) and Dionysian (heart/passion) elements. In his book *Flow*, Mihaly Csikszentmihalyi has expounded his belief that it is in complexity that we experience our most fulfilling states of mind.[30] This helps explain why, when one "gets" it, classical music becomes so totally absorbing, enthralling, and necessary. Bearing this in mind, we have to be cautious about innovations that, in trying to broaden classical music's appeal, undermine or devalue its essential nature. Classical music is never going to be an easy sell because it demands so much from its listeners. The audience (often without realizing it) is a vital component in what Benjamin Britten described as "this holy triangle of composer, performer, and listener" that is the very heart of live music-making.

If orchestras need to adapt to survive, so be it. But that they continue to play a vital, if marginal, role in American culture is essential. Any classical music enthusiast can stay at home and listen to the gamut of Western art music in high fidelity on an iPod to his/her heart's content, but there is no substitute for the shared concert experience. Orchestras must continue to provide the outlet for some of the finest manifestations of the human spirit of the past 200–300 years. As Michael Tilson **Thomas** has said recently, it is an art form which "like no other . . . unflinchingly looks at life as it actually is, as we actually feel it!"[31]

Notes

1. For a discussion of these factors see "A Dialogue on Conductor Training," *Symphony Magazine*, December 1984, 40–42+.

2. Conductors are not infrequently composers themselves (e.g., Yakov **Kreizberg**, David **Robertson**, Esa-Pekka **Salonen**, Michael Tilson **Thomas**, Osmo **Vänskä**) and sometimes work closely with composers in preparing contemporary works (e.g., Semyon **Bychkov**).

3. For an excellent description of the many facets and expectations of the modern conductor see JoAnn **Falletta**, "The Compleat Music Director," *Symphony*, November–December 2002, 40–43.

4. In a 1997 *Financial Times* (May 31) interview, Andrew **Litton**, music director of the Dallas SO, claimed: "Only 40 per cent of my job is music: the rest is PR."

5. See, for example, Donald **Runnicles** deputizing for **Levine**, Esa-Pekka **Salonen** for **Thomas**, Gisèle **Ben-Dor** for **Maazel**, and Semyon **Bychkov** for almost everyone.

6. Examples include James **DePreist** (Mitropoulos), Yakov **Kreizberg** (Stokowski), and abroad, Hans **Graf** (Karl Böhm), and Neeme **Järvi** (Besançon).

7. Benjamin Ivry, "Musical Chairs," *Christian Science Monitor*, 23 February 2001, 9.

8. Roger Dettmer, "The State of US Conductors," *Fanfare*, September–October 1982, 85–86.

9. "America Still Shuns Americans," *New York Times*, 4 November 1990, sec 2, 27.

10. "A Pied Piper Lures San Franciscans into Concerts," *New York Times*, 22 June 1999.

11. Based on the categories of member orchestras by budget in the January–February 2006 edition of *Symphony*.

12. Such cycles may vary in length anywhere from three to more than twenty-five years.

13. John von Rhein, "The Search for Maestro Right," *Chicago Tribune*, 13 August 2006, Arts & Entertainment, 1.

14. "Matchmaking; or How Conductors and Orchestras Get Together," *New York Times*, 5 May 1998.

15. "It was said to be impossible to obtain a baton in the United States without the imprimatur of Ronald Wilford of Columbia Arts Management Inc." Stephen Fay, *The Independent* (London), 17 October 1999.

16. Eije **Oue**'s appointment in Minnesota being a case in point.

17. "How to Choose a Music Director," *The Daily Telegraph* (London), 18 June 2001.

18. For example, the appointments of Michael **Christie** at the Colorado Music Festival, Christopher **Wilkins** in San Antonio (Tex.), Robert **Spano** in Atlanta (Ga.), Miguel **Harth-Bedoya** in Fort Worth (Tex.), and Daniel **Hege** in Syracuse (N.Y.). A particular example would be the appointment of the relatively unknown Keith **Lockhart** to the Boston Pops.

19. Another prevalent notion, not without foundation, is that, like fine wine, conductors improve with age.

20. Norman Lebrecht, *The Maestro Myth* (New York: Citadel Press, 2001).

21. Kurt **Masur**, "Conductors, Orchestras and Society: A Contemporary View," *Journal of the Conductor's Guild* 13, no. 1 (1992): 22–32.

22. William J. Baumol and William G. Bowen, *Performing Arts, the Economic Dilemma* (New York: Twentieth Century Fund, 1966).

23. Two of the ugliest being Saint Louis (2005) and Louisville (2006).

24. This was due, in no small measure, to the influx of highly accomplished refugees escaping the conflagration in Europe who found work teaching in colleges and universities across this country.

25. Joseph Horowitz, *Classical Music: A History of Its Rise and Fall* (New York: W. W. Norton, 2005), 397.

26. Dettmer, "The State of US Conductors."

27. "Lenny's Kids Leap Forward," *Newsweek*, 20 February 1989, 60.

28. Julian Lloyd Webber, "Why I Was Wrong to Predict Doomsday on Music," *Sunday Telegraph* (London), 8 September 2002, 11.

29. See, for example, the entries for Christopher **Seaman,** David **Robertson,** Michael Tilson **Thomas,** Leonard **Slatkin,** Benjamin **Zander,** and David **Zinman.**

30. Mihaly Csikszentmihalyi, *Flow: The Psychology of Optimal Experience* (New York: Harper & Row, 1990).

31. *Keeping Score: MTT on Music,* SFS Media, 2004, DVD.

~

Adams, John (Coolidge)
Born 15 February 1947 in Boston, Massachusetts

Although known primarily as one of the most successful and oft-performed composers of his generation, Adams has also been active as a conductor of his own and others' music. Trained as a clarinetist, he began composition lessons at the age of ten, and he conducted a community orchestra in a work he had written when he was fourteen. He attended Harvard and took composition lessons from Roger Sessions and David Del Tredici, among others. San Francisco became his home in 1971, where he taught at the conservatory and directed the New Music Ensemble. In 1978 he began a long and fruitful association with the San Francisco SO, which premiered a number of his most important compositions: *Harmonium* (1981), *Grand Pianola Music* (1981–82), *Harmonielehre* (1985), and *El Nino* (2000).

His first two operas, *Nixon in China* (1987) and *The Death of Klinghoffer* (1991), treated political themes, not without controversy, and have received many performances worldwide. A New York PO commission, *On the Transmigration of Souls*, is a twenty-five-minute oratorio commemorating the events of 11 September 2001. Other important works include a third opera, *I Was Looking at the Ceiling and Then I Saw the Sky* (1995), *Century Rolls* (1996), *Naïve and Sentimental Music* (1999), and *Guide to Strange Places* (2001). His opuses have been extensively recorded, and he has received numerous honors and awards around the world.

Adams's conducting was furthered by a period as creative chair of the Saint Paul CO (1988–90) and conductor of the Ojai and Cabrillo Music Festivals. Conducting his own compositions alongside those of mainly twentieth-century composers, he has appeared with many of the world's leading orchestras: London SO, BBC SO, Concertgebouw Orchestra, Hallé Orchestra,

1

Berlin SO, Chicago SO, Los Angeles PO, New York PO, Montreal SO, and the Ensemble Moderne. His repertoire includes music by Ives, Debussy, Ravel, Stravinsky, Sibelius, Copland, and Ellington, as well as contemporaries Steve Reich, Philip Glass, and Frank Zappa.

Website
http://www.earbox.com/

Further Reading
Marshall, Ingram. "John Adams on Conducting Ives." In *The John Adams Reader: Essential Writings on an American Composer*, edited by Thomas May, 264–80. Pompton Plains, N.J.: Amadeus, 2006.

Selected Recording
American Elegies: music of Charles Ives, Ingram Marshall, Morton Feldman, John Adams, and David Diamond; Dawn Upshaw (s); Paul Crossley (pf); Orchestra of St. Luke's. Nonesuch 79249-2.

~

Alsop, Marin
Born 16 October 1956 in Manhattan, New York

One of the most prominent and accomplished practitioners of her generation, Alsop must be viewed as a trailblazer and role model for all aspiring female conductors. She has achieved international recognition in this male-dominated profession, appearing with most of the leading orchestras in the U.S. and Europe. With her appointment as principal conductor of the Bournemouth SO in September 2002, she became the first woman to head a leading British orchestra. Her July 2005 appointment to succeed Yuri Temirkanov as music director of the Baltimore SO poked another hole in the glass ceiling that prevents women from rising to the top of the conducting profession. Her success is no fluke, but the result of innate musical ability, initiative, determination, and achievement.

The highly gifted child of professional musicians, her epiphany came at around the age of ten when she was taken to a concert conducted by Leonard Bernstein. She had already been playing the piano since the age of two and violin since age five, and she later studied classical guitar. She entered the precollege division at Juilliard when she was seven, enrolled at Yale at sixteen, and completed her formal education with a master's degree in violin performance from Juilliard in 1978. Her experience as a professional musician was eclectic from the outset, playing session violin and founding *String Fever*, a ten-piece string swing band. The Concordia Orchestra, which performed a mixture of jazz and European music, was formed later, providing an opportunity for her to cut her conducting teeth.

She studied conducting with Carl Bamberger and later with Harold **Farberman**. In 1988 she won the Stokowski Conducting Competition with the American SO and received a Leonard Bernstein Conducting Fellowship to the Tanglewood Music Center, where she worked with Gustav Meier, Seiji **Ozawa**, and Bernstein himself, who proved to be her main guiding influence. As a mentor, he taught her that communicating with musicians and the audience was the key to a successful career. Alsop relates how, in theory, Bernstein encouraged individual expression—which in practice meant conducting the way he did! This same year she became associate conductor of the Richmond (Va.) SO. The following year she won the Koussevitzky Conducting Prize at Tanglewood, and in 1990 she accompanied Bernstein to Japan to assist in the founding of the Pacific Music Festival in Sapporo. Their close association over the next few years, which resulted in her being dubbed his favorite pupil, served to bring Alsop to the public's attention.

Her first permanent directorships came in 1989 with appointments to the Eugene (Ore.) SO and the Long Island (N.Y.) PO. Guest appearances with the Philadelphia Orchestra and the Los Angeles PO followed. She was appointed music director of the Cabrillo Festival, which specialized in contemporary music, in 1991, and her career experienced a major boost with the directorship of the Colorado SO in 1993, a post she was to occupy for ten years. For her work with these organizations she received two commendations from ASCAP for adventurous and imaginative programming.

In the following ten years her reputation expanded exponentially with guest appearances throughout the USA and Europe. She embarked on a recording schedule specializing in works by American composers, including a six-CD collection for Naxos of the orchestral works of Samuel Barber with the Scottish National Orchestra. She became that orchestra's principal guest conductor in 1999, a distinction she also held at the same time with the City of London Sinfonia. She has recorded Tchaikovsky's Fourth Symphony with the Colorado forces and Saint-Saëns with the BBC PO; no doubt other recordings of the standard repertoire will follow. As well as in the UK, where she has regularly conducted the London SO and the London PO, she has appeared in Austria, Germany, France, Holland, Finland, Sweden, Italy, Australia, and Japan. Bernstein's *Candide* with the New York PO is one of a number of her concert performances of opera. She has since moved into the theater to direct *La Traviata, Rigoletto* (English National Opera), and *Nixon in China.*

Such achievements could not have occurred without a good deal of critical acclaim. The critic of the *Daily Telegraph* described her as a conductor who can make a difference and the *Times* commented that since she took over in Bournemouth "each concert has raised the roof higher and higher." Reviewing the second disc in her Barber series, which includes the Cello Concerto and the famous Adagio for Strings, the *BBC Music Magazine* praised her "keen sensitivity" in balancing rhetoric and clarity. Her debut performance with the NYPO for the 1999 Copland Festival was described as "supple, vibrant . . . an impassioned performance." The inaugural disc of a planned Brahms symphony cycle with the London PO (2005) met with universal critical approval, attracting plaudits such as energetic, lithe, deft, spirited, and gracefully pliant. An important aspect of her progress has been her ability to establish rapport with orchestral players, accounting for a considerable portion of her success in overcoming gender prejudice. More surprising and regrettable, then, was the publicly aired furor that greeted her appointment to lead the Baltimore SO. Ostensibly a conflict between the players and management over procedures, communication, and power, the former believed that more time should be taken to assess all likely candidates. This stance may have been justified since most searches take longer than six months, but it may also have been a stalling tactic. Alsop's strong personality, popular appeal, and track record as an advocate for American and contemporary music convinced the Baltimore board that it had found the right person to rejuvenate the orchestra artistically and economically (the orchestra was reportedly suffering a debt of $10–$12 million). Having made up its mind, it excluded the seven-member players' delegation from further deliberation before proceeding to make its rumored decision public. This exclusion provoked a virulent response from the players; an e-mailed memo claimed that the vast majority were opposed to Alsop's appointment "on artistic grounds" and also questioned "her offstage leadership skills." Given her sterling credentials and the fact that she had successfully collaborated with the orchestra as a guest conductor on at least seven previous occasions, this implacable hostility is hard to understand except as the players' resentment of the high-handed attitude of the board, or as a blatant case of gender prejudice—but no one would admit to that. The whole affair, in which Alsop herself played no part other than accepting the post when offered, was a publicity nightmare. One hopes any bad feeling will have dissipated as conductor and orchestra begin their professional relationship (2007), and that together they will find the chemistry to restore the lively, progressive, and innovative reputation the organization enjoyed under David **Zinman**'s directorship.

Website
http://www.marinalsop.com

Further Reading
"Alsop, Marin." In *World Musicians*, edited by Clifford Thompson, 16–17. New York: H. W. Wilson Company, 1999.

Bartleet, Brydie-Leigh. "Re-embodying the Gendered Podium." *Context*, no. 23 (2002): 49–57.

Higgins, Charlotte. "Just Call Me Maestra (Interview with Marin Alsop)." *Guardian* (London), 11 June 2001, 10.

Kellow, Brian. "Marin's Maxims (Interview with Marin Alsop)." *Opera News* 68 (June 2004): 42–43.

Valdes, Lesley. "The Maestra: Myth, Mystique, and Matters of Fact." *Symphony* 50 (July–August 1999): 24–28, 63–64.

Woestendiek, John. "Born to the Baton." *Sun* (Baltimore, Md.), 20 July 2005, 1C.

Selected Recordings
Bernstein: *On the Waterfront: Symphonic Suite*; *Chichester Psalms*; *On the Town: Three Dance Episodes*; Elizabeth Franklin-Kitchen (s); Thomas Kelly (boy sop); Victoria Nayler (a); Jeremy Budd (t); Paul Charrier (b); Bournemouth SO and Ch. Naxos 8.559177.

Brahms: *Symphony no. 1 in c*; *Tragic Overture*; *Academic Festival Overture*; London PO. Naxos 8.557428.

Concordia Chamber Ensemble; works by Carbon, Homans, McKinley. MMC 2135.

Tchaikovsky: *Violin Concerto*. Assad: *Violin Concerto*; Nadja Salerno-Sonnenberg (vn); Colorado SO. NSS, live: Denver 11/2004.

Weill: *Symphony no. 1*; *Symphony no. 2*; *Lady in the Dark: Symphonic Nocturne* (arr. Bennett); Bournemouth SO. Naxos 8.55748.

~

Amado, David
Born 26 July 1968 in Meriom, Pennsylvania

Appointed musical director of the Delaware SO in 2003, Amado is a young conductor with a track record of outreach to audiences. As cofounder, conductor, and managing director of Sequitur, a dynamic contemporary crossover group in New York City, he set about attracting an avant-garde audience not only for music but for theater and dance as well. As director of the Saint Louis SO's Community Partnership Program, he attracted a wide audience through programs designed to enrich arts appreciation in local communities and activities such as special event, outdoor, educational, family, and outreach concerts, preconcert lectures, and radio and television interviews. Similarly, in Delaware he aims to raise the orchestra's profile within the community through new and innovative programming. By involving other musical traditions than the purely classical, he is attempting to dissolve some of the formal barriers which are part of the traditional concert scene. A three-year extension to his contract, taking it to 2009, attests to his success.

Amado attended Juilliard as a piano student of Herbert Stessin and earned a master's degree from Indiana University in 1993. He then returned to Juilliard to study conducting with Otto-Werner Mueller and won the Bruno Walter Memorial Scholarship. After a stint as apprentice conductor with the Oregon SO, he became the Saint Louis SO's conducting assistant in 1997, progressing to associate conductor in 2000. He was appointed to conduct the Saint Louis SYO in 1999. He has been guest conductor with the Detroit SO, the Rochester PO, the New World Symphony (America's Orchestral Academy in Miami, Fla.), the Royal Stockholm PO, and the Orquesta Sinfónica de Xalapa (Mexico), among others.

～

Ansbacher, Charles
Born 5 October 1942 in Cincinnati, Ohio

Ansbacher is conductor of the Boston Landmarks Orchestra, principal guest conductor of the Sarajevo (Bosnia) PO, and conductor laureate of the Colorado Springs SO. This gives some indication of the interesting life he has led. After being music director of the Colorado Springs orchestra for almost twenty years (1970–89), he dutifully accompanied his wife, Swanee Hunt, to Austria upon her appointment as the U.S. Ambassador. Conducting opportunities were not easy to come by in Vienna, but he did find work at the Vienna State Opera and with the Vienna CO. Then came an invitation to conduct the SPO, which had been struggling to survive during the Balkan upheavals. Conditions were grim, but Ansbacher was able to garner enough spirit among the players that the success of the New Year's Eve concert of 1996 seemed to celebrate the end to hostilities in a very concrete way. He has since taken the orchestra on international tours, including an appearance at the prestigious Ravenna Festival in 1998. His success in Bosnia led to invitations from a number of East European orchestras, not least the Moscow SO.

The Ansbachers returned to live in the U.S. when Swanee was recruited to teach at Harvard in 1997. In the Boston area Charles saw the opportunity to fill a gap in the music scene, where little in the way of free concerts or outdoor summer events was on offer. Thus, in 2001, he created the Boston Landmarks Orchestra, made up of local professional players, to perform free concerts at venues with historical or architectural importance. By 2003 it was giving over forty concerts a year. Reviewing the opening concert of the 2006 season, *Boston Herald* critic T. J. Medrek commented on the diverse makeup of the audience, "an impressive sea of singles, couples and families, of all ages and generations (although skewing noticeably younger) out for an evening of—gasp!—Mozart," which convinced him that classical music is still a central part of the city's life.

Ansbacher was born into a family of psychologists and educated at Brown University. He received a master's degree in 1968 and a DMA degree in 1979 from the University of Cincinnati. After an apprenticeship with the Kingsport (Tenn.) orchestra, he was appointed music director of the Middletown (Ohio) SO in 1967. He moved to Colorado Springs three years later, where he was responsible for expanding the orchestra's activities and supervising its move to a purpose-built auditorium, the Pikes Peak Center, in 1982. In addition to conducting, he has been involved in the fields of design and architecture.

Further Reading

Edgers, Geoff. "Grace Notes: Conductor Ansbacher Is the Free Spirit behind BLO's Gifts of Music." *Boston Globe*, 9 August 2002, D17.

Gruber, Gerold Wolfgang. "Cross-over: Swanee Hunt und Charles Ansbacher im Gespräch mit Gerold W. Gruber." *Österreichische Musikzeitschrift* 49, no. 9 (1994): 525. [German]

"The Two Worlds of Charles Ansbacher." *Symphony Magazine* 31, no. 3 (1980): 85.

∼

Baker, Robert Hart
Born 19 March 1954 in Bronxville, New York

Baker's professional conducting career has been occupied with three appointments over roughly the same time period. Appointed music director of the Asheville (N.C.) SO for the 1980–82 season, he remained its conductor until 2004. After leading the Saint Louis PO as a guest conductor in 1981, he was chosen to be its director in 1983, the same year that he took up the post as conductor of the York (Pa.) SO. He continues to hold both appointments. Until the 1999–2000 season he regularly led the York YSO. (He had previously [1977–81] directed the New York YSO.) As a student at Harvard he conducted the Cambridge Bach Society (1972–74) and founded and directed the Connecticut PO (1974–84) while a graduate student at Yale. From 1979 to 1981 he directed the Danbury (Conn.) Little Symphony and the Putnam SO in Brewster (N.Y.). He was an assistant conductor at the Spoleto Festival of Two Worlds (1979–84), where, among his other duties, he directed Barber's *Anthony and Cleopatra* at the Italian venue. Other forays into opera have included *Carmen* at the Brevard Music Center, *Madame Butterfly* with the Connecticut Opera, and *La Traviata*, *Rigoletto*, and *Le nozze di Figaro* at the Cullowhee Music Festival.

Baker's musical education began with oboe lessons at the age of nine, expanded when piano lessons were added five years later, and extended to conducting and composition in his late teens. He spent the summer of 1971 in Europe, studying oboe at the Academie Internationale in Nice and conducting at the Mozarteum in Salzburg under the tutelage of Herbert von Karajan, where he was given the distinction of leading a concert with the Mozarteum Orchestra. He received his undergraduate degree cum laude from Harvard (1974), and two master's degrees, MM (1976) and MMA (1978), from Yale, where he studied with Leonard Bernstein. He completed his DMA at Yale in 1987.

Baker has appeared as guest conductor and clinician across the U.S. and has traveled abroad to conduct in Korea, Spain, Italy, and Switzerland. He took the opportunity afforded by the breakup of the Soviet Bloc to record with an East European orchestra. With the Szeged SO in Hungary he recorded the complete piano concertos of Liszt with pianist Richard Frank. Among his other recordings he lists: Symphony no. 1 by Ernest Bloch, Brahms's First and Third Symphonies, Symphony no. 4 by Mahler, and Mozart's Fourteenth Piano Concerto. He is engaged in making the first recordings of orchestral works by Caryl Florio, who served as composer-in-residence at the Biltmore Estate near Asheville, N.C., around the turn of the twentieth century.

On leaving the Asheville SO in 2004, he was dubbed "beloved maestro," appointed conductor laureate, and praised for consistently improving the quality and scope of the orchestra over twenty-two years.

Further Reading

Harris, Paul A. "Philharmonic: 'Oldest of Its Type.'" *St. Louis Post-Dispatch*, 23 October 1994, 4C.

∽

Barenboim, Daniel
Born 15 November 1942 in Buenos Aires, Argentina

Building on his prestige as a piano wunderkind, Barenboim established his credentials as a conductor in the late 1960s in recordings of Mozart concertos and symphonies with the English CO. He studied conducting with Igor Markevitch at the age of nine while a student at the Salzburg Mozarteum, appearing before a student ensemble during the Salzburg Festival of 1952. His professional debut occurred in 1962 when on tour in Australia, and he first conducted the Israel PO that same year. It was his close association with the English CO, lasting for some ten years, that set him firmly on the path to a dual career as pianist and conductor.

What distinguished these early Mozart recordings and performances was a fresh, romantic approach that demonstrated a fine ear for balance and texture. Already under the spell of Furtwängler and influenced by his collaboration with Klemperer, Barenboim's essays with larger forms and forces were often less successful: brilliant insights interspersed with wayward, inconsistent, and self-indulgent tempi. Even as his art has matured, his performances have always retained a sense of improvisation, for, as he himself has said, without risk music is nothing.

Barenboim was the offspring of pianists who taught him from the age of five. His must have been a prodigious talent, for two years later he was to give his debut concert playing Mozart and Beethoven (*Appassionata*) sonatas. Shortly thereafter the family moved to Salzburg, where Daniel attended the Mozarteum and worked at piano repertoire with Edwin Fischer. He then spent some time studying with Nadia Boulanger in Paris and subsequently at the Accademia Nazionale di Santa Cecilia in Rome, becoming, at age fourteen, the youngest recipient of its diploma. He made his American debut in 1957 playing Prokofiev's First Piano Concerto under the direction of Stokowski. At this stage his parents were living in Israel and wisely decided to limit his concert-giving to three months a year, allowing him to have some general education and live a "normal" life with pursuits such as chess, soccer, and even boxing! As his career as a solo pianist blossomed, he began to enjoy a reputation in a third area of musical activity, that of chamber music, where he forged a number of significant partnerships with artists such as Perlman, Zuckerman, his first wife Jacqueline Du Pré, and singers Dietrich Fischer-Dieskau and Janet Baker. He had a high profile at the opening of London's Queen Elizabeth Hall and directed South Bank Music there from 1968 to 1970.

In the meantime his conducting career was beginning to take off. His American debut occurred on tour with the Israel PO in 1967, and he first appeared on the rostrum in New York as a last-minute substitute conductor for the London SO the following year. He conducted his first opera, *Don Giovanni*, at the Edinburgh Festival in 1973 and began a long association with the Berlin PO in 1979. His first major appointment was with the Orchestre de Paris in 1975. This eventually led him to the post of artistic director of the newly opened Bastille Opera in 1985. These appointments both terminated in 1989 when Barenboim was involved in a dispute with the politically appointed intendant. In 1981 he began a close association with the Bayreuth Festival conducting *Tristan* and, five years later, his first complete *Ring* cycle. From 1993 he was director of the Berlin Staatsoper and largely responsible for its transition into a company of international stature.

Barenboim's relationship with the Chicago SO goes back almost twenty years before he was appointed its ninth music director in 1989. His appointment was a surprise to some, but at least the orchestra knew what it was getting and endorsed the choice. His predecessor, Sir Georg Solti, no doubt desirous of bolstering his own legacy, supported the candidacy of a conductor whose style and approach were so very different from his own. Barenboim set about putting his own stamp on the Chicago music scene by setting high standards for himself, players, and audiences, as well as by attempting to expand the orchestra's role through cooperation with other aspects of the city's cultural life. His commitment to contemporary music was fulfilled through the annual residency of Pierre Boulez, the Composer in Residence program, a number of important commissions, and the MusicNOW chamber series, although some critics felt that not enough attention was paid to more approachable American contemporary composers. After the honeymoon period, it began to emerge in the press and elsewhere that there was dissatisfaction with Barenboim's leadership among some of the players. They were bemused by his intensely cerebral manner, seeming to them condescending, aloof, and prickly. There were further misgivings about his imprecise beat and lapses in ensemble. Although a warmer string tone developed, the orchestra had some difficulty adjusting to his more flexible approach that expected players to take on some of the responsibility for creativity and ensemble—not an easy task after decades of being drilled to precision in the unforgiving acoustic of Orchestra Hall! What often emerged, it was claimed, were blurred, undiscriminated texture and performances lacking character. The occasional calamity notwithstanding (the Da Ponte/Mozart opera series, for example, which lost sponsorship and landed the orchestra with a hefty deficit), the public continued to support the orchestra through the mid-

1990s with ticket sales and subscriptions. The later Wagner opera series was acclaimed a triumph. His tenure with the orchestra has also been marked by frequent appearances in the dual role of pianist and conductor. He led the orchestra on a dozen international tours, including the first to South America in 2000. When the orchestra moved once more into deficit in 2001 as a result of the faltering economy, Barenboim was again embroiled in criticism that in the credibility gap between his supporters and detractors, the orchestra had somehow lost its way. His decision to resign at the end of the 2005–6 season (a surprise announcement in 2004) indicated an unwillingness to go along with the administration's wish to popularize concert-giving as a way of dealing with financial pressures. In this effort they wanted Barenboim to play a more public, non-musical role, which he was not prepared to do. It was at a time when the jet-setting lifestyle he had led for most of his career was beginning to take its toll. Health problems had forced the cancellation of several subscription concerts and recitals. The complex, edgy relationship he had had with the players also showed signs of fraying at the edges in public. After seventeen years at the helm, it was time to move on.

Never shying away from controversy, especially political, he immediately left for Jerusalem at the outbreak of the 1967 Arab-Israeli war and received a death threat the following year for putting on a concert at short notice in London's Royal Albert Hall to protest the Soviet takeover in Czechoslovakia. His biggest battle has been a persistent one, to persuade the Israeli public to accept the music of Wagner. He tried unsuccessfully for the first time in 1991, finally succeeding in 2001 when he performed the *Tristan* prelude as a second encore during the Berlin Staatskapelle's tour. The fulfillment of this "very personal and private" wish nevertheless caused a storm of protest in official circles as high as that of Israeli Premier Sharon, with the unrepentent Barenboim fielding accusations of deviousness. He also forged a close relationship over a number of years with the controversial Palestinian American literary critic and music-lover Edward Said, both men sharing a belief in the transcendence of art over political ideology. In practical terms this resulted in Barenboim giving master classes for Palestinian students in the occupied territories, and their joint founding of the West-Eastern Divan Orchestra, made up of Jewish and Arab players. Within an intractable political situation, such integration was frowned upon in some Israeli circles.

Barenboim's championing of Wagner's music in Chicago, Bayreuth, and Berlin has been one of the hallmarks of his later career. He demonstrates a love and reverence for this music which yields performances rich in color and powerful in spirit. It seems that the "Furtwängler approach" works best for him in Wagner and the later romantic repertory, where he can indulge a flexible control of tempo and conjure up a depth and nobility of expression.

Barenboim's is a brilliant and complex personality. He is a tireless musician: brisk, alert, and confident. Articulate, intellectual, eclectic, witty (a great raconteur), and prone to practical jokes, he is Siegfried-like in his fearlessness. To Edward Said, the "nature of his extraordinary music making" is that it "seems to flow from him and into the nature of music itself." The dual nature of his career as pianist and conductor has not been without its strains, however, and one suspects that the total control he exerts over the keyboard cannot be so easily commanded from an orchestra. The wellspring of his musicmaking has always been to recapture something of the spirit of Furtwängler, from whom he learned that creativity in performance depends on solid "scientific preparation in rehearsal." His performances have matured over the years; to youthful spontaneity has been added a cerebral detachment and a sense of inevitability.

Website
http://www.danielbarenboim.com/

Further Reading

"Barenboim, Daniel." In *World Musicians*, edited by Clifford Thompson, 49–54. New York: H. W. Wilson Company, 1999.

Barenboim, Daniel, Edward Said, and Ara Buzelimian. *Parallels and Paradoxes: Explorations in Music and Society*. New York: Pantheon Books, 2002.

Barenboim, Daniel, Michael Lewin, and Phillip Huscher. *A Life in Music*. New York: Arcade Publishers, 2003.

Hart, Philip. "Daniel Barenboim." In *Conductors: A New Generation*, 3–44. New York: Charles Scribner's Sons, 1983.

Kupferberg, Herbert. "Daniel Barenboim: A 50-year Career Just Keeps on Growing." *American Record Guide* 63 (November–December 2000): 6–8.

Rhein, John von. "Harmonic Divergence: After 5 Seasons Together, Barenboim and the CSO Are Still Working the Kinks Out of Their Relationship." *Chicago Tribune*, 26 May 1996, Arts & Entertainment, 1, 8.

Selected Recordings

Beethoven: *Missa solemnis*; soloists; Chicago SO. Erato 4509-91731-2.

Brahms: *Violin Concerto*; Maxim Vengerov (vn); Chicago SO. Teldec 17144.

Mozart: *Piano Concertos: No. 20 in d*, K 466; *No. 27 in Bb, Concert Rondo in D*; Barenboim (pf and cond); English CO. EMI 56517.

Tchaikovsky: *Symphony no. 5*. Verdi: *La forza del destino*: Overture. Sibelius: *Valse triste*; West-Eastern Divan O. Warner 62190.

Wagner: *Der fliegende Holländer*; Falk Struckmann (*Holländer*); Jane Eaglen (*Senta*); Robert Holl (*Daland*); Peter Seiffert (*Erik*); German State Op Ch and O, Berlin. Teldec 88063.

〰

Barra, Donald (Paul)
Born 21 August 1939 in Newark, New Jersey

Over the last twenty years the San Diego CO has become an increasingly significant cultural icon on Southern California's musical landscape. From modest beginnings in the ritzy Rancho Santa Fe suburb, the ensemble has steadily expanded its sway geographically and enhanced its reputation artistically. In 1989 the orchestra began a series of recordings that extended its notice nationally and internationally. The driving force behind this orchestra since its formation in 1984 has been Donald Barra, emeritus professor of music and director of orchestras at San Diego State University. Through hard work, dedication, and the ability to find the right niche, he can take credit for creating and sustaining a viable professional CO. From an initial season offering of seven performances, the group has dramatically expanded its output to over forty concerts a year (2003). He achieved a high standard of performance from the start by recruiting the leading players from the San Diego SO and further afield, and by attracting solo artists of high caliber, including Lorin Hollander, Jean-Pierre Rampal, and Mischa Dichter. The orchestra's debut recording of music by Ibert and Poulenc led to a contract with the Koch International label. A 1993 recording of music by Malcolm Arnold won a Grammy for its producer and a Best Chamber Orchestra Recording of the Year accolade for the orchestra. Barra relinquished the post of music director in 2004 to accept the less taxing one of conductor laureate. Future plans are to travel, write, and guest conduct.

After a thorough musical grounding via the Eastman School of Music (AB cum laude), Juilliard (MS), and Columbia University (EdD), as well as attendance at Tanglewood, Aspen, and the American Symphony Orchestra League's Summer Institute, Barra spent ten years (1973–83) as music director of the Johnstown (Pa.) SO and Chorale, and as associate director of the Bedford Springs Music Festival. Among his mentors he lists Leonard Bernstein, Seiji **Ozawa**, Richard Lert, and Jorge **Mester**. In 1983 he published *The Dynamic Performance: A Performer's Guide to Musical Interpretation*, and the book's success aided his appointment in San Diego. In addition to his recordings with the SDCO, Barra traveled to Russia where he conducted the Moscow PO in a recording of piano concertos by Schnittke and Shostakovitch, with Israela Margalit as soloist.

Website
http://www.donaldbarra.com/

Further Reading
Barra, Donald. *The Dynamic Performance: A Performer's Guide to Musical Interpretation.* Englewood Cliffs, N.J.: Prentice-Hall, 1983.
Brown, Royal S. "The San Diego Chamber Orchestra: Ten Years Young." *Fanfare* 18, no. 3 (1995): 26–34.
Willet, John. "The Little Orchestra That Could." *San Diego Metropolitan Magazine*, April 1998. http://www.sandiegometro.com/1998/apr/ear.html

Selected Recordings
Arnold: *Serenade for Small Orchestra; Sinfoniettas 1 and 2; Concerto for 2 Violins and String Orchestra*; Igor and Vesna Gruppman (vns); San Diego CO. Koch 3-7134-2H1.
Schnittke: *Concerto for Piano and Strings.* Shostakovich: *Concerto for Piano Trumpet and Strings*; Israela Margalit (pf); Moscow PO. Koch 3-8150-2H1.

∿

Bay, Peter
Born 3 March 1957 in Washington, D.C.

Music director and conductor of the Austin (Tex.) SO since 1998, Peter Bay has been credited with renewing interest in the ASO, increasing attendance, adding diversity to its programs, and generating technological recognition for the orchestra. Bay began a 45-minute weekly online live chat with Austin elementary school students. He is particularly committed to education, visiting local schools to talk about the orchestra and conducting hundreds of programs for young people. In 2000, *XL Ent*, an alternative entertainment weekly, named Bay one of the twenty-five most influential people in Austin.

Bay's résumé shows a fondness for twentieth-century composers, but he says there is very little repertoire that is not rewarding. Though he began his bachelor of music education degree at the University of Maryland with the intention of becoming a high school band director, Bay discovered his heart lay with the orchestra and all the fine literature written for it. He continued his orchestral studies at Peabody Conservatory, where he earned a master's degree in 1980. While there he was hired as assistant conductor with the Annapolis (Md.) SO under director Leon Fleisher, someone Bay credits as having had enormous influence on him. His elementary school boys' choir director and his high school band director are the other two men who he says were wonderful because they were excellent musicians and warm people.

Bay won first prize at the Baltimore SO's Young Conductors Competition in 1980 and at the Leopold Stokowski Conducting Competition in 1987. He was one of only two conductors selected to participate in the Leonard Bernstein American Conductors Program in 1994.

Bay completed a seven-year tenure with the Richmond (Va.) SO in 1989. Throughout that time he held the posts of assistant conductor, associate conductor, music advisor, and principal guest conductor. In 1985 Bay and the RSO performed the U.S. premiere of Benjamin Britten's *The Sword in the Stone* and recorded it on Opus One Records. When Bay left the RSO, the governor of Virginia lauded his "contributions to the musical culture of the Commonwealth." From 1989 to 1993 Bay was associate conductor of the Saint Paul CO, which he led on many regional tours. He received national attention in 1990 when he conducted a Copland Ninetieth Birthday Concert, broadcast live on National Public Radio. Another long-term association began in 1987 with the Rochester (N.Y.) PO when he was appointed assistant conductor. Subsequently he served as conductor-in-residence, music advisor, artistic director of educational programming, and principal guest conductor. His performances with them included the world premiere of Copland's suite for the film *The Heiress* and the U.S. premiere of Britten's *Concerto Movement for Clarinet and Orchestra*. They also recorded *Voices*, available on the Nexus label.

Bay served as music director of the Erie (Pa.) PO from 1996 to 1999 and has been music director of the Britt Festival Orchestra in Medford (Ore.) since 1993. He made his debut with the Austin Lyric Opera in 2002 with *A Streetcar Named Desire*, in which he was said to have "conducted . . . with a sensitive understanding of Previn's varied score." Reviewers of other Bay conducting performances also speak of sensitivity and passion, interpretations that are musically valid, vivid, and brilliant, and an infectious energy evidenced by the way he conducts with his whole body. Audiences and musicians alike respond positively.

Bay's guest appearances have included the National SO, Saint Louis SO, Houston SO, Dallas SO, Baltimore SO, New Mexico SO, North Carolina SO, Syracuse SO, Virginia SO, West Virginia SO, Colorado SO, Hawaii SO, Richmond SO, Alabama SO, Canton SO, Bochum SO (Germany),

Carinthian SO (Austria), Lithuanian National SO, Minnesota Orchestra, and Algarve SO (Portugal); the Louisiana, Buffalo, Rhode Island, and Tulsa Philharmonics; the Saint Paul CO; the Eastman and Aspen Opera Theaters; and the Theater Chamber Players of the Kennedy Center. His summer music festival appearances have included Aspen (Colo.), Grant Park and Ravinia (Ill.), Round Top (Tex.), OK Mozart (Okla.), and Skaneateles (N.Y.).

Further Reading
Blakeslee, Michael. "Spotlight on Peter Bay." *Music Educators Journal* 76 (December 1989): 54–56.
Polgar, Robi. "On His Toes." *Austin Chronicle*, 13 November 1998. http://www.austinchronicle.com/issues/vol18/issue11/arts.symphony.html

Selected Recordings
Britten: *The Sword in the Stone, Concert Suite*; Richmond SO. Opus One 100.
Voices: Music for Percussion and Orchestra; Nexus (perc); Rochester PO. Nexus Records 10317.

～

Beck, Crafton
Born 18 December 1956 in Memphis, Tennessee

Although Arkansas farm boy Crafton Beck's first musical instrument was the clarinet, and that not until junior high school, by college he had determined that "music was it." At Ohio State University he was "turned on by score study" and went on to earn a master's degree in conducting. He earned a doctorate at the Cincinnati College-Conservatory of Music, writing his dissertation on Debussy's extended and complex use of accentuation markings. Following this, Beck taught and conducted orchestra for a year at Carlton College in Minnesota. A year in the apprentice program (1989) at the Cincinnati SO led to six more as assistant to conductor Erich Kunzel with the Cincinnati Pops Orchestra. Many of his arrangements have appeared on the orchestra's numerous albums, two of which received Grammy nominations. He also was music director of Carnegie Opera Theater in Cincinnati for 1991.

In 1996 Beck left Cincinnati to take up the post of music director of the Boca Pops Orchestra in Boca Raton (Fla.). Boca was ready to exchange its somewhat staid reputation for a trendy one, so the city embraced Beck's initiatives such as the summer series and ambitious educational outreach for schools. He continued this focus on fun and educational concerts for children when he left Boca Raton in 2000 to assume the position of music director and conductor of the Mississippi SO in Jackson. Beck has also been music director of the Lima (Ohio) SO since 1997. In 2004 a reviewer for the *Lima News* recognized his influence there, noting, "Largely thanks to Beck's direction, the problems of intonation, dragging tempos and the times when entire sections slogged behind the whole are past. This is now a group of really good musicians playing challenging music with skill and enthusiasm. It's a huge turnaround that has happened gradually over the past few years and it needs to be acknowledged."

As a conductor he is noted for sensitivity, intensity, limitless energy, creativity, and enthusiasm. Skilled with audiences and musicians alike, Beck has developed a national reputation in the pops arena for both his conducting and his arrangements. He has appeared as guest conductor with more than thirty American orchestras, including the New World Symphony, Dayton PO, Milwaukee SO, Arkansas SO, Oregon SO, Memphis SO, New Mexico SO, Delaware SO, Sacramento SO, and the Florida Orchestra. Orchestras such as Los Angeles PO, Detroit SO, and Indianapolis SO have performed Beck's arrangements.

Further Reading

Beck, Crafton. "The Dot as a Nondurational Sign of Articulation and Accent." *Music Research Forum* 5 (1990): 63–78.

Beck, Crafton. "The Use of the Dot, Dotted Dash, and Dotted Circumflex as Markings of Accentuation in the Works of Claude Debussy." DMA diss., University of Cincinnati, 1989.

Passy, Charles. "Boca Baton." *Symphony* 47 (November–December 1996): 77–78.

⟶

Ben-Dor, Gisèle (Ivonne Buka)
Born in Montevideo, Uruguay

Born into a musical Polish-Jewish family, Gisèle (Buka) Ben-Dor began piano studies at age four. Not only did she add guitar, accordion, recorder, and Paraguayan harp to her accomplishments, she also began putting together choruses and telling friends what and how to play and sing while she was still a child. Though she had not yet had conducting training, Ben-Dor was fourteen when her school paid her a part-time salary to conduct choirs. She loved being the teacher. When the rest of the family fled to Israel in 1973, Ben-Dor's father was unable to join them for another three years. Since her mother couldn't speak the language, Ben-Dor was obliged to be the family administrator, which gave her an early taste of taking charge when she was only seventeen.

Continuing to study piano, Ben-Dor also earned an artist diploma in orchestral conducting from the Rubin Academy of Music at Tel Aviv University, where she studied with Enrique Barenboim. Meanwhile she learned the violin, cello, and clarinet! Ben-Dor came to the U.S. in 1980 when she won a full scholarship to the Yale School of Music, earning a master's degree in orchestral conducting in 1982. Six months later she made her professional conducting debut with the Israel PO. She accepted a position as music director with the Norwalk (Conn.) Youth Symphony in 1983 and won conducting fellowships at the Los Angeles Philharmonic Institute (1984) and Tanglewood Music Center (1985). In 1987 she left Norwalk to be assistant conductor for the Louisville Orchestra for one year, then headed to Texas, where she became resident conductor for the Houston SO (1988–91), music director of the Houston YSO (1988–89), and music director for the Shepherd School of Music SO (1988–90) at Rice University.

Ben-Dor went back east in 1991, accepting positions as music director for the Annapolis (Md.) SO (until 1997) and for the Boston Pro Arte CO, where she became principal conductor in 1997, then conductor emerita in 2000. Ben-Dor was only the second woman to conduct a Boston Pops concert (1994). She gained considerable attention when, in 1994 and again in 1999, she made dramatic guest appearances at the New York PO without rehearsal or scores, stepping in at the last minute for Kurt **Masur** and Daniele Gatti. In 1999 she joined the initial steering committee of the National Women Conductors Initiative, set up by the Women's Philharmonic in San Francisco to mentor and assist young women conductors. Ben-Dor held a lengthy tenure as music director for the Santa Barbara (Calif.) SO from 1994 to 2006, at which point she became conductor laureate. The multilingual conductor became an American citizen in 2001.

Known for her high artistic standards and electric energy, Ben-Dor is passionate about education and outreach to a wide variety of audiences. She has organized numerous festivals to celebrate composers (e.g., Revueltas) and types of music (malambo, tango, zarzuela) that often highlight the art of Latin America. She has designed programming that involves the whole community, including collaboration with local composers and soloists. In Santa Barbara, Ben-Dor substantially increased both the orchestra's visibility and its endowments. She conducts without a baton, preferring to use both hands as well as the rest of her body to mold sounds effectively. Described as both formidable and incandescent on the podium, she is precise, dramatic, compelling, and fiery. Ben-Dor calls herself assertive and very, very persistent. Others have added "headstrong" and "hard to get along with." While a mainstream musician with a special interest in Mahler, she also has a deep interest in music other conductors neglect. Unafraid to mix the new and unusual with old favorites, Ben-Dor believes that modern music can elicit an active response from audiences even if it is difficult, and that the orchestra can capture people's imaginations with anything done well and with conviction. She wants to share her profound love of music and help people to know that "classical music is not about old dead white men in powdered wigs."

Ben-Dor has continued her world travels as a guest conductor, appearing with the Rotterdam PO, Bern SO, Brabant SO, Jerusalem SO, Israel SO, Orchestre de Cannes, New York PO, London SO, London PO, English CO, BBC National Orchestra of Wales, Los Angeles PO, New World Symphony, Israel CO, Helsinki PO, Houston SO, Minnesota Orchestra, Orchestre de la Suisse Romande, Israeli Opera, Tanglewood Young Artists Orchestra, Bavarian RSO, Ulster Orchestra, Saint Paul CO, Orchestre National d'Île de France, Phoenix SO, Toledo SO, Pacific SO, and many others throughout the U.S., Europe, and Latin America.

Website
http://giseleben-dor.com

Further Reading
Hansen, L. "A Musician in Heart and Soul: Gisèle Ben-Dor." *The Maud Powell Signature: Women in Music* 1, no. 3 (1996): 9–12.
Hayes, Malcolm. "Waving, Not Drowning." *Classic CD* 108 (February 1999): 24–27.
Pozen, Joanna. "The 'MA' in Macho: Gisèle Ben-Dor Calls Conducting a 'Macho' Profession." *Boston Herald*, 12 June 1994, Magazine.
Reel, James. "A Conversation with Conductor Gisèle Ben-Dor." *Fanfare* 24 (November–December 2000): 12, 14, 17–18.
Valdes, Lesley. "The Maestra: Myth, Mystique, and Matters of Fact." *Symphony* 50 (July–August 1999): 24–28, 63–64.

Selected Recordings
Bartók: *For Children; Divertimento; Romanian Folk Dances*; Sofia Soloists CO; Centaur CRC 2239.

Ginastera: *Estancia; Panambi*; Luis Gaeta (b-b); London SO. Naxos USA 8557582.

Revueltas: *La Coronela; Itinerarios; Colorines*; English CO; Santa Barbara SO. Koch 3-7421-2HI.

Sims: *Quintet; Night Piece; Solo in Four Movements; Flight; Concert Piece*; Michael Curry (vc); Anne Black (va); Ian Greitzer (cl); Theodore Mook (vc); Beth Pearson (vc); Suellen Hershman (fl); Hanneke Provily (fl); Sandra Lechner Kott (vn); Katherine Matasy (cl); Boston Pro Arte CO; Composers Recordings CR643.

Villa-Lobos: *Symphony no. 10* "Amerindia"; Carla Wood (ms); Carlo Scibelli (t); Nmon Ford-Livene (br); Santa Barbara SO; UCSB Chamber Choir. Koch 7488.

Bjaland, Leif
Born 12 December 1955 in Flint, Michigan

Aspiring conductor Leif Bjaland went to college at the University of Michigan, where he studied with Gustav Meier and Elizabeth A. H. Green, earned a master's degree in music, and, from 1976–78, served as assistant director of the UM Men's Glee Club. Staying in academia, he became a professor of music at the Yale University School of Music, as well as music director of the Yale SO. In 1986, Bjaland moved west to become affiliate artist assistant conductor of the San Francisco SO and music director of the SFS Youth Orchestra until 1990. He was selected by Leonard Bernstein in 1988 to conduct the Chicago SO at several concerts as part of the American Conductors Program.

From 1989 to 1993, Bjaland was resident conductor and artistic coordinator for the New World Symphony in Miami (Fla.). He was named music director of the Waterbury (Conn.) SO in 1994. He is also currently conductor and artistic director of the Florida West Coast SO in Sarasota. Since beginning there in 1997, Bjaland has continued his commitment to music education for all ages, with a focus on bringing live performances to pre-school children. His "First Night Out" series is aimed at bringing together people who have not yet heard the symphony, creating a musical opportunity that is "a combination of a first date, college freshman orientation and a theme park ride." He is known for adventurous repertoire, mixing the unusual with the familiar. As a champion of neglected works, Bjaland has conducted world premieres such as the complete orchestral version of Ravel's work for solo piano, *Miroirs*, David Carlson's *Quantumsymphony*, and Charles Griffes's previously unfinished *Symphony 1919*. He also led the U.S. premiere of Frank Martin's *Symphony* (1937).

Descriptions of Bjaland's conducting style include galvanic, intense, athletic, explicit, charismatic, warm, and imposing. His goals are to develop the orchestra's sound, increase its finesse, and broaden its repertoire. Bjaland is also an active opera conductor with his own orchestras and others, including the Florida Grand Opera in Miami, the Ballet de l'Opera Royal de Wallonie (Liege, Belgium), the Opera Company of the Philippines, and Glimmerglass Opera. With the Waterbury SO, he presented the world premiere of George Chadwick's opera, *The Padrone*.

Bjaland's recent guest-conducting appearances include the Music in the Mountains Festival in Durango, Ravinia Festival, Chicago's Symphony II, San Francisco SO, Nashville SO, New Zealand SO, World YSO at the National Music Camp at Interlochen, Young Artists Orchestra at the Boston University Tanglewood Institute, Grand Rapids SO, Malmö SO (Sweden), Gavleborgs SO (Sweden), Kalamazoo SO, Marin (Calif.) SO, National SO, Rochester PO, Detroit SO, Virginia SO, Colorado SO, Louisiana PO, Cincinnati SO, and Utah SO, among many others.

Website
http://www.leifbjaland.com/

Further Reading
Huisking, Charlie. "Decade of Distinction: Leif Bjaland Celebrates 10 Years with Florida West Coast Symphony." *Sarasota Herald-Tribune*, 5 November 2006, G1.
Huisking, Charlie. "Gulf Coast Gem." *Symphony* 49 (May–June 1998): 43–45.

⌢

Blomstedt, Herbert
Born 11 July 1927 in Springfield, Massachusetts

Although born in the U.S., Blomstedt grew up in Sweden and has spent the majority of his professional life in Europe. The exception was his ten-year term as music director of the San Francisco SO (1985–95). Blomstedt has an unassuming, modest manner, and his accomplishments as a conductor rest on his absolute integrity and dedication to music. His success, documented by favorable reviews and a number of distinguished, prize-winning recordings, is traced by a series of increasingly prestigious appointments that were won by merit rather than ambition. His straightforward podium style and easy rapport engenders immediate respect from orchestral musicians. His performances are highly charged, without being theatrical, with his sure instinct for musical structure and innate sense of phrasing and rhythmic control.

Blomstedt's parents were Seventh-Day Adventist missionaries living in Springfield when their son was born. Two years later the family returned to live in their native Sweden. When Herbert began to show musical aptitude his mother taught him piano. Obsessed with music from an early age, he later learned violin and organ and found every opportunity to engage in chamber music and organ playing. He attended the Royal College of Music in Stockholm (1945–50), gaining a diploma in music education and later two others in conducting and organ. Tor Mann was his conducting teacher. From 1948–52, he took classes in musicology at the University of Uppsala. He also attended John Cage's classes in contemporary music in Darmstadt and studied Renaissance and Baroque performance practice at the Schola Cantorum in Basle. Deciding to concentrate on conducting, he studied with Igor Markevitch at the Salzburg Mozarteum (1950) and spent a year at Juilliard studying with Jean Morel (1953). He attended the Tanglewood Festival that summer, studying with Leonard Bernstein, and won the Koussevitzky Prize for conductors. This success was repeated when, in 1955, he won first prize at the Salzburg Conducting Competition. He made his professional debut in 1954 conducting the Stockholm PO. He was appointed music director of the Norrköping SO, where he stayed from 1954 to 1961. In 1962, he was appointed professor of conducting at the Royal College of Music, Stockholm, and music director of the Oslo PO. He held the posts conjointly for the next six years. In 1967, he began a ten-year term as music director of the Danish RSO. As his reputation grew, so did the invitations to appear as guest conductor. The most significant of these turned out to be an appearance with the Dresden Staatskapelle. So impressed were the Staatskapelle musicians that they invited him to become their music director in 1975. An orchestra with a long and distinguished history, it was hidden behind the Iron Curtain after World War II, but had retained its own distinctive sound and musical traditions, and Blomstedt's appointment was an ideal match between conductor and orchestra. With twenty years of experience, Blomstedt's credentials as a conscientious and deeply committed musician untainted by ego were well established and fit the orchestra's expectations. Despite the restriction of working in the East he was able to enhance the orchestra's reputation with tours to Western Europe and the U.S. During the Dresden period, he was also chief conductor of the Swedish RSO (1977–83).

Blomstedt made a rather late American debut with the Detroit SO in 1980 and four years later was introduced to the San Francisco SO. This collaboration led to his acceptance of an invitation in 1985 to become its music director. At first glance, the juxtaposition of a quiet, conservative, deeply religious man with the orchestra of a city famed for its liberal, easy-going ways did not seem to be a good fit! In the beginning there were tensions—what one player characterized as a "definite cultural divide." In rehearsal Blomstedt is "incredibly intense" and determined that the orchestra, through him, should achieve unanimity of purpose faithful to the composer's intentions. In a ten-year relationship there are always ups and downs, but what emerged quite quickly was an orchestra which had previously been described as sloppy becoming much more proficient technically. Hence, the orchestra's national standing began to rise. Blomstedt and the orchestra undertook a series of tours to Europe, Asia, and around the U.S., appearing at the Salzburg, Edinburgh, and Lucerne Festivals and embarking on a recording schedule for Decca/London that resulted in two Grammy awards, a Gramophone Award from the UK, and France's Grand Prix du Disque. Recording highlights from this period include a complete cycle of Nielsen symphonies, Orff's *Carmina Burana*, Strauss's *Alpine Symphony*, Mahler's *Resurrection Symphony*, and music by Hindemith, Beethoven, Bruckner, Brahms, Mozart, Mendelssohn, and Schubert. Blomstedt frequently performed works by contemporary American composers, premiered works by Wuorinen, Harbison, Perle, Carter, Reich, and Danielpour, and won the Ditson Conductor's Award from Columbia University for distinguished service to American music. But in an interview with Mark Steinbrink published in the *New York Times* (3 September 1986), Blomstedt voiced reservations he feels about today's composers: "Contemporary music rarely moves me in the way a Beethoven symphony moves me." He went on to explain that he most closely identifies with instrumental music "that suggests . . . transcendental values . . . closest to the finest aspects of ourselves, closest to God. And that's where I most love to dwell." Blomstedt's decision to quit San Francisco after ten years was, in part, because of his wish to return to Europe to be with his family and closer to his musical roots. There was also the perception that a long, intense professional relationship is subject to wear and tear, and cannot maintain a certain level of excellence indefinitely. The partnership had been mutually beneficial as Blomstedt's performances had taken on a greater warmth and humanity—some of the San Francisco spirit had rubbed off on him! Accepting the title of conductor laureate has meant frequent and very successful reunions with the orchestra he brought to worldwide prominence.

He has appeared frequently as guest conductor with the world's leading orchestras, including the Berlin PO, Boston SO, Chicago SO, Philadelphia

Orchestra, and New York PO. For two years (1996–98) Blomstedt worked as music director with the NDR SO, Hamburg. In 1998, he accepted the directorship of the Leipzig Gewandhaus Orchestra, an East German orchestra with an even more illustrious pedigree than the one in Dresden. It is an orchestra that responded well to the conscientious and deeply felt musicianship that has marked Blomstedt's fifty-year career. The partnership has produced a number of distinguished recordings on the Decca label. At the end of his contract in 2005, he indicated that he was not interested in another directorship, but would instead be contented with "shorter relationships."

Blomstedt's interpretations are distinguished by dramatic insight, structural awareness, and rhythmic control. He has often been described as a musicians' musician, but truly, he is any musical person's musician. Anyone going to hear his concerts expecting a histrionic display on the podium will be disappointed, but anyone who values concentrated listening and music allowed to speak for itself will appreciate his art. His many honors include the Anton Bruckner Prize in Linz (2001) and the Carl Nielsen Prize in Copenhagen (2002). He is a Knight Royal of the Order of the North Star, Stockholm (1971), a Knight Royal of the Order of Dannebrogen, Copenhagen (1978), and a member of the Royal Music Academy in Stockholm.

Further Reading

Johnson, Stephen. "Questions & Answers: Herbert Blomstedt." *Gramophone* 68 (August 1990): 355–56.

Knight, John Wesley. "Herbert Blomstedt Strives for Precision with Spontaneity." *Instrumentalist* 55 (March 2001): 12–16.

Steinberg, Michael Philip. "Making Music with Herbert Blomstedt." *Symphony Magazine* 36, no. 3 (1985): 69–74.

Steinbrink, Mark. "The San Francisco Symphony and Maestro Herbert Blomstedt." *Ovation* 8 (February 1987): 20–23.

Selected Recordings

Bach: *Mass in B minor*; Ruth Ziesak (s); Anna Larsson (a); Christoph Genz (t); Dietrich Henschel (b); Gewandhaus CCh; Leipzig Gewandhaus O. Euroarts 2054518 DVD.

Beethoven: *Symphonies* (complete); Helena Doese (s); Marga Schiml (a); Peter Schreier (t); Theo Adam (b); Staatskapelle Dresden. Brilliant 99793/1/2/3/4/5.

Nielsen: *Symphonies 1–3*; San Francisco SO. Decca 460985.

Sibelius: *Symphonies* (complete); San Francisco SO. Decca 00689202.

Bond, Victoria (Ellen)
Born 6 May 1945 in Los Angeles, California

Bond is esteemed as both conductor and composer. That she has chosen to concentrate on composition of late does not detract from her contributions as one of a group of pioneering women conductors (which includes JoAnn **Falletta**, Catherine Comet, Eve Queler, and Marin **Alsop**) who began to be noticed in the late 1960s and the 1970s. Without managing to break into the first ranks of this male-dominated profession, Bond warrants being taken seriously as a first-rate working musician and will serve as an inspiration to young women of subsequent generations who harbor the same ambitions.

Born into a family of musicians reaching back several generations, Bond was able to play the piano by ear from the age of three and, in early adolescence, entertained ideas of becoming an opera singer. She was taught piano first by her mother and then moved to New York City to study with Nadia Reisenberg at the Mannes College of Music. She recrossed the country to attend the University of Southern California, where she studied composition with Ingolf Dahl and worked with composer Paul Glass, graduating with a BMA degree in 1968. Back in New York at Juilliard, first as a Juilliard Scholar (1972–77) and later as a Juilliard Fellow (1975–79), she worked closely with Pierre Boulez and Roger Sessions as assistant conductor of the contemporary music ensemble. Her conducting teachers were Jean Morel and Sixten Ehrling, and she attended classes given by Herbert von Karajan, Leonard **Slatkin**, and Herbert **Blomstedt**. While still a student she was invited to participate in the Cabrillo Festival (1974) at the invitation of Michael Tilson **Thomas**, and at the White Mountains Music Festival in 1975. The first woman to graduate from Juilliard with a DMA in orchestral conducting (1977), she was appointed music director of the New Amsterdam SO (1978–80) in New York City and received an Exxon/Arts Endowment Award to work as affiliate conductor (1978–80) of the Pittsburgh SO during André **Previn**'s tenure. Her duties also included conducting the Pittsburgh YSO. In New York she took the directorship of the Empire State YO (1982–86), for which she composed two of her most popular works: *The Frog Princess* and *What's the Point of Counterpoint?* She made her European debut with the RTE National SO in Dublin (1983) and spent a year working at the Southeastern Music Center. It was at this time that she became involved in opera presentation with Bel Canto Opera (1982–88). A National Institute for Music Theater award enabled her to work as an assistant conductor at the New

York City Opera (1985–86). An important segment of her life began when she became music director of the Roanoke (Va.) SO (1986–95), and this, in turn, led to her work as director of Opera Roanoke (1989–95) and her theater activities with the Harrisburg (Pa.) Opera (1998–2003). During this period she mounted productions of the standard operatic repertoire: Le nozze di Figaro, Don Giovanni, La Bohème, and Il barbiere di Siviglia, among others. A singular achievement was the performance of her own opera Travels—a contemporary reworking of the Gulliver story—that received plaudits from the critics at its premiere in 1995. In 1993 she established another important link when she debuted with the Shanghai SO, and her association with China has continued in her work as artistic advisor to the Wuhan SO.

Bond has built up an extensive list of guest appearances with second- and third-tier orchestras, but it is rather regrettable that she has never had the opportunity to direct a top-flight ensemble. There are social, cultural, and economic factors to account for this, but it is not due to a lack of ability or enthusiasm on the part of Bond.

Website
http://www.victoriabond.com

Further Reading
Apone, Carl. "Victoria Bond: Composer, Conductor." High Fidelity/Musical America 29 (April 1979): 28–29.
Lepage, Jane Weiner. "Victoria Bond." In Women Composers, Conductors, and Musicians of the Twentieth Century: Selected Biographies, 1:1–12. Metuchen, N.J.: Scarecrow, 1980.
Singer, Rosanne, and Steve Mencher. "Bonding Elements." Symphony 44, no. 5 (1993): 63–64.

Selected Recording
Hagen (Daron): Songs of Madness and Sorrow; Paul Sperry (t); Cleveland CS. Arsis CD 127.

～

Botstein, Leon
Born 14 December 1946 in Zurich, Switzerland

Botstein's achievements are truly awesome! He is a distinguished conductor, academic administrator, and scholar. As such, he brings a unique perspective to the dilemma of concert-giving at the turn of the twenty-first century. He has commented on the ritualistic and moribund aspect of concert going and how it can leave the uninitiated feeling alienated. To address this problem he has devised a three-pronged strategy: to rethink programming and the live concert experience; to expand the repertory with new music, including neglected or difficult music from the past; and to bridge the gap between the arts and academe. Music, he argues, is only relevant as it relates to people and is made more meaningful within a historical context. Hence the didactic component has always been emphasized in his relationship with audiences. His "Classics Declassified" concerts include a lecture, a performance, and then a post-performance discussion. This is a similar formula to the one Leonard Bernstein used in his musical appreciation lectures. Purists may frown at this seemingly lowbrow approach, but, especially with decreasing music education opportunities in public schools, it seems to be valuable. Botstein and his various endeavors have attracted a loyal following and an increase in corporate and private financing. His programming initiatives have been copied elsewhere.

Botstein's forebears were Polish Jews. His parents were studying medicine in Zurich when the tide of anti-Semitism sweeping across Europe persuaded them to stay in Switzerland for the duration of the Second World War; they emigrated to the U.S. shortly afterward. Leon grew up in a lively intellectual New York émigré community and received violin lessons from the esteemed Roman Totenberg. He was sufficiently gifted to attend the New York High School of Music and Art. In 1963 he began undergraduate studies in history at the University of Chicago, where he was concertmaster of the university orchestra, organizing a chamber orchestra and playing solo recitals. In graduate school at Harvard he conducted the Boston Doctor's Orchestra and served as assistant conductor of the college orchestra. Although continuing studies in history, he nurtured his conducting ambitions by taking lessons from James Yannatos. After Harvard, he spent a year working in educational administration in New York City. By chance in 1970 he was offered the presidency of Franconia College, an obscure and unaccredited liberal arts college in New Hampshire. This made him the youngest college president in the nation. In addition to his many other responsibilities at Franconia, he found time to conduct the college choir and teach courses in orchestration. Within five years he managed to turn the fortunes of this anarchic institution around, gaining attention with a number of academic initiatives in the process. Not surprisingly, he was wooed away by another institution undergoing stressful times, Bard College, where he was installed as president in July of 1975 and where he remains to this day. In the years immediately following,

Botstein was preoccupied with academic life until, in 1981, a personal tragedy took place. His second daughter, Abigail, herself a talented violinist, was killed in a traffic accident. Resuming his conducting activities was partly to mitigate his grief, but also the result of a realization that music-making was really vital to his life. To this end he began taking conducting lessons from Harold **Farberman** and resurrected the Hudson Valley Philharmonic CO. In 1992 he was offered the directorship of the American SO, a forty-year-old freelance organization that had been founded by Leopold Stokowski. At the same time he became editor of the highly regarded journal *Musical Quarterly*.

The ASO was in need of rejuvenation, and it proved an ideal opportunity for Botstein to put his ideas into practice. The first manifestation was evident in the thematic programming he introduced during the orchestra's subscription series as part of the Lincoln Center Presents Great Performers series. One such program in 1993 took a Shakespearean theme, with Tchaikovsky's tone poem *Hamlet*, Dvořák's *Othello*, and Strauss's *Macbeth*. In line with giving forgotten works a re-hearing, the program also included *The Tempest* by Victorian New England composer John Knowles Paine. The audience was provided with an elaborate program booklet containing informative essays. Another important outlet is the Bard Music Festival Rediscoveries concerts, concentrated weekends for studying and listening to the music of a single composer. In 1999, the college featured Schoenberg, presenting lectures and chamber music recitals, as well as a performance of *Gurrelieder*. Many of these festival performances find their way back to New York City as part of the ASO's subscription series. The driving force behind the construction of a $62 million performance space at Bard College, Botstein led a performance of Mahler's Third Symphony at its inauguration in 2003. This is a concrete example of the way he believes that architecture, performing arts, and academia should interrelate.

Although Botstein's chief tilt at the "tyranny of the familiar" is his resurrection of neglected works from the nineteenth and twentieth centuries, he also champions new music with premieres of, for example, Philip Glass's *Concerto Fantasy for Two Timpanists and Orchestra* and Einojuhani Rautavaara's *On the Last Frontier*. He has performed music by two of his teachers, Wernick and **Farberman**, and music by Gerhard, Petrassi, Schnittke, Wilson, Starer, and Kupferman.

In 1995, Botstein became music director of the American Russian Youth Orchestra, made up of conservatory students from the U.S., Russia, and elsewhere, in partnership with Bard College. The same vision of an integrated educational experience which places music within a larger social and cultural milieu is applied to the way this organization functions. The orchestra, which is conducted by other eminent conductors as well, has toured extensively in the two host countries, Russia and the U.S., and around the world. In 2003, Botstein accepted a three-year term as music director of the Jerusalem SO. This was another emergency rescue operation as the orchestra was in dire straits, about to disband, and needing leadership from someone with both vision and a track record for salvage.

As a conductor, is Botstein a dilettante? At least one critic has complained how inconsistent his conducting can be, and he has certainly received some mixed reviews, especially from the New York critics. As with other musical endeavors, conducting improves with practice, so Botstein's technical control has developed over the decade during which he has put the American SO through its paces. But in any case, the musical world must be grateful for what he has done to give neglected music an airing. He is increasingly in demand as a guest conductor, although he tends to perform more standard repertoire with other orchestras. He has appeared with the London PO, Philharmonia Orchestra, Royal Scottish National Orchestra, St. Petersburg SO, NDR-Hannover Orchestra, and Düsseldorf SO. With the American SO he has recorded two neglected Strauss operas, *Der Liebe der Danae* and *Die Ägyptische Helen*, Mendelssohn's oratorio *Saint Paul* and music by Dohnanyi, Brahms, and Schubert. With the London PO he has recorded Reger tone poems and Bartók's *Concerto for Orchestra*, and with the London SO, Gliere's Third Symphony. His scholarship includes editing *The Compleat Brahms*, publishing a distillation of his doctoral thesis titled *Music and Its Public*, and writing a controversial book on alternatives to high school education, *Jefferson's Children*.

Further Reading
Scherer, Barrymore Laurence. "The Conductor as Musical Explorer." *Wall Street Journal*, 16 November 2006, D6.

Selected Recordings
Copland: *Inscape*. Sessions: *Symphony no. 8*. Perle: *Transcendental Modulations*. Rands: ". . . *where the murmurs die*. . ."; American SO. New World 80361.

Glière: *Symphony no. 3*, Op. 42 "Il'ya Murometz"; London SO. Telarc DDD CD 80609.

Strauss (R): *Die Ägyptische Helena*; Deborah Voigt (*Helena*); Carl Tanner (*Menelas*); Celena Shafer (*Aithra*); Jill Grove (*Muschel*); Christopher Robertson (*Altair*); Eric Cutler (*Da-ud*); Concert Chorale of New York; American SO. Telarc 80605, live: New York 10/6/2002.

～

Brott, Boris
Born 14 March 1944 in Montreal, Canada

The adjective that first springs to mind when describing Boris Brott is inde-fatigable. The man became a law school student in middle age, has run his own music festival for at least seventeen years, has held distinguished direc-torships with three British orchestras, has nurtured at least six orchestras in Canada, is regularly engaged by leading corporations as a charismatic moti-vational speaker, and is founder-director of the "other great orchestra of Los Angeles." Brott's has been a life singularly dedicated to the propagation of classical music, from the industrial town of Hamilton, Ontario, to the cushy suburbs of Ventura County, California. In this relentless pursuit he has been constantly involved in educational activities, community outreach programs, and the mentoring of young musicians as soloists and orchestral players.

Brott was born into a family of professional musicians and demonstrated exceptional music ability at an early age, beginning violin lessons with his fa-ther, Alexander Brott, at age three, and appearing as soloist with the Mon-treal SO at a children's matinée two years later. In addition to taking classes at the Montreal Conservatoire and McGill University, he first attended Pierre Monteux's summer school in Maine in 1956. A scholarship enabled him to study with Igor Markevitch in Mexico City, where he made his offi-cial conducting debut with the National SO of Mexico and won first prize in the Pan-American Conducting Competition in 1958. He exhibited his en-trepreneurial skills early by founding and directing the Philharmonic Youth Orchestra in Montreal (1959–61). In 1962 he took third prize at the Liver-pool Conducting Competition and then served as Walter Susskind's assistant with the Toronto SO (1963–65). The late 1960s saw his activities centered in England as conductor of the newly formed Northern Sinfonia Orchestra (1964–69) and as conductor of the Royal Ballet's touring company (1966–68). He made his Covent Garden debut with the Royal Ballet in Stravinsky's *The Soldier's Tale* in 1966. After winning the Mitropoulos Con-ducting Competition in 1968, he spent the following season as Bernstein's as-sistant with the New York PO. In Canada he served as music coordinator at Lakehead University, directing the Lakehead (ON) SO (1967–72) and the Regina (SK) SO (1971–73).

His long tenure with the Hamilton (ON) PO (1969–90), though it ended acrimoniously, was a remarkable achievement. He transformed a community orchestra into one of Canada's leading symphonic ensembles. He sallied forth into the staid community with "an evangelist's fervor" to bring his artistic vision to shopping malls, steel mills, schools, and libraries, as well as the concert hall. By devising outreach programs utilizing small chamber ensembles such as the original Canadian Brass, he was able to provide extended contracts to abler players to build the quality of the orchestra and to extend its season. In its heyday it played a forty-two-week season to 16,000 subscribers. When, after twenty-one years, the board decided not to renew Brott's contract, William Littler wrote in the *Toronto Star* that "the excitement of the early years had peaked, leading to a period of artistic stasis and audience decline." During this period Brott was conductor of the BBC Welsh Orchestra (1972–77) and the CBC Winnipeg (MB) Orchestra (1976–83), interim director of the Atlanta (Ga.) SO (1971), founder-director of Symphony Nova Scotia, and conductor of the Ontario Place Pops Orchestra (1983–91).

If Brott was down after the Hamilton debacle, he was by no means out. He and his wife, Ardyth, had founded the Boris Brott Summer Music Festival in 1988. Over the course of the next seventeen years, what began as a ten-day event centered in Hamilton became a twenty-week season with a plethora of concerts and events in venues throughout southern Ontario, extending to Toronto itself in 1998. The festival focused on classical music concerts but included a variety of events with popular appeal. The mainstay of the festival was the National Academy Orchestra, an ad hoc ensemble comprising gifted young instrumentalists drawn from leading colleges, conservatories, and universities alongside a sprinkling of seasoned professionals acting as mentors. Each year people were astonished at the quality achieved by the ensemble after such a short time together. One particular feature was the Hamilton Living Heritage Series that showcased Canadian music, emphasizing Brott's lifelong commitment to Canadian composers. Brott's work with the National Academy Orchestra is a fine example of his effort to develop young artists. In 2004 he was named principal youth and family conductor of the National Arts Centre Orchestra in Ottawa, with which he had worked for over twenty years conducting performances for Young People's Concerts and working extensively with outreach programs to schools and communities. He conducted or produced over one hundred programs for radio and television in Canada and the UK.

One result of the Hamilton departure was Brott's decision to enroll in law school at the University of Western Ontario (1992–95). What began casually as an invitation to address IBM executives after a concert in Dallas in 1991 developed into a parallel career as a motivational speaker addressing corporations around the world in any one of the five languages in which he is fluent. The theme of his presentations is the common goals shared by music and business: teamwork, creativity, and leadership. They involve participants in an interactive performance with either a small ensemble or a video recording.

Objectives that had been consistently in evidence throughout Brott's career emerged again when he created the New West SO from a merger of the financially strapped Ventura County and Conejo SOs in 1992, with no less a vision than the creation of a professional orchestra of the first rank, staffed primarily by players from the Los Angeles region. Since its inception, the orchestra has focused on the classical symphonic repertoire, although it has also paid more than lip service to American music. In addition to a seven-concert subscription series in Oxnard and Thousand Oaks, outreach and educational activities extend throughout Ventura County and beyond via Our Symphonic Adventure concerts. A notable event is the Discovery Artists Program and Concert, which serves to further Brott's mission of nurturing young talent. In 2002 he took over the leadership of the McGill CO, of which he had been co-conductor with his father since 1989.

His excursions into the theater have been infrequent. He conducted Donizetti's *Daughter of the Regiment* for the Canadian Opera Company in 1977 and later directed Hamilton Opera. Recently, he gave a much-admired concert performance of Bizet's *Carmen* with the New West SO in Ventura County. Over his long career his guest appearances have included all the major Canadian and British orchestras, and frequent trips to Central and South America, France, Germany, Italy, Scandinavia, Japan, Korea, Israel, and the Netherlands. Brott's recording career extends from 1967, when he laid down recordings of twentieth-century British music, to the recent issue of a DVD of Bernstein's *Mass*, recorded in Rome in 2000. A number of recordings with the legendary pianist Glenn Gould have recently surfaced from the archives and are being issued on CD, including Gould's own *So You Want to Write a Fugue*. Other recordings conducted by Brott have appeared on the CBC, Mace, Mercury, Pro Arte, Sony Classical, and Albany labels with orchestras that include the London SO, Northern Sinfonia Orchestra, Toronto SO, and CBC Toronto Orchestra.

Website
http://www.borisbrott.com/

Further Reading
Gee, Ken. "Regional Reports—Hamilton: Middle-of-the-Road." *Musi-Canada (Canadian Music Council)* 40 (September 1979): 6–7.
Schulman, Michael. "Boris Brott." *The Canadian Composer/Le Compositeur Canadien* 142 (June 1979): 8–15.

Stewart, Andrew. "A Classic Opportunity in Hamilton." *Classical Music Magazine* 14, no. 3 (1991): 17–20.

Selected Recordings
Brott (Alexander): *Violin Concerto*; *Arabesque for Cello and Orchestra*; *7 Minuets and 6 Canons*; *Paraphrase in Polyphony*; Angèle Dubeau (vn); Denis Brott (vc); McGill CO. Analekta 29801.
Davies (Victor): *Mennonite Piano Concerto*; *Good Times*; Irmgard Baerg (pf), London SO. Lilypad 5995.
Mozart: *Le nozze di Figaro*; Tiziana Carraro (s), José Fardilha (b), Marco Grimaldi (br), Madelyn Renée Monti (s), Rossana Potenza (s), Alessandra Zapparoli (s); Rome PO. Kultur Video 2842 DVD.
Webern: *Concerto*, Op. 24; Glenn Gould (pf), (from *Glenn Gould Edition—Berg, Krenek, Webern, Debussy, Ravel*). Sony 52661.
Weinzweig: *Dummiyah/Silence*; O der Beethovenhalle-Bonn, (from 4-CD set). Centredisques CMCCD 8002.

Brown, Justin
Born 2 March 1962 in Haywards Heath, Sussex, England

The son of amateur musicians, Justin Brown grew up in a home with two grand pianos and began playing them at age four. Five years later he began playing violin, which exposed him to chamber and orchestral music. Cricket, football, and tennis followed, but eventually music won out and he went on to earn a music degree at Cambridge University. Brown also studied with Seiji **Ozawa** and Leonard Bernstein at Tanglewood Music Center, making his conducting debut with the British stage premiere of Bernstein's *Mass*.

He gained considerable attention as staff conductor of the English National Opera and Scottish National Opera, as well as in numerous guest appearances conducting operas throughout Asia, Australia, and Europe, particularly in Scandinavia and the UK. While in Glasgow, Brown also founded the St. Bride's CO. After several years of freelancing as pianist and conductor, he accepted the full-time position of music director of the Alabama SO, beginning with the 2006–7 season.

Chosen by the ASO for his combination of talent, passion, vision, charisma, and energy, Brown came to Birmingham eager to be involved in all aspects of the orchestra's work, to give a focus and personality to the enterprise, and to become a real presence in the community. One of his priorities is to celebrate and connect with local institutions and cultural resources, particularly to bring the ASO closer to the city's black community. Brown wants to take the orchestra to varied venues and wider audiences by means of touring, recording, radio, and the internet. Hoping to dispel the perception that classical music is elitist, he passionately champions music for schools and takes the orchestra to them.

Known for his extremely physical and eloquent conducting style, Brown frequently conducts sans baton and will perform unusual antics such as playing air violin and dancing to the edge of the podium. Since coming to the ASO, Brown has reorganized the arrangement of the string section and programmed edgier, more adventurous repertoire. Critics have commented on the orchestra's cleaner, brighter sound, its energy and enthusiasm, its new silky warmth, and its color and balance. Apparently Brown's personal warmth and intensity are being absorbed and reflected by the orchestra.

A frequent guest conductor, Brown has appeared with many orchestras, including the BBC SO, Royal PO, Bournemouth SO, London SO, Malmö SO (Sweden), Norrköping SO (Sweden), Stavanger SO (Norway), Odense SO (Denmark), Trondheim SO (Norway), Dresden PO, Berlin SO, Winterthur Orchestra, Orchestre du Capitole de Toulouse, St. Petersburg PO, Danish Radio Sinfonietta, Swedish CO, Bergen PO (Norway), Lahti SO (Finland), Finnish RSO, RTL Luxembourg Orchestra, and others in Europe, Australia, and Asia.

Further Reading

Burton, William Westbrook. "Bernstein Protégés: Justin Brown." In *Conversations about Bernstein*, 94–104. New York: Oxford University Press, 1995.
Huebner, Michael. "Music to Birmingham's Ears: New Conductor Wants Orchestra to Reach Out to Wider Audience." *Birmingham News*, 29 January 2006, 1F.

Selected Recordings

Bernstein: *Candide*; Nickolas Grace (br); Scottish Opera O. Ter 1156.
Carter: *Concerto for Violin*; *Lauds*; Rolf Schulte (vn); Odense SO. From *Music of Elliott Carter Vol. 6*, Bridge 9177.
Elgar: *Cello Concerto in e*, Op. 85. Barber: *Cello Concerto in a*, Op. 22; Anne Gastinel (vc); City of Birmingham SO. Naïve V 4961.
Koch: *Memory of a Summer Day*; *Earth My Likeness*; Susanne Elmark (s); Odense SO. From *Jesper Koch: Orchestral Works*, Dacapo 8.226502.
Tavener: *The Protecting Veil*; *Thrinos*; *Eternal Memory*; Raphael Wallfisch (vc); Royal PO. Intersound 2847.

Bychkov, Semyon

Born 30 November 1952 in Leningrad, Soviet Union

Although he seldom appears in the U.S., Bychkov's inclusion in this book is warranted because he is a naturalized citizen. After a formal musical education in the Soviet system, he spent a year at the Mannes College of Music in New York City, making an immediate impression as a student conductor. An invitation to conduct *Il Trovatore* at the Art Park Festival followed and led to his appointment as music director of the Grand Rapids (Mich.) SO (1980–85). He became associate, then principal guest conductor, of the Buffalo (N.Y.) PO, and succeeded Julius Rudel as music director in 1985. Following a remarkable series of last-minute substitutions for ailing maestros—Haitink at the Concertgebouw; Kubelik at the New York PO; Muti at the Berlin PO; Rowicki at the Bamberg SO; and Chailly at the Vienna PO—he was ready to vault onto the international conducting circuit. Karajan even mentioned him as his possible successor in Berlin, and Phillips Records signed him for an exclusive five-year contract. The leap he took was to accept the conductorship of the Orchestre de Paris (1989). Since then his career has been centered in Europe.

Bychkov has always felt the need to put down musical and domestic roots and have an orchestra of his own to work with intensively. He has shaped his career around perceived opportunities for growth rather than strategically planned moves aimed toward Parnassus. In fact, there seem to have been contradictory elements at play throughout his career. On the one hand he is admired as a deeply thoughtful and passionate musician, on the other he has been called a heavy-handed, obtrusive, and superficial interpreter. Take, for example, his recording of Strauss's *Ein Heldenleben* with the WDR (Hamburg) SO (2003). It garnered very favorable reviews; Michael Kennedy (*Sunday Telegraph*, 13 April 2003) described it as "a most impressive performance . . . notable for sheer musicality and avoidance of meretricious playing to the gallery." In an interview, Bychkov explained that he and the orchestra had "refined their understanding of Strauss's epic tone poem in the course of more than 40 concert performances." However, one of these performances, at Carnegie Hall in February 2002, left the *New York Times* critic Paul Griffiths decidedly unimpressed; he found it "crude and spasmodic. Mr. Bychkov staked everything on the vulgar points he wanted to make now and then and the performance fell apart." All artists can experience an off night, especially on tour, but this is by no means an isolated example. How does one reconcile such comments as "inspired conducting, which breathed life into phrase after phrase," with "music making [that] lacked passion and impetus, that often projected an air of studied affectation?" Perhaps he has not so far made it into the highest echelons of his profession because his desire to impress in public makes him his own worst enemy—a fault of which he seems to be aware and for which he tries to compensate by becoming too restrained and inward-looking at times. His much-heralded debut at the Met in 2004 with *Boris Godunov* was seen as "subdued" and "a curiously low-key affair." With a Bychkov performance, it seems, one is either going to be transported or underwhelmed.

Bychkov showed early musical promise, possessing perfect pitch and taking piano lessons from the age of five. In 1959 he entered the Glinka Choir School, one of twenty successful applicants from a field of 2,000. Here he was much influenced by his teacher, Lina Anikova Stepenova, and by attending rehearsals of the Leningrad PO (where an early mentor, Yuri **Temirkanov**, was making his mark). Here, also, was where he first acquired a taste for conducting. Graduating with a Diploma of Honor, he continued his studies at the Leningrad Conservatory (1970–74) as a pianist and as a member of the conducting class of the legendary Ilya Musin. Winning first prize in the Rachmaninoff Conducting Competition, he began to acquire experience by conducting twenty performances of *Eugene Onegin*. He would have gone on to debut with the Leningrad PO had it not been for a brush with the KGB! He did not consider himself a dissident, but he was certainly a nonconformist and a Jew, and was clearly chafing under the Soviet system. He left Russia at the earliest opportunity, and it is shortly thereafter that we find him knocking on the door of the Mannes College of Music in 1975. His conducting of a student production of Tchaikovsky's one-act opera *Iolanta*, its U.S. debut, brought him to the attention of then-principal, famed Met mezzo-soprano Risë Stevens, who "kept a friendly eye on his advancing career." After obtaining his artist diploma in 1976, he was retained as conductor of the college orchestra (1976–80). In 1983, during his tenure as music director of the Grand Rapids (Mich.) SO, he was sworn in as a naturalized U.S. citizen on stage during a concert and promptly turned to the orchestra to lead them in *The Star-Spangled Banner*. His work with the Buffalo (N.Y.) PO (1985–89) was decidedly impressive, and his formidable personality helped pull the organization out of artistic doldrums and ensure some financial stability. When Bychkov assumed his position, the orchestra was carrying a $1 million debt and playing a reduced season. By 1986 he had turned affairs around and had the orchestra ready to tour. Its appearance at Carnegie Hall prompted critic Tim Page to describe the performance as "a musical event tinged with greatness." It was also during this time that Bychkov participated in the series of jet-setting substitutions mentioned above.

Bychkov found his removal to Paris and an orchestra subsidized by the French government challenging, to say the least. Together, conductor and orchestra made significant, if uneven, progress toward cohesiveness, although as late as February 1996, the *Financial Times* described a performance of *The Rite of Spring* in London as "a distinctly shoddy reading." During his tenure (1989–98) he was obliged to familiarize himself with the French repertoire and venture into performing more contemporary music. He found particular sympathy for the orchestral works of Henri Dutilleux. This was also the time when, under contract to Phillips, he produced a series of esteemed recordings with his own orchestra and with the Berlin PO, Concertgebouw Orchestra, London PO, Philharmonia Orchestra, and Bavarian RSO. Having centered his activities thus far in the concert hall, the 1990s saw him making distinctive contributions in the opera house, leading to his appointment as chief conductor to the Semperoper in Dresden (1999–2003). A performance of *Eugene Onegin* while he was principal guest conductor of the Maggio Musicale Fiorentino (1992–98) was particularly admired, one critic writing that it was "rare to hear an Italian orchestra play with such refinement, precision, and tonal luster." He also appeared as a guest conductor directing *Elektra* (Vienna State Opera and Covent Garden), *Salome* (Hamburg), *Tristan* (Chicago and Vienna), *Tosca* (Milan), and *The Queen of Spades* (Amsterdam), among others. However, his traditional views of opera production and his ubiquitous presence in all aspects of a production's preparation have not always endeared him to administrators, and, despite artistic success, he decided not to extend his contract in Dresden. Similarly, on the grounds that "methods used to govern the orchestra . . . are harmful to its music making," he decided not to renew his contract as principal guest conductor of the St. Petersburg PO, which originally ran from 1990 to 1994.

It has been in the slightly rarified atmosphere of the West German Radio (WDR) in Cologne, where Bychkov has been chief conductor since 1997, that he feels most comfortable and at home artistically. Here he can work with adequate rehearsal time, during which he is notoriously exacting, meticulous, and verbose. In partnership with the enterprising Avie label, he has been able to resume his recording activities with generous preparation time and first-rate audio engineering. His tenure with the orchestra has produced a viable partnership achieving considerable eminence. Playing praised for its "dramatic urgency," "tonal luster," and "romantic bloom," puts them, if not quite in the orchestral "top drawer," then very close to it. Their recordings of Shostakovich symphonies have been particularly well received. A concert performance of *Daphne* (2004) with Renée Fleming in the title role so impressed one critic that he declared: "Lucky, lucky Cologne."

Bychkov's expressed desire to take "several months a year for myself, for study and to reflect on what I'm doing" is indicative of the introverted aspect of his character and doesn't leave him much time for guest appearances. He has also expressed a desire to divide his time between concerts and opera "for the sake of balance." He conducted *Boris Godunov* at Covent Garden in 2003, followed by his Met debut with the same work the following year. That, and performances of *Tristan* in Chicago (he had to withdraw from a scheduled *Aida* due to injury), together with guest appearances conducting the Pittsburgh SO, suggest American audiences may be seeing him more often in the future.

Website
http://www.semyonbychkov.com

Further Reading
Allison, John. "Semyon Bychkov." *Opera* 51 (November 2000): 1301–04.
Jolly, James. "The French Connection." *Gramophone* 69 (September 1991): 11.
Kupferberg, Herbert. "Semyon Bychkov on Tour with His Paris Orchestra." *American Record Guide* 57, no. 2 (1994): 12–14.
Reel, James. "Conversing with Conductor Semyon Bychkov." *Fanfare* 27 (May–June 2004): 35–39.

Selected Recordings
Mahler: *Symphony no. 3*. Höller: *Der ewige Tag*; Marjana Lipovšek (a); West German R. Ch. Ladies; Cathedral Ch. Girls and Boys, Köln; West German RSO and Ch. Avie AV 0019, live: Köln 1/2002.
Shostakovich: *Symphony no. 7*; West German RSO. Avie AV 0020.
Strauss (R): *Daphne*; Renée Fleming (*Daphne*); Kwanchul Youn (*Peneios*); Anna Larsson (*Gaen*); Michael Schade (*Leukippos*); Johan Botha (*Apollo*); Cologne West German RSO and Men's Ch. Decca 000518202.
Tchaikovsky: *Symphony no. 6*; Royal Concertgebouw O. Phillips 420925.

~

Christie, Michael
Born 30 June 1974 in Buffalo, New York

Although Michael Christie's musical career didn't begin especially early, it has accelerated spectacularly. He began playing trumpet in high school and went on to earn a bachelor's degree in trumpet performance at Oberlin College Conservatory of Music (1996). While there, however, he also studied conducting with Robert **Spano** and Peter Jaffe. Despite being the youngest entrant at the first International Sibelius Conductors' Competition (1995) in Helsinki, he gained international attention when the judges awarded him a specially created prize for outstanding potential.

This gave Christie the opportunity to spend 1996–97 in an apprenticeship with Daniel **Barenboim** at the Chicago SO and the Berlin Staatsoper, followed by another in 1997–98 with Franz **Welser-Möst** at the Zurich Opera House, where he was assistant conductor. During these same years (1996–98) Christie was associate conductor at the Helsinki PO. In 2000, he was appointed music director of the annual summer Colorado Music Festival in Boulder, which had been losing audience and funding. Under his leadership the festival has attracted increasingly larger audiences and garnered additional sponsorship, bringing financial stability to a faltering organization.

Christie accepted a position as artistic director and chief conductor of the Queensland (Australia) SO from 2001 to 2004 and remains principal guest conductor. Their Sculthorpe recording was nominated for an Australian Recording Industry Association (ARIA) award in 2004. The Phoenix (Ariz.) SO appointed him music director in 2005, as did the Brooklyn (N.Y.) PO in 2006, both with great expectations.

Called mature beyond his years and bearing encomiums such as "masterly" and having "staggering talent," Christie is known for his exuberance, imagination, and a willingness to experiment. He demonstrates collegiality with the orchestra and communicates his enjoyment of the music with both musicians and audience. He gives preconcert chats and often interviews soloists onstage during intermissions. One of his innovations is a concert guide called "Keeping Score," which involves printed commentary corresponding to numbers that flash on a screen at appropriate moments. In Colorado he has added family-friendly performances such as a "Spotlight Series" of morning concerts for children and families. Some of his other efforts include the "Composer Spotlight Initiative," "Bach's Coffee House," and projects at schools. Christie wants to heighten orchestral visibility through increased community outreach and artistic excellence, and he channels his engaging energy into fund-raising and development. He says he is "trying to put a human face back on this art form and create effective bridges between the orchestra and the community."

In 2006 the American Symphony Orchestra League gave him the Helen M. Thompson Award for an emerging music director, which recognizes superior talent, exceptional musical leadership, commitment to organizational vitality, and potential for continued artistic growth..

Christie has made guest appearances across the U.S. and Europe, conducting the City of Birmingham SO, Lausanne CO, Royal Liverpool PO, Swedish RSO, the major Finnish orchestras, Luxembourg PO, Czech PO, and the symphony orchestras of Atlanta, Dallas, Indianapolis, Los Angeles, Minnesota, Pittsburgh, Saint Louis, and Vancouver, among others.

Further Reading

"1st International Sibelius Conductors' Competition: No Winner, But One Megatalent." *Finnish Music Quarterly* no. 4 (1995): 54–55.

Lewis, Zachary. "Oberlin Portrait: Michael Christie." *Oberlin Portrait*, 2 November 2006. http://www.oberlin.edu/con/bkstage200611/portrait_michaelChristie.html

Selected Recording

Sculthorpe: *Songs of Sea and Sky*; William Barton (didgeridoo); Queensland SO. ABC Classics 476 192-1.

⌒

Conlon, James
Born 18 March 1950 in New York, New York

"I conduct every performance as if it were the last one in my life, which it might be." This statement, a mixture of the deeply felt and (in the best sense) the naïve, is typical of the philosophical underpinnings that have supported Conlon's deliberate and thoughtful progress as a conductor in a career spanning over thirty years. When interviewed, he is soft-spoken and intense; friendly, if a little reserved, but never stuffy. In discussing his ideas about music and conducting he is not reticent about expressing his deeply held views, and a number of consistent threads emerge. Both on and off the podium he seems remarkably free of narcissism, with genuine humility in the service of music-making. Since his early teens, music has been his calling and way of life. He is not interested in the power conducting brings for its own sake, but he does realize the spiritual force of his art and the ability it gives him to inspire, uplift, console, and transform lives. He deplores any indulgence in personal vanity by celebrities in general, and by musicians in particular, unless they intend to use their gifts to infect others with their enthusiasm. The greatest satisfaction a musician can experience derives from a sense of service as guardian and caretaker of a great legacy. Conlon has been driven by a fierce ambition in pursuit of this end and states that his personal goal is simply to survive and keep on conducting! How can so ostensibly modest a man have enjoyed so much success? In today's world, although the conductor is still the leader of the orchestra, he or she can no longer be autocratic in the way that Toscanini and Szell were. A different psychology is required, and Conlon's strength is that he has had the perspicacity to develop it. His strategy seems to be gentle insistence and a mastery of the situation that involves not only his relationship with a given orchestra, but also the cultural grounding of the music he is performing and the ethos in which it is being made. He is acutely aware of the different ways orchestras in the Anglo-American, Teutonic, and Latin traditions work. This sensitivity is reflected in his unexpected success at the Paris Opéra, accounted for by the respect he earned from all sides and the cavalier approach (his "What have I got to lose?" attitude) he brought to the position in the first place.

He seems to have been fully aware of the pitfalls and disadvantages inherent in early success, and, for the first ten years of his professional life, made a conscious decision to work only as a guest conductor to avoid the extra-musical responsibilities of a music director. He has continued to carefully measure each step of his professional development, but his deeply serious purpose has been nurtured by an almost childlike delight in making music. He has taken the most appropriate opportunities that arose and, with each of his appointments, consistently raised the prestige of his ensembles to rank with the best.

Conlon's decision to base his career in Europe after 1980 was a complex one. Partly, it had to do with the fact that American conductors are undervalued in the U.S. (At the time of this writing, of the so-called Big Five American orchestras only one—Boston with James Levine—has an American-born music director.) He was also drawn to Europe in a Henry Jamesian way. It began as an annual trip that became a desire to stay. The influence of his Juilliard teacher, the irascible Frenchman Jean Morel, also nurtured a liking for France and things French. Professionally speaking, however, there was more to it. He senses "osmosis of place"; culture is absorbed not simply from specific places or institutions, but necessarily, as he sees it, from the sociocultural milieu in which a performer steeps himself. At the same time he regrets that classical music plays a far less significant role in the U.S., where there is a pervading climate of anti-intellectualism and the misapprehension that some sort of expertise is required when listening to music rather than just an ability to take it at face (ear!) value.

Conlon's own life history belies such trappings of elitism. Coming from a modest and not particularly musical home, he had a classic epiphany while accompanying a friend's family to an amateur performance of *La Traviata* when he was eleven years old. This fired his enthusiasm for opera and eventually his ambition to conduct, and he made a late start learning piano and violin. His enthusiasm for classical music did not sit well with his peers at school, so when he transferred to New York's High School of Music and Art in 1965, he was relieved to find contemporaries interested in the same kinds of things he was. He entered Juilliard in 1968 and, by his junior year, was assistant conductor of the school's orchestra. As an assistant at the Spoleto Festival in Italy in 1971, he was given the opportunity to conduct one of the performances of Mussorgsky's *Boris Godunov*, which he did to much acclaim. When Thomas Schippers was unable to conduct Juilliard's American Opera Theater performance of *La Bohème* in 1972, Conlon's substitution was urged by no less a personage than Maria Callas. Immediately upon graduation he was made a staff conductor at Juilliard (1972–75) and signed a contract with Columbia Records. In 1974 he was given an American National Orchestral Association Award, and, at the invitation of Pierre Boulez, became the youngest conductor to lead a New York PO subscription concert. At Juilliard he gave the first performance of Samuel Barber's revised version of *Antony and Cleopatra* in 1975. His Met debut followed with *Die Zauberflöte* in 1976; he conducted there regularly for the following four seasons and has returned frequently over the years since. Specializing somewhat in Verdi, he conducted *Macbeth* for Scottish Opera in 1976 and made his Covent Garden debut with *Don Carlos* in 1979. He did not neglect the concert platform, however, and was busy making guest appearances in the U.S. and around the world. His first appointment, which has continued for over twenty-five years, was as music director of the Cincinnati May Festival, primarily devoted to choral music and utilizing the services of the Cincinnati (Ohio) SO. His close association with France began in 1980 when he first appeared in concert with the Orchestre de Paris. More significantly, the following year, he gave his Paris Opéra debut with the double bill of *Il Tabarro* and *I Pagliacci*. When he was approached by the Rotterdam PO to become chief conductor he felt he was ready to take on his first permanent appointment, committing himself to a schedule of upwards of sixty concerts a year. He held this post from 1983 to 1991 with great distinction. By the close of the 1980s Conlon had built up the orchestra to be one of the most accomplished in Europe and toured successfully with them both there and in the U.S. He built on the strong Mahler tradition in Holland with performances that rivaled those of the more prestigious orchestras in Amsterdam and The Hague. His reading of the Sixth Symphony was particularly admired. Having appeared as guest conductor with the leading European orchestras, including the London PO and the Berlin PO, he felt ready to take on his first permanent opera house appointment as conductor in Cologne, which he held from 1989 to 2000. After two years he was appointed *Generalmusikdirektor* of the City of Cologne, which included the conductorship of the city's Gürzenich Orchester, as the opera orchestra is known. He was the first individual in over forty years to hold both posts, and this gave him the opportunity to conduct Wagner, which he had not done previously. In 1993 he appeared for the first time at La Scala, Milan, conducting Weber's *Oberon*.

The administration of the Paris Opéra, which supervises performances at the newly contructed Bastille Opera House and the nineteenth-century Palais Garnier, is intimately bound up with French cultural politics. In its short history it saw the hasty departures of the two previous music directors, Daniel **Barenboim** and Myun-Whun Chung. Conlon's appointment owed much to his having already established a good working relationship with the Opéra's dictatorial administrator, Hughes Gall. For the 1995–96 season he served as music advisor, previous engagements allowing him to conduct only two productions. During his first full season as principal conductor he quickly enhanced his public profile with performances of Puccini, Verdi, Wagner, and Debussy, winning kudos for the high quality of the performances and approval of his interpretations. His continuing tenure was due both to his shrewdness in avoiding political and power struggles and to his understanding of the temperament of French orchestral musicians. No greater compliment can be paid him than the claim that France's best orchestra resided in the pit of the Bastille. In 1996 Conlon agreed to make an innovative movie of Puccini's *Madama Butterfly* with the director Frédéric Mitterand. By using young and relatively inexperienced singers with "fresh voices and credible faces," accompanied by the Orchestre de Paris, which was unfamiliar with the music, Conlon created a performance devoid of either musical or dramatic clichés. He wound up his final season with the Paris Opéra in 2004 with Verdi's *Otello* at the Bastille and a farewell concert with the orchestra on stage at the Palais Garnier. He left to become director of the Ravinia Festival, cementing his ties to the Chicago SO. By the 2006 season, attendance levels were up to 83 percent, well above expectations, due largely to Conlon's influence.

Whenever Conlon appears in the U.S. as guest conductor he invariably wins accolades from orchestras, audiences, and critics. The *Washington Post* commented, "His visits often mean each season's sweetest musical memories." He has maintained his contacts with the Aspen Music Festival from being a student there, and he appears regularly and teaches at the Tanglewood Festival. Further indication that he intends to reposition his career in the U.S. came with his appointment as music director of the Los Angeles Opera in 2006, in addition to directing Chicago's Ravinia Festival. One suspects that he has both the Chicago SO and the Met directorships in his sights.

His performances in both concerts and the opera house are marked by discipline, sensitivity, and flair. He inspires musicians to give their best and produce passionately committed performances. He gets everything to fall into place through judicious choice of tempi, rhythmic tension, warmth, color, radiance, and contrast. His operatic performances find just the appropriate characterization and pungency to match the score. Although not averse to innovation, and encouraging it at the Paris Opéra, he believes strongly that stage directors should not go against the spirit of the score for the sake of theatrical effect. He feels the obligation to defend the intrinsic musical integrity of a work, as "the greatest dramatist is the composer."

As Conlon is such a welcomed guest conductor, his list of appearances is extensive. In North America he has appeared with the orchestras of Detroit, Houston, Cincinnati, Pittsburgh, Washington D.C., Los Angeles, San Francisco, Toronto, Montreal, and Vancouver, as well as the "Big Five" orchestras of New York, Boston, Cleveland, Philadelphia, and Chicago. In Europe he has appeared frequently with the Berlin PO, London PO, London SO, City of Birmingham SO, Hallé Orchestra, L'Orchestre National de France, Dresden Staatskapelle, and L'Orchestra di Santa Cecilia. He has conducted opera in London, Milan, Chicago, and Moscow.

Conlon has been a champion of neglected works, including the early symphonies of Dvořák, the three symphonies of Max Bruch, Liszt's oratorios and symphonies, Weill's *Propheten*, and more recently the music of Alexander von Zemlinsky (1871–1942), including three of his operas, *Die Zwerg, Die Seejungfrau,* and *Eine florentinische Tragödie.* He conducted the premiere of Tobias Picker's *An American Tragedy,* a Met commission, in December 2005. Over his career he has compiled an extensive roster of recordings that includes a distinguished series of Mozart symphonies with the Scottish CO, and music of Mozart, Weber, Liszt, Puccini, Bartók, Janáček, Stravinsky, and Poulenc with the Rotterdam PO. With his Cologne forces he has recorded Mahler, Bruch, Weber, von Zemlinsky, Goldmark, Mendelssohn, and Berg, and with French forces he has recorded Stravinsky's *Rossignol* and Puccini's *Madama Butterfly.* A number of his opera performances are available on video.

Website
http://www.jamesconlon.com

Further Reading
"Conlon, James." In *World Musicians,* edited by Clifford Thompson, 185–86. New York: H. W. Wilson Company, 1999.

Dyer, Richard. "James Conlon Has Careers in Two Continents." *Boston Globe*, 13 July 1997, N9.
Kellow, Brian. "At Home Abroad." *Opera News* 63 (June 1999): 14–18.
McClellan, Joseph. "James Conlon's Continental Connection." *Washington Post*, 4 July 1987, D1.
Smith, Patrick. "James Conlon." *Opera* 49 (February 1998): 147–52.

Selected Recordings
Dvořák: *Rusalka*; Larissa Diadkova (*Jazibaba*); Renée Fleming (*Rusalka*); Franz Hawlata (*Vodnik*); Sergei Larin (*Prince*); Eva Urbanova (*Foreign Princess*); Paris Opera O. TDK Oprus DVD.
Mahler: *Symphony no. 5*; Cologne Güzenich O. EMI 74979.
Rossini: *Semiramide*; June Anderson (s); Marilyn Horne (ms); Stanford Olsen (t); Samuel Ramey (b); Metropolitan Op C; Metropolitan Op O. ImageEntertainment 57793 DVD.
Stravinsky: *Le Rossignol*; Natalie Dessay (*Le Rossignol*); Marie McLaughlin (*La Cuisinière*); Violeta Urmana (*La Mort*); Vsevolod Grivnov (*Le Pêcheur*); Albert Schagidullin (*L'Empereur*); Laurent Naouri (*Le Chambellan*); Maxim Mikhailov (*Le Bonze*); Hugo Simcic (*L'Enfant*); O and Ch of the Opéra National de Paris; Christian Chaudet, director. Virgin 44242 DVD.
Zemlinsky: *Complete Choral Works and Orchestral Songs*; Deborah Voigt (s); Donnie Ray Albert (br); Soile Isokoski (s); Violeta Urmana (ms); Andreas Schmidt (br); Michael Volle (br); Düsseldorf Muziekvereins Ch; Gürzenich-O Kölner. EMI 5 86079 2.

⌒

Cooper, Grant
Born 18 April 1953 in Wellington, New Zealand

The son of an opera singer, Grant Cooper sang in his first opera at age four, going on to study piano and music theory, and to compose. After graduating from the University of Auckland with a degree in pure mathematics, he came to the U.S. to be assistant director of bands at Yale University. His performance on the trumpet led to fellowships from Tanglewood and the Queen Elizabeth II Arts Council of New Zealand. Cooper was principal trumpet of the Tulsa (Okla.) PO and earned a master's degree in music from the University of Tulsa. He then focused his attention on conducting. He was music director for the Fredonia (N.Y.) Chamber Players from 1983–99 and for the

Penfield (N.Y.) SO from 1993–99. Also from 1993 to 2003 he served as professor of music at Ithaca (N.Y.) College, where he directed the orchestra. Since 2001, Cooper has been artistic director and conductor of the West Virginia SO and resident conductor of the Syracuse (N.Y.) SO, where he previously was associate conductor (1997–2001). He is also artistic director for the summer Bach & Beyond Festival in Fredonia, and was artistic director and conductor for the Anchorage (Alaska) Festival of Music until 2003.

Cooper likes to program concerts around themes and is known for showcasing local talent and works by New Zealand composers. His conducting often focuses on precision, while at the same time communicates intensely the emotion of the music to both orchestra and audience. Cooper also connects with audiences at pops or family concerts, combining an atmosphere of fun with interesting music. His own compositions and arrangements, many written for young audiences, reflect his belief that orchestral music can be appreciated by people of all ages. He and the WVSO won a 2005 NEA Access to Artistic Excellence grant to support a tour introducing orchestral music to new audiences in rural and underserved communities throughout West Virginia.

Cooper was guest conductor of the fourteenth Commonwealth Games (1990) closing ceremonies in Auckland, appearing with Dame Kiri Te Kanawa as soloist. He returned to New Zealand to conduct the millennium celebrations there with the Auckland Philharmonia. Cooper has appeared regularly as guest conductor of Ottawa's Thirteen Strings and the philharmonic orchestras of Buffalo and Rochester. In recent years he has also conducted the Spokane (Wash.) SO, Erie (Pa.) PO, Kansas City (Mo.) SO, Stamford (Conn.) SO, Cayuga CO, Syracuse Opera, and the Mozart Wochen of the Heidelberger Schlossfestspiele.

Selected Recordings
Cooper: *Boyz in the Wood and Other Fables*; Deborah Montgomery (s); Steven Stull (br); Liane Hansen (narrator); Grant Cooper (narrator); Martha Hamilton (*Miller's Daughter*); Mitch Weiss (*Rumpelstiltzkin/King*); Ithaca Children's Choir; Cayuga CO. Kiwiflite.
Lilburn: *Allegro for Strings*; *Concert Overture in D*; *Introduction and Allegro for Strings*; *Four Canzonas*; *Diversions for Strings*; Ithaca College Festival O. From Kiwi Pacific CD-SLD-99, live: Ithaca 9/1996.
Ritchie: *Viola Concerto*; Timothy Deighton (va); Penn's Woods Festival O; From *Viola Aotearoa*, Atoll ACD202, live: Penn State University, 7/1/2000.

⌒

Cumming, Edward
Born 10 August 1957 in Oakland, California

Edward Cumming won the prestigious Eisner Prize for Creative Achievement in the Arts while still an undergraduate at the University of California at Berkeley (BA, 1979). He studied with Michael Tilson **Thomas** at the Los Angeles Philharmonic Institute and with Otto-Werner Mueller at Yale University, where he earned a master of arts (1985) and a doctorate (1992) in orchestral conducting.

A resident conductor of the Florida Orchestra from 1989 to 1993, he initiated popular "Champagne" and "Coffee" concert series for young adults and senior citizens. In 1993 he became the founding music director of the Pacific Symphony Institute, where he stayed until 1996. He conducted the PSI Orchestra in world premieres of Hector Armienta's *Caras del Sol* and Khoa Van Le's *Symphonic Ode to Vietnam, 1975*. The Flagstaff (Ariz.) Festival of the Arts appointed him artistic director in 1996. From 1997 to 2002, Cumming was resident conductor of the Pittsburgh SO, where he worked closely with Mariss **Jansons**. During the same years he served as music director for the Pittsburgh YSO, with which he led the world premiere performance of Tamar Diesendruck's *Every Which Wave*. While in Pittsburgh, Cumming conducted concerts for young people, outreach concerts throughout the state, and syndicated radio broadcasts.

Cumming accepted the position of music director for the Hartford (Conn.) SO in 2001. There he has continued to demonstrate his passion for outreach and educational programming. He began a "Rush Hour Classics" series aimed at young professionals, with cocktails at 5:30 followed by a 6:30 concert. The "Search for a Star" program auditions promising Connecticut artists. He explains difficult music to concert audiences, often utilizing humor or techniques such as listening guides, demonstrations, and audience participation. Cumming conducts with verve and likes to program unusual works, urging audiences to "expect the unexpected." He and the HSO won a 2003 ASCAP award for adventurous programming of contemporary music. Cumming and the orchestra have continued in this vein: In 2005 they performed the world premiere of Richard Cumming's *Aspects of Hippolytus* and both commissioned and performed Valerie Coleman's *The Painted Lady* and Michael Gatonska's *Wandering the Moon Nursery*.

Cumming has guest conducted orchestras across the United States, including the Los Angeles PO, Rochester PO, Oregon SO, Detroit SO, Buffalo

PO, Maryland SO, San Antonio SO, and Memphis SO. His credits abroad include La Orquesta Ciudad de Granada (Spain), South Bohemian State Orchestra (Czech Republic), Ulster Orchestra (Belfast, UK), and the Singapore SO.

Selected Recordings
The Star Spangled Banner/America the Beautiful [CD-single]; Whitney Houston (s); Florida O. Arista.

～

Davies, Dennis Russell
Born 16 April 1944 in Toledo, Ohio

Dennis Russell Davies is a conductor who, it seems, has always been true to himself. His track record is that of equal dedication to traditional and modern music. As he has matured and gained in experience and authority, he has become one of that small band of conductors whose programs, through an imaginative mixture of the familiar and the challenging, can attract audiences and send them away from a musical experience both enthralled and intrigued.

Davies's affinity for music emerged at an early age when he began picking out tunes on the piano. Although he came from a modest home, it was a musical one, and, at the age of six, he was sent to study piano with an excellent local teacher, Berenice McNab. Many years later when making his conducting debut with the Berlin PO, he reminded the orchestra's *intendant*, Wolfgang Stresemann (who had once been the conductor of the Toledo SO), that when he (Davies) was seven years old he had performed Mozart's K414 concerto under him. After playing in and occasionally conducting his high school orchestra and attending various music camps in his early teens, he made up his mind to become a musician and entered Juilliard in 1961, intending to become a concert pianist; Lonny Epstein and Sascha Goronitzki were his teachers. He studied conducting with Jorge **Mester** and, having an affinity for it, was accepted into the graduate conducting class of Jean Morel. His interest in contemporary music was sparked by his experience as graduate assistant to Luciano Berio. Together they founded the Juilliard Ensemble as a vehicle to perform new music and inaugurated a series of concerts, "New and Newer Music," at Lincoln Center. Davies remained with the group that came to be known simply as "Ensemble" until 1974. At the same time he was gaining valuable experience as conductor of the Norwalk (Conn.) SO

(1968–72). Nineteen seventy-two was an important year: he received his DMA from Juilliard, made a guest appearance with the Los Angeles PO, and was named music director of the Saint Paul CO. During his tenure in Minnesota he transformed a less-than-thriving organization. He found a larger performance space for it, instituted a graduated ticketing policy to help attract a larger, more diverse audience, and took the orchestra on local tours annually. He made the orchestra more flexible by dividing it into smaller ensembles to visit schools and community centers to increase the public's awareness of the group. In 1973 he participated in music festivals in Aspen and Alaska and journeyed to the Netherlands Opera to take over *Pelleas et Melisande* from an ailing Bruno Maderna. He succeeded Carlos Chávez as music director and principal conductor of the Cabrillo (Calif.) Music Festival in 1974. This was probably the country's leading venue for experimental music, and over the next seventeen years Davies commissioned and premiered numerous works. One idea that took root in association with composers Nicholas Thorne and Nicolas Roussakis was the establishment of the American Composers Orchestra, based in New York City. Its purpose was to give a hearing to new works, and a re-hearing to a whole host of neglected works by American composers of earlier generations, such as MacDowell, Griffes, Beach, Ives, Schuman, Harris, and Riegger. Davies's influence on the podium accounts for the success of this enterprise, which he continued to foster until 2002.

During the late 1970s, Davies's main sphere of activity shifted to Europe. He appeared at the Bayreuth Festival in 1978 to lead *The Flying Dutchman*, and in 1980 he accepted the post of music director at the Württemberg State Opera in Stuttgart. In this progressive theater there was ample opportunity for promoting new works in addition to the standard repertoire. Important premieres were Henze's *The English Cat* (1983) and Glass's *Akhnaten* (1984), the third opera of a trilogy which Davies secured for a complete performance three years later. His 1984 recording of Arvo Pärt's *Cantus in Memorium Benjamin Britten* was crucial in furthering this composer's reputation and was followed by a series of recordings bringing to prominence other composers from Eastern Europe, including Alfred Schnittke, Giya Kancheli, and Peteris Vasks, music that Arved Ashby described as "mellifluous and soulful postminimalism." Nineteen eighty-seven saw the premiere of *Die Kaiser von Atlantis* by Viktor Ullmann. It had been composed in a concentration camp where the composer perished soon afterward. Davies was also in Chicago that year for performances of *Lulu* at the Lyric Opera. His association with the Philadelphia Orchestra through its Saratoga Performing Arts Center began in 1985 and continued for the next three summers. In characteristic fashion,

Davies set about infusing new life into a rather staid event with his customary mixture of the novel and the familiar.

In Bonn, where he was director of civic music (1987–95), he pursued the traditional role of Kapellmeister, directing the Beethovenhalle Orchestra, which did double duty in the pit of the Bonn State Opera. As we have come to expect, Davies's tenure there mixed the traditional (including productions of *Otello*, *Freischütz*, and *Salome*) and new (a revival of Lou Harrison's *Rapunzel* and the premiere of *The Blackamoor of Peter the Great* by Alfred Lourié). Taking the Bonn orchestra on tour to the U.S., he programmed concerts that included works by Beethoven and Brahms alongside those of Schnittke, Wuorinen, and Ullmann. Because Bonn is Beethoven's birthplace, the orchestra showcased his music in its repertoire and at the city's triennial Beethoven Festival. With the orchestra, Davies has made a recording of the "new critical edition" of the *Eroica Symphony*.

Davies's ties with the Stuttgart CO go back to 1989, and his ongoing commitment with them echoes his earlier tenure in Saint Paul. He made a deep impression in 1991 with a nine-concert series devoted to Mozart as part of the European Music Festival, which led to him being offered the post of chief conductor in 1995. Once again, a healthy mix of repertory and breaking the group into component ensembles proved to be invigorating. The orchestra has embarked upon recording all 107 of Haydn's extant symphonies and has premiered Philip Glass's Third Symphony, specifically composed for it. Performances in North America serve to remind U.S. audiences what a versatile and accomplished conductor they have in Dennis Russell Davies, with concerts of music by Glass (his *Tirol Concerto* with Davies as soloist), Haydn, and Tchaikovsky (*Serenade for Strings* and *Souvenir de Florence*).

From Bonn, Davies removed to Vienna to become the chief conductor of the Austrian RSO, where he stayed from 1996 to 2002. His work with this orchestra follows the pattern we have seen elsewhere. He has recorded two symphonies of Philip Glass (2 and 5), music by Giya Kancheli, Valentin Silvestrov, and Erkki-Sven Tüür, and the symphony by the Bruckner protégé Hans Rott (1858–84), who died tragically, young and insane. After Vienna, Davies accepted the appointment at Linz, which combines the Linz Bruckner Orchestra and the Linz Opera. Originally a five-year contract, it was extended to 2014 due to the favorable impression he made and his own comfort level in the position. Meanwhile, back in the U.S. he gave the premieres of Bolcom's operas *McTeague* (1992) and *A View from the Bridge* (1999) and presented Berio's *Re in Ascolta* at the Chicago Lyric Opera. He appeared for belated debuts with the New York PO (1993), playing Walton, Beethoven, and Debussy, and at the Met in 1996, performing Glass's *The Voyage*. Considering the great diversity of music that comes under his baton, Davies's conducting style is remarkably economical and straightforward. This is not to suggest that his conducting is in any way lacking in emotion or intensity. On the contrary, his commitment and enthusiasm produce exciting performances in every style and genre. He is a conductor whose extensive experience as a pianist and chamber music player makes him a sympathetic accompanist with a sensitivity appreciated by singers and players alike. His vast experience conducting new scores, which he seems to master effortlessly, gives his performances a feeling of clarity. The breadth and scope of his activities are frankly astounding. He has been singularly loyal to the American composers he grew up with, Bolcom, Stokes, Harrison, Cage, and especially Glass, and to his European mentors, Berio, Henze, and Maderna.

Further Reading

Ashby, Arved. "A Talk with Dennis Russell Davies." *American Record Guide* 60, no. 4 (1997): 22–25.

Kupferberg, Herbert. "Dennis Russell Davies: He's No Innocent Abroad." *American Record Guide* 57, no. 3 (1994): 10–12.

Mandelbaum, Mayer Joel. "The American Composers Orchestra." *Harmony* 10 (April 2000): 47–55.

Weber, B. "The Maestro as Midwife: As Conductor, Dennis Russell Davies Brings Life to a New Opera." *New York Times*, 29 September 1999, E1, 5.

Selected Recordings

Bruckner: *Symphony no. 8* (orig. ver.); Bruckner Orchestra Linz. Arte Nova 628560.

Glass: *Symphony no. 3*; *The CIVIL Wars: Interlude no. 1*; *The Voyage: Mechanical Ballet*; *The CIVIL Wars: Interlude no. 2*; *The Light*; Stuttgart CO; Vienna RSO. Nonesuch 79581.

Kancheli: *Liturgy in Memory of Givi Ordzhonikidze* "Mourned by the Wind." Schnittke: *Concerto for Viola*; Kim Kashkashian (va); Beethovenhalle O; Saarbrücken RSO. ECM 437199.

Mcphee: *Tabuh-tabuhan*. Ung: *Inner Voices*. Harrison: *Suite for Strings*; American Composers O. Decca 444560.

Stravinsky: *Monumentum pro Gesualdo di Venosa*; *Danses concertantes*; *Concerto in D*; *Apollon musagète*; Stuttgart CO. ECM B0004886.

⌒

Davis, Andrew (Frank)

Born 2 February 1944 in Ashridge, England

Davis is one of the most versatile and admired conductors at work today. A musician of great talent and tremendous vitality, he is a quick learner who has amassed a wide-ranging repertoire. Because he is so open and forthright in expressing his views, he is an interesting case study of the way conducting reflects character. It is impossible to miss the enthusiasm, industriousness, and stamina he exudes, together with the commitment and loyalty he has brought to each of his long-term engagements. He is genuinely admired, liked, and trusted by those with whom he works. He clearly labors tremendously hard to absorb and formulate his musical conceptions so that no one ever doubts his ability to convey precisely what he wants or how to achieve it. The fluency he showed early in his career has matured over the years, and as his manner has become increasingly avuncular, so his interpretations have developed a surer sense of control and added depth. Of the key elements demanded of his art, he seems primarily attracted to such stylistic traits as clarity, balance, and the quest for variety of orchestral nuance. He consistently wins points for the luminosity and color of his readings. For example, his debut performance as music director at Chicago's Lyric Opera of Tchaikovsky's *The Queen of Spades* (2000) was praised for wringing "every drop of dark brooding atmosphere from the composer's penultimate opera." His detractors—there are a few—claim that, with all his polish, he sometimes misses out on dramatic intensity (Andrew Clark found his conducting of Wagner's *Siegfried* "a bit tepid"). There is the sense that, in the end, his music-making seems somewhat to be lacking soul. If he also seems to lack charisma on the podium, it is probably related to the fact that his conducting is torso-driven and his arm movements are rather symmetrical, but there is never any doubt that he conveys what he wants to his players very effectively.

Davis's career has had its fair share of breaks. As an adolescent, his treble voice broke just as the organist at his church left, so he took over the job, which eventually led to him winning an organ scholarship to King's College, Cambridge. Then there was the friend he had met at Cambridge, a player with the BBC Scottish SO, who surreptitiously moved Davis's application from the "maybe" to the "yes" file, thereby gaining him an audition and the job of assistant conductor. The indisposition of Israeli conductor Eliahu Inbal in 1970 led to Davis's first big break directing a concert that included Janáček's *Glagolitic Mass* with the BBC SO at very short notice. It was as a guest conductor with this piece, programmed as a tribute to the former music director Karel Ancerl, that he so impressed the powers-that-be of the Toronto SO that they offered him his first permanent directorship. A chance remark at a lunch between his wife, the singer Gianna Rolandi, and Bill Mason, general director of the Lyric Opera, led to his being approached with the offer of the music directorship—a position whose ambience seemed tailor-made for him. After two or three years immersed in theater work, he satisfied a hankering to conduct more orchestral concerts by accepting an appointment as *primus* of a triptych of conductors in an unusual arrangement to lead the Pittsburgh SO (2005), one of the most accomplished in the nation. This was an attempt to allow Davis to successfully navigate operatic and orchestral responsibilities, a dual role for which he seems particularly well suited. However, his decision not to continue with it at the completion of a three-year contract would indicate that it was a better idea in theory than in practice. If, as according to Benjamin Franklin, the mother of good luck is diligence, no one can begrudge Davis on that score!

Davis was born into a home of modest means near the town of Watford, just north of London. Demonstrating early promise on the piano, he attended the junior department of the Royal Academy of Music (facts that closely parallel those of another musical knight, Sir Elton John, who lived in nearby Pinner). Taking up the organ, he studied with Peter Hurford at Saint Albans Abbey, and, as stated above, became an organ scholar at King's College under David Willcocks. Seemingly destined for the cloistered life of a cathedral organist, he caught the conducting bug while working with student groups such as the University Music Society Orchestra. After graduation from Cambridge (1967) he won an Italian Government bursary to study for a year with Franco Ferrara in Rome. Upon his return to England he worked as a keyboard and continuo player with groups such as the Academy of St. Martin-in-the-Fields, while conducting a couple of amateur orchestras. His attendance at a seminar for young conductors sponsored by the Royal Liverpool PO in 1969 was followed shortly thereafter by the last-minute BBC SO substitution, and then his appointment as assistant conductor of the BBC Scottish SO (1971–73). He made a spectacular debut at the Glyndebourne Festival (1973) directing a much-admired production of Strauss's late opera *Capriccio*; he led a Far East tour with the English CO and debuted with the Israel PO that same year. From 1973 to 1975 he was associate conductor of the New Philharmonia Orchestra and, with a burgeoning reputation, made his North American debut in 1974 with the Detroit (Mich.) SO. He was principal guest conductor of the Royal Liverpool PO (1974–76) before assuming the directorship in Toronto, the first of his long-term commitments (1975–88).

The Toronto (ON) SO under Davis was only the second orchestra from the West to visit China (1978), and the Mahler performances they gave there caused quite a stir. The crowning achievement during his Canadian tenure was the opening of the Roy Thomson Hall in 1982, considered one of the best concert venues on the continent at the time. It may be he stayed in Canada too long and that he left a little jaded, albeit with the honorific conductor laureate. He was immediately rejuvenated as director of Glyndebourne Festival Opera (1988–2000). Characteristically, he bought a home in the Sussex countryside to be close to his work. His achievements during those years, which included cycles of operas by Mozart, Strauss, Tchaikovsky, and Janáček, were considerable, reflecting an honest, straightforward approach to music-making that was typical of his distinguished predecessor, Fritz Busch, but often underrated by critics. In 1989 he became chief conductor of the BBC SO, the third of his long-term commitments (1989–2000). Here, his versatility was a tremendous asset that allowed him to perform a wide range of repertoire, including a hefty proportion of contemporary works as well as those playing to his strengths: Elgar, Strauss, Beethoven, Mozart, Dvořák, Janáček, Berg, Schumann, Stravinsky, and Tippett. He is credited with enlivening a somewhat stale, if highly accomplished, ensemble and restoring its positive self-image. On relinquishing this post he again received the conductor laureate appellation, the first person ever to receive this title from the orchestra. In 1995 he accepted the position as principal guest conductor of the Stockholm PO in addition to his Glyndebourne and BBC duties.

It came as no surprise to find Davis attracted to the Lyric Opera post. One sees a parallel between the much-vaunted Midwestern values of industry, flair, and enjoyment and Davis's own work ethic. There is an attraction to living in North America for the English which has to do with shuffling off the claustrophobic clutch of the mother country. Davis has expressed his appreciation for working in the U.S. in general and Chicago in particular. At the same time he retains the aura of hearty Britishness that many Americans find irresistible. His previous guest appearances conducting Strauss and Mozart with the company had been well received and forged an atmosphere of mutual respect with the Lyric's excellent orchestra. In addition, the house had a reputation for being particularly well run, as well as having a solid financial footing within a surprisingly collegial and relaxed atmosphere. With a proven track record, the new music director could be expected to bring his commitment and stamina to bear in a typically hands-on way. His acceptance of the post accompanied his decision to move his home and family to Chicago from the outset. The opportunity to develop the orchestra and chorus, to work with some of the leading vocal talent, and to explore those areas of the operatic repertoire, particularly Verdi and Wagner, that had previously eluded him were some of the "carrots" that clinched the deal. Conscious of his reputation as a musical chameleon, he saw an opportunity to "pull back from this tremendous diversity and imbue it with greater depth."

As noted above, the Davis regnum got off to an auspicious start with *The Queen of Spades*, in which every aspect of the production received commendation. His first essay into Wagner with *The Flying Dutchman* (2000) was considered a success, and the well-received *Parsifal* (2002) established him as a bona fide Wagnerian. Several years later, with a complete *Ring* cycle under his belt, matters appear to have been working out well, at least artistically. He has shown himself an able Verdian with admired performances of *Otello* (2001) and *Aida* (2004). All in all, the repertoire has the authentic Davis imprimatur.

The hallmarks of his achievement have included developing the distinctive sound quality of the orchestra, which in the *Ring*, for example, produced a "luminous transparency in Wagner's often thick scoring one seldom hears in live performances." He has consistently received accolades from his musicians, who find him agreeable to rehearse with since "he has very little to say because players and singers only need to watch him to know exactly what he wants." His well-known empathy toward singers and his skill as an orchestral accompanist have also been evident even when that deference occasionally interrupts dramatic tension. This workhorse's annus mirabilis was probably 2004, when, in addition to his regular Lyric schedule (which included *Rhinegold, Cunning Little Vixen*, and *Don Giovanni*), he took on the house's *Aida* (stepping in at short notice for an indisposed colleague, never having conducted it previously), and substituted at the Chicago SO, again on short notice, for concerts in February and again in September for the injured **Barenboim**. It was in October of that year that he announced his appointment as artistic advisor to the Pittsburgh SO. It had come as rather a shock, though, when, in 2002, the Lyric company posted its first financial deficit in seventeen years, largely due to the external factors that affected all aspects of American cultural life at the time. A planned production of Berlioz's *Benvenuto Cellini* had to be shelved and replaced by a sure-fire money-maker in the *Pirates of Penzance*. Further administrative paring was necessary in 2005, and the casting of Tippett's *A Midsummer Marriage* (2005) ran into contractual difficulties; this challenge, together with a considerable amount of audience bafflement (long associated with this work), tarnished the planned celebration of the composer's centenary. Regarding the *Ring* cycle performances in the spring of 2005, *Chicago Tribune* critic John von Rhein summed up with: "Nobody could fault the high level of singing overall or the integrity and supple control with which Davis steered his orchestra through all 15-plus hours of this supremely demanding work . . . [His] soaring musical influence held the audience in rapt attention." Amid the overwhelming praise there were a few murmurings about the pacing, in the interests of narrative, being too brisk at times and some of the work's "beautiful moments" being somewhat subdued. These cavils aside, the fact that he was invited to Bayreuth to conduct *Lohengrin* (2002) and to Dresden for *Parsifal* (2003) (described as "divine") clearly indicates his emergence as a major Wagnerian conductor. He has maintained his love affair with Janáček's music at the Lyric with *Jenufa* (2001) and *Vixen* (2004). The latter, notoriously difficult to stage, is nonetheless one of the most radiant of scores redolent with nature, including the human variety, and it proved difficult for Davis to exercise his customary restraint in the pit.

Davis has been a welcome guest conductor with the Chicago SO for almost thirty years, both at Orchestra Hall, its downtown venue, and at Ravinia, its summer home, where in 2001 he conducted a dramatized version of Mendelssohn's *A Midsummer Night's Dream* incidental music. His programs have reflected the broad span of his repertoire interests, which, in recent years, have included Tippett's oratorio *A Child of Our Time* (2005), as well as music by Haydn, Mozart, Beethoven, Britten, and Stravinsky. His brief tenure with the Pittsburgh SO (which he shared with Yan Pascal Tortelier and Marek Janowski) apparently did not quite work out as expected. It was meant to benefit Davis's hectic schedule by requiring him to spend only four to seven weeks a year with the orchestra. Was that enough time to create a mutual relationship and maintain the orchestra's distinctive identity? The rationale for experimenting with a triumvirate, since no conductor is expected to excel in every style (though in Davis's case to suggest this almost amounts to an insult!), is that each would bring his own distinctive qualities to bear. It was an experiment watched closely by other institutions, and there was no doubt disappointment that it was of such short duration.

As a guest conductor, Davis has appeared at Covent Garden, La Scala, the Met, and the Paris Opéra, and with many of the world's major orchestras, including the New York PO, Boston SO, Philadelphia Orchestra, Concertgebouw Orchestra, Vienna SO, and many others. Of his many audio and video recordings, his Glyndebourne versions of Berg's *Lulu* (*Gramophone's* Best Video award, 1997) and Rossini's *Ermione* (2005) are outstanding. He has also won a Grand Prix du Disque for his recording of the Duruflé *Requiem* (1978) and *Gramophone's* Record of the Year award for Tippett's *The Mask of Time* (1987). In September 1998 his recording of Birtwistle's *Mask of Orpheus* with the BBC SO won a Gramophone Award for Best Contemporary Recording. In addition to his fine recordings of Elgar's First and Second Symphonies, his recording of Anthony Payne's completion of the composer's sketches for his Third Symphony reflect Davis's lifelong dedication to this composer. He received a CBE from Queen Elizabeth II in 1992 and a knighthood in 1999.

Further Reading
Blyth, Alan. "Andrew Davis." *Opera (England)* 48 (July 1997): 775–79.
"Davis, Andrew." In *World Musicians*, edited by Clifford Thompson, 217–19. New York: H. W. Wilson Company, 1999.
Driscoll, F. Paul. "The English Beat." *Opera News* 62 (January 1998): 12–15.
Evans, Neil. "Power behind the Proms." *Classic CD* 64 (August 1995): 28–30.
Hart, Philip. "Andrew Davis." In *Conductors: A New Generation*, 47–67. New York: Charles Scribner's Sons, 1983.
Rhein, John von. "Lyric Opera Stakes Its Future on the Highly Regarded Sir Andrew Davis." *Chicago Tribune*, 7 January 2001, Magazine, 11.

Selected Recordings
Birtwistle: *The Mask of Orpheus*; soloists; BBC Singers; BBC SO. NMC 50.
Elgar: *The Dream of Gerontius*; Philip Langridge (t); Catherine Wyn-Rogers (a); Alastair Miles (b); BBC SCho; BBC SO. Kultur Video 4082 DVD.
Janáček: *Sinfonietta*; *Balada Blanickà*; *The Fiddler's Child*; *Taras Bulba*; Royal Stockholm PO. MSI Music 2564604302.
Rossini: *Ermione*; soloists; London PO (Glyndbourne production). Kultur Video 2850 DVD.
Stravinsky: *Le Sacre du Printemps*; Toronto SO. Orpheum Masters 809.

∼

Deal, Karen Lynne
Born 7 May 1957 in Richmond, Virginia

Particularly praised for her inventive programming for children and families, Karen Lynne Deal didn't attend classical concerts when she was a child. She began playing flute at age nine, and by high school was playing in the Richmond YSO. In her senior year at Oral Roberts University, Deal had the chance to conduct, so after graduating with a degree in applied flute in 1980, she went on to earn a master's degree in orchestral conducting from Virginia

Commonwealth University (1982) and a doctorate in orchestral conducting from the Peabody Conservatory of Music (1989). From 1983 to 1984, Deal was music director for the Rockbridge (Va.) Orchestra. While doing postgraduate work at the Hochschule für Musik und Darstellende Kunst in Vienna from 1984 to 1985, she conducted the Pro Arte Orchestra (also in Vienna) and the Frankfurt State Opera.

In 1986 Deal became associate conductor for the Annapolis (Md.) SO. She joined the music faculty of Loyola College (Md.) in 1988 and founded and was music director of the Sinfonia Concertante, a professional chamber orchestra noted for its commitment to living composers. In 1988 Deal won the National Repertory Orchestra's Biennial Conducting Competition in Keystone (Colo.), and for the next season was assistant conductor for the NRO. She also founded (1990) and was music director of the Chesapeake YSO. Deal resigned all the Maryland positions in 1992 when she became associate conductor for the Nashville (Tenn.) SO and music director and conductor for the Nashville Ballet. True to form, in 1997 she took on additional responsibilities as conductor for Nashville Opera and joined the conducting faculty at Belmont (Tenn.) University. While in Nashville, Deal developed a reputation for community outreach and creative programming that brought new listeners to the symphony. She began the highly interactive "Pied Piper Series" of child-oriented matinee concerts, as well as an annual Let Freedom Ring concert which celebrated Black History Month by featuring the music of both African American composers and African American soloists. Middle Tennessee University awarded Deal the Woman of Achievement Award in 1996, and the following year *Nashville Life* magazine voted her one of the city's "Coolest People."

In 2000, Deal resigned her Tennessee posts to become music director and conductor of the Illinois SO and the Illinois CO. Here she continued her quest to quash the stereotype of "the maestro" and remove any air of intimidation surrounding the symphony, proving instead that it is inviting and accessible. Her "Sneakers and Jeans" family matinee series showcases her gifts for reaching young listeners and deftly balancing entertainment with learning, as does her "Step by Step" educational program for children in grades K–6. Outgoing and energetic, Deal holds "Concert Comments" sessions before performances and also frequently sprinkles comments and explanations throughout programs, believing repartee during a concert makes audiences feel more intimate and closer to the music, the musicians, and the composer.

She reaches out to new audiences by bringing the orchestra to unusual venues such as the Illinois State Fair, the Illinois Shakespeare Festival, and an equestrian show. She involves local talent and youth orchestras in programs. Deal promotes the orchestra in nonmusical ways as well, speaking to schools and civic groups and holding monthly "Musical Morsels" luncheons to preview concerts using musical examples, composer details, and insider information. In 2004, she was honored both with a Studs Terkel Humanities Heroes award for her leadership in music education and with a Community Service Award from the Illinois Council of Orchestras. The council also bestowed on her the Meritorious Service in Outstanding Programming Award in 2002, and the previous year Deal was given the Mayor's Award for Individual Artist of the Year from the Springfield (Ill.) Arts Council. In 2005, she was conductor-in-residence for the Conductors Institute at Bard College.

Deal's recent guest-conducting engagements have included the SOs of New Mexico, Waterloo/Cedar Falls (Iowa), Tucson (Ariz.), Sacramento (Calif.), Richmond (Va.), Springfield (Mo.), Westmoreland (Kans.), Reading (Pa.), Brevard (N.C.), and Bremerton (Wash.), as well as the Tulsa PO, the Kansas City Camerata, the National Repertory Orchestra in Breckenridge, and the Orquesta del Nuevo Mundo, where she conducted the concert premiere of *Mujeres e Musicas*, featuring female composers including Clara Schumann, Fanny Mendelssohn, Maria Grever, and Maria Martinez.

Website
http://www.karendeal.com

Further Reading
Dietrich, Matthew. "The Real Deal: Conductor Brings a New Style to the Illinois Symphony Orchestra." *State Journal-Register* (Springfield, Ill.), 16 February 2001, Magazine, 5A.

⌒

Delfs, Andreas
Born 30 August 1959 in Flensburg, Germany

Delfs is a musician of two worlds and an interesting mix of contrasts. His musical education followed the traditional path of Kapellmeister; he worked as a musical assistant in various German theaters from the age of seventeen until after he graduated from the Hamburg Conservatory (1981), a pupil of Christoph von **Dohnanyi** and Aldo Ceccato. He then decided to travel to the U.S. to enroll as a graduate student at Juilliard, where he received tutelage from Jorge **Mester** and Sixten Ehrling. At Juilliard he was awarded the

Bruno Walter Scholarship and buttonholed by André **Previn** to be his assistant in Pittsburgh. But Previn left there before Delfs arrived, so he worked instead as the William Steinberg Fellow under Lorin **Maazel** (1986–90). He returned to Europe to conduct the Swiss Youth Orchestra and appeared at the Bern Opera. Subsequently, he was appointed director of the Hannover State Opera and Orchestra (1995–2000). Maintaining his U.S. ties through guest appearances, he made a strong impression at his New York City Opera debut conducting *Carmen*. His appointment as music director of the Milwaukee (Wisc.) SO followed in 1997, and he later combined this with the directorship of the Saint Paul CO (2000–04). He was appointed principal conductor of the Honolulu (Hawaii) SO for a three-year term commencing with the 2007–8 season.

Delfs seems equally at home in the musical spheres of Europe and America, but acutely aware of their differences. Contrary to prevailing wisdom, he finds American orchestras more proficient and dedicated than their European counterparts. State subsidization there can lead to complacency and routine, especially among provincial ensembles. Programming in America is more dynamic and adventurous, he claims.

Delfs is deeply committed musically but also has a flair for marketing his product. In this respect he has been touted as a model for twenty-first-century conductors in America. He hails from a family of actors, so his bent for the theatrical is not unexpected, nor does it detract from his seriousness of purpose, which is to propagate his passion for music (he uses the metaphor of a drug dealer wanting to get everyone hooked!). He has been known to strap on an accordion when directing performances of Kurt Weill's *Kleine Dreigroschenmusik* and, for his Gershwin centennial tribute with the Milwaukee orchestra, he included a sketch with himself as a "stuffy" conductor being assailed by an actor in the role of the composer's defender, Oscar Levant. One result of his Pittsburgh tenure was his realization that orchestras in the U.S. are part of a music industry. Whereas some conductors, such as Mariss **Jansons**, find a business model appalling, and others, like Daniel **Barenboim**, find it beneath them, Delfs, at least for now, is happy to embrace it. Not only that, but he displays media and marketing know-how to a remarkable degree! His fresh approach in Milwaukee witnessed an 11 percent rise in attendance in just two years, amounting to an average 85 percent capacity in the orchestra's refurbished home, Uihlein Hall, with many performances sold out. He has been a hit with Milwaukee audiences not only because of good programming. He throws himself wholeheartedly into media and civic events, fund-raising, and educational ventures. Unlike some of his colleagues, he does not find it demeaning to make room for fun in his concerts, and no one can doubt that he takes his musicianly role seriously. Taking the Milwaukee orchestra on a millennium tour to Cuba in 1999 (the first major U.S. orchestra to go there in thirty-seven years) would, he knew, cause some controversy. The orchestra will celebrate its fiftieth season in 2008–9, and Delfs has indicated that this will be the time for him to move on. His willing agreement to resign his post with the Saint Paul CO in order for it to become a self-governing body is entirely in keeping with his collegial approach to music-making.

Delfs is certainly not lacking in musical skills. He combines a pleasing podium manner with a solid baton technique that enables him to convey all the nuances of carefully prepared and meticulously executed interpretations. His performances, thankfully free of intrusive "personality," are found to be deeply satisfying by audiences and critics alike. With a repertoire spanning all periods and genres from the Baroque to the present day, he is equally effective throughout. Performances of the standard classics are reported to be fresh and invigorating, since he has a knack of choosing just the right tempo for slow movements and a liking for fleet finales. His service to contemporary music is also exemplary. In Hannover he gave the European premiere of John Corigliano's opera *The Ghosts of Versailles*, and he has performed stage works by Henze and Ligeti. In North America he has programmed works by Boris Blacher and Bernd Alois Zimmermann, and, especially with the Saint Paul CO, specialized in performances of American composers, including the concert premiere of Philip Glass's *Suite from "The Hours,"* John **Adams**'s *Chamber Symphony*, Theodore Shapiro's *Chambers*, and works by Golijov, Higdon, and Kernis. He has also performed Garrison Keillor's pastiche opera *Mr. and Mrs. Olson*.

As a guest conductor, Delfs has appeared extensively in Europe, North America, and Asia. Some of his more prestigious credits to date include the Philadelphia Orchestra, National SO, San Francisco SO, Dallas SO, NHK SO (Japan), London PO, Zurich Tonhalle Orchestra, and the radio orchestras of Frankfurt, Berlin, and Leipzig. In the opera house he has led performances of *Die Zauberflöte*, *Rigoletto*, and *La Bohème* at the Royal Opera House in Stockholm; *Le nozze di Figaro* and *Il trittico* at the Aspen Music Festival; and *Cavalleria rusticana*, *I Pagliacci*, and *Die Lustige Weiber von Windsor* at the Württemberg State Opera in Stuttgart. His recordings include a disc of music by Schoeck with the Swiss Youth Orchestra, jazz-inspired concertos by Erwin Schulhoff with the Deutsche Kammerphilharmonie, ballet music scenes by Prokofiev and Tchaikovsky with the Milwaukee SO, and a performance of *Hansel and Gretel* in English, with soloists Heidi Grant Murphy and Susanne Mentzer, released in 2004. His most recent assignment is a CD and DVD accompanying Renée Fleming in a recital of sacred music with the Royal PO.

Further Reading
"Bases Loaded." *Symphony* 49 (March–April 1998): 6.
Strini, Tom. "Showman of Substance." *Symphony* 50 (March–April 1999): 28–32.

Selected Recordings
Humperdinck: *Hansel and Gretel*; Susanne Mentzer (*Hansel*); Heidi Grant Murphy (*Gretel*); Judith Forst (*Witch*); Janice Taylor (*Mother*); Robert Orth (*Father*); Anna Christy (*Sandman/Dew Fairy*); Milwaukee SO and Ch and Children's Ch. Avie AV0050.
Mozart: *Requiem in d*, K 626. Süssmayr: *German Requiem in Bb*; Maria Jette (s); Jennifer Larmore (ms); James Taylor (t); Eric Owens (b); Saint Paul CO; St. Olaf Ch (Anton Armstrong, dir). Limestone E-2802.
Schulhoff: *Concerto for Piano and Small Orchestra*, Op. 43; *Double Concerto for Flute and Piano*; *Concertino for String Quartet and Winds*; (+ piano music); Bettina Wild (fl), Alexander Madzar (pf); Hawthorne SQ; Deutsche Kammerphilharmonie. Decca 444819.

～

DePreist, James
Born 21 November 1936 in Philadelphia, Pennsylvania

For one who began his conducting career at the rather advanced age of twenty-six, DePreist's achievements have been considerable. His reputation is derived chiefly from his lengthy tenure as music director of the Oregon SO (1980–2003), as well as his guest-conducting appearances with many of the world's leading orchestras. However, given his undoubted talent and achievements, it is disappointing that he never progressed to an appointment at one of the major U.S. orchestras. In making this assessment, one cannot avoid taking the race factor into account. Why, for instance, was DePreist, who is black, made to wait twenty-five years after his successful debut concert with the Boston SO at Tanglewood in 1973 before being invited back to conduct it at Symphony Hall, Boston, in 1997? This is not to belittle in any way his achievement in Portland, the home of the Oregon SO, where during his twenty-three-year tenure he was regarded with admiration and affection, and where he transformed a respectable regional ensemble into a world-class orchestra.

Not that his tenure in Portland was always fair sailing. After an initial period of expansion which resulted in the orchestra's elevation to a "major" status rating by the American Symphony Orchestra League, financial difficulties during the 1985–86 season resulted in a deficit amounting to $1.2 million. It took a year of intensive fund-raising, in which DePreist took a major role within the community, to return to solvency. Beginning in 1987, the orchestra's progress was reflected in several commercial recordings. The first album, titled *Bravura*, contained showpieces such as Respighi's *Feste romane*, Strauss's *Don Juan*, and Lutosławski's *Concerto for Orchestra*, and reviews praised not only the work of the Delos engineers but also DePreist for his "penetrating, vivacious readings." He continued to expand the scope of the Oregon SO's activities in terms of resources, concerts, and repertoire. As well as mainstream repertoire, he consistently included new and challenging music when designing his programs. Over the years he built up a loyal following, enjoying one of the highest per-capita subscription attendances of any major U.S. orchestra. He worked hard to increase the orchestra's educational and community programs and inaugurated a series of free local park concerts in 1996. Of the latter, he later reflected ruefully that "[park] concerts tend to be, let's say, excessively accessible!"

His authoritative and technically assured conducting style was developed early. He relies primarily on meaningfully choreographed hand gestures and, as he usually conducts from memory, eye contact to convey his strongly envisioned concept of the score to the players. His interpretations are noted for their rhythmic precision, graceful phrasing, warmth, energy, and joie de vivre. His rehearsal manner is informal and players normally address him by his first name, but he gives directions in a clear, strong voice and commands authority through his artistic commitment and innate musicality.

His 2001 recording of Stravinsky's *Rite of Spring* and *Firebird Suite* elicited comments from the critics that reflect DePreist's principal qualities as a conductor. Jim Sveda, commenting on the refinement of the performances, wrote, "One is almost tempted to call it a delicacy." Jonathan Swann, in the *Gramophone*, described it as "a very balletic performance" and complimented the conductor on its clarity, a quality also remarked upon by Michael Oliver, who praised the ravishing orchestral sound and the way that "DePreist allows his solo players to phrase beautifully."

DePreist is a man of deep humility, and yet he is confident in his abilities. He needed both these qualities to overcome the double prejudice of being black and American in the field of orchestral conducting, which is almost exclusively dominated by Europeans. Add to this the physical trauma of having contracted polio and been left disabled by it. Growing up in a female-dominated family (his father died when James was young), he admits to having been spoiled. A gifted child, he demonstrated early musical abilities that were encouraged by the household and especially by his aunt, the pioneering contralto Marian Anderson. He learned to play the piano and drums and showed interest in a variety of music, popular as well as classical. He performed in jazz groups in high school and college and even made an appearance on *The Tonight Show*. Planning to become an attorney, he declined a college music scholarship and entered the University of Pennsylvania as a pre-law major, graduating with a BS in economics in 1958. By then his legal ambitions had faded and he went on to earn a master's degree in film studies from the Annenberg School of Communications. At the same time, he attended the Philadelphia Conservatory of Music, where, encouraged by the success of a score he had composed for the Philadelphia Dance Academy, he took lessons in composition from Vincent Persichetti. In 1961 the U.S. State Department sent him on a Far East tour as a kind of cultural ambassador to give jazz workshops and recitals of his own compositions. While in Bangkok, Thailand, in 1962, he was invited to conduct a rehearsal of Schubert's Symphony no. 9 with the university orchestra. The experience was a revelation and convinced him to become a conductor. Just two months later he contracted polio (not having had the required number of shots) and was flown back to the U.S. with a paralyzed lower torso. During his convalescence, he devoured all the scores he could lay his hands on, composed another ballet, and became even more determined to embark on a conducting career. Through his aunt he had made the acquaintance of Leonard Bernstein, and at his suggestion, DePreist entered the 1963 Mitropoulos International Competition for Conductors, making it through to the semifinal round. Undaunted, he was determined to gain as much experience as possible and emerged an outright winner in the competition the following year. This success led to an invitation to become an assistant conductor of the New York PO for the 1965–66 season, and he conducted the Philadelphia Orchestra in Marian Anderson's farewell concert. However, other invitations were few and far between, and he decided to try his luck in Europe. ("I thought it would be better to starve slowly over there than instantly over here.") He made a notable debut with the Rotterdam PO in 1969 that led to invitations from other European orchestras. Throughout his career, thus far, he had struggled to stand while conducting, due to his disability, but he adopted a seated posture in concerts after 1969. He forged a particularly close link with the Stockholm PO. After its then–music director, Antal Dorati, moved to the National SO in Washington, D.C., DePreist became principal assistant conductor (1971–74) and then principal guest conductor (1975–76). Because of Dorati's respect for DePreist, the job involved more responsibility and more performances than is usually allotted to a number-two position, including planning the summer concert series and conducting most of its concerts. During this period DePreist appeared for the first time with the Chicago SO (1973) and the Cleveland Orchestra (1974), and conducted his first full programs with the New York PO and the Philadelphia Orchestra. He also made his debut with the Boston SO at Tanglewood. In 1976 he accepted a position as music director with the Quebec SO that lasted until 1983. His ambition to expand this modest organization's horizons was constantly frustrated, however, whereas his appointment to the Oregon SO in 1980 gave him much more scope, and, as we have seen above, he made the most of the opportunity.

During his tenure in Portland, DePreist's other activities included the principal conductorship of the Malmö SO in Sweden (1991–94) and of the Monte Carlo PO (1994–98). In 1993 he made his debut with the Helsinki PO, with whom he was to embark on an acclaimed series of Shostakovich recordings. His health problems were exacerbated when his kidneys began to fail in the late 1990s, but a generous kidney donation from a longtime admirer gave him a new lease on life. In 2000 he was awarded Columbia University's Ditson Conductor's Award. The Oregon SO's 2002–3 season was billed as the James DePreist Tribute Season, and at its conclusion he was named the orchestra's laureate music director. The following season he acted as artistic advisor to the Phoenix (Ariz.) SO and was appointed director of conducting and orchestral studies at Juilliard. As well as making his London SO debut in 2005, he became permanent conductor of the Tokyo Metropolitan SO in May of that year. There is no indication that retirement features in his future plans.

DePreist has over fifty recordings to his credit. In addition to those with the Oregon SO and the Helsinki PO, he has recorded with the Chicago SO, Monte Carlo PO, Malmö SO, Royal PO, Royal Stockholm PO, Los Angeles CO, and the Juilliard Orchestra. His recorded opus includes the music of Mozart, Glinka, Tchaikovsky, Rachmaninoff, Prokofiev, Shostakovich, Sibelius, Strauss, Bizet, Fauré, D'Indy, Saint-Saëns, Hindemith, Martinů, Lutosławski, Respighi, and Menotti. He can boast of laying down a good number of scores by contemporary American composers, including Tomas Svoboda, Joseph Schwantner, Norman Dello Joio, Ellen Taaffe Zwilich, Robert Daugherty, Vincent Persichetti, Nicolas Flagello, and George Tsontakis. From among non-American contemporary composers he has recorded music by Richard Rodney Bennett, Sofia Gubaidulina, Giya Kancheli, Aulis Sallinen, Harre Merikanto, and Alfred Schnittke. As a guest conductor he has appeared with all the leading North American orchestras and the principal ensembles in Amsterdam, Berlin, Budapest, Copenhagen, Helsinki, Manchester, Melbourne, Munich, Prague, Rome, Rotterdam, Seoul, Stockholm,

Stuttgart, Sydney, Tel Aviv, Tokyo, and Vienna. He appears regularly at the Aspen Music Festival, with the Boston SO at Tanglewood, and with the Philadelphia Orchestra at the Mann Music Center. He is the recipient of honorary doctorates from thirteen institutions, including the University of Pennsylvania, Juilliard School, Oregon State University, and Portland State University. In November 2005, he received the National Medal of Arts from President Bush in the Oval Office. He is the author of two books of poetry.

Website
http://www.jamesdepreist.com

Further Reading
Glass, Herbert. "From Oregon to Sweden." *Gramophone* 70 (January 1993): 18–19.

Passy, Charles. "Heart and Mind: The Musical Ascent of James DePreist." *Symphony Magazine* 40, no. 1 (1989): 52–56.

Reel, James. "An Interview with James DePreist." *Fanfare* 19, no. 2 (1995): 102.

Tucker, Tyffany. "James DePreist Looks Back." Associated Press, 15 July 2002.

Tuska, Jon. "An Interview with James DePreist." *Fanfare* 13, no. 1 (1989): 66.

Selected Recordings
Bravura: Lutosławski: *Concerto for Orchestra*. Respighi: *Feste romane*. Strauss (R): *Don Juan*; Oregon SO. Delos 3070.

Mahler: *Symphony no. 5*; London SO. Naxos 8557990.

Persichetti: *Symphony no. 4*. Lees: *Passacaglia*. Daugherty: *Hell's Angels*; *Symphony no. 3* "Philadelphia Stories"; *Sundown on South Street*; Oregon SO; Bassoon Brothers. Delos DE-3291.

Sallinen: *Symphony no. 4*, Op. 49; *Symphony no. 5*, Op. 57 "Washington Mosaics"; *Shadows*, Op. 52; Malmö SO. BIS 607.

Stravinsky: *Le Sacre du Printemps*; *Firebird Suite*; Oregon SO. Delos 3278.

∿

Diemecke, Enrique Arturo
Born 9 July 1955 in Mexico City, Mexico

Enrique Arturo Diemecke was born into a very musical family, the son of professional musicians. He began playing violin at age six, adding French horn, piano, percussion, and composition to his skills before pursuing conducting. Diemecke earned a BA degree in violin performance from Catholic University in 1980, then a master's degree in conducting from the same institution. His first conducting positions were in Mexico: assistant conductor of the Mexico City PO (1980–83), associate conductor of the Philharmonic Orchestra of the National Autonomous University of Mexico (1982–85), music director of the Xalapa SO (Orquesta Sinfónica de Xalapa) (1986–87) and the Bellas Artes Opera (1984–90), and artistic and music director of the National Opera of Mexico (1986–90). Diemecke's commitments were international from an early stage. From 1983 to 1986, he served as Exxon/Arts Endowment assistant conductor for the Rochester (N.Y.) PO, then from 1986 to 1990 as resident conductor of the Saint Paul CO. In 1990 he began two new music director positions: one for the Flint (Mich.) SO at the Flint Institute of Music, the other for the National SO of Mexico (Orquesta Sinfónica Nacional de México). While continuing in both positions, the well-traveled Diemecke became artistic advisor for the Tulsa (Okla.) PO in 2000 and music director for the Long Beach (Calif.) SO in 2001. He added yet another position in 2005, music director of the Buenos Aires Philharmonic of the Teatro Colon.

In recognition of his outstanding career in Mexico, Diemecke was given the Laurel de Oro a la Calidad award in 1993. He won the 2000 Orphée d'Or award for Best Opera Conductor from the French Académie du Disque Lyrique for his live recording of Mascagni's *Parisina*. The Academy also awarded him the Orphée d'Or in 2002 for conducting the recording of Donizetti's *The Exiles of Siberia*. In 2003, Diemecke was nominated for a Latin Grammy in the "Best Classical Album" category for his recording, *Chávez: Concertos for Violin and Piano*.

Diemecke is passionate about the classical tradition in which he was nurtured, and has a preference for Mahler. A noted interpreter of Mahler's works, he has been awarded a Mahler Society medal for his performances of the composer's complete symphonies. He has also shown a commitment to promoting his native traditions, performing and recording works by Mexican composers. Classical traditions are kept fresh by doing things better and with a new attitude, he believes. Most of all he is dedicated to quality, which he sees as the key to improvement for himself as well as his orchestras and their programs.

As a guest conductor, Diemecke has continued his global travels, leading the Los Angeles PO, National Orchestra of Colombia, BBC SO, Valladolid Symphony (Spain), ORCAM Madrid, Orchestre National d'Île de France, Royal PO, Orchestre de Paris, Orchestre Philharmonique de Montpellier (France), Opera Pacific, National SO, and the symphony orchestras of

Chautauqua (N.Y.), Charlotte (Va.), Winnipeg (Manitoba), Phoenix, Columbus (Ohio), Hartford (Conn.), Baltimore, Houston, Minnesota, Colorado, and Fort Worth. He also frequently conducts at festivals such as the Lincoln Center Summer Festival, the Hollywood Bowl Festival, Finger Lakes (N.Y.), Wolf Trap, Autunno Musicale a Como (Italy), Europalia (Brussels), World Fair Expo Sevilla (Spain), and Festival International Radio France.

Further Reading
Holston, Mark. "Wielding a Far-Reaching Baton." *Americas* 44 (May–June 1992): 56–57.

Selected Recordings
Chávez: *Concierto para Violin*; *Concierto para Piano*; Jorge Federico Osorio (pf), Pablio Diemecke (vn); State of Mexico SO. Prodisc Records.
Donizetti: *Gli Esiliati in Siberia*; O National de Montpellier. Actes Sud 34108.
Mahler: *Symphony no. 1*. Brahms: *Tragic Overture*; Flint SO; Flint Institute of Music, live: Flint 4/20/2002.
Mascagni: *Parisina*; O National de Montpellier; Actes Sud OMA 34103.
Villa-Lobos: *Symphony no. 4*; *Cello Concerto no. 2*; *Floresta do Amazonas*; Andres Diaz (vc); Simón Bolívar SO of Venezuela. Dorian 90228.

～

Dohnanyi, Christoph von
Born 8 September 1929 in Berlin, Germany

Von Dohnanyi is regarded as one of the most confident and accomplished conductors of his generation. He is admired for his conducting skills and for giving distinctive performances of repertoire across the full sweep of music from the Baroque era to the present day. His association with the U.S. falls into two periods. The first, a brief one (1951–52), was as a student attending Florida State University, where his grandfather, the distinguished Hungarian musician Ernö von Dohnanyi, was composer-in-residence. He spent the following summer at the Berkshire Music Center in Tanglewood, where he took lessons from Leonard Bernstein. The second period, a considerably longer one, was his tenure as music director of the Cleveland Orchestra (1984–2002). In addition, he has been a frequent guest conductor of the leading American orchestras in Boston, Philadelphia, Pittsburgh, Chicago, New York, and Los Angeles, and has also conducted at the Metropolitan and Chicago Lyric opera houses.

Between these two American periods, von Dohnanyi pursued the classic training for a conductor, progressing through the ranks of provincial German opera houses, each one more prestigious than the last. He began with a five-year stint (1952–57) as a coach at the Frankfurt-am-Main Opera working under the directorship of Georg Solti. He was first in charge in Lübeck (1957–63), where he became the youngest *Generalmusikdirektor* in Germany. From there he moved to a post in Kassel (1963–66), which he held for a time with the conductorship of the Cologne RSO (1964–70). With the reputation as a conductor of contemporary music, he gave the premiere of Henze's opera *Die Junge Lord* in Berlin in 1965, which was also the year he made his UK debut with the London PO. In 1966 he followed up with the premiere of Henze's opera *The Bassarids* at the Salzburg Festival. From 1968 to 1977 he was in charge at the Frankfurt Opera. His tenure there included a much-admired production of *Moses und Aaron*. It was during this period that he made his Met debut with *Falstaff* (1972) and his Covent Garden debut with *Salome* (1974). He reached the peak of his progression through the German opera houses at the Hamburg State Opera (1977–84). However, during his tenure he had to weather a series of administrative and artistic crises, and his acceptance of the Cleveland Orchestra directorship allowed him to resign three years before his contract expired.

The unique character of the Cleveland Orchestra, whose history goes back some eighty years, was laid down during the conductorship of Georg Szell, who, by dint of fearsome discipline, inculcated a style of playing of tremendous precision, literalness, and vitality. The orchestra continued to play brilliantly under Szell's successors, Boulez and **Maazel**, but the abrasive personality of the latter caused a good deal of discontent among its ranks. What the orchestra needed was a disciplinarian to maintain its standards, a musical imagination to produce fresh and challenging performances, and a personality, both sympathetic and corporate, to create a pleasant and amicable working environment. In Christoph von Dohnanyi they got an ideal fit. Not only was he an experienced and disciplined classicist, but also an avowed proponent of contemporary music. His appointment was a tremendous gamble, however, for he had not been among the original front-runners; in fact, he had only conducted the orchestra on one previous occasion, albeit one that made a deep impression. On taking up his appointment, he was clear-headed enough to realize that his task was to maintain those distinctive qualities upon which the orchestra's reputation rested, while injecting it with new spirit and personality. He also knew that to preserve his audience and the financial and social standing of the orchestra, he would have to be pragmatic about pursuing his desire to program and commission new music. He was circumspect, certainly, but he was not willing to give up his belief that music-making should be stimulating and challenging, with a judicious mix of the classics and contemporary fare.

The other means to promote the orchestra were touring and recording. Von Dohnanyi embarked on a veritable orgy of recording (he had done relatively little previously), laying down versions of much of the mainstream nineteenth- and twentieth-century repertoires, as well as a smattering of more avant-garde pieces. Four or five years into his term he had complete symphony cycles of Beethoven, Schumann, and Brahms under his belt, together with the better-known symphonies of Schubert, Tchaikovsky, Bruckner, and Mahler, and important works by Strauss, Berlioz, Ravel, and Bartók. He proved his commitment to American music by scheduling and recording works by Ives, Varèse, and **Adams**. A ten-disc CD set of recorded live performances taken from his twenty-year tenure and issued by the Cleveland organization gives a good indication of the varied and imaginative slate of works he programmed and reflects the orchestra's consistently high standard of performance.

The orchestra was a very persistent presence on the international scene. It toured overseas annually and appeared frequently at the most prestigious concert venues and festivals. Its residency at the 1992 Salzburg Festival was the first by an American orchestra. While touring programs tended to be conservative, the repertoire for the 1989 European visit is typical of the imaginative and balanced programs performed by the orchestra. It included Tippett's *Triple Concerto*, Schoenberg's *Variations Op. 31*, Webern's orchestration of Bach's *Ricercar*, and symphonies by Schubert (no. 9) and Mahler (no. 5). The statistics for the von Dohnanyi era speak for themselves: over 1,000 concerts, 109 works recorded, 15 international tours, 24 world premieres, and 7 U.S. premieres. He also made 73 appointments during his tenure. Few would dispute that his reign was an illustrious one. He left the orchestra in as good, if not better, shape than he found it. It now bore the von Dohnanyi stamp, and if the spectre of Szell still hovered over the orchestra, it must at least have been a benign one! It was a great era because it was a great partnership.

The question as to whether or not von Dohnanyi is a great conductor is probably irrelevant, but he certainly is a very good one. Criticism of his performances has always been that there is something, often a lot, held back. In a sense, this reflects a deliberate approach on his part. He has a very rational intellect that appreciates that music is of the mind as well as the heart; it informs as well as uplifts and entertains. His performances are lucid (some would say clinical) yet at the same time honest, faithful, fresh, and strong, given by the orchestra in almost flawless and sumptuous presentations. His interpretations of the classics are stylistically relevant without attempting to be stylistically "historical." These interpretations are inspirational, his approach is selfless, and his conducting devoid of mannerism to ensure that the music is the first priority. To some he appears as a "Prussian Puritan," stern and austere, but he would probably counter this criticism in his eminently erudite and quotable way by saying, "Don't make it too easy for feelings to call themselves feelings. If you control them, you have a chance to reach the truly great feelings."

Von Dohnanyi has always been an eloquent conversationalist and sometimes a vicious critic (see his famous interview with Richard Morrison in the *Times*, 25 August 1994). In part because of the disruptions of his early childhood—the Nazis murdered his father and his uncle, the famous theologian Dietrich Bonhoeffer—his many interviews reveal a serious and humane mind genuinely concerned with the political and cultural issues of the day. He worries that the internationalizing of music, its inevitable detachment from its cultural roots, will make it less relevant. He feels a responsibility to the music of our time to give it a hearing to find out what is good: "You cannot do only great music." He understands that it is personality, not ego, that goes into the making of a conductor. More importantly, his Cleveland experience has proved that what constitutes a great orchestra is the collective consciousness of talented instrumentalists with the commitment to play together and listen to each other.

During von Dohnanyi's tenure in Cleveland, his other activities included regular appearances at the Salzburg Festival and a much-admired rendition of *Fidelio* at Covent Garden (1990), in addition to his conducting of *Wozzeck*, *Die Frau ohne Schatten*, and *Die Meistersinger* there. In 1993 he made his first appearance at the Vienna State Opera with Wagner's *Ring Cycle*. He began a close partnership with the Philharmonia Orchestra as principal guest conductor in 1994, becoming principal conductor in 1997, and opening the Edinburgh Festival with them in 2002. From 1998 to 2000 he was the principal guest conductor of the Orchestre de Paris. In 2004 he accepted the post of chief conductor of the NDR SO, Hamburg.

Further Reading

"Final Bows (a Brief Retrospective of the Careers of the Mighty Maestri of Boston, New York, and Cleveland)." *Symphony* 53 (May–June 2002): 21–27.

"High Notes: Christoph von Dohnanyi." *Musical Opinion* 119 (Winter 1996): 186.

Jaffé, Daniel. "From Where I Sit: Christoph von Dohnányi (interview)." *Gramophone* 79 (May 2002): 21.

Jolly, James. "Christoph von Dohnanyi Talks." *Gramophone* 67 (June 1989): 20–21.

Knight, John. "Freedom with Discipline." *The Instrumentalist* 54 (March 2000): 12–17.

Selected Recordings

Bartók: *Miraculous Mandarin*, Op. 19/Sz 73. Stravinsky: *Pétrouchka*; Vienna PO. MSI Music 4762686.

Beethoven: *Symphony no. 9*; Carol Vaness (s); Janice Taylor (ms); Siegfried Jerusalem (t); Robert Lloyd (b); Cleveland O and Ch (Robert Page, dir). Telarc CD 80120.

Christoph von Dohnanyi: Compact Disc Edition; Cleveland O; 10-CD boxed set. SKU MAA01032, live performances: 1984–2001.

Mendelssohn: *Die erste Walpurgisnacht*, Op. 60; *Symphony no. 3 in A minor*, Op. 56 "Scottish"; soloists; Cleveland O. Telarc 80184.

Schoenberg: *Variations for Orchestra*, Op. 31; *Five Pieces for Orchestra*, Op. 16; *Erwartung*, Op. 17; *Orchestral Songs*, Op. 8; Anja Silja (s); Vienna PO. Decca 448279 (from 2-CD set).

～

Eschenbach, Christoph (Ringmann)
Born 20 February 1949 in Breslau, Germany

Eschenbach is one of a number of musicians who have made the transition from pianist to conductor, although, like **Barenboim**, it seems that he intended to be a conductor all along. After a distinguished career as a pianist, his conducting transition was bumpier than most, but, having made it, he has come to be regarded as one of the most impressive practitioners of his generation. Even during the transition period when he chiefly led concerto performances from the keyboard, he showed the potential to be a fine conductor. He is particularly admired for his spectacularly successful work as music director of the Houston (Tex.) SO (1988–98).

Houston had gotten to know Eschenbach fairly well through his guest appearances. On one notable occasion he stood in at the last minute for the music director Sergiu Comissiona, and, on only a single rehearsal, achieved a memorable performance of Bruckner's Symphony no. 6. It was evidently a partnership that produced good vibes, and when the director's position became vacant, Eschenbach seemed to possess the strength of character and musical accomplishment needed to take on the formidable task of lifting the orchestra out of the doldrums. Indeed, the situation was dire, with the orchestra facing a deficit of $2.3 million, dwindling audiences, and low morale brought about by a reduction in the number of players and salary cuts for the remaining ones. Nevertheless, there was some attraction to the position for Eschenbach. He valued the special rapport with the players and the potential to effect a renaissance in a situation relatively removed from the limelight, where he could consolidate and build his skills as an orchestral trainer and creative conductor. Having committed to the task of rejuvenating the orchestra's fortunes, he launched himself into it heart and soul, prepared to devote as much time and effort as necessary. What was most surprising was the way he assumed the mantle of handling the socioeconomic aspects of the job successfully, a role totally alien to someone used to working with the subsidized orchestras of Europe. He was known to have the knack for motivating people, however, and, after remarkably few years, he could claim to have made considerable progress and was enjoying what may best be described as a prolonged honeymoon. He could boast a recording contract, international tours, and approval from audiences and critics alike.

Eschenbach's success depended primarily on his ability to galvanize the players, present appealing programs, and give riveting performances. He used his orchestra-building skills to encourage a shared, productive mentality among players and to impress them with his artistic integrity. By introducing this stronger sense of cohesiveness, hiring the best new players, and stripping away some of the deadwood, he forged an ensemble able to claim its place as one of the nation's most respected musical organizations. This productive partnership had staying power and didn't suffer from the disillusionment that often sets in after the initial euphoria.

One critic described Eschenbach as "a dynamic conductor with a mercurial musical sensibility." His interpretations invariably achieve musical excellence, are often interpretively challenging, and are sometimes wayward, though always interestingly so. His astonishing intellect and musical sensibility never allow things to get quite out of hand. His podium manner is a blend of the restrained and the balletic, at the same time assertive and self-effacing. His physical gestures, always intending to convey musical meaning, remind one at times of Leonard Bernstein, one of his heroes. The clear and communicative aspect of his style probably derives from the influence of Georg Szell, with whom he had concentrated study during the late 1960s. His approach to the complexity of musical expression, combining emotional intellect, spiritual depth, and physical energy, probably reaches back to the impression made on him as a ten-year-old boy by the performances conducted by Furtwängler. Like von Karajan, with whom he also studied briefly, he aims to break down the "tyranny of the bar line" and reach beyond slavish attention to the score. There is a seriousness bordering on severity in Eschenbach's music-making that is also Karajan-esque. In rehearsal he has learned to limit his natural bent for verbal explanation and now relies far more on gesture and an occasional "keyword" to attain his musical ends, which, after all, are beyond words. Perhaps the most crucial influence was derived from his adoptive mother, his first piano teacher and also a teacher of singing. From her he absorbed the principle that later led him to exclaim: "Breathing is the soul of my conducting style!" To achieve the mutual interlistening of chamber music on the scale that is the hallmark of a great orchestra, he leads his players (and sometimes allows himself to be led by them) toward a level of expression which combines a sensitivity for sound quality, detail, lyric and dramatic contrast, and musical architecture. It was to be expected that his Houston programs would present a wide diversity of music, with adequate attention paid to the contemporary scene. He demonstrated a particular commitment to the composers of the Second Viennese School (Schoenberg, Berg, and Webern), for whose music he has a close affinity.

Touring, as much as any other factor, helps solidify an orchestra's stature at home and abroad. The second European tour in the spring of 1997 seemed to sum up the orchestra's achievement under Eschenbach's leadership. It saw them performing in the most prestigious venues in Vienna, Berlin, Amsterdam, and London, as well as giving concerts in five other German cities and France. As for recording, Eschenbach was hit by the downturn in the industry, and a number of ambitious projects failed to materialize. Preserved, though, are sets of Brahms and Schumann symphonies on the Virgin label, and one each of Mahler (no. 1) and Bruckner (no. 2) issued by Koch. For BMG/RCA he led the orchestra (with soloist Renée Fleming) in a recital of Strauss orchestral lieder and a disc of Schoenberg transcriptions. They also recorded music by Picker for Virgin and Rouse for Telarc.

After a decade of devotion to Houston, Eschenbach felt the need to explore new challenges in Europe, although he would deny the assertion that it was a need to return to his roots. In fact, his early childhood was severely disrupted by the close and aftermath of World War II. His mother had died in childbirth and his father, a musicologist and dissident, had been conscripted into the army and sent to certain death at the Eastern Front. To escape the advancing Red Army, his grandmother hauled the five-year-old through a number of countries before the two of them ended up in a refugee camp and she succumbed to a typhoid epidemic. Christoph, who barely survived, was

rescued by his mother's cousin, adopted by her and her husband, and taken
to live in Mecklenberg. He was so severely traumatized that he was unable to
speak for over a year. His new mother taught piano and voice and his new father was a competent amateur violinist, so Christoph found himself living in
an intensely musical environment. The music-making proved a spur to his
convalescence, and he was recovered enough to begin piano lessons at the
age of eight. Showing considerable promise, he took lessons from a distinguished teacher, Eliza Hansen (a pupil of Schnabel and Fischer), in Hamburg. The indelible impression made on Christoph by witnessing a Furtwängler concert led to his stated ambition to become a conductor. To encourage
this, his mother suggested he learn an orchestral instrument as well, so he began taking violin lessons. His success as a pianist was marked by twice winning the annual Steinway Piano Competition, and he removed to Cologne
for further study with Hans-Otto Schmidt-Neuhaus. On his return to Hamburg he enrolled in the Hochschule für Musik, resumed his piano studies with
Hansen, and took conducting lessons from Wilhelm Brückner-Rüggeberg.
He was a prizewinner at the 1962 Munich International Competition, but
made his reputation by winning outright of one of the stiffest of all piano
competitions, the Clara Haskil Prize, in Switzerland in 1966. This led to,
among other opportunities, an exclusive recording contract with DGG and
a guest appearance and three-month residency with Georg Szell and the
Cleveland Orchestra in 1968. That same year, as the dedicatee, he gave the
first performance of Henze's Second Piano Concerto, and about this time
formed a very successful duo with the pianist Justus Frantz. He began to realize his other ambition by appearing as conductor/soloist, and his official
conducting debut in Hamburg in 1972 was a performance of no less a work
than Bruckner's Symphony no. 3. Pursuing the dual role of soloist and conductor, he gave his U.S. debut with the San Francisco SO in 1975 and conducted his first opera, La Traviata, in Darmstadt in 1978. His first appointment was to the Rheinland-Pfalz State PO (1979–81). In 1981 he became
principal guest conductor of both the London PO and the Tonhalle Orchestra of Zurich, and the next year saw his debut with the New York PO. He first
appeared with the Houston SO in 1983, again in 1985, and in 1986 he participated in Houston's Mostly Mozart Festival. Meanwhile, he gave his
Covent Garden debut with Cosi fan tutte (1984). After becoming Houston's
music director he made annual appearances with Houston Grand Opera, beginning with a performance of The Marriage of Figaro. Among the other
works he gave subsequently were the remaining two Mozart/Da Ponte operas,
Lohengrin, Elektra, Der Rosenkavalier, and a much admired Parsifal. In 1995 he
became music director of the Ravinia Festival (1995–2003), cementing a

close relationship with the Chicago SO, and he worked jointly with Michael Tilson **Thomas** to head the Pacific Music Festival. His return to a European base came with his appointments as music director of the NDR SO in Hamburg (1998–2003) and director of the Schleswig-Holstein Music Festival. In 2000 he became chief conductor of the Orchestre de Paris.

Philadelphia presented Eschenbach with a different sort of challenge. This was not a rescue operation and it placed him much more in the spotlight. One of the most "institutionalized" of American orchestras, the Philadelphia Orchestra's decision to appoint him as music director (2003) was risky. He had had but little contact with the orchestra previously, and the announcement of his appointment was greeted by the orchestra with bemused silence. It was for the attributes that had worked so well in Houston that he was hired. Although schooled in the Germanic tradition, his musicality is more eccentric and wide-ranging than that of his staid predecessor (Wolfgang **Sawallisch**). Carrying the tag of innovator, he arrived with a stronger motivation to change than to preserve the Philadelphia heritage. He planned to modify the orchestra's opulent sound to make it more versatile in a wider range of repertoire. He was expected to foster closer ties to his audience through innovative programming, preconcert talks, and community outreach. The expectations that he would break down the barrier between audience and orchestra, make a direct appeal to the young, both players and audience, and prepare and energize the organization to play a relevant role in the twenty-first century were only partially fulfilled. His attempt to introduce less formal concert attire was resisted by the players. He did introduce challenging repertoire, continuing his support for those composers he had championed in recent years and for whose music he has a genuine enthusiasm, including Christopher Rouse, Augusta Read Thomas, Matthias Pintscher, Wolfgang Rihm, Marc-André Dalbavie, and Peter Lieberson. However, there were early murmurs of discontent as players tried to understand what he was trying to convey. This led to a sense of insecurity, with reports of the conductor losing his place in the score, squandering rehearsal time, and indulging in unexpected agogic flights of tempi. Never the subtlest of conductors, his eccentricities and mannerisms, which sometimes resulted in performances fraught with miscalculations, came under much more intense scrutiny. Nonetheless, even the most unforgiving critics were obliged to concede "an occasional magical performance." Also to his credit, he was influential in securing a recording contract for the orchestra after a lapse of ten years. When it ends in 2008, his tenure will have been the briefest directorship the orchestra has had in a hundred years.

Website
http://www.christoph-eschenbach.com

Further Reading
Erk, Wolfgang. *Für Christoph Eschenbach zum 20. Februar 1990: eine Festgabe.* Stuttgart: Radius-Verlag, 1990. [German]
Eschenbach, Christoph. "From Where I Sit." *Gramophone* 81 (Awards Issue 2003): 21.
Johnson, Lawrence A. "An Interview with Christoph Eschenbach." *Fanfare* 22 (November–December 1998): 113–116.
Jolly, James. "Interview." *Gramophone* 82 (February 2005): 16.
Miller, Sarah Bryan. "Zen Master." *Opera News* 61 (January 1997): 32–33.
Wright, David. "A Talk with Christoph Eschenbach." *American Record Guide* 65 (May–June 2003): 14–17.

Selected Recordings
Dalbavie: *Color*; *Concerto for Violin*; *Ciaccona*; Eiichi Chijiiwa (vn); O de Paris. Naïve Montaigne MO 782162.
Mahler: *Symphony no. 6*; Philadelphia O. Ondine 1084.
Rouse: *Symphony no. 2*; *Concerto for Flute*; *Phaethon*; Carol Wincenc (fl); Houston SO. Telarc 80452.
Schumann: *Symphonies 1–4*; Bamberg SO. Virgin Classics 61884.
Strauss (R): *Four Last Songs*; *Orchestral Songs: Befreit, Muttertändelei, Wiegenlied, Waldseligkeit, Cäcilie*; *Der Rosenkavalier: Orchestral Suite*; Renée Fleming (s); Houston SO. RCA 82876-59408-2.

⁓

Falletta, JoAnn (Marie)
Born 27 February 1954 in New York, New York

JoAnn Falletta brings a feminine slant to two aspects of modern conducting. The first is the debunked myth of the male maestro as a dictatorial martinet. She has succeeded so brilliantly in her chosen profession precisely because this notion has gradually eroded over the past fifty years and, where it survives at all, is only a generational legacy. The second and more important is the way that she has articulated better than anyone else the range of challenges the modern maestro faces. The skill-set that a music director must possess, aside from those of the podium, includes: a leadership role in the nurturing of the organization, especially in difficult times; an ability to manage personnel; administrative and planning skills; a commitment to community outreach; exceptional communication skills; and "the vision thing." Being focused primarily on the players, the music director is responsible for fostering an environment where artistic excellence and integrity thrive, and in which each individual player is given the opportunity to become self-realized within a larger artistic conception. It is the players, more than the audience or administration, who respond on a daily basis to the director's musicianship, talent, and insight. These aspects, when one stops to think about it, are fairly self-evident, but it has taken someone of Falletta's perspicacity to express them as lucidly as she did in an address entitled "The Compleat Music Director," delivered at the Fifty-Seventh National Conference of the American Symphony Orchestra League. It is doubtful any man could have done it so thoroughly!

The gender issue cannot be ignored. When she set out upon her chosen profession she faced double-jeopardy odds against making a success of it. Until very recently, orchestral conducting at the higher levels has been an almost exclusively male preserve. Added to this is the prejudice against American-born conductors securing top-flight appointments in the U.S. Although music lags behind the other professions, the cultural revolution of the 1970s did open up possibilities for a woman as utterly dedicated and determined as Falletta. In this respect, she is to be regarded as a pioneer, if not exactly a trailblazer. She claims she never really thought about the odds against her and, with typical determination, overcame the well-meaning discouragement she met with at the Mannes College of Music, understanding early on what it would take to succeed. Her aim was to be so well prepared and project such an aura of professionalism that the gender issue would become subsumed in the process of music-making. Ultimately, it is by being oneself, with all the musical integrity and sincerity that one has accrued, that one achieves the necessary respect and authority that are still the hallmarks of a good conductor.

Falletta was born into a music-loving family. A shy child, she began to learn the guitar and piano from the age of seven. Later she took up the cello to experience orchestral playing. When she was old enough, she was taken to concerts at Carnegie Hall regularly, and it was at one of these, at the age of about twelve, that she received enlightenment. At a performance of Beethoven's Sixth Symphony—she doesn't remember by whom—she became aware of what she wanted to be; it was "the moment when I felt I had to be involved in *that* repertoire in *that* way." From then on she immersed herself in music, attending concerts and rehearsals, listening to recordings, and playing scores. She soon began to feel that, given the opportunity, she had the ability to shape the sound patterns she was studying. She entered Mannes College of Music in 1972 to study guitar, and with persistence became a conducting student in her second year. She studied principally with Sung Kwak and Carl Bamberger. She then went on to graduate study jointly at Mannes and Queens College. At Queens she was given the opportunity to conduct the student orchestra while taking lessons from Semyon **Bychkov**. Outside of school, she took on a very unpromising ensemble calling itself the Jamaica SO. She transformed this group and renamed it the Queens PO, with which she continued to be associated until 1991. Transferring to Juilliard in 1983 and receiving its Bruno Walter Scholarship, she worked extensively with Jorge **Mester** and privately with Sixten Ehrling, as well as took part in master classes given by Leonard Bernstein, whom she found very inspiring. Her first foray away from New York City was to Denver, where she acted as music director of the Denver (Colo.) CO (1983–92). In 1985 she won the Stokowski Conducting Competition and a concert with the American SO in Carnegie Hall. She also won the Toscanini Prize and was appointed associate conductor of the Milwaukee (Wisc.) SO (1985–88). By this time she was already giving around one hundred performances per year. Falletta conducted the Women's PO, an organization in San Francisco devoted to performing works by women composers, from 1986 to 1996, performing and recording a great deal of new and unfamiliar music. In 1989 she obtained her DMA in conducting from Juilliard and became music director of the Long Beach (Calif.) SO, where she enjoyed an eleven-year stay. From 1985 onward she embarked on a heavy conducting schedule, holding up to five positions simultaneously; while acting as artistic advisor to the Santa Cruz (Calif.) SO (1990–91), she also became music director of the Virginia SO in 1991. As well as accepting guest appearances with American orchestras, she began to be known in Europe, most famously making her debut (1992) with the Mannheim Orchestra, the first female conductor in its three-hundred-year history!

Her most prestigious appointment came in 1999 as music director of the Buffalo (N.Y.) PO, the same year she was awarded Columbia University's Ditson Conductor's Award. The BPO has a proud pedigree and a distinguished succession of music directors, including Josef Krips, Lukas Foss, and Michael Tilson **Thomas**. At the time of Falletta's accession, however, it was experiencing some severe budget problems. She quickly demonstrated her mettle by calling for support from the community to endorse the orchestra as a valued cultural asset. This, in turn, persuaded local corporations to increase their donations. The orchestra's outreach is impressive and includes a "Family

Concerts" series, preconcert lectures, and over one hundred community performances throughout the region. This approach mirrors ones she had taken
previously in Long Beach and Virginia, where both orchestras had been faltering when she took over. By focusing on the orchestras as community assets that provide a blend of inspiration, pleasure, entertainment, and education, she was able to turn their fortunes around. She has always been
prepared to devote the necessary time to being an ambassador for music to
her constituencies, showing genuine concern about the decline in classical
music audiences and finding innovative ways to reverse the trend, hence the
skill she has developed in programming a judicious mixture of the familiar
and unfamiliar, the old and the new. It is a mistake, she believes, to depend
on the established repertory masterpieces to attract audiences, because, ultimately, the organization's ambience becomes that of a stale museum art. On
a personal level, the amount of unfamiliar music and number of premieres
she performed with the Women's PO helped invigorate her approach to more
familiar scores. When the BPO returned to Carnegie Hall in 2004 with Falletta at the helm, it was after an absence of sixteen years. The program,
which consisted of music by Kodály, Barber, Griffes, and Zemlinsky, is typical of the innovative scheduling that has been a consistent feature of her career. At last count, she had performed nearly three hundred works by American composers, including sixty world premieres, and received eight
consecutive awards from ASCAP for creative programming. In 2002 she was
the recipient of the Seaver/NEA Conductors Award, and in 2005 acted as
artistic advisor to the Honolulu (Hawaii) SO during its search for a new music director.

Her programming flair is reflected (commercial considerations notwithstanding) in her legacy of over thirty recordings. Again, there is the mixture
of the familiar and the unknown; composers range from Moussorgsky, Debussy, and Sibelius through Schumann (Clara) and Waldteufel, to Germaine
Tailleferre, Schreker, and Lyadov. She has championed American music in
recordings of Copland, Morton Gould, Converse, Griffes, Rathaus, Moross,
and Elinor Armer (in association with Ursula LeGuin), among others. The
recording of Griffes's orchestral music won the Editor's Choice award from
the Gramophone. She has similarly compiled a number of imaginative collec-
tions on themes such as Impressions of French Music, Seascapes, and Pictures.
In addition to the orchestras of which she has been director, she has recorded
with the English CO, London SO, New Zealand SO, and Czech National
SO. She appears on a video recording, Behind the Scenes with JoAnn Falletta,
which shows how symphony orchestras use layers of sound to create music.
She has also published a volume of poetry, Love Letters to Music.

Although Falletta has guest conducted extensively on five continents and with many fine orchestras, one feels she deserves exposure with the most prestigious ensembles. Of the so-called Big Five American orchestras, for instance, she has appeared only with the Philadelphia Orchestra. One senses a lingering prejudice at play here, since her accomplishments merit the opportunity to prove herself in front of the very best ensembles.

Website
http://www.joannfalletta.com

Further Reading
Brown, Royal S. "Call Her Maestra: An Interview with JoAnn Falletta." *Fanfare* 21 (November–December 1997): 108–22.
Dubins, Jerry. "JoAnn Falletta: Fanfare for the Uncommon Women." *Fanfare* 27 (March–April 2004): 81–86.
Falletta, JoAnn. "The Compleat Music Director." *Symphony* 53 (November–December 2002): 40–43.
Ginell, Richard S. "JoAnn Falletta." *Musical America* 110 (September 1990): 10–12.
Kozinn, Allan. "An American Woman Conductor on the Way Up." *New York Times*, 25 March 1985, H23.

Selected Recordings
Copland: *The Red Pony Suite*; *Rodeo*; *Prairie Journal*; *Letter from Home*; Buffalo PO. Naxos 8.559240.
Fuchs (Kenneth): *An American Place*; *Eventide (Concerto for English Horn)*; *Out of the Dark (Suite for CO)*; Thomas Stacy (Eh); Timothy Jones (cor); London SO. Naxos 8.559224.
Pictures at a Gallery: Reger: *Four Tone Poems after Arnold Böcklin*. Schreker: *The Birthday of the Infanta* (exc). Rachmaninoff: *The Isle of the Dead*. Berlioz: *Overture to 'Benvenuto Cellini'*; Buffalo PO. Buffalo Philharmonic CD.
Seascapes: Bax: *Tintagel*. Ibert: *Ports of Call*. Britten: *Four Sea Interludes from "Peter Grimes."* Glazunov: *The Sea*, Op. 28. Mendelssohn: *Beautiful Melusine*; Virginia SO. VSO HRC004.
The Women's Philharmonic: Mendelssohn (Fanny): *Ouverture*. Schumann (Clara): *Piano Concerto in a*, Op. 7. Tailleferre: *Concertino for Harp and Orchestra*. Boulanger (Lili): *D'un Soir Triste, D'un Matin de Printemps*; The Women's Philharmonic. Koch 3-7169-2 H1.

⌒

Farberman, Harold
Born 11 November 1930 in New York, New York

During a long and distinguished conducting career, Farberman, who is also a noted composer, has made significant contributions as a teacher of conducting and as a propagator of new and unfamiliar music. He is one of the leading Mahlerians of the post–Bruno Walter generation and a most ardent champion of the music of Charles Ives. For his research, performance, and recording of Ives's music he was awarded a grant from the National Institute of Arts and Letters (1972), as well as the Ives Medal. He has focused on encouraging American conductors, and encouraging them to perform music by American composers. To this end, he was founder-president of the Conductors Guild (1975) under the auspices of the American Symphony Orchestra League, and, in 1980, he founded the Conductors Institute, first at the University of West Virginia, then at the University of South Carolina, and latterly at Bard College. In 1990 he was appointed professor of conducting at the Hartt School of Music at the University of Hartford (1990–2000). His pedagogical experience is encapsulated in a book and video: *The Art of Conducting Technique.*

Farberman was born into a musical family. His father and brother played drums in klezmer bands. After obtaining his diploma from Juilliard in 1951, he spent the following twelve years as percussionist and timpanist with the Boston SO. During this time he was active as a composer and earned his master's degree in composition from the New England Conservatory of Music (1957). Summer composition study with Copland at Tanglewood also included participation in Eleazer de Carvalho's conducting class. From 1955 to 1963 he was conductor of Boston's New Arts Orchestra, and from 1967 to 1970, interim director of the Colorado Springs SO, where he introduced contemporary and American music and established high musical standards. He served as music director of the Oakland (Calif.) SO (1971–79) and was chief guest conductor of the Denver (Colo.) SO and the Bournemouth (UK) Sinfonietta. He has been a frequent guest conductor and has recorded extensively with orchestras in Europe. His recordings of Mahler symphonies with various London orchestras are much admired, and he made the first recording, with the Philharmonia Hungarica, of Clinton Carpenter's 1966 performing edition of the uncompleted Tenth Symphony. He has made a specialty of recording percussion ensemble music (including his own), the music of Michael Haydn, and New York composer Irving Bazelon (1922–95). His recording of Glière's Third Symphony with the Royal PO, released in 1978, was awarded Belgium's Saint Cecilia Award.

Further Reading

Farberman, Harold. "The Art of Conducting Technique: A Fresh, Original Look at the Art of Conducting, Including Pattern Cubes, a Three-Dimensional System for Charting Baton Movement." *Choral Journal* 43 (September 2002): 76–77.

Farberman, Harold. *The Art of Conducting Technique: A New Perspective.* Miami, Fla.: Warner Bros., 1997.

Farberman, Harold. "Training Conductors." In *The Cambridge Companion to Conducting,* edited by José Antonio Bowen, 249–61. Cambridge: Cambridge University Press, 2003.

Starr, William W. "The Conductors Institute." *Musical America* 107, no. 6 (1988): 25–27.

Selected Recordings

Bazelon: *Symphony no. 6; Taming of the Shrew Overture; Symphony no. 2* "Testament to a Big City"; Rousse PO. Albany 370.

Gliere: *Symphony no. 3,* Op. 42; *Concerto for Cello,* Op. 87; Serguey Sudzilovski (vc); Royal PO; USSR Cinematographic O. Regis 2068.

Haydn (M): *Symphonies*; Bournemouth Sinfonietta. Vox CDX 5020.

Ives: *Symphony no. 2*; New Philharmonia O. Vanguard VBD10033.

Mahler: *Symphony no. 5*; London SO. Vox 97205.

〜

Figueroa, Guillermo
Born 5 April 1953 in Puerto Rico

Born into a musical family, Guillermo Figueroa studied violin with both his father and his uncle at the Conservatory of Music in Puerto Rico. He went on to attend Juilliard, where he won the Victor Herbert Prize for excellence in violin playing. In 1979, he also won first prize for violin playing at the Washington International Competition. Figueroa studied conducting in New York with Harold **Farberman**, yet it was many years before that became his career. He was a founding member (1972) and concertmaster of the conductorless Orpheus CO until 2001. He also spent ten years as concertmaster and guest conductor for the New York City Ballet Orchestra before stepping down in 2001. Figueroa became principal guest conductor for the Puerto Rico SO (Orquesta Sinfónica de Puerto Rico) in 1993, becoming its first native music director in 2001. Under Figueroa the PRSO made its debut at both Carnegie Hall (2003) and the Kennedy Center (2004). He recently announced that he will not renew his contract with the PRSO when it expires in 2007.

In 2001, he was also appointed music director of the New Mexico SO, becoming the first Puerto Rican-born conductor to lead an orchestra of that caliber. Figueroa says he is energized by the education initiatives and partnerships the NMSO is forging with the Hispanic and Native American communities. In 2002, the orchestra received a Met Life Award for Excellence in Community Engagement. He is passionate about Berlioz, whose music affects him deeply. The Berlioz Festival he initiated in 2003 is a testament to his enthusiasm and strong leadership. Figueroa is also an advocate for new music, premiering (as conductor and violinist) the works of composers such as Roberto Sierra, Daron Hagen, and German Caceres. He conducted the first recording of Sierra's oratorio, *Bayoan*, with the Bronx Arts Ensemble Orchestra. In 2003, Figueroa was conductor-in-residence for the Conductors Institute at Bard College. He cofounded (2004) and is co-artistic director of the annual Festival de Musica Rondena chamber series in Albuquerque.

Figueroa has appeared as a guest conductor with the New Jersey SO, Memphis SO, Phoenix SO, Iceland SO, Colorado SO, El Salvador SO, Xalapa SO (Mexico), Tucson SO, Juilliard Orchestra, Santa Fe SO, and frequently the New York City Ballet at Lincoln Center.

Further Reading

Trotter, Herman. "An Unlikely Spot for Berlioz." *American Record Guide* 66 (September–October 2003): 21–23.

Selected Recordings

Berlioz: *Le Corsaire Overture*. Tchaikovsky: *Symphony no. 4 in F minor*. Ravel: *Daphnis and Chloé, Suite 2*; New Mexico SO. NMSO 5, live 4/2001, 9/2001.

Sierra: *Bayoan*; Wonjung Kim (s); Peter Stewart (b); Bronx Arts Ensemble. Albany Records 514.

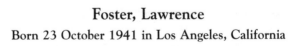

Foster, Lawrence
Born 23 October 1941 in Los Angeles, California

Lawrence Foster was born into a not particularly musical Romanian-Jewish family. It was customary in that culture, however, for offspring to learn a musical instrument—forcibly, if necessary! So it was that the reluctant Lawrence began piano lessons at the age of six—an experience that may have cowed but did not extinguish his musical genes! A concert he attended at the age of thirteen, given by the Los Angeles PO under Alfred Wallenstein, proved to be an epiphany and set his determination to become a conductor. Los Angeles in those days was a gathering point for many émigré Jewish musicians, and it was from within this group that Foster found his earliest teachers, particularly Fritz Zweig, his first conducting teacher. It was also in this milieu that Foster was able to meet Bruno Walter. He attended Black-Foxe Military Academy, where a classmate was the son of the film composer Franz Waxman, and when he conducted his first orchestra concert with the Young Musician's Debut Orchestra (1960), it was to share the podium with Miklos Rosza. When an opportunity to work with the San Francisco Ballet opened up, Foster, absenting himself from the university, worked as an assistant conductor, and later as music director. In this role, he undertook extended nationwide tours with Fonteyn and Nureyev, which were proving grounds for his trade as a conductor. During this period, he attended master classes at the Bayreuth Festival (1961–63) and took conducting lessons from Karl Böhm. In 1964 he made an appearance conducting the Stuttgart Opera and attended the Berkshire Music Center at Tanglewood, where he won the Koussevitzky Prize.

His growing reputation earned him an assistantship to Zubin Mehta with the Los Angeles PO (1963–68). In 1967 he made his London debut with the English CO. The following year he gave his first performance with the Royal PO and impressed sufficiently to be offered the post of chief guest conductor, which he held from 1969–74. In 1969, the orchestra made a North American tour in which he shared the conducting with the orchestra's principal conductor, Rudolf Kempe. The touring schedule had Foster conduct the RPO concert in Houston, which led to an invitation to lead a series of concerts with the Houston (Tex.) SO, and this in turn led to his appointment there as conductor-in-chief, which lasted from 1971 until 1978. He also appeared frequently with the Houston Opera, conducting the U.S. premiere of Handel's *Rinaldo* and a staging of Berg's *Lulu*. In 1974 he began a close partnership with Scottish Opera and in 1976 made his Covent Garden debut with the revised version of Walton's *Troilus and Cressida*.

After resigning from his post in Houston in 1978, Foster's sphere of operation centered in Europe, specifically Monte Carlo, where he conducted the Orchestre National (renamed the Orchestre Philharmonique) de Monte Carlo (1979–90). The orchestra's duties included accompanying the annual opera season. In addition, he became *Generalmusikdirektor* for the City of Duisberg (1981–88) and music director of the Lausanne CO from 1985 to 1990. Beginning in 1998, he was a frequent guest conductor of the Jerusalem SO and became its designated music director, but, owing to a misunderstanding with management, he never took up the appointment. In 1992 he resumed the directorship in Monte Carlo for a couple of seasons, and he assumed the position of music director of the Barcelona SO in 1996, which he held until 2002. He renewed his association with the Jerusalem SO, becoming music adviser for a three-year term beginning in 2001, and, retaining his Iberian connection, he became music director of the Gulbenkian Orchestra in Lisbon in 2002.

In 1986, he renewed his U.S. ties during the inaugural season of the Los Angeles Opera with a production of *Otello* starring Placido Domingo, the company's artistic director, and he has maintained an active relationship with them. Subsequent productions have included: *La Bohème*, Prokofiev's *Fiery Angel*, *The Marriage of Figaro*, a much-praised *Elektra*, *Cosi fan tutte*, *Don Giovanni*, *Faust*, *Pagliacci*, *The Magic Flute*, and *Nabucco*. From 1990 to 1998 he took on the duties of music director of the Aspen Festival and School.

For the most part, Foster uses detailed and precise conducting gestures based on solid musicianship to convey his musical intentions. His interpretations exhibit a strong sense of structural intelligence, which pays dividends in works that many conductors find challenging, such as Schumann's *Rhenish Symphony*. He excels in colorful and exotic music from Berlioz, de Falla, Stravinsky, and Hindemith to Copland. This repertoire allows him to enliven his performances with vigor, excitement, and clarity. He brings emotional commitment to works with which he feels a close affinity: the music of Enesco and Strauss, for example. His conducting of the classics has been less well received, however, and the critics have found his Mozart performances rather dull. He has been a champion of new music and has given a number of premieres, most notably of that Paul McCartney's oratorio, *Standing Stone*, which he also recorded.

He has recorded with the Berlin RSO, Philharmonia Orchestra, London SO, and City of Birmingham SO, in addition to those orchestras with which he has held appointments. His recording of Enesco's opera *Oedipe* in 1991 won critical praise and was awarded the Grand Prix du Disque. A disc of piano concertos by obscure composers Emil von Sauer and Franz Xaver Scharwenka with pianist Stephen Hough and the CBSO was given Record of the Year by the *Gramophone* magazine in 1996. As guest conductor he has appeared with many leading orchestras, including those in Los Angeles, Pittsburgh, Montreal, Chicago, Paris, Helsinki, and with the RSO in Berlin. He has also conducted opera at Covent Garden, the Met, the Opera Comique and Bastille in Paris, and in Los Angeles, Houston, and Monte Carlo.

Further Reading

Brown, Royal S. "An Interview with Lawrence Foster." *Fanfare* 22 (January–February 1999): 40.

Kolodin, Irving. "Music to My Ears (N.Y. Philharmonic Conductorial Debut)." *Saturday Review* 3 (10 January 1976): 66.

Selected Recordings

Dukas: *Symphony in C*. Fauré: *Pelléas et Mélisande*, Op. 80; Monte Carlo PO. Claves 9102.

McCartney: *Standing Stone*; London SO. EMI 56484.

Saint-Saëns: *Piano Concerto no. 5* (from *Pnina Salzman v. 3*); Pnina Salzman (pf); Jerusalem SO. Doremi 7840.

Waxman: *The Song of Terezin*. Zeisl: *Requiem ebraico*; Deborah Riedel (s); Della Jones (ms); Michael Kraus (b-b); Berlin Radio Symphony Ch; Berlin Radio Children's Choir; Berlin RSO. Decca 460211.

Weber: *Overtures: Ruler of the Spirits, Peter Schmoll, Preciosa, Abu Hassan, Jubilee, Turandot (and March); Invitation to the Dance* (orch. Weingartner); City of Birmingham SO. Claves 9605.

⌒

Freeman, Paul (Douglas)
Born 2 January 1936 in Richmond, Virginia

In a field of activity dominated by white males, it is inevitable that race should prove to be a significant issue in the career of Paul Freeman, an American conductor of African descent. Race has played a role in the shaping of his career, the repertoire he has championed, and the ethnic and cultural shift he has effected through the Chicago Sinfonietta. To deal with the latter first; the mid-sized orchestra which Freeman helped found in 1987 and continues to conduct is probably the most diverse in existence. It boasts a membership that is 55 percent female and 25 to 35 percent people of color, but more importantly, it has attracted a loyal multiracial following. It has proved a useful vehicle for performing and recording established and new work by black composers, following on the tradition that Freeman began in the 1970s with his nine-LP *Columbia Black Composers Series*. If prejudice has hindered his career path, Freeman has also benefitted from the role of "token black." As he himself is quoted as saying, however, "I may get an engagement as a guest conductor because of the color of my skin, but never have I been invited back simply because I was black." Race may have played a significant role in his career, but his critically acclaimed music-making has relegated it to a secondary consideration. Having conducted more than one hundred orchestras in over thirty countries and being one of the most prodigious of classical recording artists (over two hundred releases to date), he leaves little doubt of that!

Freeman is the next-to-youngest of a large family, all of whom were set to learn a musical instrument. His opportunity came at the age of seven, when he was arbitrarily handed a clarinet. He made sufficiently rapid progress that his orchestra teacher convinced his parents that he should take private lessons. When he was fifteen, he stepped up to direct his school orchestra for a short program because the director of music was sick. From that moment he was sold on the idea of becoming a conductor. In pursuit of this ambition, he added piano and cello to his endeavors. He entered the Eastman School of Music to pursue a major in clarinet, and graduated with a BM in 1956. He played in the Eastman school orchestra under Howard Hanson and went on to earn a master's degree (1957) and a doctorate (1963) in music theory, all the while taking conducting classes. In 1959 he was awarded a Fulbright scholarship that took him to the Hochschule für Musik in Berlin, where he studied orchestral and operatic conducting with Ewald Lindermann. During his stay he took full advantage of the rich musical life of the German city and attended a conducting seminar given by Herbert von Karajan. Returning to the U.S., he was appointed music director of the Rochester Opera Theatre (1961–66), and he took conducting lessons with Monteux at his Ecole and with the renowned German émigré Richard Lert in California. He conducted the San Francisco Conservatory Orchestra (1966–68) and the San Francisco Little SO (1967–68). His career received a big boost when he won the Mitropoulos Conducting Competition in 1967. As winner of the Spoleto Festival of Two Worlds Award in 1968, he conducted the festival's production of Tristan und Isolde that year. From 1968 to 1970 he was associate conductor of the Dallas (Tex.) SO, then conductor-in-residence of the Detroit (Mich.) SO (1970–79). He also served as chief guest conductor of the Helsinki PO, and it was during this period (1974–77) that he produced the groundbreaking series of recordings of music by black composers for CBS. His first major directorship was with the Victoria SO in British Columbia (1979–89). He also began an association with the Saginaw (Mich.) SO as music director (1979–88), eventually leaving with the title of music director emeritus and a relationship with the organization that continues to this day. The first of the two most significant events in his career took place in 1987 with the founding of the Chicago Sinfonietta. The second was his appointment in 1996 as music director of the Czech National SO in Prague.

The Czech National SO was formed as a result of the chaotic situation in Czech musical life following the Velvet Revolution of 1989 and the loss of state subsidies to artistic institutions. The orchestra was founded in 1993 to provide a vehicle for meeting inexpensive foreign recording contracts and during its earliest years was led by the respected Czech conductor Zdenek Kosler. Since Freeman assumed the directorship in 1996, the orchestra has demonstrated consistent progress and acquired the versatility one associates with orchestras in the West. It has made more than fifty CDs, embarked on several European tours, and plans to visit Asia and America in the near future.

Of the more than one hundred orchestras with which Freeman has appeared as guest conductor, space constrains mention to only the most prestigious: in the U.S. he has appeared with the symphony orchestras of Chicago, Cleveland, Baltimore, Houston, San Francisco, and Saint Louis, as well as the New York PO and the Minnesota Orchestra. He has appeared with the Tonkünstler Orchester in Vienna, Leningrad (now St. Petersburg) PO and Moscow PO in Russia, Oslo PO in Norway, Warsaw PO in Poland, and L'Orchestre de la Suisse Romande in Switzerland. In Great Britain he has conducted all the major London orchestras and the Scottish CO, and in Germany he has conducted orchestras in Berlin, Leipzig, and Stuttgart. Similarly, for his extensive discography, it will be sufficient here to mention a few recent highlights as he has probably recorded more American music than any other conductor. His 3-CD set *African Heritage Symphonic Series* with the Chicago Sinfonietta on the Cedille label recaps and extends his earlier CBS series and demonstrates his particular effort to promote the work of black composers. Represented are works by William Grant Still, Samuel Coleridge-Taylor, Fela Sowanda, David Baker, Adolphus Hailstork, Hale Smith, Roque Cordero, Michael Abels, Ulysses Kay, Coleridge-Taylor Perkinson, and William Banfield. Critics have praised the quality of the music as well as that of the performances. In an extensive collaboration with the Chinese American pianist Derek Han, he has recorded complete piano concerto cycles by Mozart (London PO), Haydn (English CO), Beethoven (Berlin SO), and Tchaikovsky (St. Petersburg PO). With the Czech National SO, which has its own recording studio and label, he plans to record a complete cycle of Mahler symphonies, of which the first and fifth are already extant, and for which he was awarded the Mahler Prize by the European Union of Arts. Another major product of this partnership has been an extensive series of recordings of orchestral music by the American composer Meyer Kupferman (1926–2003).

Further Reading

Blank, Christopher. "Rhapsody in Black." *Commercial Appeal* (Memphis, Tenn.), 20 February 2003, E1.

Denton, David. "An American in Prague: A Conversation with American Conductor Paul Freeman." *Fanfare* 24 (March–April 2001): 58–61.

Selected Recordings

Baker: *Cello Concerto*. Perkinson: *Sinfonietta for Strings no. 2* "Generations." Abels: *Global Warming*. Banfield: *Essay for Orchestra*; Katinka Kleijn (vc); Chicago Sinfonietta. Cedille CDR 90000 066, *African Heritage Symphonic Series*, vol. 3.

Beethoven: *Piano Concertos 1 and 3*; James Johnson (pf); Royal PO; St. Petersburg PO. Centaur 3580.

Kupferman: *Icon Symphony*; *Concerto for 2 Clarinets*; Stanley Drucker (cl); Naomi Drucker (cl); Czech National SO. From Soundspells Productions 133 (2-CD set).

Mozart: *Complete Piano Concertos*; Derek Han (pf), Philharmonia O. Brilliant Classics 99476.

Sibelius: *Violin Concerto*; *Romance*, Op. 26; Sergiu Schwartz (vn); London SO. Vox 8199.

～

Gilbert, Alan
Born 23 February 1967 in New York, New York

Imitating his parents, who were both violinists in the New York PO, Alan Gilbert began playing the violin as a little boy. (He was not the only one: his younger sister is concertmaster of the Orchestre National de Lyon.) Even now, with a full-time conducting career, he continues to perform chamber music as a violinist and violist. At Harvard, where he earned his bachelor's degree, he was assistant conductor for the Harvard-Radcliffe Orchestra and music director for the Harvard Bach Society Orchestra. Gilbert also won the Sadler Award and the Holbrit Award for Performing Musicians. He studied violin at the New England Conservatory of Music, but when he went on to the Curtis Institute of Music in Philadelphia, he chose to pursue conducting and studied with Otto-Werner Mueller to get his artist diploma. Meanwhile, he won a fill-in position with the Philadelphia Orchestra as an "extra violin" for two seasons. As a result he played almost every week, which he says was one of the best things that could have happened to his conducting development. He earned a master of arts degree in conducting from Juilliard in 1994.

That same year, he won the Helen M. Thompson Award for promising young conductors from the American Symphony Orchestra League, the Suisse Award and first prize at the Geneva International Music Competition, the Bunkamura Orchard Hall Award, and the Sir Georg Solti Prize.

From 1992 to 1997 he was music director for the Haddonfield (N.J.) Symphony. In 1994, he went to work for the Cleveland Orchestra and for the next three years was assistant conductor. Gilbert won the prestigious Seaver/NEA Conductors Award in 1997. He is a member of the Royal Swedish Academy of Music and since 2000 has been chief conductor and artistic advisor for the Royal Stockholm PO, where his contract extends through the 2007–8 season. In 2001, he cofounded the Music Masters Course in Kazusa, an annual international music festival dedicated to artistic cross-cultural exchange. Gilbert remains artistic director of MMCK. He became the first music director of the Santa Fe (N.Mex.) Opera in 2003. Not only had he been a frequent performer and guest conductor there, but in 1993 he was assistant concertmaster to longtime concertmaster Michael Gilbert, his father. In 2004, Gilbert became principal guest conductor at the NDR SO in Hamburg. New York PO music director Lorin **Maazel** also chose Gilbert to conduct the NYPO for two weeks every season from 2006 through 2009.

Gilbert enjoys making bold moves and doing things for the first time, such as taking on the American premiere of Thomas Adès's difficult setting of *The Tempest.* He makes brave choices, thinks big, shows good technical control, and demonstrates strong baton technique. As comfortable with standard orchestral works as cutting-edge contemporary ones, Gilbert wants to perform a wide range of music, so he looks forward to expanding the SFO's repertoire.

Although not yet forty, he has already conducted all of the "Big-Five" orchestras, something many superb conductors never achieve. Even so, it was a rather stunning announcement that he would be appointed the next music director of the New York PO, commencing with the 2009–10 season! A guest conductor in demand, Gilbert has also appeared with the Los Angeles PO, Los Angeles Opera, San Francisco SO, Royal Concertgebouw Orchestra, Deutsches SO Berlin, Berlin PO, Zurich Opera, Atlanta SO, Baltimore SO, Minnesota Orchestra, National SO, Toronto SO, Orchestre Philharmonique de Radio France, Tonhalle Orchestra (Zurich), Bavarian RSO (Munich), Orchestre National de Lyon, Mahler CO, Tokyo SO, Sapporo SO, New Japan PO, and China Broadcasting SO.

Further Reading

Lunden, Jeff. "Young Conductor at Home with N.Y. Philharmonic." *All Things Considered,* NPR, 15 March 2007.

Van Sant, James A. "Keeping an Eye on Alan Gilbert: A Young Conductor Is Making Waves." *American Record Guide* 65 (March–April 2002): 8–9.

Selected Recordings
Börtz: *En gycklares berättelser* (*A Joker's Tales*), Concerto for Recorder and Orchestra; Dan Laurin (recorder); Royal Stockholm PO. From *A Joker's Tales: 21st-Century Music for Recorder*, BIS 1425.
Mendelssohn: *Symphony no. 3 in A minor*, Op. 56, "Scottish." Mahler: *Symphony no. 5 in C♯ minor* (Adagietto); Mahler CO. From *Gustav Mahler Musikwochen 2003*, Real Sound 116, live: 7/30/2003.

~

Gittleman, Neal
Born 29 June 1955 in Ancon, Panama

Neal Gittleman grew up in Brooklyn (N.Y.) with two passions: music and sports. Though he manages to occasionally combine the two in concerts such as "Pops Goes Out to the Ballgame," including sports-related music, speaking parts performed by local sports notables, musical play-by-play and color commentary, cheerleaders, and film footage, his career has been all about music. He graduated from Yale University in 1975 with a bachelor's degree in music before pursuing his study with teachers in Paris, at the Manhattan School of Music, the Pierre Monteux Domaine School, and the Hartt School of Music, where he earned his arts diploma in orchestral conducting in 1983. Gittleman began his professional conducting career in 1981 as assistant conductor of the Hartt SO and the Hartt Opera Theater, and in 1982 he was awarded the Karl Böhm Conducting Scholarship.

Upon graduation from Hartt, Gittleman moved west to become assistant conductor of the Oregon SO until 1986 under the Exxon/Arts Endowment Conductors Program. During this time he won second prize at the Ernest Ansermet International Conducting Competition in Geneva (1984) and third prize at the Leopold Stokowski International Conducting Competition in New York (1986). He accepted a new position as associate conductor with the Syracuse (N.Y.) SO (1986–89) and the following year that of music director of the Marion (Ind.) PO (1987–96). In 1989, Gittleman began a ten-year association with the Milwaukee (Wisc.) SO, as associate conductor until 1995 and then as resident conductor until 1998.

Music director of the Dayton (Ohio) PO since 1995, he continues to conduct for opera, ballet, and theater in addition to the concert stage. Gittleman's innovative "Classical Connections" programs, in which he offers audiences a guide to understanding classical music with a "behind the scenes" look at symphonic masterpieces, have been popular from Milwaukee to Phoenix to Dayton. From 2000 to 2005 he led the Indianapolis SO in a series of "Disney Concerts" and initiated diversified non-subscription special events, broadening the orchestra's repertoire.

Gittleman, described as playful, authoritative yet informal, easygoing, and enthusiastic, is appreciated for both his artistic accomplishments and his people skills. He hosts a regular program on Dayton's classical radio station and fosters community support by collaborating with area arts groups and creating programming that appeals to both audience and orchestra. ASCAP has given Gittleman and the DPO four awards for programming of contemporary music, most recently in 2004 and 2005. Throughout his ten years with the DPO, Gittleman has pushed for improvement and achieved it, while at the same time establishing a sense of allegiance within the organization among musicians, board members, and volunteers alike. In 2006, he agreed to extend his contract through the 2009–10 season.

As guest conductor, Gittleman has appeared with numerous orchestras, including the symphonies of Chicago, Indianapolis, Oregon, New Jersey, Phoenix, Saint Louis, San Antonio, San Francisco, and Seattle; the Minnesota, Philadelphia, and National Repertory Orchestras; the Buffalo and Rochester POs; the ensembles of Anchorage, Bangor, Baton Rouge, Chattanooga, Cincinnati, El Paso, Eugene, Green Bay, Jacksonville, Knoxville, New Haven, Omaha, San Jose, Springfield; and Chicago's Grant Park and Oregon's Britt Music Festivals. Also active internationally, Gittleman has led the Orchestre de la Suisse Romande, Edmonton SO, Orchestra London (ON), Orquesta Filarmónica de la Ciudad de México, UNAM PO, Orquesta Cámara Bellas Artes, Sarajevo PO, and Augsburg PO. Beyond the orchestral podium, he has conducted for the Dayton Opera, Human Race Theatre Company, Syracuse Opera Company, Hartt Opera Theater, Milwaukee's Skylight Opera Theatre, Milwaukee Ballet, Hartford Ballet, Chicago City Ballet, Ballet Arizona, and Theater Ballet of Canada.

Further Reading
Campbell, K. "Tending His Garden." *Symphony* 46, no. 1 (1995): 73–74.
Simmons, Carol. "Maestro: Neal Gittleman Begins His Tenth Season as Musical Director of the Dayton Philharmonic Orchestra." *Dayton Daily News*, 10 October 2004, F1.

Selected Recordings

A *Celebration of Flight*; Mary Elizabeth Southworth (s); Dayton PO. Albany Troy 672.

Gershwin: *Rhapsody in Blue*; *Concerto in F*; Norman Krieger (pf); Prague National SO. Artisie 4 1005.

Nocturnes: 20th Century Music for Voice, Horn and Piano; Cantecor Trio. Equilibrium.

Sierra: *Piezas Caracteristicas*; William Helmers (b. cl); Dennis Najoom (tp); Thomas Wetzel (perc); Stefanie Jacob (pf); Catherine Schubilske (vn); Scott Tisdel (vc); Milwaukee SO. Subito Music CRI 725.

Svoboda: *Piano Concerto no. 1*, Op. 7; *Piano Concerto no. 2*, Op. 134; Tomas Svoboda (pf); Norman Krieger (pf); Dayton PO. Artisie 4 1006.

～

Graf, Hans
Born 15 February 1949 in Marchtrenk, Austria

It seemed only a matter of time before Graf, one of the most highly regarded and experienced European conductors of his generation, would become the director of a prestigious American orchestra. He achieved this by succeeding Christoph **Eschenbach** in Houston (Tex.) in 2001. Graf had made his American debut with the Buffalo (N.Y.) PO as long ago as 1989 and had both impressed and disappointed on tours to the U.S. with the Mozarteum Orchestra of Salzburg (1987 and 1991). It was said that he had been a leading contender for the Dallas (Tex.) SO post that went to Andrew **Litton**. However, it was as music director of the Calgary (Alberta) PO (1995–2003) that he made his reputation as a mover and shaker. These were years of impressive artistic achievement but financial instability for the orchestra. In 2001, with a record of performances that were vibrant and deeply revealing, Graf was the unanimous choice of the Houston musicians. His ability to establish instant rapport with, and the respect of, his players is a trait that has run throughout his career, and it creates a performance chemistry that percolates to the audience. Although he is inevitably caught up in the whoop of Houston's Tex-Americana and the orchestra's marketing division (a 2003 performance of Beethoven's Ninth Symphony was accompanied by big-screen video), Graf is essentially a serious musician with a sober and somewhat restrained podium manner (he struck one critic as a "cherubic boxer"). His interpretations are thoughtful and well prepared, and he has an impeccable ear. Although it seems like a cliché to say that his performances of the standard orchestral repertoire are fresh and exhilarating, this is the consensus of many reviews.

Graf was born near Linz in Upper Austria to a family of professional musicians and received instruction at an early age in piano and violin from his father, who taught at the Bruckner Conservatory. During his adolescence, his sister and brother-in-law introduced him to the orchestral music of Debussy, Ravel, Bartók, and Stravinsky, turning his ambition toward conducting. He studied for four years at the Hochschule für Musik in Graz and graduated with diplomas in piano and conducting in 1971. He went on to take conducting lessons with Franco Ferrara in Siena (1970–72), Arvid Yansons in Leningrad (1972–73), and, briefly, Sergiu Celibidache in Bologna. In a *Boston Globe* interview with Richard Dyer he explained, "Ferrara taught me how to conduct; Yansons showed me how to be a conductor. These are not the same things." He spent a season as conductor of the Iraqi National SO in Baghdad (1975–76) and then worked as a coach at the Vienna State Opera (1977–84), making his conducting debut with the company in 1981. His big break came when he won the Karl Böhm Conducting Competition in 1979, after which guest-conducting invitations began to come in. He first appeared at the Vienna Festival in 1978 and conducted the Vienna SO for the first time in 1980. For the ten years from 1984 to 1994 he was music director of the Mozarteum Orchestra and the Landestheater in Salzburg. He was also chief guest conductor of the VSO and conductor of the Orquesta Sinfónica de Euskadi in Spain. In 1998 he was appointed conductor of the Orchestre National de Bordeaux-Aquitaine and Opéra de Bordeaux. In Houston he is also artist-in-residence at the School of Music of Rice University. He made his New York PO debut in 2005 with music by Lyadov and Tchaikovsky.

Graf has an extensive itinerary of guest-conducting appearances throughout Europe, North America, and Japan. These include the Vienna PO, St. Petersburg PO, Orchestre National de France, Leipzig Gewandhaus Orchestra, Royal Liverpool PO, and the Boston SO, with which he has enjoyed an especially close relationship since his debut there in 1995. He has also appeared with orchestras in Oslo, Rome, Copenhagen, Baltimore, Cleveland, Dallas, Detroit, Saint Louis, Pittsburgh, Tel Aviv, and elsewhere. In the opera house he has performed in Munich, Berlin, Rome, Paris, and Venice, and appears regularly at the world's leading music festivals: Florence, Breganz, Vienna, Salzburg, Aix-en-Provence, Orange, Tanglewood, Blossom, and Wolftrap. His recordings appear on EMI, Orfeo, Erato, JVC, Capriccio, and CBC Records labels. He won praise for his tasteful and stylish recordings of the complete symphonies of Mozart and Schubert and for the premiere recording of Zemlinsky's opera *Es war einmal*. In Bordeaux, he is recording the complete orchestral works of Henri Dutilleux, and he was made Chevalier de l'ordre de la Légion d'Honneur for services to French music in 2002. His concert and operatic repertoire is far-reaching but, naturally enough, with an emphasis on the Austro-German masters. Equally at home in the Russian and French repertoire, his programs in recent years have embraced a number of twentieth-century American composers. The HSO is commissioning a concerto each year for its section principals, leading up to its centennial year in 2013. Graf directed the first of the series in January 2002, a bassoon concerto by Larry Lipkis called *Pierrot*.

Further Reading
Scherzer, E. "Portraet." *Opernwelt* 26, no. 4 (1985): 68. [German]
Ullman, Michael. "Mozart as Symphonist: The Hans Graf Recordings." *Fanfare* 14, no. 3 (1991): 125–27.

Selected Recordings
Bartók: *The Wooden Prince*. Stravinsky: *The Fairy's Kiss: Divertimento*; Houston SO. Koch KIC-CD-7594.
Lehár: *Der Rastelbinder*; Helga Papouschek (*Mizzi*); Elfie Hobarth (*Suza*); Heinz Zednik (*Janku*); Adolf Dallapozza (*Milosch*); Fritz Muliar (*Pfefferkorn*); Margarita Hintermeier (*Babuschka*); Austrian RSO and Ch. CPO 777 038-2.
Liszt: *Piano Concertos 1–3*; Janina Fialkowska (pf); Calgary PO. CBC SM 5000 Series 5202.
Mozart: *Symphonies: no. 1; nos. 4–36; nos. 38–48; nos. 50–52; no. 55; in a; in F; in D; Menuet in C*; Salzburg Mozarteum O. Capriccio 49 288.

～

Hanson, George (Robert)
Born 24 January 1958 in Iowa City, Iowa

A fourth-generation trumpet player, young George Hanson nevertheless planned on a career in medicine. In high school, however, he joined a rock band and changed his mind. He attended Concordia College (Minn.), Indiana University, the Curtis Institute of Music, and the Vienna Academy of Music. In 1986, he won the Hungarian International Conducting Competition in Budapest. Hanson was associate conductor for the Atlanta (Ga.) SO from 1988 to 1993, during which time he was named Young Musician of the

Year by *Musical America* (1990) and won the Leopold Stokowski Conducting Competition (1991) in New York. He served as assistant conductor of the New York PO under Kurt **Masur** from 1993 to 2000, and music director of the Anchorage (Alaska) SO from 1994 to 1999.

Since 1996 Hanson has been music director and conductor of the Tucson (Ariz.) SO. From 1998 to 2004 he was also general music director of the Wuppertal (Germany) SO and Opera, reducing his commitment to principal guest conductor in 2005, then to conductor laureate. Hanson believes his bi-continental work contributes to artistic enrichment because he can carry styles and approaches between orchestras and let them influence each other through him. He enjoys mixing well-known works with contemporary pieces that have an emotional appeal. Subscription growth in both Tucson and Wuppertal indicates audiences are enjoying such combinations as well. In 2004 Hanson and the TSO received an ASCAP award for programming of contemporary music. His recordings with the Wuppertal SO have also won prizes, including the Discophage award from the French music magazine *Repertoire* for the 2001 recording of Respighi, and the German Echo Klassik award for the music of Rubinstein in 2003.

Hanson has appeared with nearly ninety symphony orchestras and opera companies in numerous countries, including the New York PO; the orchestras of Warsaw, Stuttgart, Budapest, Indianapolis, Atlanta, and Charlotte; the Berlin RSO, Hamburg RSO, Saint Paul CO, South African NSO, National SO of Mexico, Osaka SO, Nuremberg SO, Bremen SO, Orchestre Symphonique de Mulhouse (France), and Arizona Opera.

Selected Recordings

Bruch: *Serenade for Strings; Schwedische Tänze*, Op. 63; *Schön Ellen*, Op. 24; Claudia Braun (s); Thomas Laske (br); Kantorei Barmen-Gemarke; Wuppertal SO. MDG 3351096.

Draeseke: *Symphony no. 3 in C major* "Symphonia tragica," Op. 40; *Symphonic Prologue to "Penthesilea,"* Op. 50; *Overture to "Gudrun"*; Wuppertal SO. MDG 335 1041-2.

Respighi: *Rossiniana P148; Metamorphoseon modi XII P169; Burlesca P59; Bach's Passacaglia and Fugue P159*; Wuppertal SO. MDG 335 1030.

Rubinstein: *Cello Concerto in A*, Op. 63; *Don Quixote*, Op. 87; *The Demon: Ballet Music*; Alban Gerhardt (vc); Wuppertal SO. MDG 335 1165-2.

Rubinstein: *Symphony no. 2* "Ocean" (orig); *Ouverture Triomphale; Sérénade Russe no. 1* (arr. Müller-Berghaus); *Valse caprice* (arr. Müller-Berghaus); *Trot de Cavalerie*; Wuppertal SO. MDG 335 1240-2.

〰

Harth-Bedoya, Miguel
Born 13 May 1968 in Lima, Peru

Frequently heralded as "one of the most exciting conductors of his generation" (what promising young conductor isn't?), Harth-Bedoya has experienced a meteoric rise to prominence in his chosen profession. This is all the
more surprising because, apart from taking piano lessons and performing with
a chorus of employees of AeroPeru organized by his mother, he showed no
extraordinary musical talent or ambition. During his last year in high school
he worked as general factotum for the Lima Opera Company, and the experience of rehearsing and accompanying, together with an urge to control,
triggered his ambition to become a conductor. Some of his now much-fêted
dynamism must have been in evidence when he was accepted into the undergraduate conducting program at the Curtis Institute of Music in Philadelphia. Upon graduation, he transferred to the Juilliard School and soon made
his mark there. He subsequently led the Juilliard Orchestra on tours of France
(1993) and Japan (1995) and has kept close ties with the school as conductor and teacher. While completing his master's degree he obtained his first
appointment as conductor of the New York YSO (1994) and attracted the
notice of Michel Schmidt, a leading artists' agent, who has been a guiding
force in the development of his career. It was with the NYYSO that he
demonstrated his ability to perform new scores in the orchestra's "First Music" series. While still maintaining ties to Peru as artistic director of the
Orquesta Filharmonica de Lima and the capital's New Opera Company, he
got his career proper underway with his appointment as music director to the
Eugene (Ore.) SO (1995–2003). Setting out to attract a younger audience to
the orchestra in Eugene, he established two signal traits: a liking for innovative programming and an ability to engage his audience through short
preperformance talks. He was recruited as one of three associate conductors
of the Los Angeles PO in 1998. The encouragement and support of music director Esa-Pekka **Salonen** led to the creation of the position of associate conductor specifically for Harth-Bedoya, who served in it from 1999 to 2004.
One of the most memorable events of his tenure was the sold-out April 2004
concert in the Walt Disney Concert Hall when he conducted the premiere
of *Dear Friends—Music from Final Fantasy* by Nobuo Uematsu, derived from
the music the composer wrote for the popular *Final Fantasy* games.

His early achievements in Los Angeles solidified his reputation, and the
next few years proved to be highly peripatetic ones as Harth-Bedoya became
a sought-after guest conductor. Within a few years he had mounted podiums

to face the leading North American orchestras, including the New York PO (debut 2000), Chicago SO, Philadelphia Orchestra, Boston SO (Tanglewood 2003), Cleveland Orchestra (Blossom Festival 2003), Orchestra of Saint Luke's, and the orchestras of Baltimore, Cincinnati, Detroit, Indianapolis, Houston, Saint Paul, and Toronto. Abroad he has conducted the London SO, BBC Concert Orchestra, City of Birmingham SO, Bamberg SO, NDR SO Hamburg, Munich PO, Royal Stockholm PO, and Buenos Aires Philharmonia.

In 2000 he took on the directorships of the Fort Worth (Tex.) SO and the Auckland Philharmonia in New Zealand. For the latter, a relatively young organization, he has created a special niche with a repertoire that blends both familiar and more challenging pieces, notably those of local composers. In a 2003 concert, for example, he paired the premiere of *Alice* by New Zealand composer Gillian Whitehead with Beethoven's Ninth Symphony. For several years now the audience has revelled in the orchestra's "gorgeous sound." Characteristically, he achieved an instant rapport with the players: "I felt useful when I played with this orchestra. A conductor needs to feel useful, otherwise there's no point to us being there." Fort Worth, on the other hand, provided an opportunity to establish a home base, and to consolidate and hone his skills. He soon had the orchestra playing at a much higher level of excellence than at any time in its history. As a result, his contract was extended first to 2008 and then to 2011.

Harth-Bedoya is naturally drawn to the music of Latino composers, to whose stylistic diversity he brings a particular sympathy. He frequently programs music by Piazzolla, Ginastera, and Moncayo, and has made a point of propagating the music of his friend and contemporary, Argentinian composer Osvaldo Golijov. His performances reflect a belief in the intrinsic value of these works that goes deeper than any superficial gloss, and he conducts them with an infectious enthusiasm that audiences and players find irresistible. He gave the New York premiere of Golijov's chamber opera *Ainadamar* at the Brooklyn Academy of Music in 2003, and in August 2006 he led the premiere of *Azul*, a work for cello and orchestra, with Yo-Yo Ma as soloist. He has also demonstrated his ability to conduct complex scores by American composers such as Theodore Shapiro, George Tsontakis, and John Corigliano, and by the Antipodeans Juliet Palmer and Peter Sculthorpe. He conducted the premiere of Stephen Paulus's *Heloise and Abelard* at the Juilliard Opera Center. His operatic repertoire, which includes Stravinsky's *Le Rossignol* and *Oedipus Rex*, is not confined to twentieth-century works, however. With the New Opera Company of Peru he has given *La Bohème*, *Le nozze di Figaro*, *Xerxes*, *Die lustige Witwe*, and *La sonnambula*. He revived

Martin y Soler's *Il tutore burlato* in Bologna, Italy, a performance recorded for the Bongiovanni label. In 2002, he was the recipient of the Seaver/NEA Conductors Award.

Website
http://www.miguelharthbedoya.com/

Further Reading
"A Fantasy Come True: Videogames in Concert (Fort Worth Symphony Orchestra Performs Uematsu's Music from 'Final Fantasy' Series, Conducted by Miguel Harth-Bedoya)." *Film Score Magazine* 10 (September–October 2005): 10.
Ferman, Dave. "A Slower Tempo: With a New House and a Baby on the Way, Miguel Harth-Bedoya, the Fort Worth Symphony's Continent-Hopping Conductor, Tries to Ease the Pace." *Fort Worth Star-Telegram*, 22 July 2001, Arts 1.
Somerford, Peter. "Dancing to the New World Beat." *BBC Music Magazine*, 1 February 2003: 7.

Selected Recordings
Alma del Peru; Orquesta Filarmonica de Lima. Filarmonika Fila 0101.
Prokofiev: *Peter and the Wolf*. Saint-Saëns: *Carnival of the Animals*; Michael York (narrator); Miguel Harth-Bedoya (narrator); Fort Worth SO. Filarmonika.
Tchaikovsky: *Symphony no. 5*; *Pezzo in forma da sonatina* from 'Serenade for Strings'; Fort Worth SO. Filarmonika.

⁓
Hege, Daniel
Born 4 September 1965 in Denver, Colorado

Hege, who is one-quarter Nez Perce Indian, grew up in the Golden/Arvada area of Colorado. When he was ten his family moved to Aberdeen (Idaho), and not long after he began taking piano lessons. As he grew older it became clear that music was going to play a primary role in his life. With no pretensions to becoming a virtuoso pianist, he found that the piano was the medium through which he began analyzing the way music works. His parents were very supportive of his musical inclinations, and his local church provided him with frequent opportunities to perform. He also took up the oboe. He attended

Bethel College (1983–87) in Kansas, a Mennonite institution where he studied history and music and was active in voice and oboe-playing. He went on to gain a master's degree in orchestral conducting from the University of Utah, and during his time there he founded the University CO, was assistant conductor of the University Orchestra, and was music director of the Utah Singers. Following this, he studied with Daniel Lewis at the University of Southern California and with Paul Vermel at the Aspen Music Festival.

His career received a major boost in 1990 when he won the Young Musicians Foundation Debut Orchestra's Conducting Competition and was subsequently appointed the organization's music director. The following year he began a thirteen-year association as conductor of the Newton Mid-Kansas SO, an organization affiliated with his alma mater, Bethel College. In addition, he was appointed assistant conductor of the Pacific (Calif.) SO and worked as director of music for the Orange County High School for the Arts. He also served as principal conductor of the Disney Young Musicians SO, where he worked with such artists as Henry Mancini, John Williams, Doc Severinsen, and Dudley Moore in concerts that were televised nationally to more than fifty million viewers. His initial role as conductor of the Chicago YSO (1994) expanded when the leading players from the ensemble formed the Encore CO, which became the resident youth orchestra of Chicago's Grant Park Festival and toured Europe in 1995 and 1997 under Hege's leadership. He was associate conductor of the Kansas City (Mo.) SO during the 1995–96 season and began a six-year association with the Baltimore SO in 1995, progressing from assistant to associate to resident conductor in 2001. He was appointed music director of the Haddonfield (N.J.) SO for a three-year stint in 1998, and the following year became music director of the Syracuse (N.Y.) SO, which he led in a Carnegie Hall Concert in 2003. He made his operatic debut that same year leading *La Traviata* with the Syracuse Opera.

Hege is considered one of the most promising conductors of his generation and has been praised for a firm grasp of the stylistic characteristics of the music as well as performances of impressive ensemble and robust dynamic shading. With a commanding, if respectful, presence on the podium, he makes no secret of the analytical approach he brings to scores. His performances bear the hallmark of thorough preparation. He continues to progress to more prestigious guest-conducting invitations, with recent appearances in Indianapolis, Detroit, Seattle, and Rochester in the U.S., and Singapore, St. Petersburg (Russia), and Auckland (New Zealand) abroad. He has also appeared at the Aspen and Grand Tetons music festivals. He has begun to expand his discography, which currently includes music by Adolphus Hailstork and a disc of violin concertos by black composers of the eighteenth and nineteenth centuries, with soloist Rachel Barton. The first release by the Syracuse SO is a live recording on the Classics Concert label of music by Verdi, Barber, Debussy, Respighi, and James Johnson. He followed this with a *Holiday Pops* collection. He has also laid down his credentials as a conductor of contemporary music—he has made a specialty of the works of Robert Daugherty, and, as music director of the Chicago YSO, he was twice honored by the American Symphony Orchestra League for innovative programming.

Further Reading

Hall, J. T. "Conduct Most Becoming." *Syracuse New Times*, 23 March 2003, Cover.

Herron, Frank. "Past, Present and Future: Different Views of the Syracuse Symphony Orchestra." *Post-Standard* (Syracuse, N.Y.), 6 September 2006, Special Section 5.

Selected Recordings

Big Band Bash; Syracuse SO. Syracuse SO.

Violin Concertos by Black Composers of the Eighteenth and Nineteenth Centuries; music by Saint-Georges, White, Coleridge-Taylor, de Meude-Monpas; Rachel Barton Pine (vn); Encore Co. Cedille 35.

~

Ioannides, Sarah
Born 2 April 1972 in Canberra, Australia

Born to a Cypriot conductor-composer father and a Scottish mother, Sarah Ioannides grew up in England, where she studied violin, piano, and French horn. She was a violinist in the National Youth Orchestra and CO. Her educational achievements include bachelor and master of arts degrees in music theory/history from Oxford University (1993), an advanced certificate in conducting and the Conducting Prize from the Guildhall School of Music in London (1994), a diploma in conducting from the Curtis Institute of Music (1998), and an MM degree in orchestral conducting from Juilliard (2000). There she also won the Bruno Walter Scholarship and a position as assistant conductor to Otto-Werner Mueller. Other awards from this period include the Janet Watson Prize (1995) and the Alice Horsmann Travelling Fellowship (1995) from Oxford, a Wingate Scholarship (1996), a Fulbright Scholarship (1996), the Presser Foundation Scholarship (1997), and the Kenneth Tyghe Memorial Prize (1999) at the Leeds Conducting Competition.

Ioannides accepted a variety of short-term positions throughout these educational years: music director for the Oxford Philharmonia (1990–93), music director for the Oxford University Opera (1994–95), assistant conductor for the Opera Company of Philadelphia (1997–98), and principal guest conductor for the Oxford University CO (2001–2). She also toured extensively as assistant conductor to composer Tan Dun (1999–2003) and from 1997 to 2000 was music director for the Swarthmore College Orchestra.

In 2001, she received the JoAnn Falletta Award from the Women's Philharmonic Committee. Ioannides was the first female to join the conducting staff of the Cincinnati (Ohio) SO in 2002 when she became assistant conductor, as well as music director for the Cincinnati Symphony YO. During her two-year tenure she won one of the two Bruno Walter Assistant Conductor Chair awards for the 2003–4 season. She was guest music director for the Dessoff Choirs (N.Y.) for the 2004–5 season. In 2005 Ioannides accepted two music director posts, for the El Paso (Tex.) SO and for the Spartanburg (S.C.) PO. Active in both communities, Ioannides is noted for creative programming, a high energy level, artistic vision, vitality, and an infectious passion for music, as well as for cultivating partnerships with artists of all kinds and putting on educational events.

Ioannides has made guest-conducting appearances with a variety of ensembles, including the Daejeon PO (Korea), Orquesta Sinfónica Municipal de Caracas (Venezuela), Flemish RSO, New World Symphony, SWR Vokalensemble, RIAS Kammerchor, Oregon Bach Festival Orchestra, Oxford University Orchestra, Naumburg Orchestra, Annapolis SO, Gothenburg SO, BBC Concert O, Los Angeles PO, London SO, Beata Moon Ensemble, Curtis Opera, Guildhall SO, Millennium Chamber Symphony, British Youth Opera, and many others.

Website
http://www.sarahioannides.net

Further Reading
Hicks, Ann. "A Twenty-first Century Maestra." *Greenville News*, 4 September 2005, F1, F3.
Roedl, Kim. "Introducing Ioannides." *El Paso Times*, 28 August 2005, 1F, 8F.

Itkin, David
Born 2 May 1957 in Portland, Oregon

David Itkin began taking piano and percussion lessons when young and started his musical life in jazz, musical theater, and rock. He discovered orchestral music at sixteen, when he accompanied his grandmother to a symphony concert. Itkin went on to earn both bachelor's (1980) and master's (1982) degrees from the Eastman School of Music. He also did some doctoral work at Indiana University, where he was appointed assistant conductor of the Indiana University Opera Theater.

From 1988 to 1993 Itkin was associate conductor for the Alabama SO. While there he was named honorary lieutenant governor of the state of Alabama for outstanding service to the arts. He became music director and conductor for the Kingsport (Tenn.) SO and music director for the Birmingham Opera Theater, remaining in both positions from 1992 to 1995. In 1993 he took on two more assignments, music director and conductor of the Arkansas SO, where he remains, and music director for the Lucius Woods Festival Concerts in Solon Springs (Wisc.), which he kept through 2000. His tenure as music director and principal conductor of the Lake Forest SO in Chicago, which had begun in 1997, also concluded in 2000. Itkin's newest position is music director and conductor of the Abilene (Tex.) PO, which he accepted in 2005.

A charismatic leader, Itkin is considered unusual because he commits to memory most of his scores. Itkin talks to audiences informally about the music before concerts, emphasizing the importance of live music and its sensory purpose. He also reminds listeners that there are no tests at the end of the concert! He speaks frequently to civic organizations and has a regular radio program in Little Rock to publicize concerts.

In addition to conducting, Itkin serves as juror for numerous competitions and composes a variety of music, including two works that have been nominated for the Pulitzer Prize, *Jonah* in 2001 and an oratorio, *Exodus*, in 2006. Both the *Exodus* CD and the film for which Itkin composed the score, *Sugar Creek*, are expected in 2007.

Itkin's guest-conducting engagements have taken him to most states and multiple countries in Europe, the Middle East, and Asia, where he has led, among others, the Winnipeg SO, Slovenska Filharmonija (Slovenia), Las Vegas PO, Seoul PO, San Diego SO, Colorado PO, and the Indianapolis, Baltimore, and Reno COs.

Jackson, Isaiah (Allen)
Born 22 January 1945 in Richmond, Virginia

During the early years of the new millennium, Jackson has been active as music director of two complementary organizations: the Youngstown (Ohio) SO (1996–2006) and the Pro Arte CO of Boston (2001–present). The former, a minor-league regional orchestra, is concerned with building its audience through traditional and popular programming. The latter, a self-governing musicians' cooperative, is known for its innovative repertoire. Jackson is well suited to be the figurehead of both. His elegant manner and amiable personality adapt well to the kind of wooing that keeps audiences enthralled in Youngstown, and it is hard to imagine a more sympathetic collaboration than that between him and the Pro Arte CO. In performance he lends his versatility and finely honed musicianship to both organizations.

Presumably, the Pro Arte programming is a shared process between orchestra and conductor, and they have the knack of devising programs that are a judicious blend of the known and the new. By honoring tradition and celebrating music-making as a living art form, they provide a role model for what a twenty-first-century orchestra should be. This is seen to good effect, for example, in Earle Brown's "concept" piece *December 1952*, where the performance requires the players to have devised in rehearsal how they will play the piece. Add to this Poulenc's quirky ballet score, *Aubade*, Michael Daugherty's intriguing *Le Tombeau de Liberace*, and Brahms's *Serenade in A* and you have a typical Pro Arte program of beautifully executed performances.

Born into the upper echelons of what was then referred to as Negro society, albeit in the segregated city of Richmond (Va.), Jackson was set to learn the piano at the early age of four. Apparently this was not due to a display of prodigious musical talent, but was prescribed therapy for an injured left hand. However, the musical seed was planted, and, as he grew into adolescence (having added clarinet to his musical armory), he nurtured the ambition to be a professional musician. At fourteen he was sent to the progressive Putney School in Vermont. The experience of traveling with his high school class to the USSR resulted in his enrolling at Harvard, where he graduated cum laude in Russian studies (1966). But Harvard also provided encouragement for his musical aspirations, first as a member of a glee club and the university choir, then as the conductor of a student performance of *Cosi fan tutte* and the Bach Society Orchestra. That clinched it, and when he came to Stanford in 1966 it was to major in music. The following summer was spent at

Fontainebleau in France, studying with the renowned teacher Nadia Boulanger. He then attended Juilliard, where he founded and conducted the Juilliard String Ensemble and served briefly as assistant to Leopold Stokowski at the American SO. His debut with a major orchestra at a leading venue (Kennedy Center) was with the National SO in 1972, and he also became an assistant conductor of the Baltimore SO and conductor of the New York YSO. Once he obtained his DMA from Juilliard in 1973, his career blossomed as he debuted with the Vienna SO and stayed on to direct Vienna's Youth Music Festival. Returning to the U.S., he accepted the appointment as associate conductor of the Rochester PO (1973–87). His work as conductor of the Dance Theater of Harlem was noticed when the ensemble toured Europe, and he was invited to be a guest conductor for London's Royal Ballet in 1985. He so impressed there that he became its principal guest conductor in 1986 and then was made the company's music director (1987–91). He was, of course, the first black conductor to hold the appointment. He gave up the directorship of the Flint (Mich.) SO (1982–87) in favor of the Dayton (Ohio) PO (1987–93) during the period when he lived in England. He also made frequent visits to Australia, after which the Queensland SO made him its principal guest conductor in 1993. Jackson's attempt in 1996 to found his own flexible musical organization, Music America, floundered from lack of support, and that same year he accepted the directorship of the Youngstown orchestra. He spent nine years with the YSO, during which time he is credited with making significant improvements in the ensemble's quality, though the board decided not to renew his contract when it expired in 2006.

As a guest conductor, Jackson has appeared with the New York PO and Los Angeles PO, and the orchestras of Cleveland, Detroit, San Francisco, Houston, Dallas, Baltimore, Indianapolis, Toronto, and Oakland. In Europe he has guest conducted with the Helsinki PO, Czech SO, Orchestre de la Suisse Romande, BBC Concert Orchestra, and Royal Liverpool PO. He has been guest conductor of the Berlin SO, with whom he has made three recordings: a CD of film scores by Waxman, Hermann, and Rosza, another of ballet music by William Grant Still, and one of a live New Year's Eve concert (1991). The Koch label issued a recording of harp concertos by Ginastera and Mathias, with soloist Ann Hobson Pilot accompanied by the English CO, and ABC Classics produced a CD of the Melbourne SO performing music by Australian composer Nigel Butterly. Jackson is closely identified with the Gospel Project, which, in collaboration with choral director Alvin Parris III, attempts to blend gospel and orchestral music. This project, which includes the release of a CD of gospel choirs and the

Louisville Orchestra, has traveled to twelve U.S. cities as well as to the Brisbane Biennial Festival in Australia and Liverpool's Anglican Cathedral in the UK.

Jackson's achievements in music, despite the double disadvantage of being an American and black, have been considerable. He is a highly cultivated and deeply committed individual whose extraordinary talent and abilities, together with a gracious demeanor, have won praise and admiration worldwide. His performances are noted for attributes such as lyricism, clarity, and finesse, if occasionally criticized for lack of emotion. In evaluating his achievements to date, however, one cannot avoid the sneaking suspicion that he is yet to fulfill his early promise.

Further Reading
Jackson, Isaiah. *As We Forgive Those*. Boston: Boston Athenaeum, 2003.
Schwarz, K. Robert. "Black Maestros on the Podium, but No Pedestal." *New York Times*, 11 October 1992, Arts & Leisure 1, 27.
Story, Rosalyn. "Have Baton—Will Travel." *American Visions* 8 (February–March 1993): 42.
Whitaker, Charles. "Music Man of the Royal Ballet." *Ebony* 43 (April 1988): 86, 90, 92.

Selected Recordings
Gospel at the Symphony; Gospel Choir, Louisville O. Koch 3-7246.
Still: *La guiablesse*; *Quit dat fool'nish*; *Summerland*; *Danzas de Panama*; Alexa Still (fl), Susan DeWitt Smith (pf); Berlin SO. Koch 3-7154-2.

〜

Jansons, Mariss
Born 14 January 1943 in Riga, Latvia

Arvid Jansons's (Yansons's) conducting career was taking off as his son Mariss was growing up. When Mariss was nine, his father was appointed third conductor of the Leningrad PO. His mother was a distinguished opera singer, and the boy spent many childhood hours in the theater at rehearsals and performances observing his parents at work. Although he felt under no great pressure from either to become a musician, living in such a milieu clearly left its mark. At the Leningrad Conservatory, which he entered in 1957, he took conducting lessons from Nikolai Rabinovich and studied violin, viola, and piano. After graduating with honors, he attended the Vienna Academy of

Music, where he pursued conducting studies with Hans Swarowsky and Karl Österreicher, and then went on to Salzburg to work under Herbert von Karajan. He was a prizewinner at the Karajan Competition in West Berlin in 1971. After the Soviet authorities summoned him home, he was taken under the wing of Yevgeny Mravinsky, the principal conductor of the Leningrad PO, and became an associate conductor in 1973. Later he was promoted to associate principal conductor of the orchestra, from 1985 to 1997.

His first directorship was as principal conductor of the Oslo PO. It was in this situation that he began to make a name abroad through international tours, recordings, and radio and television broadcasts. When he arrived in 1979, the state-subsidized Oslo orchestra had national but very little international standing. It was an orchestra of enthusiastic, mainly Norwegian, mainly young players, and it gave Jansons the scope to apply his considerable orchestra-building skills: "I had to make many changes . . . raise their morale, and do a lot of work with them at rehearsal stage," he said in a 2000 interview in *Fanfare*. The transformation was soon apparent, and, in pursuit of a recording contract, the orchestra made a demo tape of Tchaikovsky's Symphony Number Five. The Chandos label agreed to issue the performance, which Jansons describes as "one of the best," and offered to record them in other Tchaikovsky symphonies.

Truly, the Jansons/Oslo story is a remarkable one. Over a twenty-year span the partnership earned international respect through recordings and extensive tours in Europe, North America, and Japan. They appeared at the principal concert venues in London, Vienna, Amsterdam, New York, and Tokyo, and played at the Lucerne, Salzburg, and Edinburgh festivals and at London's Promenade Concerts. They received glowing reviews for their recordings on the Chandos, Simax, and EMI labels, with repertoire ranging from Bartók to Respighi and from Mahler to Saint-Saëns. Their Sibelius symphony cycle is particularly admired. To account for such success, one must acknowledge Jansons's ability to develop rapport with his players based on mutual respect and understanding, and his willingness to devote the necessary time and effort to building up a cohesive ensemble. Norman Lebrecht, writing in the *Daily Telegraph* (18 July 2001), summed up this achievement by saying: "The ensemble that Jansons has built over twenty years has a sound all of its own, a rich and sweet-sour resonance that stands out like a silk topper among a sea of baseball caps."

Perhaps even more astonishing is what Jansons was able to accomplish during the four years he was principal guest conductor of the BBC Welsh Orchestra, long regarded as the poor relation of all the British orchestras. The magic that Jansons wrought was nothing short of miraculous. The most stunning legacy is a complete cycle of Tchaikovsky symphonies recorded for BBC Television. In ferociously passionate interpretations, he had the orchestra "playing like demons."

Jansons is one of the most eminent conductors working today and one of the most (possibly *the* most) popular among orchestral musicians. Qualities that distinguished his work in the past seem to have become even more pronounced since he suffered two severe heart attacks in 1996. One of the qualities most frequently mentioned is the ability his mere presence has to transform the sound of the music. Transformation is the word that applies not only to the physical changes he is able to make to an orchestra's sound, but also, on a higher plane, to his ability to alter the listener's perception and sense of being. Jansons is very aware of a spiritual (not necessarily religious) dimension that is accessible through music. He is able to tap into this aspect of the music for his own inspiration and can convey it via the players to the listener. It goes without saying that all the orchestras he conducts are technically efficient, but he seems to be able to infuse extra warmth of feeling almost instantly. This seems to happen through the energy—cosmic as well as physical— he generates. From where does this mesmeric power come? The answer, as Sir Thomas Beecham once quipped, is "inspiration and perspiration!" Jansons works very hard to prepare each concert and each rehearsal and is always armed with a strong sense of what he wants to accomplish. He immerses himself in the culture surrounding each score through background reading and study, and he draws upon his vast experience and musical insights to make each performance fresh and revealing. He understands how to apply the "palette" that a conductor uses to realize his conception: atmosphere, phrasing, vitality, color, balance, and warmth. It is the added energy and enthusiasm, finally, which galvanizes his musicians. This is achieved in the spirit of cooperation and shared responsibility. He encourages players to be more involved and responsive to his conception, not just to do as they are told. On the other hand, he conducts as if he were a member of the orchestra and is always sensitive to players' concerns. Thus, Jansons's performances are never routine, as he is always seeking some new insight, not for the sake of novelty, but in pursuit of a deeper spiritual dimension beyond the notes. His rehearsal technique is thorough and painstaking, and he micromanages every phrase, *luftpause*, ritardando, and dynamic shading, but all this careful preparation is subsumed in the white heat of performance. This is a heavy responsibility, because every concert becomes more important and carries greater expectations than the previous one. Due to the precarious state of his health, it is almost as though every concert takes on the intensity of a farewell performance. His positive response to his near-death experiences has been to strengthen his attitude toward spirituality, bringing ever-deeper insights to bear and especially imbuing slow movements with more serenity at slower tempi. Following heart surgery and a long convalescence, he decided to make his return to conducting away from the spotlight among his old friends of the BBC Welsh Orchestra. After leading half a rehearsal with medically approved, low-key conducting, he realized that could never work for him and he threw off all restraint in order to be true to himself and the music.

A conductor's ability to change the character of an orchestra was most clearly demonstrated during Jansons's seven-year tenure as music director of the Pittsburgh SO (1997–2004). Almost immediately, listeners noticed the change to a warmer, richer, more balanced sound, as well as interpretations of added depth. Pittsburgh concertgoers were treated to one revelation after another. He stamped his imprint, urgency, and (yes) charm on the orchestra with heart and hand (he conducted without a baton for a time), although his all-embracing, inclusive approach came as something of a surprise to the players at first. His serious medical problems, coming between the announcement of his appointment and the beginning of his first ten-week residency, must have been a cause of great anxiety to the Pittsburgh administration, but his return to the podium (equipped with a heart defibrillator for safety's sake!) seemed to usher in an even more vibrant presence than before. The orchestra immediately responded to his congenial personality; good chemistry and positive vibes were felt all around, and the notoriously conservative Pittsburgh patrons greeted him with genuine warmth and enthusiasm. Jansons later stated that it had taken him a year of adjustment to glean the necessary information about the orchestra, the organization, the public, and the educational activities needed to hone his approach. The question remained, though, why had he come to Pittsburgh and not taken a position with one of the world's top-flight orchestras? The answer, it is presumed, is that he needed a change from Oslo and wanted to test the waters in the U.S. A top-ranking orchestra would have left him overexposed. Pittsburgh, a very fine orchestra snapping at the heels of the so-called Big Five, gave him some room to maneuver. One of his major challenges was programming. Jansons is not known to be overenthusiastic about most contemporary music, although he conducted quite a bit of it in Oslo. On the other hand, the Pittsburghers were notorious for their "know what we like, like what we know" attitude. As well as performing those romantic stalwarts Tchaikovsky, Dvořák, and Rachmaninoff and the Scandinavian repertoire, which seemed to pour heart and soul from him, he was eager to extend his repertoire backward to the classics, to Haydn and Beethoven particularly, and forward to contemporary composers with a reputation for accessibility. The orchestra set up a Composer-in-Residence program with Rodion Shchedrin (2000–01) and Michael Hersch (2001–2). Jansons also programmed music by Robert Daugherty, Roberto Sierra, David Stock, and Michael Moricz, among others. He was keen to support the outreach of the orchestra, which runs one of the nation's most active and highly regarded education programs in a city where the public school system has virtually abandoned music education.

Touring was an important priority. Jansons contended that to claim equal footing with the top orchestras, Pittsburgh should emulate them. The higher the status enjoyed in the musical world, of which touring is a principal measure, the easier it is to sustain the morale of the players and attract the most talented applicants when vacancies arise. The orchestra embarked on a West Coast tour in 2000, a South American tour in 2001, and a world tour in 2002. In March 2002 the orchestra appeared at Carnegie Hall in New York City for the seventh time.

It is a matter of profound regret that Jansons's tenure with the Pittsburgh SO should have coincided with stagnation in the recording industry. Only as the result of a groundswell movement in Pittsburgh was EMI (with whom Jansons had an exclusive contract) persuaded to issue a recording of Shostakovich's Eighth Symphony based on live performances. To document his close affinity with the composer's music, excerpts from the rehearsals were also included. It is to be hoped that many of the subscription series and touring concerts that were recorded digitally and broadcast by WQED-FM will one day become available as a memorial to a remarkable partnership.

Why did Jansons decide not to renew his Pittsburgh contract? He claims there was nothing really wrong there, and that he had appreciated the orchestra and the Pittsburgh environment. Clearly there were his health concerns, the high stress levels associated with the duties of a music director, and the long commute from his home in St. Petersburg, Russia. As well as his heart condition, he had begun to experience bouts of shoulder strain—a serious impediment to conducting. Approaching his sixtieth birthday, he determined that he needed a change. He had been passed over for the New York PO job (too hardened a bunch to have any truck with Jansons's "spirituality"), and prestigious appointments were on the horizon for him in Europe. His insistence on yearly renewals of his contract was an early indicator of a lack of long-term commitment to Pittsburgh. It is evident that Jansons disliked many of the manifestations of unbridled capitalism in the U.S. and the low status that classical music and orchestras, in particular, enjoy in American culture. The lack of appreciation and support for what the orchestra could and should be doing to bolster Pittsburgh's image around the world particularly galled him. Since it appeared that goals he publicly announced for the orchestra in February 2001 were not likely to be fully realized, this became a major factor in his decision to leave. Every case is unique, of course, but it augurs ill that a musician of Jansons's caliber has been lost to the U.S. and may never be persuaded to return, or only to appear in New York and other prestigious venues as a guest or with visiting orchestras.

Jansons was appointed music director of the Bavarian RSO in 2003 and principal conductor of the Concertgebouw Orchestra in 2004.

Further Reading

Croan, Robert. "Meet the Man behind the Baton . . . Mariss Jansons." *Pittsburgh Post-Gazette*, 14 September 1997, G1.
Denton, David. "An Interview with Mariss Jansons, Conductor of the Oslo Philharmonic Orchestra." *Fanfare* 23 (March–April 2000): 111–15.
Kimberley, Nick. "A True International." *Gramophone* 71 (July 1993): 24–25.
Norris, Geoffrey. "Musician, Magician." *Daily Telegraph* (London), 12 September 2002, 24.

Selected Recordings

Mussorgsky: *Pictures at an Exhibition* (orch. Ravel); *Night on Bare Mountain* (orch. Rimsky-Korsakov); *Khovanshchina: Prelude* (orch. Rimsky-Korsakov). Rimsky-Korsakov: *Scheherazade*; *Capriccio espagnole*; Joakim Svenheden (vn); Oslo PO; London PO. EMI 50824.
Rachmaninoff: *Orchestral Works*; St. Petersburg PO, Leningrad PO. EMI 75510.
Shostakovich: *Symphony no. 8*; Pittsburgh SO. EMI 57176.
Tchaikovsky: *Complete Symphonies*; Oslo PO. Chandos 10392.

∼

Järvi, Kristjan
Born 13 June 1972 in Tallinn, Estonia

Any discussion of Kristjan, the least known of the Järvi troika, is bound to focus on his work as the conductor of Absolute Ensemble, a groovy, flexible, crossover performing group of ten to eighteen players that was formed in 1994 with composers and instrumentalists from the Manhattan School of Music in New York City. However, he has also established his credentials as a "regular" symphonic conductor. The *Australian* (11 March 2004) described his rendition of *Pictures at an Exhibition* with the Adelaide SO as a "magnificently gripping performance that had the audience on the edge of their seats. Occasionally orchestral concerts hit supreme highs: this was one." In fact, he claims that splitting his time between the wild and improvisatory world of Absolute and the more sedate, traditional one of the concert hall and opera house makes him a better conductor. He is certainly a charismatic and technically proficient one!

Järvi is the younger son of maestro **Neeme Järvi**, music director of the New Jersey SO, and his older brother is **Paavo Järvi**, music director of the Cincinnati (Ohio) SO. The family left its native Estonia in 1980, so it is perhaps not surprising that Kristjan, who was only eight at that time, should have become the most eclectic and adventuresome member of an adventurous family. After formal training as a pianist at the Manhattan School of Music, he went on to study at the University of Michigan, but, finding the ambience there too traditional and restrictive, he dropped out and returned to New York City to concentrate on working with Absolute Ensemble. It was as a graduate student at Ann Arbor that he was drawn into conducting when composer friends needed someone to conduct their new pieces. He did not entirely relinquish the traditional path taken by his father and brother, spending two years (1998–2000) as assistant to Esa-Pekka **Salonen** at the Los Angeles PO. He began fulfilling guest appearances with orchestras that, thus far, have included the Bamberg SO, Frankfurt RSO, Hallé Orchestra, Japan PO, Dresden PO, Netherlands PO, Royal Stockholm PO, and WDR Cologne SO, among others. His first appointment was as principal conductor of the Norrlands Opera and SO in Sweden, and he became chief conductor of the Vienna Tonkünstler Orchester in 2004.

Absolute Ensemble is a group of classically trained and skilled improvisatory instrumentalists who aim to break down the barriers that exist between the genres of twentieth-century music: rock and its offshoots, folk, Broadway, jazz, and classical. Its versatility is demonstrated by the fact that it can devolve into five different subgroups, each with its own emphasis and programming niche: Scratchband, Absolute Mix, Music in Chamber, Architechtonics, and Blood on the Floor. These are categorizations aimed at breaking down categories! An audience drawn to a particular genre or venue might then be tempted to hear the group in one or more of its other manifestations. The philosophy behind this assault on musical segregation is the belief that traditions become sterile traps, and that innovation and vitality rejuvenate and liberate the performing experience. It opens up to a wider audience by blurring stylistic boundaries and encouraging classical devotees to become more "unbuttoned." The group's performance venues run the gamut of pubs, jazz clubs, and concert halls. The repertoire consists of music by some of today's leading young composers, such as James MacMillan, Mark-Anthony Turnage, Daniel Schnyder, Charles Coleman, and Michael Daugherty, as well as by more established composers, including John **Adams** and Steve Reich. The repertoire reaches back to earlier classical roots with "weird transcriptions" of Mahler, Debussy, and Schoenberg. It borrows from Gershwin and is heavily influenced by the pop music of the Beatles, Frank Zappa, and Jimi Hendrix, the funk of James Brown, and the jazz of Miles Davis and Duke Ellington. Such fusions, which often include light shows and other paraphernalia, are not new, of course, but seldom have they been so convincingly presented, and with such verve, as they are by this group, of which Järvi is the driving force. His versatility proves that he has the potential to become an outstanding conductor and an influential presence on the music scene for many years to come.

Website
http://www.kristjanjarvi.com/

Further Reading
Tommasini, Anthony. "Putting Music Back Together Again; for the Absolute Ensemble, It's Time to Break Up All the Categories That Are Breaking Up Music." *New York Times*, 27 October 2000, 5.
Whiting, Melinda. "Sons of Järvi: Paavo and Kristjan Follow in Their Father's Footsteps . . . Mostly (interview)." *Symphony* 52 (September–October 2001): 16–20.

Selected Recordings
Adams: *Chamber Symphony* (1992). Schoenberg: *Chamber Symphony*; Absolute Ensemble. CCN'C 00492.
Rosenberg: *The Isle of Bliss*; Patrik Forsman (*Astolf*); Agneta Eichenholz (*Felicia*); Lisa Gustafsson (*Zephyr*); Norrlands Opera SO and Ch. Phono Suecia PSCD 722.
Gruber (HK): *Rough Music*; *Zeitstimmung*; *Charivari*; Vienna Tonkünstler O. BIS 1681.

Järvi, Neeme
Born 7 June 1947 in Tallinn, Estonia

Neeme Järvi is probably the most prolific conductor in the history of recorded sound, with over 350 CDs to his credit! Many of these discs are of unfamiliar or neglected music issued by small-scale or specialist record companies with orchestras not generally regarded as top flight. This says a lot about Järvi: his character, his enthusiasms, and his success. With an affable, ebullient, and phenomenally industrious personality, he is obsessed with bringing forward music that has been neglected and with coaxing the best possible performances of it from his players. Not all of his endeavors are successful, but there are enough successes to make a valuable contribution to the universe of orchestral music and to justify his childlike enthusiasm for exploration. This joyous profligacy annoys some critics who question his musical discrimination. One could say, perhaps, that he is not a perfectionist or visionary seeking to refine his interpretations over a lifetime; rather he is an artist who strives for excellence in whatever endeavor he is currently engaged. Where he succeeds, it is through a spirit of collaboration with players, his respect for their professionalism, and their willingness to respond to his spontaneity. Dubbed "the human superconductor" and "charisma in tails," his performances work, in part, because of his physical presence and an inexplicable gift of "conveying musical wishes by physical attitude." It is not only his recorded legacy that demands accolades, but also the recognition and degree of financial security he has brought to his orchestras. The reasons for his success are complex: his personality and ability are foremost, but the excellent (though not always comfortable) basic training and experience he received from the Soviet system during the early part of his career should also be taken into account. The Estonian conductor Eri Klas paid him perhaps the greatest compliment when he said, "Success in no way changed him. He is still the same person he used to be when we were both students."

Järvi's parents were amateur musicians, and his older brother Vallo became a professional musician. Neeme must have been something of a prodigy, as he made his debut on Estonian radio as a xylophonist at the age of four. He studied percussion and choral directing at the Tallinn School of Music, and then went on to the Leningrad Conservatory, where his conducting teachers were Nicolai Rabinovich and Evgeny Mravinsky. After graduation in 1960, he returned to Estonia as a percussionist in the Radio Orchestra, founded the Tallinn CO, and conducted at the Estonian Opera Theater. He was soon conducting the Estonian RSO and accepting guest appearances for opera and ballet in Moscow and Leningrad. In 1963 he was appointed music director of the renamed Estonian Radio and Television SO. From these early days Järvi made it his mission to program, as much as he was allowed, music by the leading Estonian composers: Eduard Tubin, Heino Eller, Rudolf Tobias, Veijo Tormis, Artur Lemba, and Arvo Pärt. During this time he made guest appearances throughout the Eastern Bloc countries. In 1971, at the age of thirty-four, he won first prize in the Accademia Nazionale

di Santa Cecilia conducting competition in Rome, which led to guest appearances in Western Europe, Canada, Mexico, and Japan, and his Met debut with *Eugene Onegin* in April 1972. He toured the U.S. with the
Leningrad PO in 1973, and in 1976 was made chief conductor and artistic director of the newly formed Estonian State SO. In 1977 he accompanied the
Leningrad SO on a U.S. tour. He ran afoul of the Soviet authorities in 1979
when he gave the premiere of Arvo Pärt's *Credo* without receiving the necessary permission. This incident, which resulted in the firing of several colleagues, and the years of being burdened by bureaucracy convinced him that
it was time to emigrate. The family moved first to Vienna and then to the
U.S. Järvi, his wife Lillia, their two teenage sons (**Paavo** and **Kristjan**—both
destined to become conductors), and daughter Maarika arrived with two
suitcases and $100 apiece. The family settled in New Jersey, and Järvi was
soon able to capitalize on his reputation and accept invitations to appear
with the leading U.S. orchestras (New York, Philadelphia, Boston, etc.). After deputizing for Mariss **Jansons** at short notice with the Gothenburg (Göteburg) SO, he agreed to lead it on a tour to the UK in 1980, which resulted
in the offer and his acceptance of the post of principal guest conductor of the
City of Birmingham SO (1981–84). The following year he accepted the directorship of the Gothenburg SO, a partnership that was to last twenty-two
years (1982–2004) and produce the bulk of Järvi's recorded oeuvre with the
Swedish company BIS. In 1981 he returned to the Met with *Samson and
Delilah* and made his first appearance at the Swedish Royal Opera with *Salome*. As principal conductor from 1984 to 1988, he enjoyed a very fruitful
relationship with the Scottish National Orchestra, which saw a significant
improvement in the quality of the playing, particularly among the strings,
and an extensive recording schedule that included a complete Prokofiev
symphony cycle and the popular tone poems of Richard Strauss. In 1984 he
was granted U.S. citizenship, and the following year he returned to the Met
to conduct Mussorgsky's *Khovanshchina*.

   Under his directorship, the Gothenburg SO came to be regarded both by
reputation and in fact (it was renamed the National Orchestra of Sweden in
1997) as Sweden's premier orchestra. It grew from 80 players in 1982 to 116
in 2002. When he took over, the orchestra was experiencing financial problems, but Järvi saw that the route to improving its standing was via touring
and recording. To negotiate a successful recording contract in a fiercely competitive market, it was necessary to find a niche and to persuade the players
to accept reduced, economically realistic fees in the recording studio. The focus of his efforts was Scandinavian (not only Grieg and Sibelius but Nielsen,
Stenhammer, and Berwald) and Slavic music.

In 1990, the year he accepted the post as first principal guest conductor of the Japan PO, he realized the long-cherished hope of achieving an American appointment to be closer to his new home, becoming the music director of the Detroit (Mich.) SO. In 1989 the Detroit orchestra was in dire straits. True, it had just moved back into the renovated and acoustically excellent Orchestra Hall, but it faced a budget deficit of over $8 million and the players were obliged to take a salary cut of nearly 10 percent in order for the orchestra to stay solvent. Järvi plunged into this situation with his sleeves rolled up, and the way that he and the orchestra's board were able to turn things around is the stuff of legend! In his first season he played forty-four concerts to sold-out houses, a vast improvement over the previous year, and, in order to negotiate a five-disc recording contract, he appealed directly to the orchestra's constituency to raise the necessary financial support. Remarkably, two of the first three recordings, a disc of music by Barber and Beach and one of Charles Ives, showed up on the *Billboard* classical bestseller list. What Järvi realized was that the Detroit orchestra, despite its many travails, was still a fine ensemble with dedicated musicians who played "from the heart." The situation suited his chameleon-like ability to adapt to his circumstances and indulge his passion for rooting out obscure yet worthwhile repertoire. In this instance it not only included American music from composers such as Amy Beach and George Whitfield Chadwick, who existed virtually only in the pages of music encyclopedias, but also music by the African American composers William Grant Still, Duke Ellington, and Olly Wilson. One of the orchestra's innovations was to host an annual black composer's forum. During the time when the orchestra was under a heavy financial burden there was little opportunity for touring. They took up a residency in Lucerne in 1995, but it wasn't until 1998 that they were able to embark on a major "Eurotour" with sponsorship from Guardian Industries, a Detroit-based multinational glass manufacturer. They visited nine countries in just under four weeks, including Estonia for a stop at Järvi's hometown of Tallinn. The other circumstance that helped to turn the orchestra's fortune around was the development of Orchestra Place, an urban renewal project on land surrounding Orchestra Hall. This was a major factor in making the Detroit SO relevant culturally and civically. The arts and education campus includes the "Max" Center, a multipurpose performing space, a high-rise office building whose occupancy provides much-needed income, and a Performing Arts High School. The orchestra has also been fortunate to be able to continue its weekly radio broadcasts across the NPR Network, thanks to support from General Motors. However, Järvi laments the downturn in the market for recorded music, which he blames not only on the economy but also on the restrictive practices of the Musician's Union that make recording economically unviable.

Since the fall of the Soviet Union, Järvi has renewed ties with his native Estonia, where he founded an international conducting seminar in the resort town of Parnu in the summer of 2000. Unfortunately his manic lifestyle eventually caught up with him, and he suffered a serious stroke there in July 2001. He made a rapid recovery, and four months later he was performing and recording with his Swedish orchestra and resuming his schedule of guest appearances. It was a warning call, however, and he decided to relinquish both the Detroit and Gothenburg posts in 2004–5. In 2003 his appointment as music director of the New Jersey SO was announced, scheduling him to take up full duties in the 2005–6 season and serve as conductor designate in the meantime. This post, close to the home he has in New York City, involves much less traveling. It is hard to imagine, though, that an orchestra of only eighty players and with a small operating budget will be any less of a challenge to the redoubtable Järvi. And, as if to betoken his complete recovery, he signed a four-year contract to lead The Hague Residentie Orchestra in 2005.

Website
http://www.neemejarvi.com/

Further Reading
Brezina, Ales. "Interview with Neeme Jaervi." *Czech Music* 2 (1999): 6–7.
Hansson, Martin, and Pia Naurin. "A Passionate Affair: The Story of Neeme Järvi and Göteborgs Symfoniker." *Gramophone* 81 (March 2004): 93.
Johnson, Lawrence B. "Neeme Jaervi." *Stereo Review* 55 (September 1990): 90–92.
Malitz, Nancy. "Into America." *Gramophone* 69 (1992): 33–34.
Wiser, John D. "Neeme Järvi and Chandos in Detroit: The Search for the New, the Great, and Lots of It." *Fanfare* 15, no. 3 (1992): 139–44.

Selected Recordings
Chadwick: *Symphonies 2 and 3*; Detroit SO. Chandos 9685.
Prokofiev: *Complete Symphonies*; Royal Scottish National O. Chandos 8931.
Schmidt: *Complete Symphonies*; Chicago SO; Detroit SO. Chandos 9568.
Sibelius: *Andante lirico*; *Pohjola's Daughter*; *Rakastava*; *Tapiola*; Gothenburg SO. BIS 312.
Stravinsky: *Jeux de cartes*; *Orpheus*; *L'Histoire du soldat*; Royal Concertgebouw O. Royal Scottish National O. Chandos 10193.

Järvi, Paavo
Born 30 December 1962 in Tallinn, Estonia

Mariss **Jansons** and Paavo Järvi, two of today's brightest conducting talents, are both sons of famous conductor fathers (also the case with Carlos Kleiber). This is a situation that has both advantages and drawbacks! One advantage is to be steeped in the conducting milieu from an early age. Järvi admits that as far back as he can remember, he always wanted to be a conductor. When he was five years old he almost brought his father's rehearsal of *La Traviata* to a standstill by standing behind him and conducting away in imitation. He was in no way pressured into following in his father's footsteps, nor was he discouraged. In fact, it was his father's suggestion that he take up percussion as the quickest way to achieve the requisite standard of instrumental playing to join an orchestra. This proved to be the entrée that enabled the teenager to play with a number of local orchestras and observe many conductors at work, and also to experience the adrenaline high of playing in rock bands. Another advantage, it may be presumed, was enjoyed upon graduation from music school. When looking for conducting opportunities, he found it helpful to have a father with many useful contacts. The disadvantages, of course, are charges of nepotism and invidious comparisons, especially because father and son share the same repertoire specialties of Russian and Baltic composers.

In Järvi's case, being steeped in music at an early age is putting it mildly! He began piano and percussion lessons when he was five, and, as did his father (q.v.) before him, made something of a name for himself as a xylophone prodigy, appearing in a television performance at the age of seven. He attended many of his father's rehearsals and concerts, often because there was no one left at home to babysit him. He entered the Soviet music education system that required attendance at music school as well as regular elementary and high school. His turning seventeen, when he would have expected to enroll at the Tallinn Conservatory, coincided with his family's decision to leave the Soviet Union and settle in the U.S. It was a period of considerable adjustment for a teenager from the Soviet Bloc who didn't speak any English. Living in New York, however, he was soon able to attend the pre-college division at Juilliard. He then enrolled at the Curtis Institute to study with Max Rudolf and Otto-Werner Mueller. With these two strong, if different, personalities he began to study the art and craft of conducting. Rudolf was a lovable personality who taught his students the importance of communication both as a performer and an orchestral trainer—how to convey one's wishes to an orchestra clearly and concisely. Mueller's strength was to insist his students were well prepared technically after thorough study of the score. What Järvi had to learn for himself was that personality is what makes a conductor, and that experience, rather than learning, confirms this. Close observation of Leonard Bernstein and Michael Tilson **Thomas** while attending summer classes at the Los Angeles PO's Summer Institute helped to reinforce that fact. Upon graduation from Curtis, Järvi's task was to build a career in a musical environment that he found was an "uptight and unfriendly scene for a young musician." Not surprisingly, then, he moved to Europe to get a start, making his debut with the Trondheim Orchestra in Norway in 1982. He gradually built up contacts and eventually became principal guest conductor of the Malmö SO in Sweden. In 1994 he was appointed chief conductor there and also made an important debut with the City of Birmingham SO. Back on the North American continent, he worked with the Lyra Borealis CO in Toronto (Ontario), an organization specializing in performing the music of Estonian composers. His reputation was enhanced by his appointment to principal guest conductor of the Stockholm PO (1995–99) and to the same position with the City of Birmingham SO (1996–99). He made his operatic debut at La Scala and gave debut concerts with the New York PO and the Berlin PO in 1999. In 2000, he began an association with the Verbier Music Festival in Switzerland and also appeared with the Pittsburgh SO for the first time. He emerged as the winning contender for the music director post of the Cincinnati (Ohio) SO in 2001. In his considered way, Järvi was not entirely sure he was ready for a directorship, but his initial reluctance was overcome by the enthusiastic response he received from the orchestra. He soon realized that it was a situation in which he could make a real contribution toward enhancing the reputation of an orchestra that had existed for too long in the shadow of its more illustrious neighbor in Cleveland. In 2006, he also became chief conductor of the Frankfurt RSO.

Järvi is a voluble personality and still regarded as youthful and dashing, qualities exploited by the Cincinnati PR department. He is not a particularly demonstrative conductor, but his essentially graceful gestures can become highly charged at times. He combines intelligence and taste with a fund of innate musicianship to create real and dynamic performance experiences. He has certainly generated more than the usual enthusiasm for a new appointee and earned the respect of his players without the formality that often exists between maestro and orchestra. Although his interpretations are carefully crafted and attentive to detail, Järvi understands that technical excellence alone is not sufficient; he moves his audience by creating vivid excitement on stage. "A performance full of unexpected pleasures" was the comment of one critic. His performance of Schumann's Second Symphony was described as "marvelously shaped, intensely expressive, and beautifully balanced in every way." When his performances are criticized, it is for being somewhat clinical, described by one critic as "tame and tidy." It follows that with his talents and temperament he is considered an ideal interpreter of the music of Stravinsky.

Although he expects to devote most of his time to Cincinnati and signed an extension to his contract in 2003 which will take him through the 2008–9 season, he is in great demand as a guest conductor. As such he has appeared with the Philadelphia Orchestra, Orchestra of the Age of Enlightenment, the philharmonics of London, Berlin, Munich, Prague, St. Petersburg, and Israel, Orchestre de Paris, Orchestra National de France, Orchestra di Accademia di Santa Cecilia, RAI-Turin Orchestra, Tokyo SO, and Sydney SO. He has given concerts regularly with the Estonian State SO and conducts the Los Angeles PO, New York PO, and the symphony orchestras of Houston, Detroit, San Francisco, Pittsburgh, and Philadelphia. In addition to establishing himself in Cincinnati and taking the orchestra on its first U.S. tour (2003), Järvi accompanied the American Russian Young Artists Orchestra on its 2002 tour of Russia and acts as artistic advisor to the Estonian National SO. He has built up an extensive list of recordings on the Telarc, Virgin Classics, BIS, and Koch labels that reflect his championing of Baltic composers: the Estonians Pärt, Tuur, Sumera, Kasemets, and Tubin, in addition to Sibelius and Stenhammer. His recorded repertoire extends to Dvořák, Prokofiev, Stravinsky, Ravel, and Gershwin.

Website
http://www.paavojarvi.com/

Further Reading
Anderson, Colin. "Paavo Järvi—Growing Up and Soaring Upward." *Fanfare* 29 (September–October 2005): 92–95.
Brown, Royal S. "An Interview with Paavo Jaervi." *Fanfare* 18, no. 3 (1995): 14.
Quinn, Michael. "Strange Bedfellows (Interview with Paavo Järvi on Some Unlikely Programming)." *Gramophone* 80 (February 2003): 28–29.

Selected Recordings
Berlioz: *Symphonie Fantastique*; Love Scene from *Romeo and Juliette*; Cincinnati SO. Telarc CD 80638.
Bernstein: *Prelude, Fugue, and Riffs*; *Facsimile*; *West Side Story: Symphonic Dances*; *Divertimento for Orchestra*; City of Birmingham SO. Virgin 63301.

Pärt: *Summa*; *Trisagion*; *Symphony no. 3*; *Fratres*; *Silouans Song*; *Festine lente*; *Cantus in memoriam Benjamin Britten*; Estonian Natl SO. Virgin 7243 5 45501 2 6.

Sibelius: *Snöfrid*; *Our Native Land*; *Väinö's Song*; *Sandels*; *Hymn to the Earth*; *Song to Lemminkäinen*; *Finlandia*; Ellerhein Girls' Choir; Estonian Natl Male Choir; Estonian Natl SO. Virgin 5455612.

Stravinsky: *Le sacre du printemps*. Nielsen: *Symphony no. 5*; Cincinnati SO. Telarc 60615.

～

Jean, Kenneth
Born 25 October 1952 in New York, New York

When he was a student at San Francisco State University, Jean's childhood ambition to become a violinist faltered, and he began to nurture the idea of becoming a conductor instead. Applying to the Juilliard conducting program, he was, at the age of nineteen, the youngest successful applicant and the last student to be admitted into the class of the legendary Jean Morel. Born into a Chinese American family, Jean spent his formative years from four to fourteen in Hong Kong. He began piano lessons at age seven and later added the violin, for which he felt a greater affinity. He enrolled at SFSU after the family moved to San Francisco in 1967. Upon graduating from Juilliard in 1976, he joined the conducting staff of the Cleveland Orchestra as assistant to Lorin **Maazel**. Meanwhile, he had made his Carnegie Hall debut with the New York YSO in 1972 and been appointed its music director. He was invited by Antal Dorati to be resident conductor of the Detroit SO from 1979 to 1985, where he progressed from the most menial to more substantial assignments. He rounded off this stage of his career by winning the American SO's Stokowski Conducting Competition in 1984. In 1986, he was appointed an associate conductor of the Chicago SO and remained with that ensemble until 1993. Within months of this prestigious appointment he secured the leadership of his first professional orchestra by becoming music director of the Florida SO in Orlando (1986–92). In addition, he served as principal guest conductor of the Hong Kong PO. In 1990 he was recipient of a Seaver/NEA Conductors Award. His second directorship was with the Tulsa (Okla.) PO (1997–2000), and he served as music advisor to the New Mexico SO during its interregnum (1999–2001).

Both of Jean's directorships began promisingly, achieved remarkable things, and ended sourly. In Orlando, where the orchestra was under-strength and played in an acoustically poor auditorium, Jean was frustrated at never being able to produce the opulent sound he craved for the late-romantic scores he loved. He was, perhaps unfairly, criticized for not realizing the full potential of symphonies by Mahler, Rachmaninoff, Tchaikovsky, and Sibelius, but he shares some of the blame for not choosing repertoire better suited to his forces and venue. In all fairness, though, it must be noted that he served for six of the most difficult years in the financially strapped orchestra's history, culminating in a four-month players' strike in 1990. Afterward, he was obliged to deal with a number of player defections, as well as woo back an audience by programming popular works rather than more contemporary and less familiar ones, as was his inclination. He found the Tulsa orchestra better equipped to handle big romantic blockbusters and showed his mettle early on with a sterling performance of Mahler's Second Symphony. A performance of the Verdi *Requiem* the following year was equally impressive. The subscription series concerts generally received critical approval, with particular praise for the staples of Tchaikovsky and Brahms. Even the adventurous works garnered some appreciation, such as Robert McDuffie's performance of the violin concerto of Philip Glass. Season ticket sales increased during the first two years, the second of which was the orchestra's fiftieth anniversary. By the third season, however, things were not going so well, and Jean decided not to extend his three-year contract. He felt frustrated at the level of support for the orchestra and the arts in general by the Tulsa community and at the lack of support from the orchestra's board for his ideas for growth through imaginative programming and outreach initiatives.

Jean's conducting style has frequently been described as exuberant: "Bobbing, weaving, waving, lunging . . . like a parody of the hyperactive maestro." However, it is a style that orchestral musicians find easy to follow, which inspires confidence and elicits their full potential. Also, often overlooked is the significant role a conductor's "antics" can play in focusing the attention of the audience to the music's expressive twists and turns, and Jean, it seems, has the knack of engaging his audiences in that way. He has exploited his musicianship and developed his professionalism to the point of exercising total control over his forces, and, whereas in his younger days he was sometimes criticized for being too rigid and literal in his interpretations, he has latterly found the rhythmic and melodic flexibility that reflects both a secure and an expressive hand. This is particularly evident as a sympathetic concerto partner.

Jean is a well-rounded and sensitive artist who can produce "zesty" and stylish performances of Baroque and classical music, but it is in works that

require fire and brilliance that he is most in his element. Within the limitations imposed by the provincial classical music milieu and the fashion for
thematic program design, he has a knack for finding the right "feel" for cohesive groupings. He pays more than lip service to contemporary scores. As
well as works by Philip Glass, he has featured American scores by John
Corigliano, John Harbison, Dan Welcher, Libby Larsen, Jacob Druckman,
Robert Beaser, Arthur Bloom, Richard Adams, and Christopher Rouse,
among others. In 1993, Jean led the Chicago SO's eightieth-birthday tribute
to Morton Gould with the first performance of a suite from his ballet *Fall
River Legend.*

During his association with the Hong Kong orchestra Jean recorded a
number of works by Chinese composers Du Ming-xin, Hua Jan Jun, and Zhao
Yuan Ren. One of these albums, *Colorful Clouds,* achieved best-seller status.
Jean was one of the conductors able to take advantage of recording opportunities afforded by the collapse of the Iron Curtain. In the early 1990s, he
made a number of recordings with the Slovak PO and the Czechoslovak
RSO for the Naxos label. These include ballet scores by De Falla and a Ravel
program which features *Rapsodie Espagnole, Daphnis et Chloé Suite Number
Two,* and *La Valse.* With Japanese violinist Takako Nishizaki he recorded the
violin concertos of Beethoven, Mendelssohn, and Tchaikovsky. More recent
discs include Berlioz overtures with the Polish State PO (2000) and, upon his
returning to lead the Hong Kong PO, the *Cendrillon* and *Esclarmonde* suites
of Massenet (2002).

Whereas Jean may well thrive for the time being as a busy freelance conductor, sooner rather than later he needs to secure a permanent appointment
with an ensemble that is financially stable, and where he can showcase his
considerable talent to the full.

Further Reading
Brown, Steven. "Jean Legacy." *Orlando Sentinel,* 3 May 1992, F1.
Marum, Lisa. "Kenneth Jean, Conductor." *Ovation* 6 (January 1986): 34.
Watts, James D. "Rewarded for Good Conduct." *Tulsa World,* 6 June 1997,
16.

Selected Recordings
Berlioz: Overtures: *Le corsaire; King Lear; La Carnival Romain; La damnation
de Faust: Rákóczy March; Menuet des follets; Romeo and Juliette: Love Scene;*
Polish State PO. Amadis 7158.
Massenet: *Orchestral Suites: Cendrillon; Esclarmonde;* Hong Kong PO. Naxos
8555986.

Ming-xin: *Festival Overture*; *Great Wall Symphony*; Hong Kong PO. Marco
Polo 223939.
Viva Espana! The Music of Spain; Czecho-Slovak RSO. Naxos 550174.

⌒

Kahane, Jeffrey (Alan)
Born 12 September 1956 in Los Angeles, California

Jeffrey Kahane successfully begged his parents for piano lessons at age five,
started the guitar at age ten, and at fourteen was accepted as a scholarship
student for intense private study with pianist Jakob Gimpel. At sixteen he
left high school to attend the San Francisco Conservatory of Music, where
he earned a bachelor's degree in 1977. He transferred to Juilliard briefly along
the way, but soon returned to the "less stifling" atmosphere in San Francisco.
Over the next decade he won numerous keyboard prizes, including second
place at the Clara Haskil Competition (1977), fourth place in the Van
Cliburn Competition (1981), an Avery Fisher Career Grant (1983), and first
place in the Artur Rubinstein Competition (1983). In 1987 he won the first
Andrew Wolf Chamber Music Award.

Kahane's conducting debut came in 1988 at the Oregon Bach Festival,
and he has pursued a dual career since. His dedication to working with young
musicians led to cofounding the Gardner CO, an ensemble of outstanding
students and recent alumni of major schools of music in the Boston area,
where he served as artistic director and conductor from 1991 to 1995. Since
1992, Kahane has been associate conductor at the San Luis Obispo (Calif.)
Mozart Festival. He was music director of the Santa Rosa (Calif.) SO from
1995 to 2006, leaving behind a more than 50 percent increase in subscribers
and three consecutive years of budget surpluses, the final one reaching six figures. He has been music director of the Los Angeles CO since 1997. He and
the LACO won an ASCAP award for programming of contemporary music
in 2005. Known in both cities not only for innovative programming but also
for using the orchestra to inspire young people and bring communities together, Kahane instigated series and events that have attracted wider audiences to the classical concert hall. His preconcert talks at SRSO concerts
drew an average of five hundred people. He believes orchestra music directors have a responsibility to interact with the children in their community
and that the orchestra is central to the life of a community. The SRSO won
a national Met Life award for excellence in community engagement for a collaborative project based on Sir Michael Tippett's oratorio, *A Child of Our
Time*, involving five hundred Santa Rosa High School students and teachers.

In 2001, Kahane became artistic director of the newly formed Green Music Festival in Sonoma County (Calif.). He took over the position of music director for the Colorado SO in 2005. He is known for a striking lack of ego and a low-key demeanor that makes him popular with musicians and audiences alike. Ever the teacher, Kahane in his first season experimented with a concert that began with a very detailed lecture on various aspects of Beethoven's Fifth Symphony, continued with a rousing performance of the symphony, and ended with an invitation from Kahane to the nearly full house to step up to the microphone with questions. He likes to program works that the orchestra has not played before, tries to honor a wide range of constituencies, and looks for ways to weave the orchestra and its repertoire into the fabric of the community by sharing the joy of music. Kahane won a second ASCAP award for programming of contemporary music in 2006, this one with the CSO.

Kahane also finds the time to make guest appearances as pianist and conductor. Among others, he has conducted the Aspen Chamber Symphony, Los Angeles PO, Minnesota Orchestra, New York PO, San Francisco SO, Saint Louis SO, Toronto SO, Detroit SO, Dallas SO, Houston SO, Seattle SO, Saint Paul CO, National Arts Centre Orchestra, Camerata Salzburg, Academy of St. Martin-in-the-Fields (London), and Royal PO of Galicia (Spain).

Further Reading

Green, Barry. *The Mastery of Music: Ten Pathways to True Artistry*. New York: Broadway Books, 2003.

Kahane, Jeffrey. "Half-Full and Rising: Is the Orchestra in Decline? Not from My Vantage Point . . ." *Symphony* 52 (November–December 2001): 53–58.

Selected Recordings

Bach: *Violin Concertos: No. 1 in A; No. 2 in E; Concerto for 2 Violins in D; Concerto for Oboe and Violin in C*; Hilary Hahn (vn); Margaret Batjer (vn); Allan Vogel (ob); Los Angeles CO. Deutsche Grammophon B0000986-02.

Rorem: *More Than a Day; Water Music; From an Unknown Past*; Brian Asawa (ct); Margaret Batjer (vn); Gary Gray (cl); Los Angeles CO. BMG/RCA 09026-63512-2.

⌒

Kalmar, Carlos
Born 26 February 1958 in Montevideo, Uruguay

Born to Austrian parents, Carlos Kalmar began violin lessons at age six, then at fifteen went to the Vienna Academy of Music to study conducting with Karl Österreicher. In 1984, he won the Hans Swarowsky Conducting Competition in Vienna. Kalmar accepted the position of conductor of the Vienna Volksoper for 1987 and also began a four-year tenure as music director with the Hamburg SO. He left there in 1991 to become music director of the Stuttgart PO until 1995. From 1996 to 2000 Kalmar was music director of the Anhaltisches Theater Dessau and the Philharmonie Dessau. In 2000 he began two new positions, music director of the Vienna Tonkünstler Orchestra and principal conductor of the Grant Park Music Festival in Chicago. Kalmar resigned his Viennese position in 2003 to accept a second position in the U.S., that of music director of the Oregon SO, where he has a contract through the 2008–9 season.

According to critics, Kalmar has effected a transformation in the sound quality of the OSO, thanks to his style, his emphasis on the basics of rhythm, intonation, articulation, and phrasing, and his personnel changes. Some of those decisions have been controversial, but Kalmar remains focused on his mission to challenge and refine the orchestra.

Kalmar is credited with sensitive musical interpretation and an ability to elicit an emotional range of expression from the orchestra. He is also known as a champion of American music, programming the offbeat and the neglected. One *Chicago Tribune* reviewer opined, "The idiomatic authority that Carlos Kalmar . . . brings to American music puts the comparatively half-hearted efforts of many a native son to shame." His Kurka recording with the Grant Park Orchestra received a 2004 Grammy nomination.

Kalmar's guest-conducting engagements reflect his international interests, taking him to the Czech PO, Prague SO, BBC National Orchestra of Wales, Berlin RSO, Orquesta Nacional de España, ORT Orchestra of Florence, Bournemouth SO, Hamburg State Opera, Residentie Orchestra, Vienna State Opera, Yomiuri Japan Orchestra, Flemish RSO, Zurich Opera, and others. In North America he has led numerous ensembles, including the Dallas SO, Houston SO, Baltimore SO, Kansas City PO, the San Francisco SO, Los Angeles PO, Philadelphia Orchestra, Saint Louis SO, Vancouver SO, Milwaukee SO, New World Symphony, Minnesota Orchestra, Cincinnati SO, Phoenix SO, National Arts Centre Orchestra in Ottawa, and others.

Further Reading
Barreiro, Diego. "Desde Rusia y Austria a Montevideo." *Sinfónica* 7, no. 78 (2001): 14–15. [Spanish]

Selected Recordings
American Works for Organ and Orchestra; music by Barber, Piston, Sowerby, Colgrass; David Schrader (org); Grant Park O. Cedille CDR 90000 063.
Dohnanyi: *Konzertstück*. Enescu: *Symphonie concertante*. D'Albert: *Cello Concerto*; Alban Gerhardt (vc); BBC Scottish SO. Hyperion CDA 67544.
Joachim: *Violin Concerto no. 2 in D*, Op. 11. Brahms: *Violin Concerto*; Rachel Barton (vn); Chicago SO. Cedille CDR 90000 068.
Kurka: *Symphony no. 2*; *Julius Caesar*; *Music for Orchestra*; *Serenade for Small Orchestra*; Grant Park O. Cedille CDR 90000 077.
Szymanowski: *Violin Concerto no. 1*. Martinů: *Violin Concerto no. 2*. Bartók: *Two Portraits*; Jennifer Koh (vn); Grant Park O. Cedille CDR 90000 089, live: Chicago 7/1–2/2004, 7/1–2/2005.

～

Kreizberg (born Bychkov), Yakov
Born 24 October 1959 in Leningrad, Soviet Union

Born in the Soviet Union and developing a major career in Europe, Kreizberg (he assumed another family name to avoid confusion with his older brother, the conductor Semyon **Bychkov**) owes to the U.S. the start of his conducting career. Subsequent visits include a Bournemouth SO tour and occasional guest appearances. He arrived in New York as an émigré at the age of sixteen with prodigious keyboard skills and having studied briefly with the eminent conducting teacher Ilya Musin. During his early teenage years he had studied composition and had several works performed. Learning the piano from the age of five, he had become a proficient sight-reader and an expert at playing from orchestral scores. In his adopted country he earned a living as an accompanist in New York voice studios. He attended the University of Michigan, becoming the first student there to earn a doctorate in both orchestral and operatic conducting, and was winner of the Eugene Ormandy Conducting Prize. Awarded a fellowship to the Berkshire Music Center at Tanglewood, he was tutored by **Ozawa**, Bernstein, and Leinsdorf. A further scholarship took him to the Los Angeles Philharmonic Institute, where he also worked with Bernstein and was invited to become an assistant to Michael Tilson **Thomas**. He served as conductor of the Mannes College of Music orchestra (1985–88) and won the Stokowski Conducting Competition in 1986. If his years in the U.S. served to complete his formal music education and gave him his start as a conductor, his real apprenticeship began in 1988, when, at the age of twenty-seven, he became the youngest *Generalmusikdirektor* in Germany with an appointment to the opera house of Krefeld-Mönchengladbach and conductor of the Niederrheinischer SO. There followed six years of hard work learning the repertoire and improving the orchestra—the classic way that conductors in Germany have learned their craft. He continued to enhance his reputation in Europe with appointments as chief conductor to the Komische Oper in Berlin (1994–2001), as principal conductor of the Bournemouth SO (1995–2000), as chief conductor and artistic advisor of the Netherlands PO and Netherlands CO (2003–present), as principal guest conductor of the Vienna SO (2003–present), and as artistic advisor to the Jeunesses Musicales (2000–present). He has been circumspect in considering a permanent appointment in North America, and although there was some mutual interest shown in conductor searches in Atlanta, Houston, and Toronto, nothing came of them.

By the time he emerged from the relative obscurity of his first permanent appointment (but not before he had made a considerable impression at his Glyndebourne Festival debut with *Jenufa* in 1992), Kreizberg had honed his conducting skills. He has since been consistently praised for an impeccable stick technique that is taut, precise, well-articulated, and highly disciplined. There is never any question that he has prepared each performance thoroughly and meticulously, with every phrase and nuance considered. The resulting interpretations exhibit clear and imaginative ideas and a firm grasp of structure. His podium manner, the opposite of flamboyant, is not without charisma, and his deferential manner to soloists goes hand-in-hand with his reputation as an expert accompanist of both instrumentalists and singers. Reviewers have remarked on the sensitivity, passion, intensity, and immediacy of his performances. But the emotion is always held tautly in check, and it is this sense of control that has led other critics to find his readings cold and lacking atmosphere and spontaneity at times. This criticism aside, his achievements cannot be overrated. His five-year tenure with the Bournemouth SO lifted it to a higher plane. Under his rigorous training, the sound quality and ensemble were impressive. *American Record Guide* critic Faubion Bowers, reviewing a Carnegie Hall stop during its eight-concert tour of the eastern U.S. in 1997, was so impressed as to admit that Kreizberg had the orchestra sounding as if it were one of the world's greatest. In Berlin, as the *Generalmusikdirektor* at the Komische Oper, it was soon evident that his commitment and dedication enhanced the company's reputation in a wide variety of

repertoire. He reveled in a milieu where the music and the staging were prepared with equal care. Unfortunately, it was striving for high standards that
brought him into conflict with the house's management and resulted in a
premature, acrimonious, and very public severance. Working at the Glyndebourne Festival, where, after his very successful debut in 1992, he returned to
conduct a much-admired *Don Giovanni* in 1995 and *Katya Kabánova* in 1998,
he especially appreciated conditions that allowed for ample preparation and
the total dedication of all participants. His conducting of *Der Rosenkavalier*
for the English National Opera in 1994 was praised for its "magnificent sensitivity." There is a body of repertoire, indeed, where his interpretations come
close to being unsurpassed: Tchaikovsky's Sixth Symphony, Rachmaninoff's
Second Symphony, Shostakovich's Eleventh Symphony, and Stravinsky's
Firebird spring to mind.

Having composed music in his youth and worked with a number of composers performing their works, Kreizberg claims insight into the creative
process of interpretation. He belongs to the school that believes that slavish
adherence to the composer's markings, other than the actual notes, is not always appropriate. The composer may believe passionately that his tempo indications, dynamic markings, and so forth, are the right ones, but there is a
physicality involved in performance that may require adjustments. In an interview with Bruce Duffie in the June 2002 issue of the *Opera Journal*,
Kreizberg states that "with composers present I sometimes did things com-
pletely different to what was notated . . . they often agreed that my feelings
were correct and it was better that way. There is no such thing as an authentic interpretation . . . a piece of music will only live if it is recreated by
a creative mind." His service to contemporary music includes works by
Peteris Vasks, Jonathan Harvey, Aribert Reimann, Siegfried Matthus, and Judith Bingham, among others. He has aired less well-known works by the likes
of Ernst Krenek, Franz Schmidt, Kurt Weill, Karol Szymanowski, and Igor
Markevitch.

Kreizberg has appeared extensively as a guest conductor in Europe. His engagements include the Berlin PO, Concertgebouw Orchestra, BBC SO,
Leipzig Gewandhaus Orchestra, Dresden Staatskapelle, Czech PO, Philharmonia Orchestra, London SO, London PO, Bavarian RSO, Tonhalle Orchestra, Orchestre de Paris, Russian National Orchestra, Oslo PO, Orchestra
Sinfonico di Milano, and many others. In North America he has conducted
the New York PO, Chicago SO, Boston SO, San Franciso SO, Los Angeles
PO, and the orchestras of Baltimore, Philadelphia, Pittsburgh, Dallas, Minneapolis, Cincinnati, Detroit, Atlanta, Saint Louis, Washington, Toronto,
and Montreal. As well as touring with the Bournemouth SO to the U.S.,

Germany, and Austria (1996), he has led tours with the Netherlands PO to Germany (2005) and the Vienna SO to Japan (2004), Spain, and Germany (2005). His recordings have appeared on the Decca, Oehms Classics, and Pentatone Classics labels. They include selections by Tchaikovsky, Dvořák, and Wagner with the Netherlands PO; Liszt's piano concertos and *Totentanz* (soloist: Alfredo Perl) with the BBC SO; violin concertos by Beethoven and Mendelssohn (soloist: Vesko Eschenazy), and Glazunov, Prokofiev, and Khachaturian (soloist: Julia Fischer) with the Russian National Orchestra; and Bruckner's Seventh Symphony with the Vienna SO. The performance of *Don Giovanni* from the Glyndebourne Festival was issued on video.

Website
http://www.yakovkreizberg.com/

Further Reading
Duffie, Bruce. "Conversation Piece: Conductor Yakov Kreizberg." *Opera Journal* 35 (June–September 2002): 29–46.
Finch, Hilary. "Kreizberg Steps Forward." *Opera* 45 (July 1994): 798–99.

Selected Recordings
Bruckner: *Symhony no. 7*; Vienna SO. Pentatone 5186051.
Dvořák: *Symphony no. 9* "From the New World." Tchaikovsky: *Romeo and Juliet*; Netherlands PO. Pentatone 5186 019.
Khachaturian: *Violin Concerto in d*. Prokofiev: *Violin Concerto in D*, Op. 19. Glazunov: *Violin Concerto in a*, Op. 82; Julia Fischer (vn); Russian Natl O. Pentatone 5186 059.
Liszt: *Piano Concertos 1 and 2*; *Totentanz*; Alfredo Perl (pf); BBC SO. Oehms 316.
Strauss, (J., II): *Emperor Waltz*; *Tales from the Vienna Woods*; *Artist's Life*; *North Sea Pictures*; *On the Beautiful Blue Danube*; *Roses from the South*; Vienna SO. Pentatone 5186 052.

⌒

Lane, Louis
Born 25 December 1923 in Eagle Pass, Texas

Lane has served as artistic advisor and conductor at the Cleveland Institute of Music since 1982. Toward the end of a long and distinguished conducting career he held an endowed chair in music performance at the University of

Alabama (2001–2). Previously he was director of orchestral studies at Oberlin College (1995–98), senior lecturer in music at the University of Texas (1989–91), and codirector of the Blossom Festival School (1969–73).

After receiving his BM degree from the University of Texas (1943), Lane was on active service with the army. Upon demobilization, he spent the summer of 1946 at the Tanglewood Festival, taking composition lessons from Bohuslav Martinů. He continued composition studies with Bernard Rogers and earned his MM degree from the Eastman School of Music in 1947. Then he began a quarter-century association with the Cleveland Orchestra as player and conductor. He served as assistant to George Szell (1956–60), as associate conductor (1960–70), and as resident conductor (1970–73). In 1950 he took a class in opera with Sarah Caldwell; later he directed the Lake Erie Opera Theater (1964–72). He was music director of the Akron (Ohio) SO from 1959 to 1983 and principal guest conductor of the Dallas (Tex.) SO from 1973 to 1978. A close association with the Atlanta (Ga.) SO began with his appointment as co-conductor (1977–83) and continued when he became principal guest conductor (1983–88). He spent the 1984–85 season as principal guest conductor of the South African Broadcasting Corporation SO in Johannesburg. As a guest conductor he has appeared in North and South America, Scandinavia, and Eastern Europe. He has recorded for Telarc and Columbia Records; most of his available recordings are on reissued compilations. Lane's performances are appreciated particularly for their structural cohesion and refinement, the latter of which also characterizes his conducting style. He has championed many less familiar treasures of the orchestral repertoire and the music of American composers such as Aaron Copland, Ned Rorem, and David Diamond.

Selected Recordings

Copland: *Fanfare for the Common Man*; *Rodeo: 4 Dance Episodes*; *Appalachian Spring: Suite*; Atlanta SO. From Telarc 60648.

Respighi: *The Birds*; *Fountains of Rome*; *Pines of Rome*; Atlanta SO. Telarc 80085.

Rorem: *Sunday Morning*; *String Symphony*; *Eagles*; Atlanta SO. From Telarc 80353.

Scarlatti, arr. Tommasini: *The Good Humored Ladies*; Cleveland O. From Sony 60311.

Levine, James
Born 23 June 1943 in Cincinnati, Ohio

Levine is identified most closely with New York's Metropolitan Opera, with which he has been associated for more than thirty years. It is not merely the longevity of the partnership, but the extent of it that is remarkable. Spending up to seven months of the year there, he has a legendary dedication to all aspects of the institution's activities and has single-handedly steered the Met forward to a position of preeminence in the world of opera. His training and nurturing of the Met's orchestra over so many years has brought it on par with the world's finest, such as the Vienna PO, the Berlin PO, and the Chicago SO, three orchestras with which Levine has also had long and productive relationships. In manner and appearance he is far from the traditional image of the maestro. Described in *The New Grove Dictionary* as bluff and ebullient, his conducting style and baton technique, though decisive and compelling, are far from flamboyant. His demeanor in rehearsal might be described as persuasive and enthusiastically low-key. He is not prone to outbursts or tantrums but achieves results by coaxing and by impressing singers and instrumentalists alike with his thorough knowledge of and dedication to the music.

Levine's is a life almost totally absorbed in music. Before he was two he could pick out tunes at the piano and had began displaying the attributes—memory and aural imagination—of a musical prodigy. He began receiving piano lessons at the age of six and was giving recitals when he was eight. He made an appearance with the Cincinnati (Ohio) SO playing Mendelssohn's Second Concerto when he was ten. His parents, however, resisted efforts to exploit his precocity. Meanwhile, he had discovered a strong attachment to opera. He would conduct along with recordings and performances he attended and demonstrated the ability to learn operas from the score. Walter Levin, the German expatriate leader of the La Salle Quartet, undertook his formal musical training until he was ready to enter Juilliard in 1961 to study conducting under Jean Morel. His conducting ambitions had been fuelled the previous year at the Marlboro Festival, where he had gone to study piano with Rudolf Serkin, only to find himself fortuitously directing the offstage band in performances of *Cosi fan tutte*. The next summer he attended the Aspen Festival to work with conducting teacher Wolfgang Vacano and, as a result of the impression he made, was invited to join the festival staff and engaged to conduct *The Pearl Fishers* the following year (1962). As a finalist in the Ford Foundation's American Conductor's Project, Levine met his chief mentor, Georg Szell, who was one of the judges. Szell persuaded Levine to abandon his studies at Juilliard to become his apprentice with the Cleveland Orchestra. This subjected the pupil to a vigorous education for which he was more than equal. Becoming the orchestra's assistant conductor, he was also invited to teach at the Cleveland Institute of Music, where he seized the opportunity to found and direct the University Circle Orchestra.

Szell's death in 1970 brought an end to Levine's apprenticeship. By a stroke of luck, he was recruited to conduct the season's remaining performances of *Tosca* at the San Francisco Opera. This same year he inaugurated his international career with performances of *Aida* for the Welsh National Opera. Symphony orchestra guest appearances began to open up with engagements in Philadelphia, Chicago, Pittsburgh, Los Angeles, Cincinnati, Saint Louis, Toronto, Boston, Washington, and New York. The most significant of these was his Metropolitan Opera debut in 1971, where he again directed *Tosca*. As guest conductor the next season he was entrusted with *Otello*, *Rigoletto*, and *The Barber of Seville*. Two important events followed: the Met named him principal conductor (a specially created post under music director Raphael Kubelik) and he began a twenty-year association with the Chicago SO as director of the Ravinia Festival. He also returned to his native city for a four-year stint as director of the Cincinnati May Festival. Recordings of *Giovanna d'Arco*, *I Vespri Sicilani*, and performances of *Otello* at the Met confirmed his standing as a conductor of Italian opera, but he was soon branching out into Mozart and Strauss, adding *Wozzeck* to his roster in the 1974–75 season. In 1974 he was back in Europe for his Covent Garden debut, conducting *Der Rosenkavalier*. The omens were auspicious when he became music director of the Met in 1975. He was able to fill the vacuum left by the death of the autocratic general manager, Rudolf Bing, into whose shoes no one else had been able to step. He now had virtually a free hand to institute his own policies and procedures, which involved not only choosing repertoire, singers, producers, and guest conductors, but also overseeing all the additional trappings involved in producing a full season of opera. Above all it allowed him to mold and nurture the orchestra, with the result, so it is said, that audiences often attend the Met as much to hear it play as to hear and see the action on the stage! Levine's absorption into all aspects of the Met's life was recognized when, in 1985, he was designated artistic director. One of the tasks he set himself in leading the Met into the 1990s was to break away from the institution's conservative image by enhancing the repertoire with new and less-performed works. Responsible for the production of the first new work to be put on at the Met in over a quarter of a century during its centenary celebration in 1983 (Corigliano's *The Ghosts of Versailles*), he made further commitments to twentieth-century opera with productions of *Lulu, Capriccio, Moses und Aaron*, and *Susannah*, and operatic works by Poulenc, Stravinsky, Weill, Gershwin, Janáček, and Britten. To celebrate his twenty-fifth anniversary at the Met, he commissioned *The Great Gatsby* from John Harbison. Nor did he neglect the standard repertory. There have been three performances of the *Ring* cycle, a much-admired production of *Tristan*, and an economically strapped one of *The Trojans*, as well as important revivals of *Otello, Der Rosenkavalier*, and *The Tales of Hoffmann*. There have been commissions for composers Tan Dun and Tobias Picker. Over a thirty-year span it is difficult to think of any standard works in the operatic repertory that Levine has not conducted or scheduled at one time or another! While his achievements with the Met have been acknowledged, his work with the chorus and promoting singers, especially through the Young Artists Development Program, begun in 1980, should not be underestimated.

Because his career has been so centered at the Met, it is easy to overlook his achievements elsewhere. As guest conductor with the London SO he made his debut at the Salzburg Festival in 1975. The following year he was back to conduct *La Clemenza da Tito* in association with renowned producer Jean-Pierre Ponnelle, with whom he collaborated on a celebrated production of *Die Zauberflöte* in 1978. A long and fruitful relationship with the Bayreuth Festival was begun in 1982, where he has conducted *Ring* cycles and become particularly identified with *Parsifal*. Levine has been a guest conductor for many years with the Vienna PO, the Berlin PO, and, in more recent years, with the Philharmonia Orchestra and the Dresden Staatskapelle. These partnerships are well documented in a series of recordings that have elicited such superlatives as "exhilarating," "electric," "exquisite," and "supple, fleet and full of unexpected shapeliness" from the critics. In 1999, Levine accepted the post of chief conductor of the Munich PO, which improved significantly under his care. He relinquished this position in 2004 to become music director of the Boston SO, with which he had established a fruitful relationship over many years as a guest conductor.

Since he was perceived as being somewhat cocooned at the Met, there was much speculation as to how Levine would fare out in the open as music director of such a venerated institution as the BSO. Expectations were high, and he was definitely the players' pick to inspire them and lift them out of a period of underachievement. Additionally, he was expected to enliven the repertoire and enthuse the audience. Early on in his tenure it was clear that he was fulfilling such predictions, if not to everyone's liking. He programs contemporary works for which he feels a genuine commitment, regardless of how tough they are. Composers the likes of Elliott Carter and Charles Wuorinen are not easy to digest at first hearing, and it is part of Levine's trust that a cadre of composers he believes in will have its works repeated. There was nothing to cavil about in his mainstream repertoire performances; music by Haydn and Strauss was singled out for special accolades. Even more noticeable was the willingness shown by Levine to bond with the public through question-and-answer sessions at concerts, a weekly program note, and intermission commentaries on radio broadcasts. By the second season it was clear that he was pursuing his unique, if controversial, vision for the orchestra, and any drop in the number of subscriptions was offset by single-ticket sales to musical enthusiasts of various ilk, some new and others lapsed concertgoers. The end of the season was marred by an unfortunate onstage stumble after a performance of Beethoven's Ninth Symphony, which required rotator-cuff surgery and a three-month convalescence. On successfully recuperating, he was much in evidence at Tanglewood for almost a month, where his charisma was felt equally. His third season was colored by the revelation that he was the most handsomely remunerated of all American conductors, with an annual joint income from the Met and Boston at over $3 million. Whatever one may think of the ethics of such a distinction, commentators were beginning to speak of the Levine era in Boston as transformative—a great orchestra that "truly makes a difference." When he first accepted the post, the players agreed to extra rehearsal time to prepare for demanding programs. Dubbed the "Levine Premium," when the players negotiated a new contract in 2006, this provision was dropped. By this time, the orchestra had grown accustomed to Levine's methods and expectations, and he himself said the extra rehearsal time was no longer necessary. His ongoing vision was encapsulated by the bold juxtaposition of music by Schoenberg and Beethoven, which, in the context of their shared roles as musical trailblazers, made perfect sense. The concert performance of Schoenberg's incomplete opera *Moses und Aaron* gave the Boston audience its sternest test. Levine's injury had forced him to relinquish the orchestra's first tour of his tenure, but a new European venture was planned for the summer of 2007, with repertoire including music by Ives and Carter, two of the conductor's particular favorites. In 2006 the orchestra released its first recording of the present collaboration, Peter Lieberson's *Neruda Songs*, in a live performance sung by the composer's wife, the late-lamented Lorraine Hunt Lieberson.

Further Reading

Bernstein, Jamie. "A New Chapter: Looking Forward—and Back—with James Levine." *Symphony* 56 (May–June 2005): 18–24.

Hart, Philip. "James Levine." In *Conductors: A New Generation*, 221–66. New York: Charles Scribner's Sons, 1983.
Kellow, Brian. "A One-Man Band? (State of the Met)." *Opera* 55 (August 2004): 923–28.
Marsh, Robert C. *Dialogues and Discoveries: James Levine: His Life and His Music*. New York: Scribner, 1998.

Selected Recordings
Lieberson: *Neruda Songs*; Lorraine Hunt Lieberson (s); Boston SO. Nonesuch 79954.
Mozart: *Idomeneo*; Placido Domingo (t); Cecilia Bartoli (ms); Thomas Hampson (br); Heidi Grant Murphy (ms); Bryn Terfel (b-b); Carol Vaness (s); Frank Lopardo (t); Metropolitan Op O and Ch. Deutsche Grammophon DG447737.
Schoenberg: *Gurrelieder*; Deborah Voigt (*Tove*); Waltraud Meier (*Wood Dove*); Ben Heppner (*King Waldemar*); Eike Wilm Schulte (*Peasant*); Matthew Polenzani (*Klaus the Fool*); Ernst Haefliger (*Speaker*); Munich PO and Ch. Oehms OC 501.
A *Tribute to James Levine*: Leontyne Price (s); Renata Scotto (s); Margaret Price (s); Lorin Hollander (pf); Chicago SO. CSO From the Archives, Volume 18, CSO CD04. 1973–95 recordings from the Ravinia Festival.
Wagner: *Parsifal*; Waltraud Meier (*Kundry*); Siegfried Jerusalem (*Parsifal*); Kurt Moll (*Gurnemanz*); Bernd Weikl (*Amfortas*); Franz Mazura (*Klingsor*); Jan-Hendrik Rootering (*Titurel*); Metropolitan Op O and Ch. Deutsche Grammophon DG 440 073 032-9, live: New York 3/1992.

⌐

Levine, Joel
Born 26 June 1948 in Lakewood, New Jersey

Joel Levine grew up in a musical family, started taking piano lessons at an early age, and as a teenager played clarinet in the local civic orchestra. Yet he went to college at Rensselaer Polytechnic Institute, planning to become an electrical engineer. Even there, however, he conducted the school orchestra. After graduating from RPI, Levine went back to school as an undergraduate, this time at the Eastman School of Music. He majored in music theory and conducting, and graduated with honors in 1976.

Immediately upon graduation, he became conductor for the Maryland Ballet and music director and conductor for Oklahoma City's Lyric Theatre

Orchestra. In 1979, he was also named associate conductor of the Oklahoma
SO. Levine remained at the Lyric until 1990 and at the OSO until it dis-
banded in 1988. He helped found the Oklahoma Philharmonic Society to
create a replacement orchestra, becoming music director and conductor of
the new Oklahoma City PO. For those efforts he won the Governor's Arts
Award in 1989. Levine also was named Oklahoma Musician of the Year for
1992 by the Oklahoma Federation of Music Clubs.

Believing symphonic music can be interesting for almost everyone, Levine
talks to audiences to bring context to the music. He initiated a "Family Series" with music designed to entertain, educate, and introduce the whole
family to orchestral music. Each concert is preceded by an "instrument petting zoo." Levine and the OCPO offer youth concerts, play in varied venues,
and involve themselves in the community. He likes to create programs interesting not only to audiences, but also to the orchestra, which means combining the standard repertoire with rare and challenging selections. Levine
has worked with classical dancers throughout his career, as well as with other
guest artists from across the musical spectrum. Collaborating with choreog-
rapher Alvin Ailey, he conducted the Kansas City Ballet in the first contemporary performance of a "lost" Balanchine ballet, *Divertimento*.

He has been a guest on the podium with orchestras around the world, including the Brandenburg SO, Czech National SO, SO of Portugal, Mexico
City PO, and orchestras in Spain, Israel, and Bucharest. Across the country
he has led the National SO and the orchestras of Saint Louis, Detroit, Minneapolis, Baltimore, Indianapolis, Seattle, Denver, and New Orleans.

Further Reading
Gandy, Peggy. "Leader of the Band: Following Destiny's Lead; Philharmonic's
　Joel Levine Happy with Life, Career." *Daily Oklahoman*, 9 April 2000,
　Lifestyles 1.
Lackmeyer, Steve. "Philharmonic Conductor Credits Work, Luck, Timing."
　Oklahoman, 19 March 2006, Business 2D.

Selected Recordings
Gershwin: *Girl Crazy: I Got Rhythm*; Xalapa SO. From *Crazy for Gershwin*,
　Classics.
Hollywood Favorites; Xalapa SO. Hallmark Classics.
Oklahoma City Relief: A Time of Healing; Oklahoma City PO. Warner
　Bros/WEA.

Ling, Jahja (Wang-Chieh)
Born 25 October 1951 in Jakarta, Indonesia

In the search for a music director, what superhuman qualities are orchestras looking for? Recently, the San Diego (Calif.) SO sought a music director who would: inspire musicians and impart artistic vision; have immediate rapport with the players; possess a significant knowledge of broad repertoire; provide professional leadership; exhibit a strong stage presence; and devise imaginative programming. Considered highly accomplished in all of these categories, Ling was the successful candidate. On hearing of Ling's appointment, his former mentor, Christoph von **Dohnanyi**, was quoted as saying: "He is not only one of the best trained conductors in this country, but also a truly remarkable person—he has a wonderful character, is a great human being, and is a phenomenally musical individual." Best trained, certainly: he was a piano prodigy in his native Indonesia, and a conducting student of John **Nelson** and Otto-Werner Mueller at Juilliard and Yale, respectively. He also came under the tutelage of Leonard Bernstein, first as a conducting student at Tanglewood and later as a conducting fellow at the Los Angeles Philharmonic Institute. Moving north, he was "arguably the most successful of all the conducting assistants" the San Francisco SO ever had. From there he moved on to Cleveland, first as an assistant conductor and then, for a remarkable seventeen years, as its resident conductor under Christoph von **Dohnanyi** and Franz **Welser-Möst**. He served as director of the orchestra's summer season at the Blossom Music Festival for six years, led the Florida Orchestra in Tampa for twelve years, and served as music director of the National SO of Taiwan.

In an August 1994 piece in the *Los Angeles Times*, critic Martin Bernheimer wondered whether Ling was "a bona fide personality conductor or just a tasteful stylist and a highly competent technician." In response, one can list those qualities which are frequently used to describe his performances: energetic, passionate, intense, expressive, stylish, and meticulous, including readings that are propulsive and fastidious. His podium style is demonstrative with athletic gestures and an abundance of cues amounting almost to fussiness. Faithful to the score, he achieves clarity through careful balance, crisp articulation, and considered pacing. On the other hand, in a review of a 1999 Hollywood Bowl performance with the Los Angeles PO, a critic complimented the conductor for "knowing when to leave music alone and when to let the orchestra do its best without meddling." None of these comments, complimentary as they are, necessarily takes him into the "bona fide personality" category, however. Ling's other attributes? He is extremely well liked by his colleagues and associates, and, because he is invariably polite and respectful, even seasoned members of the Cleveland Orchestra regard him with affection. His industriousness, his evangelizing zeal for classical music, the patience he has shown working with youth orchestras over the years, his determination to firmly, if gently, promulgate new music, his evident modesty, and his honest self-awareness are virtues that earn respect. In addition, he has a reputation as an effective organizer and an able administrator. To all of his enterprises he brings a remarkable degree of commitment: "I want to go wherever I can make a difference. I try my best to make the greatest music I can."

Ling began to play the piano at the age of four, displaying such a remarkable aptitude that, as a seventeen-year-old high school student, he was the 1978 winner of Indonesia's national piano competition. It is said that his piano teacher in Jakarta strongly dissuaded him when he expressed some early interest in becoming a conductor, considering it would divert his concentration from becoming a concert pianist. Having received a Rockefeller Grant, Ling came to the U.S. to study piano with Mieczyslaw Munz and Beveridge Webster at Juilliard. A devout Christian, he took a position as organist/choir master at a Chinese American church in New York City and enrolled in John **Nelson**'s conducting class to better his choir-directing skills. He received his BM degree in 1974 and his MM degree the following year. Pursuing a career as a pianist, he won a Bronze Medal at the Artur Rubinstein International Piano Competition in 1977 and came away from the Tchaikovsky Competition in Moscow with a certificate of honor a year later. However, **Nelson** had detected well-above-average potential in his student and encouraged him to apply to the graduate conducting program at Yale. He graduated from there with a DMA degree in the spring of 1980, and the following summer he was awarded a conducting fellowship at Tanglewood, where Bernstein became his most influential mentor. During his early years there he also received coaching from Seiji **Ozawa**, Colin Davis, André **Previn**, Gunther Schuller, and Joseph Silverstein. In 1982 he won a fellowship for further study with Bernstein at the Los Angeles Philharmonic Institute. He began his tenure as assistant conductor in San Francisco in 1981, and it was there that he began working intensively with youth orchestras and founded the San Francisco YSO. Promoted to associate conductor in 1983, he also worked with the San Francisco Conservatory Orchestra and the Tanglewood Young Artists Orchestra. His genuine interest in working with young musicians paid off in terms of his career when his work with the SFYSO was heard by Kurt **Masur**, leading to an invitation to make his European debut with the Leipzig

Gewandhaus Orchestra (1988), and by Christoph von **Dohnanyi**, at whose instigation he became associate conductor of the Cleveland Orchestra. Shortly after taking up this post, he founded the Cleveland Orchestra's youth orchestra. He has continued to nurture youthful talent by working with, among others, the Aspen Music Festival Orchestra, the orchestras of the Curtis Institute and the Juilliard School, and the National Orchestral Institute Philharmonic based in College Park (Md.). He was the recipient of a Seaver/NEA Conductors Award in 1998. Seeking his first directorship, he was unsuccessful in New Haven (Conn.) (1987) and San Diego (Calif.) (1988), but was appointed to the Florida Orchestra in Tampa in 1988.

In a highly competitive field with many excellent candidates chasing fewer jobs, Ling must have been pleased to have secured the Tampa position, but he must also have known he was facing a stiff challenge. During its twenty-one years of existence the orchestra had been run in a hand-to-mouth fashion, acquiring a hefty deficit along the way. This weight of debt become so critical during the 1990–91 season that visiting English conductor Christopher Hogwood suggested that the orchestra reconstitute at half the size as a chamber ensemble. The situation further deteriorated such that conflict with management led the musicians to file a grievance with the National Labor Relations Board for breach of contract. The organization faced regular financial crunches, including one in 1994 in which it was bailed out by no less a personage than New York Yankees owner George Steinbrenner, a Tampa resident. The later 1990s saw a little more stability, but the orchestra suffered the indignity of being frequently bumped out of its principal venue, the Marsoni Auditorium, by commercially viable touring groups such as *The Phantom of the Opera*. By the time of Ling's valedictory season (2001–2), the orchestra was once again finding it hard to make ends meet. And yet, throughout his tenure, he managed to stay aloof from such mundane distractions to achieve remarkably high artistic standards. Nor did he skimp on the repertory, which regularly included such heavyweights as Bruckner and Mahler, when the temptation must have been to stack it with potboilers to attract a crowd. From the outset he molded the ensemble into a tighter, more cohesive whole that compared favorably with any in its peer group of regional orchestras. Although community support for the arts in the Tampa Bay area tends to be lukewarm, those who attended Ling's concerts were treated to performances of power, focus, and refinement. But having battled for twelve years (1990–2002), he knew when it was time to move on, both for his own and the orchestra's sake. In appreciation of his unstinting service, he was appointed conductor laureate.

In view of his experiences in Florida, one might have looked askance at Ling's acceptance of the music directorship of the San Diego SO in 2004, which itself had emerged from bankruptcy just six years earlier. In fact, he was taking on a very different situation, thanks to the intervention of fairy godparents in the persons of Qualcomm mogul Irwin Jacobs and his wife Joan, who had donated a record $120 million under conditions of strict fiduciary responsibility to build the orchestra's endowment and ensure its day-to-day running. In light of this rosy financial prospect and the niche the orchestra had carved out for itself in the community, Ling was willing to cut his eighteen-year ties with the Cleveland Orchestra to make San Diego and the development of its orchestra his main focus. Although he had spent his Cleveland years in a subsidiary role, this had amounted to several hundred performances and a warm relationship with the players. He had been given free rein as director of the Blossom Festival, where, for six summer seasons, he had nurtured the orchestra's spirit and produced performances of a consistently high standard in a setting of idyllic parkland that has been referred to as "music's best kept secret." His intimate knowledge and experience of what made the "Big Five" Ohio orchestra tick served to shape his ambitions for his new orchestra.

Throughout his career, Ling has been a sterling champion of new music. For his 2004–5 season in San Diego he programmed a contemporary score in five out of his ten subscription concerts, including premieres by Augusta Read Thomas and Inouk Demers. The other composers represented were John Corigliano, Peter Maxwell Davies, and Marc-André Dalbavie. He made his New York PO debut in 1993 (taking over from Kurt **Masur**, who was ill) in a program that included the first performance of Ellen Taaffe Zwilich's Third Symphony. Over the years he has led premieres by Gordon Getty, James Horner, William Bolcom, George Perle, Alvin Singleton, and Mark Anthony Turnage, and he has programmed works by, among others, Bernard Rands, Olly Wilson, Tobias Picker, Lou Harrison, Stephen Albert, Peter Lieberson, Libby Larsen, Lowell Liebermann, and Mark O'Connor. He has also fostered the work of earlier generations of American composers: Bernstein, naturally, but also William Schuman and Charles Ives. Of mainstream composers, he has shown a special affinity for the music of Gustav Mahler. He presented a cycle of his symphonies in Tampa and intends to do the same in San Diego. Indeed, it was his "audition" performance in 2003 of Mahler's Fifth Symphony that clinched his latest appointment.

As a guest artist, Ling can claim a long list of appearances. In North America he has led over twenty of the leading orchestras (including the "Big Five"), from Atlanta to Vancouver. In Germany, in addition to frequent returns to the Gewandhaus, he has led the radio orchestras of Hamburg, Hannover, Berlin, and Leipzig, and the Bochum SO. Elsewhere in Europe he has conducted the Netherlands RSO, Toulouse Capitol Orchestra, Stockholm PO, Royal PO, and Scottish CO (which he led on tour to Hong Kong in 1997). In Asia he has given concerts with the Singapore SO, Malaysian PO, Shanghai SO, Yomuri Nippon Orchestra of Tokyo, China Broadcasting SO, and the Sydney SO in Australia. He has not had the opportunity to record extensively but intends to do so with his San Diego orchestra. For Telarc he recorded Dupré's *Organ Symphony* and the First Organ Concerto by Rheinberger with Michael Murray and the Royal PO (1987). He made recordings of Baroque music with the Scottish CO, featuring trumpeter Rolf Smedvig (1993). The Continuum label issued a recording of music by Stephen Montague including the Florida Orchestra's performance of *From the White Edge of Phrygia* with Ling conducting (1994). The same forces put out a disc of symphonic dances (by Bernstein, Richard Strauss, and Ravel) on the Azica label (1998). From their archives, the NYPO has made available the live recording of the premiere of Zwilich's Third Symphony, and the Cleveland Orchestra issued Ling's performance of Saint-Saëns's "Organ" Symphony commemorating the rededication of the Norton Memorial Organ in Severance Hall. Ling continues to appear occasionally as a solo pianist with orchestra and in chamber music. He played concertos by Grieg and Beethoven with the Florida Orchestra. His piano playing, like his conducting, displays energy and clarity.

In 1998, just a few days after his first wife died tragically of cancer, Ling conducted a performance of Beethoven's *Eroica Symphony* with the Cleveland Orchestra that Donald Rosenberg, music critic for the *Cleveland Plain Dealer*, called "intensely realized . . . something of a miracle." He went on to say: "The orchestra responded to Ling's leadership as they do to few others, which says volumes for the resident conductor's ability to bond with musicians even as he bonds with Beethoven." Is this enough to answer Martin Bernheimer's question?

Further Reading
Marum, Lisa. "Jahja Ling, Conductor." *Ovation* 9 (May 1988): 50.

Selected Recordings
Dupré: *Symphony for Organ and Orchestra in G minor*. Rheinberger: *Concerto for Organ no. 1 in F major*; Thomas Murray (org); Royal PO. Telarc 80136.
Haydn: *Concerto for Trumpet in E♭ major, H 7e no. 1*. Tartini: *Concerto for Trumpet in D major*. Hummel: *Concerto for Trumpet in E♭ major, S 49/WoO*

1. Torelli: Concerto for Trumpet in D major. Bellini: Concerto for Oboe in E♭ major (arr.); Rolf Smedvig (tp); Scottish CO. Telarc 80232.

∽

Litton, Andrew
Born 16 May 1959 in New York, New York

With his boyish good looks and a privileged background—he attended the elite private Fieldston School in the Bronx—it is perhaps somewhat surprising that Litton's attitude toward the suzerain world of conducting should be so democratic! Trained as a pianist, he has never been an orchestral player, although he spent many hours as a teenager sitting at the back of the Metropolitan Opera Orchestra pit during rehearsals and performances, observing how players think and react. He regards his players as his equals but, despite his amiable personality and natural desire to make the hard work of rehearsing pleasant, he is not a person of whom orchestral players would try to take advantage. With his acute musical insights he merits too much respect for that, and he commands a sufficiently expressive and efficient baton technique to dispense with unnecessary verbiage in rehearsal, an ability much appreciated by hardened professionals. From his remarkable early success, his career has flourished because he has always been able to draw the best out of his players and produce dynamic performances that audiences find exhilarating.

Litton's parents were both musical, and he was encouraged to learn the piano at an early age; lessons on cello and violin were added soon afterward. At the age of ten his main enthusiasms in life were fire trucks and music. It was one of Leonard Bernstein's Young People's Concerts that included a performance of Respighi's *The Pines of Rome* which planted the seed of his conducting ambitions and gave music an edge over fire trucks. He was fortunate that his godfather was the timpanist of the Met Orchestra and could allow him to sit in on many productions and observe many conductors at work. However, he pursued his studies as a pianist and entered Juilliard as a student of Nadia Reisenberg. He gave his Carnegie Hall debut recital in 1979 and appeared as soloist in *Rhapsody in Blue* with the USSR SO in Moscow in 1980 while still a student. After graduating with a bachelor's degree, he spent a year in Milan as a *repetiteur* at La Scala. When he returned to Juilliard to work on a master's degree, he studied conducting with Sixten Ehrling and later received lessons from Walter Weller in Salzburg (as a recipient of the Bruno Walter Scholarship), Neeme **Järvi** in Hilversum, and Edoardo Müller in Milan. Then, "on a lark," he entered the 1982 BBC/Rupert Foundation International Conductors Competition and won. This led to an engagement with the BBC SO shortly afterward and an invitation to work with the Royal PO the following year.

In the meantime, his early success was marked in America by the award of an Exxon/Arts Endowment Scholarship and an invitation from Mstislav Rostropovich to become an assistant conductor of the National SO. This also gave him the opportunity for guest appearances elsewhere, including his first appearance with the Bournemouth SO and at the Minnesota Orchestra's Sommerfest in 1984—two events which augured well for the future. Although many of his duties as a National SO apprentice were mundane, there was always the possibility of being called on to fill in for a late indisposition, as in fact happened when he took over a program from Rostropovich that included Schubert's *Great C Major Symphony*. Not surprisingly, the program for his scheduled NSO debut concert included, in addition to Weber's *Euryanthe Overture* and the MacDowell Piano Concerto, Respighi's *Pines of Rome*. During this period he was also principal conductor of the Virginia CO and the Chappaqua (N.Y.) SO. In 1985 he was promoted to associate conductor of the National SO, and, after a second successful guest appearance, he accepted the role of principal guest conductor of the Bournemouth SO (1986). He returned to Moscow in 1987, this time to conduct the USSR SO in an uncut version of Rachmaninoff's Symphony no. 2. By the time he accepted the appointment as the youngest—and the first American—principal conductor and artistic adviser of the Bournemouth SO, he had already appeared with the Scottish National Orchestra, English CO, Royal Liverpool PO, Orchestre National de France, and RAI Milan Orchestra.

Litton's years with the Bournemouth SO were exceptionally fruitful. The orchestra is regarded as the "country cousin" of British orchestras and its unique role as a regional West of England orchestra means it plays at a number of regular venues throughout the region, involving the players in an inordinate amount of travel. It tends to have an older and more conservative following than the orchestras based in London and the larger cities. The orchestra can boast some distinguished music directors in its past—Constantin Silvestri, Paavo Berglund, and Sir Charles Groves—but Litton's appointment proved singularly auspicious and mutually beneficial. It was an opportunity for him to consolidate his reputation and establish his credentials as a demanding orchestral trainer. It was also a learning experience that rejuvenated the orchestra, exploited its versatility, and elevated its artistic standards. Together the orchestra and conductor's energy and commitment engendered loyalty from the audiences, which, in turn, allowed Litton to

expand the repertoire, especially to include more music by American composers such as Bernstein, Copland, and Barber. Litton was a convincing interpreter of British music and called upon his specialties of Russian and late
romantic music in general. His success is verified by comments such as those
made by the *Observer* in 1991, "Morale is high . . . the band is in very good
shape . . . due to the invigorating presence . . . of Litton," and by a recorded
legacy which includes Walton's orchestral music, a cycle of Tchaikovsky and
Rachmaninoff symphonies, and symphonies by Copland and Harris. The
partnership culminated in the U.S. tour of 1994, after which Litton moved
to Dallas, but he continues to maintain a close association with the
Bournemouth orchestra as its conductor laureate.

During the Bournemouth period Litton ventured into the field of operatic
conducting. At the Met he conducted *Eugene Onegin* (while suffering from
appendicitis!), made his Covent Garden debut with *Porgy and Bess*, and appeared at the English National Opera with *Falstaff* and *Salome*. He conducted
Donizetti's *Rita* in Milan and Offenbach's *La Périchole* in San Diego.

When Litton took over as conductor of the Dallas (Tex.) SO, he found
himself in a situation similar to the one in Bournemouth: leading a good orchestra in need of the self-confidence to upgrade its "hick" image. But
whereas the Bournemouth orchestra existed on a shoestring, Dallas had the
advantage of solid financial support and a modern, purpose-built auditorium
(the Meyerson Center, opened in 1989). As one of the few Americans leading a U.S. orchestra, Litton set as one of his main goals the raising of its profile at home and abroad. To succeed, he needed to maintain and improve the
standard of playing through training orchestra members (rehearsal and repertoire), replacing weaker players, and retaining the best of the existing ones.
(Over a six-year period there were twenty new hires.) A second priority was
securing a financially solid home base through ticket sales and endowments.
A third was to bolster the orchestra's profile within the community by making the programs appealing to a more diverse audience through the introduction of "Family Concerts" and other educational endeavors. The first few
seasons realized the hoped-for expansion, with five thousand new subscriptions for the 1995–96 season and many younger faces in the audience. Even
when the economic downturn hit, the orchestra seemed to weather it better
than most. A reported operating deficit of $847,000 in 2002 was reduced to
a fraction of that amount the following year. Improved media coverage including an innovative educational series, "Amazing Music," which combined
music and animation to introduce children to the classics for the A&E net-
work, and the orchestra's annual residency at Vail (Colo.) increased its exposure. The fine acoustics of the Meyerson Center played a significant role

in developing the orchestra's sound but proved less than ideal for recording. Fortunately, the Delos company was able to deploy its Virtual Reality Recording (VR2) technology to produce results that closely resembled the live sound. One of the first successes was a "breathtaking version" of the *1812 Overture*. In truth, it is in this "high romantic" repertoire that Litton excels, and cycles of Tchaikovsky, Shostakovich, and Mahler have comprised the bulk of his recorded output of over twenty sessions with the DSO. His collaborative approach has produced the distinctive, less inhibited quality of orchestral sound he wanted. The orchestra made four trips to Carnegie Hall to convince the New York critics of its worth and embarked on three world tours, each one commanding better venues and more appreciative audiences. The downside of touring is having to adjust quickly to unfamiliar playing conditions, often resulting in less flattering facets of performance upon which foreign critics are quick to comment—"neat and noisy" was one critic's quip. Some suspect that Litton has had it a little too easy during his Dallas years, and that he has become almost complacent by relying on a core of sure-fire blockbusters (Masters of the Romantic Era was the theme for the 2002–3 season). This may hurt his chances of leading one of the big-fish orchestras in the future. However, he has made a real effort to broaden the fare on offer by programming three to five premieres each season and championing English and American music. His decision not to renew his contract after the 2005–6 season but to become director emeritus suggests that, after twelve years, he realizes the danger of outwearing his welcome. Among his stated reasons for leaving is a wish to concentrate on other interests: to conduct more opera, develop more television shows for children along the lines of *Amazing Music*, and take up more guest appearances. Other activities during his period in Dallas have included the directorship of the Minnesota Orchestra's Sommerfest (2003–5), a highly controversial *Porgy and Bess* at the 1997 Bregenz Festival, a *Rigoletto* (2001) for Dallas Opera, and a return to the English National Opera for performances of *A Masked Ball*. Having served as principal conductor of the Bergen PO in Norway since 2004, he was appointed to be its next music director, effective 2008–9.

"Exuberant," "exciting," and "electrifying" are just three of the adjectives that have frequently been used to describe Litton's performances. His dynamism is based on solid musical grounds. He aspires no less than "to achieve the greatest possible artistic ends" and in this quest he commands a clear, uncomplicated conducting technique that conveys almost all of the expressive elements of the music without ostentatious display or gratuitous virtuosity. He is particularly committed to being faithful to the score and striving to get to the heart of the music. Another distinguishing feature is his attention to textural concerns: translucence and the clarity of inner voices. Balance, breathed phrasing, rhythmic vitality, and structural unity also contribute to his performances' sense of refreshing and compelling conviction. Although he has performed and recorded extensively, he recognizes that no interpretation is ever definitive: "There's always something you missed the first time." And even the best conductors have their off days, as when one disappointed London critic found the overall result to be "a touch underwhelming." Sensitive to the particular context of performances, he chooses repertoire that seeks to balance the familiar and unfamiliar, understanding that theme and contrast can both be used to create effective programs.

Website
http://www.andrewlitton.com/

Further Reading
Haverstock, Gwendolyn. "An Interview with Andrew Litton." *Fanfare* 12, no. 1 (1988): 444–46.
Jolly, James. "Orchestra as Moral Force." *Gramophone* 78 (June 2000): 17.
Rabinowitz, Peter J. "'Without Conviction, It's Going to Be Worthless': Stephen Hough and Andrew Litton Record the Rachmaninoff Concertos." *Fanfare* 28 (September–October 2004): 28–30.
Scherer, Barrymore Laurence. "Andrew Litton." *Gramophone*: 66 (April 1989): 1566–67.
Stearns, David Patrick. "Andrew Litton." *High Fidelity/Musical America Edition* 34 (July 1984): 4–5.

Selected Recordings
Brahms: *Piano Concerto no. 2 in B♭; Pieces (4) for Piano*, Op. 119; Marc-André Hamelin (pf); Dallas SO. Hyperion 67550.
Mahler: *Symphony no. 4*; Ann Murray (s); Royal PO. Virgin 63277.
Rachmaninoff: *Piano Concertos 1–3*; Stephen Hough; Dallas SO. Hyperion 67501/2.
Tchaikovsky: *1812 Overture; Voyevoda; Moscow; Sleeping Beauty Suite*; Vassily Gerelo (br), Svetlana Furdui (ms) Dallas SO. Delos 3196.
Walton: *Symphony no. 2; Violin Concerto; Scapino Overture*; Tasmin Little (vn); Bournemouth SO. Decca 444114.

Llewellyn, Grant

Born 29 December 1960 in Tenby, Wales

Grant Llewellyn grew up in a family that sang everything from Welsh hymns to rugby songs. At the age of eleven, he entered Chetham's School of Music in Manchester, where he studied cello and piano. After graduating in 1979, he went to study cello for a year in Perugia, Italy, at the Conservatorio di Francesco Morlacchi, earning money for living expenses through the unusual route of playing semiprofessional soccer. Returning to England to enroll as a choral scholar at Cambridge University (1980–83), Llewellyn began to pursue conducting. He went on to study conducting with Norman del Mar at the Royal College of Music in London, winning the Tagore Gold Medal in 1984. The following year he won a conducting fellowship at the Tanglewood Music Center, giving him the opportunity to work with Leonard Bernstein, Seiji **Ozawa**, Kurt **Masur**, and André **Previn**. In 1986 he won first prize in the Leeds Conductors' Competition.

After numerous guest appearances in the U.S. and Europe, Llewellyn accepted two positions in 1990, assistant conductor for the Boston SO and associate guest conductor for the BBC National Orchestra of Wales. In 1993, he completed his term with the BSO and began a three-year stint with the Stavanger (Norway) SO as principal guest conductor. From 1995 to 1998 he was also principal conductor for the Royal Flanders PO. Llewellyn returned to Boston in 2001 to become music director and principal conductor for the Handel and Haydn Society. He remains principal conductor, though gave up the post of music director in 2006. To great local acclaim and excitement, Llewellyn became music director of the North Carolina SO in 2004.

Called magnetic, assured, engaging, charming, and passionate, Llewellyn conducts with confidence and visible joy. He provides humorous commentary for concert audiences, sometimes quoting from period reviews and historical documents. Though he has earned a reputation as a formidable interpreter of Baroque and classical music, he challenges orchestras and audiences alike with unconventional programming, even devoting whole concerts to twentieth- and twenty-first-century music. Indeed, he and the NCSO won an ASCAP award for programming of contemporary music in 2006. Llewellyn says there is nothing worse than a safe performance, preferring risk to comfort and security. He values a smooth, integrated sound, and under Llewellyn's leadership the orchestra's playing is frequently described as crisp, precise, elegant, rich, full, and well-balanced.

Some of his practices include physically rearranging the orchestra to max-
imize blend and asking certain players to stand or lift up their instruments
during major passages. He has held public signing sessions for recordings,
taken the orchestra all over the state, and participated in intermission interviews during live local radio broadcasts of concerts. He enjoys getting young
people involved in music, directing singers of all ages, and the challenge of
conducting opera, which he calls the ultimate music-making experience. His
outreach appears to have benefitted not only the NCSO's image, but also its
bottom line; ticket sales have risen since he arrived and a budget deficit has
disappeared. Llewellyn recently signed a contract extended through 2012,
saying he would like to attract and keep additional top-class players for the
orchestra, and he still has broadcasting, recording, and touring on his larger
agenda.

Llewellyn's guest engagements include, among others, the Frankfurt RSO,
SWR SO Stuttgart, Helsinki PO, Boston SO, Calgary PO, Colorado SO,
Florida Orchestra, Houston SO, Montreal SO, Milwaukee SO, Saint Louis
SO, and Toronto SO. In the UK, he has appeared with the Hallé Orchestra,
City of Birmingham SO, and Royal Liverpool PO, and retains close links
with the BBC SO and BBC National Orchestra of Wales.

Further Reading
Waleson, Heidi. "Handel & Haydn Maps Out a New Era." *Early Music America* 7 (Winter 2001–2): 18–21, 42–43.

Selected Recordings
American Trombone Concertos, Vol. 2; music by Rouse, Chávez, Thomas;
Christian Lindberg (tb); BBC Nat'l O of Wales. BIS-CD-788.
Coleridge-Taylor: *Ballade for Orchestra in A minor*, Op. 33; *Symphonic Varia-
tions on an African Air*, Op. 63. Butterworth: *English Idylls (nos. 1 and 2)*; *A
Shropshire Lad*; *Banks of Green Willow*. MacCunn: *Land of the Mountain and
the Flood*; Royal Liverpool PO. Decca 436401.
Mathias: *Symphony no. 3*; *Oboe Concerto*; BBC Nat'l O of Wales. Nimbus NI
5343.
Peace; music by Barber, Delius, Elgar, Górecki, Lauridsen, Rachmaninoff,
Schoenberg, Tavener, Thompson, Victoria; Handel and Haydn Society O
and Ch. Avie 39.
Ryelandt: *Agnus Dei*, Op. 56; Ingrid Kapelle (s); Lucienne Van Deyck (ms);
Joseph Cornwell (t); Hubert Claessens (b), Stephan Macleod (b); Au-
dite Nova Vocal Ensemble; Flanders PO; Altra Voce Choir. Marco Polo
223785.

Lockhart, Keith
Born 7 November 1959 in Poughkeepsie, New York

There was a great deal of hype following the appointment of the relatively unknown Lockhart to lead the Boston Pops Orchestra, one of the most exposed conducting posts in the nation. To mitigate the risk, the publicity machine went into high gear to exploit his good looks and debonair manner with countless articles, interviews, and posters. Fortunately, an inherent flair for showmanship and his solid musicianship made Lockhart an inspired choice—not only to handle all the brouhaha but also to be a success on the podium, able to maintain and enhance the eminence of the Pops organization. In the decade following his appointment in 1995 he has conducted the Pops and Esplanade orchestras in over 150 concerts and sixty television appearances, recorded eight albums (including two that won prestigious awards), and led twenty-five national and international tours. Peak media exposure was achieved when the orchestra took part in the Super Bowl XXXVI extravaganza in New Orleans (La.) (2002).

Lockhart is fortunate to possess a number of qualities that have enabled him to preserve his spontaneity and integrity as both a media personality and a serious musician. To maintain a balance with Pops, he has always kept a second appointment to pursue more serious musical endeavors, first with the Cincinnati (Ohio) CO and then, since 1998, as music director of the Utah SO. In his approach to the Pops he has successfully combined a non-elitist proselytizing zeal for orchestral music with a natural bent for entertainment. He campaigns vociferously for music both on and off the podium and shamelessly uses his position as a bully pulpit to advocate support for arts organizations and arts education. He believes that all of classical music is entertainment in competition with other activities, and will not hesitate to indulge in pranks and gimmicks (which he undoubtedly enjoys) if they serve the purpose of attracting a larger, "younger, and hipper crowd" to concerts. He enjoys celebrity but manages to keep it in perspective and uses it to further the conductor's role as intermediary between the audience and the music. The danger here, of course, is overemphasizing the visual element to concerts (which has always been a part of the enjoyment) in what is certainly the least visual of activities in the entertainment spectrum. While applauding his aim to humanize and democratize concert going and break down its stereotype as a preserve of the "enfranchised, moneyed, and educated," some observers see the risk of exchanging one formulaic format with another that is equally prosaic. For the most part Lockhart has avoided this trap by preserving a healthy set of musical convictions. Thus, his approach to concert planning and rejuvenation has been to build on the Pops's one-hundred-year tradition by introducing change in small increments and making the traditional tripartite program formula more thematic and integrated. Realizing early on that the novelty and glitz surrounding his appointment were bound to fade, he has done well to maintain high standards in a situation that could easily have turned stale. Critics for the most part have avoided the temptation to be condescending, appreciating the sterling qualities of his music-making. There have been the occasional cavils, naturally, one critic going so far as to describe the 1999 *Holiday at Pops* concert as "a nadir of the commercial, tasteless, and slipshod."

Lockhart was born to music-loving parents, both IBM-ers, and when their son showed musical promise, they were supportive but not fanatically so. He was fortunate, from the age of seven, to have a particularly gifted piano teacher who, over the succeeding years, was able to engage and focus the sometimes wayward activities of a normal, healthy child. He played clarinet in his state-renowned high school band and, as its assistant conductor, began to demonstrate a natural aptitude, also conducting student performances of *Babes in Arms* and *The Pajama Game*. He attended Furman University in South Carolina (1977–81), pursuing studies in German and piano performance, and graduating summa cum laude. More significantly, he spent his junior year (1979–80) at the Hochschule für Musik in Vienna and attended the intermediate conducting class at the Aspen Festival the following summer. On the advice of Otto-Werner Mueller he enrolled in graduate school at Carnegie-Mellon University, studying conducting with Istvan Jaray and Werner Torkanowsky. Among his student assignments were directing performances of *The Mikado* and *Die Fledermaus*. During the summers he enrolled in the American Symphony Orchestra League's workshops in Morgantown (W.Va.). Graduating with an MFA in orchestral conducting (1983), he was immediately appointed to the music faculty at Carnegie-Mellon, where he remained for the next six years. During this period he was music director of the Pittsburgh Civic Orchestra (1985–90), attended master classes of the Dutch RSO in Hilversum, and was appointed assistant conductor of the Akron (Ohio) SO under Alan Balter. He conducted the Akron YSO and was a part-time faculty member in the Akron School of Music. His big break came with the appointment as "general dogsbody" to the Cincinnati (Ohio) SO in 1990, serving for two years as assistant to López-Cobos, then as associate conductor (1992–95), when his musical evangelizing introduced the concept of "Casual Concerts." His duties also included conducting the youth orchestra and serving for a year as artistic director of education and outreach (1995–96). But his most significant activity in Cincinnati proved to be his work with the Pops orchestra. Its conductor, Erich Kunzel, became a crucial mentor who encouraged his development and versatility. Another important aspect of the Cincinnati years was his work with the chamber orchestra, emphasizing the serious side to his conducting. During his seven-year tenure (1992–99) his programming proved a judicious blend of the familiar (lots of Haydn and Mozart) and the innovative: Joel Hoffman's *Self-Portrait with Gebertig*, for example. It was the reputation he built as a "crossover-guy" and his five years of solid work building up nontraditional audiences in Cincinnati, together with the fact that he had clearly impressed in Boston as a guest conductor, which recommended him for the Boston Pops job.

Some of the earliest reviews comment on Lockhart's sensitivity as an accompanist and praise his snappy, lively conducting as particularly suited to "loose-limbed American idioms." Kunzel likened his progress in Cincinnati to the growth of a sunflower, "quick and bright," and, removed from the intense media scrutiny in the geographically removed location of Utah, he imbued performances of major works by Strauss, Mahler, and Verdi with an expressiveness ranging from "heightened drama" and "restless tension" to "sculpted phrases with warm musicality." While his Pops experience had given him a mastery of diverse styles and quick-change acts, it has also given him the ability to handle the huge forces needed for, say, Mahler's Eighth Symphony. Yet what often appealed to audiences most were this composer's smaller, more intimate moments, as, for example, his performance of the slow movement of the Sixth Symphony. Indeed, one should not underestimate the quality of the well-rounded Utah orchestra; Lockhart was able to lead it on a successful European tour in 2003, even though it is the smallest of the country's full-time symphonic ensembles. However, it was not all that surprising to learn that he intends to step down from this post at the end of the 2008–9 season, citing a desire to spend more time with his family and to accept more guest appearances, especially in Europe. He has ventured infrequently but successfully into the opera house, conducting the *The Ballad of Baby Doe* for the Washington National Opera in 1997 with "marvelous sweep and flexibility," and *Tosca* for the Boston Lyric Opera in 2004, where, while not stinting on the blood and thunder, he "lavished unusual care on the lyrical moments." He was also engaged to lead Britten's *Midsummer Night's Dream* and Berg's *Wozzeck* with Utah Opera. In addition to dovetailing his duties in Cincinnati, Boston, and Salt Lake City, he has also appeared as a guest conductor with the Chicago SO, New York PO, Cleveland Orchestra, Philadelphia Orchestra, Saint Louis SO, Minnesota Orchestra,

Indianapolis SO, Houston SO, Dallas SO, and Milwaukee SO, among others, and abroad in Berlin, Amsterdam, Canada, Singapore, and Argentina.

Website
http://www.keithlockhart.com

Further Reading
Mahlmann, J. J. "Keith Lockhart on Reaching Audiences." *Music Educators Journal* 84 (September 1997): 38–40.
Lockhart, Keith. "Address to National Press Club Luncheon." Federal News Service transcript, 24 January 1996.
Lockhart, Keith. "Conversation: Responsibility Junkie (interview)." *Harvard Business Review* 84 (October 2006): 30.
Passy, Charles. "New Day at the Pops." *Symphony* 46, no. 6 (1995): 22–24.

Selected Recordings
Bernstein: *West Side Story*; *Symphonic Dances*. Frank (Gabriela): *Latin American Dances*. Rachmaninoff: *Symphonic Dances*; Utah SO. Reference RR-105.
Encore!; music by John Philip Sousa, Ferde Grofé, et al.; Boston Pops O. RCA 63662.
Sapp: *The Four Reasons*; *Imaginary Creatures*; *The Women of Trachis*; Eiji Hashimoto (harpsichord); Cincinnati CO. CRI 765.
Sleigh Ride; music by Leroy Anderson, Handel, et al.; Tanglewood Festival Ch, Boston Pops O. Boston Pops Records 4.

～

Lockington, David (Kirkman)
Born 11 October 1956 in Dartford, England

David Lockington received his first cello at age ten and within three years was playing in the National Youth Orchestra. His musical heritage includes a father who played cello, organized a youth orchestra, and directed choral societies; an uncle who led an orchestral and choral society; an aunt who was a violin prodigy; and a brother with whom he played in their father's youth orchestra. While at Cambridge University, where he earned a BA in music (1978), Lockington was a choral scholar and got his conducting start with the university's Purcell Society. Winning a scholarship, he came to the U.S. after graduation to attend Yale University, where he earned a master's degree in cello performance (1981), studied conducting with Otto-Werner Mueller, and played in the New Haven (Conn.) SO. In his second year, he won the Yale School of Music's concerto competition.

Upon graduation Lockington won the post of assistant principal cellist in the Denver (Colo.) SO (predecessor of the Colorado SO). While in this position he founded the Academy in the Wilderness CO, which included forming a board, raising funds, and serving as its conductor. He also became conductor of the Denver Young Artists Orchestra, and with them recorded *Making Music: The Symphony Orchestra*, a CD that documents three months of rehearsals and concert preparation. In 1984 Lockington officially traded the cellist's chair for the podium, becoming assistant conductor of the Denver SO and Opera Colorado.

He took his first music director post in 1987, for the Cheyenne (Wyo.) SO. Lockington accepted a position as assistant conductor of the Baltimore SO in 1992. The following year he left the CSO and became the BSO's associate conductor as well as music director of the Ohio CO. In 1995 he left the BSO and became music director of the New Mexico SO. The Long Island (N.Y.) PO selected him as music director in 1996. He bid the Ohio CO farewell in 1997, the same year that he became an American citizen. Citing his musical passion and charisma, the Grand Rapids (Mich.) SO appointed Lockington music director in 1999. To focus his energies in one place, he subsequently resigned from his New York and New Mexico positions (2000). After he left Albuquerque, the local paper referred to him as "the charismatic showman who brought the orchestra back from years of stalled paychecks and threatened walkouts."

Known as a superb musician, a people person, and an artist who cares deeply about his craft and his musicians, Lockington thinks his experience sitting in the orchestra has made him a more sympathetic and sensitive conductor. Equal trust between conductor and musicians is key to an ensemble reaching musical heights. Lockington also believes an orchestra needs to reflect its community and demonstrate interest in it. Programming must be varied and excellent and taken to nontypical places to reach populations not usually served by orchestras. His now-annual concert, "Young, Gifted and Black: Gospel Night at the Symphony," has developed a following. He took the orchestra on tour through northern Michigan and the Upper Peninsula. Collaborating with local artists, introducing new music and composers, and holding radio conversations about symphony events are other examples of his efforts to reach as many people as possible. During his first two years at the GRSO, ticket sales increased 23 percent and contributions rose 25 percent. In 2005 he and the GRSO worked with composer and harpist Debra

Henson-Conant to create *Invention and Alchemy*, a highly reviewed live DVD and CD which was nominated for a 2007 Grammy in the "Best Classical Crossover Album" category.

Lockington's guest-conducting engagements include appearances with the Saint Louis, Houston, Detroit, Seattle, Tulsa, Toronto, Vancouver, Virginia, Edmonton, Phoenix, Columbus (Ohio), North Carolina, Indianapolis, Nashville, San Diego, Kansas City, Syracuse, Alabama, Colorado, and Oregon SOs; the Buffalo, Calgary, Rochester, and Louisiana POs; and the Orchestra of St. Luke's, China Broadcasting SO in Beijing and Taiwan, National Arts Centre Orchestra in Ottawa, English CO, Orquesta Sinfónica del Principado de Asturias in Spain, and Northern Sinfonia in Great Britain. He has also conducted at the Grand Teton, San Luis Obispo Mozart, Interlochen, Summer Music, Eastern Music, and Chautauqua Music festivals.

Further Reading
Kaczmarczyk, Jeffrey. "The Sunday Profile: GR Symphony Music Director David Lockington." *Grand Rapids Press*, 18 June 2005, J1.
McManus, Drew. "An Interview with David Lockington—Music Director, Grand Rapids Symphony." *Partial Observer*, 30 August 2004. http://www .partialobserver.com/article.cfm?id=1218

Selected Recordings
Copland: *American Images*; Kevin Deas (narrator); Richard DeVos (narrator); Grand Rapids SO. GRSO.
Hailstork: *Symphony no. 2*; *Symphony no. 3*; Grand Rapids SO. Naxos American 8.550295.
Henson-Conant: *Invention & Alchemy* (CD/DVD); Deborah Henson-Conant (hp); Grand Rapids SO. Golden Cage Music, filmed and recorded live: Grand Rapids 11/2005.
Making Music: The Symphony Orchestra; Denver Young Artists O. Clearvue.
Prokofiev: *Romeo and Juliet* (Suite). Poulenc: *Gloria*; Janice Chandler (s); New Mexico SO and Ch. NMSO, live: Albuquerque 1999.

～

Loebel, David
Born 7 March 1950 in Cleveland, Ohio

David Loebel, son of a longtime Cleveland Orchestra violinist, went to college as an accomplished pianist intending *not* to become a professional musician. At Northwestern University he majored in speech and did some broadcasting on the student radio station, where he had a late-night program playing everything from bluegrass to Mahler to Zappa. Loebel earned a bachelor's degree in communications (1972), but stayed in school to earn a master's degree in music (1974). In 2000 the Northwestern Alumni Association presented him with an Alumni Merit Award, which "honors alumni who have distinguished themselves by outstanding professional and personal achievement and loyal service to their alma mater."

He began his career as assistant conductor of the Syracuse SO from 1974 to 1976. In 1976, he won third prize at the Baltimore SO Young Conductors' Competition. Two years later he shared first prize at the same competition. From 1977 to 1982 Loebel was music director at the Binghamton (N.Y.) SO, followed by a stint as music advisor for the Anchorage (Alaska) SO (1983–86). In 1982 he accepted the position of assistant conductor at the Cincinnati (Ohio) SO and rose to associate conductor in 1986. He left Ohio in 1990 for the Saint Louis SO, where he worked under Leonard **Slatkin** and Hans **Vonk** as associate conductor until 1994, then as associate principal conductor until he resigned in 2000. While in Saint Louis, Loebel enjoyed serving as artistic director of the summer festival Classics in the Loop and as music director of the Saint Louis Symphony Youth Orchestra. From 1997 to 1999 he also worked with young musicians as the resident conductor of the New World Symphony in Miami (Fla.).

In 1999, Loebel accepted the position of music director and conductor of the Memphis (Tenn.) SO. Together they have won four ('00, '01, '05, '06) ASCAP awards for programming of contemporary music. (Loebel won a fifth back in 1981 with the BSO.) He says, however, that he responds most naturally to mainstream German music, which is part of his own ethnic heritage. When in 1992 he won the Seaver/NEA Conductors Award, he used part of his prize money to study German language and culture. When programming, though, he explores the orchestral spectrum from the Baroque to the newly published. He says an orchestra needs a highly developed sense of ensemble to have the right sound, and he believes its job is to serve the composer and his music. Loebel demonstrates a facility with choral conducting and communicates well with singers as well as orchestras.

Equally articulate off the podium, his writings on music, including program notes for Telarc recordings, have been widely published. He hosts the *Memphis Symphony Radio Hour* on local public radio and is a popular speaker at community events. As a mentor to conductors, he has served on the faculties of the American Symphony Orchestra League's Conducting Workshop, the Kennedy Center's National Conducting Institute, and the University of Cincinnati College-Conservatory of Music.

Loebel has traveled widely as a guest conductor, appearing with the Opera Theatre of Saint Louis, Opera Memphis, Symphony San Jose Silicon Valley, Orchestra of St. Luke's, Calgary PO, Pro Arte CO of Boston, Tokyo PO, Philadelphia Orchestra, National SO, Minnesota Orchestra, Saint Paul CO, Brooklyn PO, Buffalo PO, Rochester PO, Louisville Orchestra, the symphony orchestras of Juilliard, Indianapolis, New Jersey, Chicago, San Francisco, Seattle, Baltimore, Milwaukee, Kansas City, Syracuse, Grand Rapids, Richmond, and Long Beach, and North Carolina, among many others. In a tour of Australia, he conducted the Sydney, Adelaide, Queensland, Western Australian, and Tasmanian SOs.

Further Reading
Philpott, L. R., comp. "MLA in Memphis, Tennessee (interview)." *CAML Review/Revue de L'ACBM* 34 (April 2006): 18–21.
Sigman, Matthew. "Paying the Rent." *Symphony* 43, no. 2 (1992): 46–47.

Selected Recordings
Independence Eve at Grant Park; Elizabeth Norman (s); Grant Park SO and Ch. Chicago Park District/GPMF.

～

Maazel, Lorin (Varencove)
Born 6 March 1930 in Paris, France

For one who was dubbed "a legend in his time" as long ago as 1960, Maazel has certainly lived up to predictions! He has been conducting orchestras more or less continuously for sixty years to great acclaim. He has conducted all of the world's leading orchestras, held some of the most prestigious appointments, made over three hundred recordings, and received numerous awards. In addition, he also appears as violin soloist and increasingly devotes himself to composition (his opera *1984*, based on the Orwell novel, was produced at Covent Garden in May 2005).

Maazel's story is that of an infant prodigy who, when the novelty wore off, was able to create a successful career virtually from scratch. His parents were studying music in Paris when Lorin was born and then returned to the U.S. to live in the Los Angeles area, later moving to Pittsburgh. The boy revealed exceptional musical propensities at the age of four and a year later began to learn the violin. He received his first conducting lessons from Vladimir Baleinikov, made his conducting debut with the University of Idaho orchestra at the age of eight, and led the Interlochen National Music Camp Orchestra at the New York World's Fair in 1939. Shortly afterward he shared a concert with Stokowski, directing the Los Angeles PO in the Hollywood Bowl. Two concerts with the NBC SO followed in 1941 at the invitation of Arturo Toscanini. Wishing for some semblance of normality in their child's upbringing, his parents wisely limited his concert-giving and sent him to public school. With his phenomenal memory and intelligence, Maazel was an exceptionally gifted pupil but also enjoyed such youthful activities as games, swimming, and bicycle riding. He entered the University of Pittsburgh at fifteen to study math, philosophy, and languages. Deciding to devote himself to music, he entered the profession as a violinist in the Pittsburgh SO and formed and led the Pittsburgh Fine Arts Quartet. Opportunities for rejuvenating his conducting career were few, but he does appreciate the opportunity he had to work closely with the Italian maestro Victor de Sabata. After a well-received performance with the Boston SO led nowhere, he accepted a Fulbright scholarship to study Baroque music in Rome (1953).

Gradually Maazel's conducting career took flight in Italy, culminating in a series of concerts at La Scala; thereafter, invitations to make guest appearances flooded in. The next milestone was an invitation to conduct at Bayreuth in 1960, where he was entrusted with *Lohengrin*. The following year his highly acclaimed recording of Ravel's *L'Enfant et les sortilèges* with the National Orchestra of France was issued. An extended tour of North America with this orchestra took place the next year, as did eight concerts with the New York PO. Nineteen sixty-three saw his debut at the Met with *Don Giovanni* and *Der Rosenkavalier*, and a successful Russian tour. He returned to Bayreuth to direct the complete *Ring* cycle for the 1968 and 1969 festivals. In 1965, he took the post of music director of the Deutsche Oper in Berlin, opening with a well-received production of *La Traviata*. With his activities centered in Berlin, he was also conductor of the Berlin RSO, a post which lasted ten years. In 1970, he began a close association with the New Philharmonia Orchestra, first as associate principal conductor and later as principal guest conductor.

His appointment to the Cleveland Orchestra (1972) as successor to Georg Szell was controversial, but he soon established a rapport with the orchestra that inaugurated a successful ten-year partnership. He left Cleveland to become the first American general manager and artistic director of the Vienna State Opera but only completed two years of a four-year contract. A return to La Scala in 1983 began the association on which his operatic activities would subsequently center. He resumed his acquaintance with the Pittsburgh orchestra in 1988, remaining its music director for the next eight years. At the same time, another earlier relationship with the National Orchestra of France was renewed. In 1993 he was appointed to lead the Bavarian RSO in Munich. The Vienna PO invited him to present the famous New Year's Day concerts for 1994 and 1996. His return to the U.S. to lead the New York PO in 2002 came as something of a surprise because of his age and his reputation for having an abrasive personality, but his credentials as one of the most experienced and dedicated of conductors could not be questioned. One of his first acts was to conduct the premiere performances of John **Adams**'s oratorio tribute to the victims of 9/11: *On the Transmigration of Souls*.

Maazel's career has not been without criticism, and he has been accused of being brash and insensitive at times. However, his success cannot simply be attributed to his phenomenal talent and his prodigious feats of memorization—he almost always conducts from memory. He commands a strong presence on the rostrum, and he possesses a strong sense of rhythmic pulse and a fine ear for balance, melodic line, and phrasing. His readings are clean and meticulously faithful to the score.

Recording contracts with DGG, London, and BMG Classics/RCA Victor Red Seal have garnered many accolades, including ten Grand Prix du Disques. His catalog of recordings includes complete symphony cycles of Beethoven, Brahms, and Mahler; the complete orchestral works of Debussy and Richard Strauss; and operas by Puccini, Verdi, Beethoven, and Gershwin. In addition to recording, Maazel has been involved with popularizing opera through movies, conducting Joseph Losey's *Don Giovanni* and Zeffirelli's *Otello*, among others. A number of his operatic performances are available on video and DVD. Recent work for television has involved writing and directing "visualizations" of Holst's *The Planets* and Vivaldi's *Four Seasons*. He has been generous in devoting his energies to charitable causes through benefit concerts and is also an active environmentalist.

Website
http://www.maestromaazel.com

Further Reading
Greenfield, Edward. "Long Past, Longer Prime." *Gramophone* 78 (June 2000): 13.
"Lorin Maazel Talks to Katharine Copisarow." *Gramophone* 63 (December 1985): 735.
"Maazel, Lorin." In *World Musicians*, edited by Clifford Thompson, 595–98. New York: H. W. Wilson Company, 1999.

Oestreich, James R. "A Maestro of Many Gifts Returns, On and Off the Podium." *New York Times*, 8 November 2000, 5.

Sell, Catherine. "Lorin Maazel on Orchestras and Music Education." *Instrumentalist* 49 (November 1994): 16–20.

Service, Tom. "'1984'; Royal Opera at Covent Garden, May 3." *Opera* 56 (July 2005): 854–56.

Tommasini, Anthony. "Why to Expect the Best of an Unexpected Maestro." *New York Times*, 25 February 2001, 51–52.

Vroon, Donald Richard. "State of the Orchestras XI: Pittsburgh." *American Record Guide* 57, no. 4 (1994): 6–8.

Selected Recordings

Adams: *On the Transmigration of Souls*; New York Choral Artists; Brooklyn Youth Ch; New York PO. Nonesuch 79816.

Berlioz: *Symphonie fantastique*. Tchaikovsky: *The Nutcracker: Suite*; Cleveland O. Telarc 60650.

Mussorgsky: *Pictures at an Exhibition*. Ravel: *Boléro*; *La Valse*; *Pavane pour une infante défunte*; *Miroirs: Alborada del gracioso*; Philharmonia/New Philharmonia O. EMI 73567.

Rimsky-Korsakov: *Symphony no. 2 "Antar."* Tchaikovsky: *Symphony no. 2 "Little Russian"*; Pittsburgh SO. Telarc 80131.

Thomas: *Gathering Paradise*. Druckman: *Summer Lightning*. Hartke: *Symphony no. 3*; Heidi Grant Murphy (s); Hilliard Ensemble; New York PO. New World 80648.

⌐〜

Macal, Zdenek
Born 8 January 1936 in Brno, Czechoslovakia

Macal was appointed to a three-year term as chief conductor of the Czech PO in 2003. He had debuted with this same orchestra at the Prague Spring Festival in 1966, having just returned from the U.S. as the winner of the prestigious Mitropoulos Conducting Competition. He led it on a tour to West Germany, Austria, and Switzerland the following year. After fleeing his native land following the Russian occupation of 1968, he was little known as a conductor in the reconstituted Czech Republic. However, after earning a reputation as one of the most vibrant and dramatic conductors of his generation in Western Europe and the U.S. in the intervening years, his achievements with the orchestra in just a few months were considered "little short of miraculous."

The impression made in Prague merely mirrored the impact he made during his twenty or so years in the U.S., where, as music director, he had transformed the Milwaukee (Wisc.) SO (1986–95) and the New Jersey SO (1993–2002). In both instances he demonstrated his orchestra-building credentials by developing a characteristically robust string tone and wind sections with equally distinguished ensemble and solo playing. He was appreciated by players for his musicianly abilities, baton control, dedication, and spontaneity, and by audiences for his histrionic podium antics, intensity, and ability to present fresh readings of the standard classics. Occasionally he received criticism for his "voluble high-Czech manner" and for performances so emotionally charged that they seemed to lack analytical insight and, particularly in slow movements, so indulged that they seemed devoid of poignancy.

In Milwaukee he proved himself adept at fund-raising, budget balancing, and audience building. In New Jersey he was hailed as "Prometheus bringing fire" and his charisma attracted to the orchestra some of the finest musicians from the pool of players in the New York area. His claim to have transformed the regional orchestra into one of national standing is probably justified and reinforced by the recording contract with the Delos label. He shepherded the orchestra into its new auditorium in the New Jersey Performing Arts Center in 1997.

Born in Brno, then Czechoslovakia, in 1936, Macal began taking violin lessons from his father when he was four. He studied conducting at the Brno Conservatory (1951–56) and at the Janáček Academy (1956–60), graduating with honors. From 1963 to 1967 he was conductor of the Moravian PO and made his mark as the 1965 winner of the international conducting competition in Besançon, France. The following year he won the Mitropoulos Competition in New York, with Leonard Bernstein as chairman of the jury. He was appointed principal conductor of the Prague SO (1967–68) and seemed destined for a distinguished career in Czechoslovakia. After fleeing the Russian invasion, however, he lived in Switzerland for a time before being appointed Generalmusikdirector of the Cologne RSO (1970–74) and of the Hannover RSO (1975–81). He was appointed music director of the Sydney SO in 1984 before becoming a U.S. citizen in 1986. He had made his U.S. debut with the Chicago SO in 1972 and enjoyed a close relationship as guest conductor of the Pittsburgh SO from 1973 to 1989. Later, as music director of the New Jersey SO, he taught the graduate conducting class at the Manhattan School of Music. He returned as principal conductor of the Prague SO for two years before taking up the chief conductorship of the Czech PO.

In all, Macal claims to have appeared before over 160 orchestras world-wide, including most of the principal orchestras on four continents, such as the New York PO, Berlin PO, Royal PO, and NHK SO in Tokyo. Since his days at the Cologne RSO, where he championed the music of Penderecki and Ligeti, he has been a forceful advocate for the less radical new music, including works by Ellen Taaffe Zwilich, Roberto Sierra, Ned Rorem, Dominick Argento, and George Crumb. He premiered the first symphonic work of film composer Marvin Hamlisch, *Anatomy of Peace*.

With the Milwaukee SO he recorded Beethoven's Ninth Symphony; Kodály's *Dances of Galanta*, *Hary Janos Suite*, and *Variations on a Hungarian Folk Song*; Prokofiev's cantata *Alexander Nevsky*; Dvořák's First and Fifth Symphonies; and a disc of music by Roberto Sierra. With the New Jersey SO he has laid down an acclaimed account of Dvořák's *Stabat Mater*, a disc of Glière (Symphony no. 2 and the *Red Poppy Suite*), the *Symphonie Fantastique* of Berlioz, and a Mussorgsky disc, which includes, as well as *Pictures at an Exhibition*, the premiere recording of a choral and orchestral version of *Night on Bald Mountain*, arranged by Shebalin and retitled *The Dream of Peasant Gritzko*. He also leads the Philharmonia Orchestra in a collection of music by the American composer Richard Danielpour: *Celestial Night*, *Urban Dances*, and *Toward the Splendid City*. In Europe he has recorded extensively for the EMI, French Decca, Supraphon, and Deutsche Grammophon labels.

Further Reading

Passy, Charles. "Zdenek Macal & the Milwaukee Symphony." *Ovation* 9 (November 1988): 16–18.

Pilátová, Agáta. "Zdenek Macal: The Hardest Thing Is to Make the Right Decision at the Right Time (interview, English)." *Czech Music*, no. 1 (2004): 2–5.

Spencer, Peter. "State of the Orchestras XIX: The New Jersey Symphony." *American Record Guide* 59, no. 2 (1996): 6–8.

Selected Recordings

Dvořák: *Symphony no. 5*; *Golden Spinning Wheel*; Milwaukee SO. Koss 1026.

Dvořák: *Symphony no. 9*; *Symphonic Variations*; London PO. Classics for Pleasure 74943.

Glière: *Symphony no. 2*; *Red Poppy Suite*; New Jersey SO. Delos 3178.

Mussorgsky: *Pictures at an Exhibition*; *Khovanshchina* (excpts); *Scorochinsky Fair* (excpt); Clayton Brainerd (b-b), Westminster Choir; New Jersey SO. Delos 3217.

Sierra: A *Joyous Overture*; *Tropicalia*; *Idilio*; *SASIMA*; *Prèambulo*; Milwaukee SO. Koss 1021.

∽

Masur, Kurt
Born 18 July 1927 in Brieg, Silesia, GDR (now Brzeg, Poland)

Masur believes emphatically that music expresses tangible feelings akin to human experience: life, death, love, poetry, etc. He has admitted that he is drawn to "expressive music, work I can draw humanistic ideas from," and he sees that his primary function in performance is to somehow convey this message. He attempts to do so by formulating a vision of a work that fulfills the composer's wishes (to the extent that this can be deduced) and convincing the orchestra of it. He then exerts all his talent and experience to realize that vision through a meaningful and heart-touching performance. Based on his own life experiences, Masur believes that music has an absolute value, especially evident in difficult times, and that conductors find artistic validity by revealing spiritual truths. Since this meaning runs deep, it often eschews the superficial and visceral excitement so prevalent in today's music-making, especially in the U.S. This may help to explain why, his many achievements aside, he spent so much time at loggerheads with the New York PO's administration during his tenure as music director (1991–2002) and why so much of his work, while of a consistently high quality, was perceived as pedestrian and unglamorous.

It could be argued that Masur's tenure was flawed by unfulfilled expectations and his achievements diminished by a publicly aired power struggle which revealed some negative character traits, as well as his indomitable will. It became clear that his contract would not be renewed past 2002, although his tenure was resolved into a celebratory dénouement, presumably prompted by guilt and regret on both sides. In all of this Masur revealed himself clearly as a product of the German Kapellmeister tradition. His humanitarian instincts incline him to take a democratic approach to the orchestra by allowing it its own identity while at the same time impressing upon it his own strength of personality. A good analogy is that of a family, but a family in which the father is an authority figure dispensing tough love! Indeed, it was this image as an experienced musician and a no-nonsense martinet that recommended him to fill the vacancy with the NYPO following Zubin Mehta's departure. He was well known to the orchestra, having appeared as a guest conductor nearly thirty times since his debut in 1981, and his appointment enjoyed the strong support both of the players and the administration. Although the handover went smoothly, it was quite clear that Masur had work to do. The orchestra's morale was not high and much of the playing had slipped to the level of the mundane. His influence to the good was felt swiftly. Morale improved, as well as orchestral discipline, and a gradual process to refine the ensemble's sound was begun. Although the orchestra's players were not immune to the effects of the intrigues going on about them, Masur is credited with building up a relationship of mutual respect and trust among them. Nevertheless, a sense of disappointment pervaded his term because many performances of the core repertoire, regarded as his strength, were deemed adequate but lackluster. Reviews of individual performances that belie this abound, however: a 29 May 1999 performance of Beethoven's *Missa Solemnis*, for example, provoked one critic to declare that he had "never heard it make such a beautiful sound"; a 17 July 1999 performance of the *Emperor Concerto* with soloist Emmanuel Ax earned the epithet "a splendid performance"; and the 12 July 2000 performance of Shostakovich's *Leningrad Symphony* was described as magnificent, with Masur praised for keeping the ninety-minute span "taut as a noose." On the other hand, Bernard Holland, while generally approving his 5 September 1999 performance of Tchaikovsky's Fifth Symphony, described it as "an earnest but loving lecture on sober living: a characteristic this music does not usually advertise." Reviewing a New York PO concert during its European tour of 2000, Andrew Clark in the *Financial Times* wrote of Masur, "When the time comes for him to exchange the New York PO for its London counterpart, it will be London's gain."

A criticism frequently leveled at Masur during the New York years was his apparent lack of support for new and American music. Not as enthusiastic an advocate as, say, Christoph **Eschenbach**, certainly, but the statistics which refute the former claim are quite impressive. He conducted some twenty-seven world premieres, a substantial number of which were inherited from his predecessor as part of the orchestra's 150th anniversary celebrations. He will primarily be remembered for commissioning *Messages for the Millennium*, a series of works on millennial themes from six composers: Thomas Adès, John Corigliano, Hans Werner Henze, Giya Kancheli, Kaija Saariaho, and Somei Suto. He has also given performances in recent years of compositions by, among others, Aaron Jay Kernis, Michael Torke, Richard Danielpour, Siegfried Matthus, Christopher Rouse, Tan Dun, Minora Miki, Susan Batti, Joseph Turrin, Dov Seltzer, and Wynton Marsalis.

Masur's recorded output was curtailed by the economic downturn in the industry after making over thirty recordings with the NYPO on the Teldec label, including music by Britten, Strauss, Gershwin, Liszt, Kodály, Ravel,

Debussy, and Tchaikovsky. Two of these recordings, Shostakovich's Symphony no. 13, *Babi Yar*, and Mahler's Symphony no. 9, won Record of the Year awards from *Stereo Review* magazine. He also recorded Brahms, Schumann, and Beethoven concerto albums with violinist Anne-Sophie Mutter for DGG. During his tenure the orchestra made thirteen tours, which included stops in twenty-seven countries, culminating in a tour to Germany and Asia in June 2002.

Masur regards his time with the NYPO as the crowning achievment of a long and distinguished career, and he regrets that it ended too soon. Among the projects he failed to accomplish was the establishment of a venue for a summer festival equivalent to that of the Boston SO's at Tanglewood. He also pushed to have a pipe organ installed in Avery Fisher Hall without success. But if he was regarded as a lame duck conductor, he certainly went out with a bang rather than a whimper! His valedictory season was interrupted by ill health, yet less than two months after receiving a kidney transplant he was back on the podium to conduct an impressive performance of Wagner's opera *Tristan und Isolde*. He felt strongly that a few more years would have provided the opportunity to groom a younger American conductor to succeed him, as had happened when Leonard Bernstein succeeded Mitropoulos in 1958.

Brieg, Silesia, Masur's birthplace, was somewhat of a cultural backwater, so he was sixteen before he heard his first orchestral concert. His musical awakening had begun much earlier, however, at about the age of seven, when he taught himself to play the piano. Later he learned to play the cello. He attended the Landesmusikschule in Breslau from 1942 to 1944, until his education was interrupted by the war and he spent six months in the German army, one of only 27 out of his unit of 130 to survive. He resumed his studies in 1946 at the Hochschule für Musik in Leipzig, originally intending to be a composer but also studying conducting with Heinz Bongartz. His first appointment was as orchestra coach and *repetiteur* at the Landestheater in Halle (1948–51), followed by appointments as first Kapellmeister at the Erfurt City Theater (1951–53) and the Leipzig City Theater (1953–55). He then became conductor of the Dresden PO (1955–58) and *Generalmusikdirektor* of the Mecklenburg State Theater (1958–60). The Komische Oper in Berlin, headed by the distinguished director Walter Felsenstein, enjoyed an international reputation for excellence when Masur was appointed senior director of music in 1960. They collaborated on a number of celebrated new productions and took the company on tours abroad. This led to a number of invitations for Masur to appear as guest conductor in the West, and his prestige and forceful character enabled him to overcome bureaucratic restrictions on travel that the East German regime attempted to impose on him

during the 1960s. He left the theater in 1964 to devote himself to developing his knowledge of the symphonic repertoire and to accept guest-conducting invitations. He returned to the Dresden PO as chief conductor for
a five-year stint in 1967. In 1970 he was appointed to lead the Leipzig
Gewandhaus Orchestra, the oldest and most prestigious orchestra in the
East German sector. He was to retain this post for the next twenty-six years,
and, with increasing exposure to the West through recordings and international tours, the reputation of both orchestra and conductor were enhanced.
In 1972, as the result of an injury sustained in a serious car accident, he gave
up using a baton. His UK debut with the New Philharmonia Orchestra took
place in 1973. The following year saw him lead the Gewandhaus Orchestra's
first tour to the U.S. and make his debut with the Cleveland Orchestra.
From 1976 to 1980 he was principal guest conductor of the Dallas (Tex.)
SO. Nineteen eighty-one saw the reopening of the Gewandhaus in Leipzig,
the hall from which the orchestra takes its name, and it was also the year of
Masur's debut with the New York PO. His first appearance at the Tanglewood Festival in 1982 strengthened his bond with the U.S. and heralded
subsequent close ties both there and with the other leading summer festivals
at Ravinia and Blossom. In 1989 he was appointed principal guest conductor of the London PO.

Such was Masur's standing in East Germany that he played a significant
role as mediator at crucial events leading to the peaceable breakup of the
GDR and the fall of the Berlin wall. He had come a long way from the ap-
paratchik role he had been obliged to assume when the wall went up in 1961!

During the New York years he was made honorary guest conductor of the
Israel PO (1992) and, on his retirement from the Gewandhaus in 1994, was
named the orchestra's conductor laureate, the first conductor to receive the
title. In 2001 he became chief conductor of the Orchestre National de
France. In addition to guest appearances with the world's leading orchestras,
he has been a professor at the Leipzig Conservatory since 1975 and has
taught conducting at various venues, including Tanglewood, New York, and
Wroclaw (Poland).

Website
http://www.kurtmasur.com/

Further Reading
Brown, Royal S. "Kurt Masur Today: A Brief Profile." *Fanfare* 16, no. 3
    (1993): 35–36.
Hemming, Roy. "Two Years In." *Gramophone* 70 (May 1993): 28–29.

Knight, John Wesley. "My Real Idol Was Bruno Walter: An Interview with Kurt Masur." *Instrumentalist* 54 (November 1999): 12–17.

Kupferberg, Herbert. "Kurt Masur." *Stereo Review* 57 (May 1992): 55–57.

Sullivan, Jack. "The Masur Legacy." *American Record Guide* 65 (May–June 2002): 5–7.

Tommasini, Anthony. "A Master Steeped in the Core Works." *New York Times*, 24 September 1998, 5.

Selected Recordings

Beethoven: *Symphonies* (complete); Anna Tomowa-Sintow (s); Annelies Burmeister (a); Peter Schreier (t); Theo Adam (b); R Ch Leipzig; Leipzig Gewandhaus O. Pentatone PTC 5186 159.

Britten: *War Requiem*; Christine Brewer (s); Anthony Dean Griffey (t); Gerald Finley (br); Tiffin Boys' Ch; London PO and Ch. London Philharmonic Orchestra 10.

Franck: *Symphony in d*; *Les Eolides*; New York PO. Apex 41372.

Mendelssohn—*Gala Concert from the Gewandhaus: Midsummer Night's Dream Overture*; *Concerto for Violin*; *Symphony no. 3 in A minor*; *Midsummer Night's Dream: Wedding March*; Frank-Michael Erben (vn); Leipzig Gewandhaus O. Arthaus Musik 100031 DVD.

Shostakovich: *Symphony no. 13* "Babi Yar"; Sergei Leiferkus (b); New York Choral Artists, New York PO. Teldec 90848.

〜

Mechetti, Fabio
Born 27 August 1957 in São Paulo, Brazil

Born into a long line of musicians, Fabio Mechetti remembers scenes from the first opera he saw, at age four, conducted by his grandfather. On the professional opera stage he sang some of the same boys' roles that his father had sung before him. He started piano lessons at age five, attending music school in addition to regular school, and by fourteen he was conducting madrigals and chamber music. Although Mechetti won piano competitions, he went to São Paulo University to study journalism. After two years, however, he succumbed to his passion for music, switching his major and working as an assistant conductor for the São Paulo Municipal Opera Theater (1979–81), where both his father and grandfather had conducted. After graduating in 1981, Mechetti came to the U.S. to attend Juilliard, where he earned master's degrees in both conducting and composition (1984).

While finishing at Juilliard, he spent a year as associate conductor for the Spokane (Wash.) SO (1984–85), then went across the country to the other Washington to hold the same position at the National SO from 1985 to 1989. In 1985, his NSO children's programs won the National Endowment of the Arts Award for best educational programming in the U.S. He was also resident conductor for the San Diego (Calif.) SO from 1986 to 1987 and in the early 1990s led the Virginia CO. In 1989 he won first place at the Nicolai Malko Competition for Young Conductors in Denmark. He also began a ten-year tenure with the Syracuse (N.Y.) SO, first as associate conductor until 1993, then as music director until 1999. In Syracuse he again was known for children's programming, conducting Saturday morning concerts that introduced youngsters to classical music by blending it with comedy, mime, and other elements appealing to those under the age of ten.

Mechetti returned to Spokane in 1993, this time to become music director, a position he held until he became music director laureate in 2004. Here he continued his track record of taking a hands-on approach to educational outreach and audience support, inspiring musicians, and being involved in the symphony's programming. He accepted two new music director positions in 1999, one with the Jacksonville (Fla.) SO and a one-year contract for the Theatro Municipal opera house in Rio de Janeiro. As he had in previous positions, Mechetti looked for ways to reach new audiences and gain their support. He and his wife, concert pianist Aida Ribeiro, led a Brazilian tour to benefit the Symphony Association; he was one of the local notables to read in a special presentation of *The Night before Christmas*; he holds morning "Coffee Series" programs and question-and-answer sessions; he attends postconcert parties with audience members; and he and his wife performed a four-hands-one-piano concert at a local church. Mechetti also cohosts *89.9 Presents the Jacksonville Symphony*, a weekly one-hour radio program featuring symphony highlights and conversations with guest artists. Under his leadership the orchestra joined forces with a local swamp-rock band to present a concert and has sponsored "Fresh Ink," a popular competition for local composers.

Mechetti says the composer's thoughts should define the performance, so his job as conductor is to see that the orchestra is honoring the composer's intentions. His style on the podium is conservative and low-key, which he says is due to his respect for his excellent musicians and their level of musicianship. No ranting is necessary. Described as polite, clear with the baton, a man of few words but choice and powerful ones, and a consummate musician, Mechetti's goal is for the JSO to gain a national reputation as an orchestra of distinction, with the effort and reputation recognized and appreciated by the whole community. In 2006 the JSO produced its first commercial recording.

As a guest conductor Mechetti has made numerous symphonic and operatic appearances, including with the Buffalo PO, New Jersey SO, Seattle SO, Pacific SO, various orchestras in Mexico, Brazil, and Venezuela, Utah SO, Rochester PO, Quebec SO, San Antonio SO, Helsingborg SO (Sweden), San Jose SO, Colorado SO, North Carolina SO, Austin SO, Phoenix SO, Auckland Philharmonia, the Japanese orchestras of Tokyo, Sapporo, and Hiroshima, Charlotte SO, Omaha SO, Long Island PO, Danish RSO, Alabama SO, Kalamazoo SO, and Washington National Opera.

Website
http://fabiomechetti.com

Selected Recording
Orff: *Carmina Burana*; Andrea Matthews (s), Christopher Pfund (t); Kurt Loft Willett (br); Jacksonville Symphony Ch; Jacksonville Children's Ch; Jacksonville SO. JSO.

∽

Mester, Jorge
Born 10 April 1935 in Mexico City, Mexico

The wordplay coined by *Los Angeles Times* critic Martin Bernheimer, "Mester is a Master," seems appropriate for this musician. A sixty-year veteran of his trade, his skills are "equally at home in the classical and modern repertory, in symphonic music and opera." In addition, he has always been a staunch proselytizer for living composers, considered innovation and outreach the lifeblood of music-making and its future survival, and been one of the leading mentors of young performers. His conducting temperament—that unique blend of qualities and emotions that defines his performances—is frequently characterized as intuitive, colorful, exuberant, radiant, precise, elegant, graceful, and balanced. What criticism there is tends to view his approach as fussy and too detail-oriented, with a tendency to "miss the wood for the trees." In 1998, after hearing Mester on a number of occasions, the *Seattle Times* critic summed him up as "never less than musical and often a great deal more than that." Now entering his eighth decade, he continues to relish the "high" of conducting. Maturity has given him a deeper insight into music and, with less to prove, more confidence and freedom. He claims: "[You use] a different part of your brain when you're performing" as an older man. Noted for his eclectic tastes and imaginative programming (not many conductors would present an all-Beethoven concert without including one of the symphonies!), his lengthy tenure with the Pasadena (Calif.) SO (since 1984) has allowed him to become a cultural icon within the community and attract an audience expecting performances "with equal amounts of unanimity and excitement" from a wide range of repertory choices.

Born in Mexico City of Hungarian stock, Mester began to take piano lessons at the age of five, but a fascination with his parents' recordings of Hungarian Gypsy music steered him toward the violin. His teachers included members of the famed Lener Quartet, fellow expatriates domiciled in Mexico during World War II. At age eleven he was sent off to military school in San Francisco, where, as luck would have it, one of his classmates was the son of the great Russian cellist Gregor Piatigorsky. It was he who urged Mester to attend the Berkshire Music Festival at Tanglewood in the summer after his junior year in high school. There he first became a protégé of Leonard Bernstein. When Bernstein decided to take his Christmas vacation in Mexico later that year, Mester gathered a local group to play chamber music with him there, quickly filling a void in the group by learning to play the viola himself. Abandoning plans to become a psychiatrist, he enrolled at Juilliard in the fall of 1952 and entered the conducting class of Jean Morel. He also played first-chair viola in the Juilliard Orchestra. He made his professional conducting debut with the National SO of Mexico (1955). Completing his MS degree in 1958, he was immediately engaged as the youngest member of the Juilliard staff on the conducting faculty, with responsibility for the opera theater, and soon became violist of the Beaux Arts Quartet (1961–65). During his initial ten-year tenure, noteworthy among the American premieres he gave were Hindemith's *Long Christmas Dinner*, Henze's *Elegy for Young Lovers*, and Cavalli's *Oromindo*. He was briefly music director of the Greenwich Village SO in New York (1961–62). About this time (1965) he first collaborated with a young music student by the name of Peter Schickele, who was "discovering" works by a hitherto obscure member of history's most distinguished musical dynasty, P.D.Q. Bach. His collaboration with Gian Carlo Menotti began with the Spoleto Festival of 1960, at which he conducted Strauss's *Salome*. This phase of his career was rounded out when he was awarded a Naumberg Prize in 1968.

His next move, when he succeeded Robert Whitney as music director of the Louisville (Ky.) Orchestra in 1967, was to prove pivotal. Whitney, together with the orchestra board's chair, Charles P. Farnsley, and supported by a grant from the Rockefeller Foundation, had eschewed the accepted concert format of engaging a guest soloist in favor of performing and recording five commissioned works each year. On his own account, Mester conducted above two hundred premieres and made seventy-two recordings of both new and neglected music. Although this legacy of recordings is not without blemish, it remains a remarkable and unique archive of twentieth-century music, much of which was shamefully neglected by most other orchestras at the time. Looking back, however, Mester is far from starry-eyed about a period of his career that made him one of the most recorded conductors in America, for, despite this accolade and subsequent recordings, Roger Dettmer, writing in *Fanfare* in 1982, lamented the fact that Mester was never given the chance to record "repertoire that suggests how powerfully, for example, he has been heard to lead Beethoven's Ninth Symphony." Claiming only that his legacy was "right for its time" Mester recalls that the Louisville patrons were less than enthusiastic about being a pioneering audience and that "eventually ticket sales began to go kaput."

Having established his credentials as a skilled and reliable executant of contemporary music, Mester went on to champion new music with organizations such as the American Composers Orchestra, the American SO (which premiered Joan Tower's Clarinet Concerto in 1988), and the sixty-year-old National Orchestral Association's reincarnation as the New Music Orchestral Project in partnership with the Mannes School of Music. During the late 1980s and early 1990s the NMOP promoted concerts of new music by Christopher James, Brian Fenelley, Joel Phillip Friedman, Anne LeBaron, and Lawrence Widdoes, among others. This close association with contemporary music, which also resulted in premieres of works by composers such as Philip Glass, Michael Daugherty, Carl Ruggles, and George Tsontakis, has had another effect. Working closely with composers to understand how their music is put together in terms of tempo, balance, and musical structure led Mester to a keener insight into "how other composers from the Classical and Romantic eras may have thought about their music."

Mester's close association with the Aspen Music Festival began in 1969. During his twenty-one-year reign as music director he developed its unique profile: a combination of imaginative programming, distinguished faculty, and guest artists, all of which attracted a slew of gifted young musicians. He remains the festival's conductor laureate. He served a year as artistic advisor to the Kansas City (Mo.) PO before becoming its music director (1973–79). In 1976 he returned for a brief stint to teach at Juilliard and was then appointed principal guest conductor of the Saint Paul (Minn.) CO (1978–79). On relinquishing his Louisville post in 1979 he took over and rejuvenated the Casals Festival in Puerto Rico (1979–85).

For his third term teaching at Juilliard, Mester returned in 1980 as chair of conducting studies. Acknowledging the debt he owed to those who most influenced his own musical progress—Gregor Piatigorsky, Leonard Bernstein, Albert Wolff, Jean Morel, and William Schuman—he has been a dedicated teacher and mentor of young musicians. Included among his pupils are James **Conlon**, Dennis Russell **Davies**, Andreas **Delfs**, JoAnn **Falletta**, John **Nelson**, Eugene Frederick Castillo, and Beatrice Jona Affron, all of whom have had or are on the verge of having distinguished conducting careers. In addition to his work at Juilliard, Mester has been associated with the Mannes School of Music, the Curtis Institute in Philadelphia, and the Thornton School of Music at the University of Southern California. As a conducting coach and orchestral trainer he has given workshops with the Buffalo (N.Y.) PO and the Orquesta Sinfónica Carlos Chávez (the training orchestra in Mexico City). His approach to teaching conducting has been notably canny. He is an exacting teacher but understands what can be taught and what is instinctive, and carefully tries to avoid blunting natural talent.

The longevity of Mester's term with the Pasadena SO is a clear indication of a successful partnership. Made up of top instrumentalists, many of whom work in the nearby Hollywood studios, the orchestra will "actually outplay the lordly Los Angeles PO" on occasion. The ad hoc nature of the group restricts the number of concerts per season, although this has increased from four to eight over the years. Nonetheless, the orchestra has established a remarkable rapport within this up-market, small-town feeling community within the Los Angeles metropolis. Its loyal following in the charmingly dated Civic Auditorium has allowed the orchestra to be largely self-supporting. These factors—quality players, community support, financial stability—have enabled Mester to play to his strengths, crafting wide-ranging repertoire. A typical concert consisting of von Reznicek's zestful *Donna Diana* overture, Brahms's serious Violin Concerto, William Schuman's purgative *Symphony for Strings*, and Respighi's opulent *Pines of Rome*, reviewed by Richard Ginell in the *American Record Guide* in 1993, illustrates the juxtapositions of mood and character that work musically in a complementary and contrasting way, similar to a well-thought-out menu. (The critic's verdict, by the way: "By any standards one could apply, these were tremendous performances.") The years (now over twenty) have seen ambitious cycles of works by Berlioz, Shostakovich, and Mahler interspersed with lesser-known fare. Another noteworthy feature has been the championing of up-and-coming soloists, especially of violin virtuosi, of whom Nadia Salerno-Sonnenberg is the best-known example. It was shortly after taking up the appointment in Pasadena that Mester received the Ditson Conductor's Award "for the Advancement of American Music" (1985). Continuing their long relationship, Peter Schickele was appointed the orchestra's "Composer in Residence" and given the opportunity to perform his own "serious" music, which included a Viola Concerto (2002) and "Symphony no. 1," composed in 1995. The outlook for classical music in its traditional concert-based form, which has long been Mester's concern, has increasingly occupied his mind in recent years as the support for orchestras in general has waned. This worry has occasioned a number of innovations, including attracting younger listeners by inviting schools to come and watch the orchestra rehearse, hosting the Los Angeles County Arts Open House, which was attended by over 20,000 local residents, doubling the number of elementary schools served in its educational "TEMPO!" program, and by playing concerts in less formal settings, including rock venues. Another strategy has been to meld evenings of music, dance, and drama in collaboration with writer and director John de Lancie, designed to entice a wider audience to attend PSO concerts. These have included Shakespeare's *A Midsummer Night's Dream* with music by Mendelssohn and Korngold (2001), Molière's *Le Bourgeois Gentilhomme* with the incidental music by Richard Strauss (2002), and Shakespeare's *Romeo and Juliet* with a potpourri of music from eight composers (2003). And then, of course, there have been the ubiquitous pops concerts with film scores and symphonic versions of rock albums.

Mester's travels to the Antipodes as principal guest conductor of the Adelaide SO (1988–90) led to his appointment as chief conductor of the West Australian SO in Perth (1991–93). Upon the completion of L.A.'s Getty Museum in 1997, he was asked to conduct at the opening ceremonies and was invited to act as artistic director of the center's classical music series. He returned to his native home in 1998 to lead the Mexico City SO (Orquesta Filarmónica de la Ciudad de México). A survey conducted among the players had placed Mester in the final group of three contenders from a pool of twenty possible candidates. Once more he set about placing his individual stamp through innovative programming and support of young solo talent. One such instance was when Philip Quint stepped in at short notice to perform William Schuman's Violin Concerto, having learned it from memory in a matter of days (the performance led to a recording for which he received a Grammy nomination). Perhaps Mester's most remarkable achievement to date was presenting a whole season devoted entirely to music of the twentieth century, with each of ten concerts covering one of its decades. Alas, such an enterprising partnership was fated not to last and he was forced to throw in the towel after just four years when the city's arts funding dried up.

A much happier chapter began in 2004 when Mester quite unexpectedly found himself at the head of the Naples PO in Florida. Making a guest appearance in April 2002, he immediately established a rapport with the orchestra that impressed players and audiences alike. Well-drilled during the twelve-year tenure of music director Christopher **Seaman**, a fine orchestral trainer, the orchestra responded enthusiastically to the energy and excitement the guest conductor generated. In turn, Mester was impressed by the orchestra's flexibility and cohesiveness. When the directorship became available the following year, Mester was a virtual shoo-in. There was great appeal, too, in the fact that the orchestra flourishes in the community of retirees with the distinction of being named among the "100 best art towns in America." The organization operates in the black and, in the Philharmonic Center, has a performance space to rival any in the nation. Since he signed a contract in 2006 renewing his contract for another five years, one assumes the "chemistry" has been right.

The indefatigable Mester runs the risk of attracting the appellation "Comeback Kid." Perhaps one of the most surprising announcements of 2006 in the musical world was his appointment as music director of the Louisville Orchestra twenty-seven years after relinquishing the post. No doubt this is a stopgap measure while the orchestra's search committee gets its act together (none of the seven candidates who auditioned was found acceptable). Local journalist Andrew Adler recalled the way Mester had "connected with listeners in a big way . . . many people still recall his blend of new-fangled programming and old-fashioned charisma."

As a conductor of opera in the Juilliard theater, Mester performed *Cosi fan tutte* (1964), *L'Elisir d'amore* (1964), *La vide breve* (1980), *Manon* (1982), *Beatrice et Benedict* (1988), and *Le Rossignol* (1988), as well as the works by Hindemith and Henze mentioned above. At the Wheeler Opera House in Aspen, he conducted, among others, *Le nozze di Figaro* (1984), *The Rake's Progress* (1987), and *Cosi fan tutte* (1991). Appearances with the New York City Opera have included *The Rake's Progress* (1987) and *Madame Butterfly* (2000). He has also led performances at the Sydney Opera House, the Spoleto Festival, and with Washington National Opera. His guest appearances with orchestras worldwide include the Royal PO (London), Boston SO, Philadelphia Orchestra, Detroit SO, Cincinnati SO, Seattle SO, Oregon SO, Milwaukee SO, Rochester PO, Buffalo PO, Cape Town SO, Jerusalem SO, and the Lausanne CO.

The Naxos company is planning to release the bulk of Mester's Louisville Orchestra recordings on its First Edition label, remastered in excellent sound for CD. Of the discs issued so far, highlights include Henry Cowell's *Hymn and Fuguing Tune no. 3*, George Crumb's *Echoes of Time and the River* and *Echoes II*, Karel Husa's *Music for Prague 1968*, William Schuman's Symphony no. 4 and *Prayer in Time of War*, Ned Rorem's Piano Concerto with Jerome

Lowenthal as pianist, and Peter Mennin's Cello Concerto with cellist Janos Starker. As a specialist in an earlier generation of American composers, he includes samplings from Samuel Barber, Morton Gould, Roy Harris, Alan Hovhaness, Wallingford Riegger, Henry Brant, and Walter Piston. Yet to be released at the time of writing are some unusual and lesser-known works by Granados (the symphonic poem *Dante*), Bruch (Symphony no. 2), Joachim (*Hungarian Concerto*), and Gottschalk (*Cakewalk Ballet*, in an orchestration by Hershey Kay). Also included in the catalog is music by Richard Strauss, Malcolm Arnold, John Addison, Peter Maxwell Davies, Boris Blacher, Hindemith, Honegger, Ibert, Frank Martin, Milhaud, as well as first recordings of works by Dallapiccola, Penderecki, Petrassi, Schuller, Shostakovich, Weisgall, and even a rock-jazz crossover piece by Ezra Lademan. Drawing on his Latino heritage, he also features works by Leonardo Balada, Carlos Chávez, Alberto Ginastera, Carlos Surinach, Joaquin Turina, and Heitor Villa-Lobos. A collection of pieces by New England composers Frederick Converse, George W. Chadwick, Arthur Foote, and Arthur Bird has appeared on CD from the Albany company. One of his most critically acclaimed readings on disc is the 1961 recording of Menotti's Piano Concerto with pianist Earl Wild reissued by Vanguard Classics. In addition, Mester leads recordings of three of Menotti's operas: *The Medium, The Telephone,* and *The Old Maid and the Thief*. From Canada come performances of the *Symphonic Ode* by John Weinzweig on the Contredisques label and a performance of Beethoven's Violin Concerto with Henryk Szering as the soloist accompanied by the Radio Canada Orchestra on a VAI DVD.

Since Louisville, Mester's recorded oeuvre is regrettably thin. It includes Rachmaninoff's *First Piano Suite* in an orchestration by Rebekah Harkness, performed by the London PO and pianist Lee Hoiby. With the Pasadena SO he recorded Strauss's *Also sprach Zarathustra* and Saint-Saëns's Third (*Organ*) Symphony in 1994, described by the *Washington Post* as "world-class performances." In 1996 they recorded Stravinsky's *Sacre du printemps* coupled with Rachmaninoff's *Symphonic Dances*. And then, of course, there are all those P.D.Q. Bach recordings. Reissued on the Vanguard label, such titles as *Concerto for 2 Pianos vs. Orchestra*, Cantata: *Iphigenia in Brooklyn, Concerto for Horn and Hardart, The Seasonings,* and the *Unbegun Symphony* require no further comment!

This perusal of Mester's long and distinguished career reinforces his reputation as a versatile, eclectic musician whose multifaceted activities extend to all branches of the conductor's art; alongside his vast knowledge and experience, he is still able to muster that degree of energy and excitement that has been a consistent feature of his lifelong music-making.

Further Reading

Ginell, Richard S. "Pasadena." *American Record Guide* 56, no. 2 (1993): 39–40.

Hanani, Hannah. "Transmitting the Art of Conducting: Jorge Mester." *Instrumentalist* 41 (May 1987): 18–22.

Naderi, Zeinab Yakouboff. "An Analytical Study of Rehearsal Techniques of Three Professional Orchestra Conductors." EdD diss., Columbia University, 1985.

"The Versatile Jorge Mester." *Instrumentalist* 36 (June 1982): 16–19.

Selected Recordings

An Hysteric Return: PDQ Bach at Carnegie Hall; soloists; Okay Chorale; Royal PDQ Bach Festival O. Vanguard 79223.

Cowell: *Hymn and Fuguing Tune no. 3*; Louisville O. From First Edition ADD FECD-0003.

Husa: *Music for Prague, 1968*; *Apotheosis of This Earth*; Louisville O. First Edition 9.

Strauss (R): *Also sprach Zarathustra*. Saint-Saëns: *Symphony no. 3*; Hector Olivera (org); Pasadena SO. Newport Classic 10010.

Stravinsky: *Le Sacre du printemps*. Rachmaninoff: *Symphonic Dances*; Pasadena SO. Newport Classic 10002.

Weisgall: *A Garden Eastward*. Saminsky: *The Vision of Ariel: Scenes I and III*; Barcelona SO/Catalonia Natl O. From Milken Archive, Naxos 51.

~

Nagano, Kent (George)
Born 22 November 1951 in Berkeley, California

Nagano is a conductor of contradictions. He combines a laid-back, soft-spoken image of California cool with the reputation as a relentless pursuer of perfection. As the composer John **Adams** puts it, "Kent's gift is his dogged determination to get it right." Nagano himself has said, "There really aren't any excuses for mistakes. Ever." Some critics feel that by concentrating on details, he sometimes misses the big picture. He combines technical facility and an intellectual vigor that is directed toward an Apollonian ideal, but sometimes leaves his listeners disappointed by a lack of emotional depth. He is at his best with scores whose fullest realization requires focus, which is why he is particularly successful conducting the music of Messiaen, Schoenberg, **Adams**, and Poulenc, among others, and is one of the leading champions of new music.

Nagano grew up near Mauro Bay in California. His parents had abandoned teaching careers at Berkeley to sustain the family produce farm that his grandparents, immigrants from Japan, had established. He learned piano from his mother from the age of four. In elementary school, by one of those curiously serendipitous chances, his music classes were taught by a German émigré who imposed rigorous standards in the European tradition. By the time he graduated from high school in 1970, he was proficient on the koto, viola, clarinet, and electric guitar. Growing up in the late 1960s, it was perhaps not surprising that Nagano should choose a double major in sociology and music at the University of California Santa Cruz. By the time he was ready for graduate school, however, his true vocation had asserted itself; he studied conducting with Laszlo Varga at San Francisco State University and received his master's degree in 1975. His apprenticeship really began when he moved east and worked with Sarah Caldwell for four years at the Opera Company of Boston. He made his conducting debut there in Cavalli's *L'Oromindo* in 1976 and the following year was entrusted with Janáček's *Cunning Little Vixen*.

In 1978, he returned to California to reestablish his reputation in the Bay Area, working as assistant conductor to Calvin Simmons at the Oakland SO and as music director of the Oakland Ballet. He landed his first permanent appointment with the Berkeley Promenade Orchestra, the local community orchestra. Nagano made an immediate impact and before long was expanding the organization's scope to include concert performances of operas by Busoni, Janáček, and Pfitzner. He renamed the orchestra the Berkeley SO and replaced casual dress with formal wear for concerts. Thus began a partnership that lasted for thirty-one years. Questioned about this degree of loyalty when, in the meantime, he had become one of the leading figures on the international podium, Nagano replied, "I am where I want to be." The orchestra was close to where he grew up and gave him an invaluable learning experience. He knew all the players personally, grew up with the orchestra, and forged a strong bond to it. There was something unique about the culture that attached to it and its place in the community. It was an ideal proving ground for the kind of innovative programming that has been one of Nagano's distinguishing traits. Here he tried out new repertoire and new composers in front of an audience appreciative of almost any musical experience from Frank Zappa to Unsuk Chin. At Berkeley, too, he enjoyed a major coup. Nagano had scheduled a concert of music by Messiaen and wrote to him for advice. The composer was so impressed that he volunteered to travel with his wife, Yvonne Loriod, to take part in the performance of his *Transfiguration of Our Lord Jesus Christ*. At Messiaen's recommendation, Nagano was invited to assist Seiji **Ozawa** in preparation of the composer's opera *St. Francis of Assisi*, which was to receive its premiere at the Paris Opera in 1983. Nagano conducted the final performance and has subsequently conducted it in Bonn, Madrid, London, and Salzburg. He returned to Boston as assistant to **Ozawa** at the Boston SO, and when that conductor became indisposed, made a dramatic debut in a performance of Mahler's Ninth Symphony. Having made his mark, Nagano won a Seaver/NEA Conductors Award and chose to use it studying with "polar opposites" Boulez and Bernstein. Nagano's reputation in Europe grew and he made his La Scala debut in 1987. In 1989 he accepted an appointment as music director at the Opéra de Lyon in France. Taking over the company from John Eliot Gardiner, who had concentrated on eighteenth- and nineteenth-century repertoire, Nagano was anxious to expand the organization's scope and introduced a remarkable series of new productions and recordings, including Carlisle Floyd's *Susannah*, John **Adams's** *Death of Klinghoffer*, Poulenc's *Dialogue of the Carmelites*, Prokofiev's *Love of Three Oranges*, Martinů's *Les trois souhaits*, and Strauss's *Salome* in French. In 1991, he was made assistant principal guest conductor to the London SO and then accepted the music directorship of Manchester's Hallé Orchestra. His nine-year tenure with the latter brought mixed reviews. Having weathered a financial crisis that threatened the orchestra with bankruptcy, he oversaw the orchestra's move to a new concert hall, and the climax of their partnership came with the performance and recording of *St. Francis of Assisi* at the Salzburg Festival. His pop idol image did help raise attendance at the Hallé, but he was forced to temper some of his more adventuresome programming, partly for financial reasons. With Nagano's meticulous drilling, the orchestra improved technically, but equivalent interpretive insight was felt to be somewhat lacking. If the Hallé and Lyon are now seen as stepping-stones, then his appointments with the Deutsches SO, Berlin, and the Los Angeles Opera, both of which came in 2000, marked further progress.

It was an interesting choice to bring Nagano in as principal conductor to assist Placido Domingo (in the role of administrator) as he attempted to boost the West Coast opera company. His goal was to develop a company imbued with a unique character that reflected the Pacific Rim's vitality. The Los Angeles connection, it was thought, could encourage the use of Hollywood technology and the talents of Hollywood directors. For example, *Lohengrin*, the opera that began Nagano's tenure, was directed by the actor Maximillian Schell. Nagano was keen to perform *Moses und Aaron* because much of it was composed by Schoenberg when he was living in California. Though he made a name for himself in Lyon as an innovator and conductor of obscure repertoire, he has taken the opportunity in Los Angeles to conduct more mainstream repertoire, with a hefty dose of Strauss (*Ariadne, Die Frau ohne Schatten, Rosenkavalier*) as well as the standard Mozart and Puccini.

Nagano has done some wonderful work with the Deutsches SO, Berlin, and is especially praised for his Schoenberg performances. The recording of the oratorio *Jacob's Ladder* was described as a "superb reading, full of humanity," and a performance of the Piano Concerto was praised for clarifying Schoenberg's orchestral writing. Although the critics have sometimes been less enthusiastic about his standard repertoire performances such as those of Bruckner's Third Symphony in its original uncut version, Schubert's *Great C Major Symphony*, and Mendelssohn's *Scottish Symphony*, there is no question that his performances of the Germanic repertoire matured considerably during his Berlin tenure. This may be due in part to the fact that, with his European reputation already established, he sought instruction from one of the orchestra's most revered former conductors, Günter Wand. At the end of a relatively brief six-year era, leading German critic Jörg Königsdorf declared "Kent Nagano has matured into one of the great conductors."

In the meantime, he returned each year to Berkeley to continue the mix of new and standard repertoire with the Berkeley SO. The 2002–3 four-concert season, for example, included music by Ligeti, Messiaen, Galina Ustvolskaya, John Manduell, Unsuk Chin, and the world premiere of Nodaira's Piano Concerto, along with Beethoven's early oratorio *Christ on the Mount of Olives*, his *Eroica Symphony*, Mozart's C-Minor Piano Concerto (K491), and Brahms's Fourth Symphony. His announcement that he would finally renounce the role of music director in 2009 was an admission that his hectic schedule was taking a toll on him. He felt he could no longer keep in touch with the essential "pulse" of the organization and its constituency.

Nagano has supporters and detractors, and his listeners are often both. His strengths lie in his ability to draw out orchestral playing that is clean, transparent, detailed, and objective, which is why he is particularly convincing in so many modern scores. This has been especially true of his collaboration with John **Adams**, many of whose orchestral works he premiered. The chief complaint seems to be that his performances display a lack of spatiality and temporal structure. Proceeding by fits and starts, they tend to lack fluency. However, his track record and experience indicate he should be equal to his new demanding appointments with the Bavarian State Opera and the Montreal (Quebec) SO, begun in 2006.

Website

http://www.kentnagano.com

Further Reading

Driscoll, F. Paul. "The Return of the Native (Interview with Los Angeles Opera Conductor Kent Nagano)." *Opera News* 67 (September 2002): 18–22.

Ginell, Richard S. "Cherishing Nagano, While Possible." *American Record Guide* 68 (January–February 2005): 6–9.

Moor, Paul. "Kent Nagano & the Berkeley Symphony." *American Record Guide* 55, no. 4 (1992): 44–45.

Rabinowitz, Peter J. "'To Enrich Our Whole Lives': A Conversation with Kent Nagano." *Fanfare* 15, no. 3 (1992): 121–26.

Searson, Charles. "The Double Life of Kent Nagano." *Classic CD* 51 (August 1994): 24–25.

Tommasini, Anthony. "Orchestras Continue to Ignore the Obvious." *New York Times*, 19 November 2000, Arts & Leisure 1, 30.

Selected Recordings

Beintus: *The Butterfly Tree*; *The Animal Singers of Bremen*; Julia Butterfly Hill (spoken vocals); Joy Carlin (spoken vocals); Joan Baez (voice); Berkeley SO. Summit 1018.

Bernstein: *Mass*; Jerry Hadley (t); Sigurd Brauns (org); Tobias Lehmann (perc); Rundfunkchor Berlin; Staats- und Domchor Berlin; Pacific Mozart Ens; Berlin RSO. Harmonia Mundi HMC 901840.41.

Messiaen: *Saint François d'Assise*; José Van Dam (b-b); Dominique Kim (Ondes Martenot); Chris Merritt (t); Dawn Upshaw (s); John Aler (t); Tom Krause (br); Guy Renard (t); Jeanne Loriod (Ondes Martenot); Valerie Hartmann-Claverie (Ondes Martenot); Arnold Schoenberg Choir; Hallé O. Deutsche Grammophon DGG 445176.

Rimsky-Korsakov: *Le coq d'or*; Olga Trifonova (*Queen of Shemakha*); Barry Banks (*Astrologer*); Albert Schagidullin (*King Dodon*); Maryinsky Theater Ch; O de Paris. Chatelet DVUS-OPLCO DVD.

Schoenberg: *Die Jakobsleiter*; *Friede auf Erden*; Dietrich Hensel (*Gabriel*); Salomé Kammer (*One Who Is Dying*); Jonas Kaufman (*One Who Is Called*); Berlin RSO and Ch. Harmonia Mundi HMC 80121.

∿

Nelson, John (Wilton)
Born 6 December 1941 in San José, Costa Rica

John Nelson was born to Protestant missionaries working in Costa Rica, and the faith he inherited has remained an important element throughout his life and career as a conductor. His earliest performing experience was as part of a trio, playing accordion with his father and brother, on preaching missions. He was blessed with a good voice and loved to sing. His early musical proclivities were such that his parents laid out $50 to purchase a secondhand Steinway piano. Piano teachers were a mixed bag, but one of them, the wife of a miner, was a graduate of the New England Conservatory of Music; he was later influenced by another pianist, this one Juilliard-trained. When he was twelve he was sent to a parochial boarding school in Orlando (Fla.), where sports were rated more highly than music. At the close of his junior year, he attended summer school at Westminster Choir College and was considerably impressed by the venerable John Finley Williamson, the school's founder. The flame of music burning brightly, he began his college career in 1959 at Wheaton College, a conservative Christian institution in the Chicago suburbs which has a strong reputation for music. He enrolled as a piano major and was actively involved in choral activities. His first directing position was at a local Baptist church, where he conducted his first performance of *Messiah*. When he removed to Juilliard for graduate study in 1963, he was already contemplating the shift from the piano bench to the podium. A shortened little finger, the result of an accident, exacerbated his doubts about whether he could make it as a pianist. He obtained a master's degree in choral conducting and then entered Jean Morel's orchestral conducting class, which, that year, was a distinguished assemblage that included Leonard **Slatkin**, Dennis Russell **Davies**, and Catherine Comet. In 1965 he began an important association as the director of the New Jersey–based Pro Arte Chorale. The next year, he was appointed conductor of the Greenwich PO. On graduation and having received the Irving Berlin Award for conducting, he spent a year working on a postgraduate diploma. He became a member of the Juilliard conducting faculty, worked with the Juilliard Opera Theater, and appeared at the New York Mozart Festival.

During his ten years with the New Jersey choir, he brought it on regular visits to New York City to sing the great choral masterpieces at Lincoln Center and Carnegie Hall. He formed the Aspen Music Festival Chorus (1968) and was appointed director of the Aspen Choral Institute (1968–73). Toward the end of this period, which culminated in a European tour with the Pro Arte Chorale, he began to see himself as stuck in a rut and was advised by his agent to do "something spicy and interesting that'll make a splash in New York." This turned out to be an uncut Carnegie Hall performance of Berlioz's *Les Troyens*, with a cast that included Evelyn Lear and Richard Cassilly with the Pro Arte Chorale. It was a successful, if reckless, venture that amassed a debt of $50,000, which took ten years to pay off! Such high expectations had been generated by this audacious project that the audience included all the leading New York critics and conductors from the Metropolitan Opera. The result was opportunities to conduct at the Santa Fe Opera and the New York City Opera, where he debuted with *Carmen*. He was also invited to assist in the Met production of *Les Troyens* conducted by Raphael Kubelik. Due to Kubelik's ill health, Nelson conducted the final two performances, and he went on to conduct the work at the Grand Théâtre in Geneva. These events set in motion what were to become two of his specialties: the music of Berlioz and a return to the music of Handel.

In shifting from choral to orchestral conducting, Nelson made a shrewd decision to accept the directorship of the Indianapolis (Ind.) SO. This gave him the opportunity to learn the ropes of being in charge of an orchestra and building up his repertoire. His tenure there, which lasted from 1976–87, was one of growth and achievement. He rejuvenated a demoralized organization, transforming it into a vibrant one despite a limited market and budget. He increased the audience, built up a flourishing relationship with the community, and presided over the move to a new concert hall. However, with the burden of administration and the fear of becoming stale and routine, he knew that, after eleven years, it was time to move on. In 1981 he accepted the post of music director of the Saint Louis Opera, which he held until 1991, and he became the director of the Caramoor Festival in Katomah (N.Y.) (1983–89).

Several years of freelancing followed his departure from Indianapolis, a period which he used to concentrate on his artistic development. He was in demand as a guest conductor with top-flight orchestras and opera companies, and first made his mark in the recording studio. He appeared with the Opéra de Lyon in 1981 conducting *Beatrice and Benedict*, the first of many subsequent appearances with that company. He debuted at the Rome opera six years later with *Benvenuto Cellini*. He became a familiar visitor at the Grand Théâtre in Geneva and began a distinguished series of Handel opera performances at the Lyric Opera in Chicago with *Xerxes* in 1996 and *Alcina* in 2000. He conducted Mozart's *Idomeneo* there in 1998 and gave a much-praised rendition of Handel's *Giulio Cesare* at the Met in 1999. His ambition to lead a European orchestra was fulfilled when he was appointed music director of the Ensemble Orchestral de Paris in 1998. His recording of *Beatrice and Benedict* (1992) with the forces of the Opéra de Lyon received a Diapason d'Or award, and he followed this with an admired recording of Handel's *Semele* (1993) with a cast that included Kathleen Battle, Marilyn Horne, and Samuel Ramey, and which won a Grammy for Best Opera Recording. He has also been the distinguished accompanist on recital records by Kathleen Battle, David Daniels, and Vivica Geneaux. This reflects the special affinity he feels for singers because of his own love of singing. In addition to opera, he has recorded music by Górecki (1993), Paul Schoenfield (1994), Handel's oratorio L'Allegro, il Penseroso ed il Moderato (2001), and a complete version of the incidental music by Mendelssohn to Shakespeare's A Midsummer Night's Dream (2003).

In a 1991 interview, Nelson expressed his frustration at not being able to perform the great Baroque masterpieces, as he had been used to doing earlier in his career, because "authentic performance" groups had cornered that niche. After working with such groups and finding a way to instill more "communicativeness" into their performances—a quality he felt to be lacking—his great achievement was to meld the sensibility and style of original instrument performances with ensembles playing on modern instruments. To achieve this, he worked with a musicologist to define aspects of authenticity with respect to tempo, rhythm, and ornamentation. Despite some resistance from the players of the English CO, this synthesis was successfully realized in his recording of Semele. Regarding the recording of L'Allegro with the Ensemble Orchestral de Paris, the critic for the American Record Guide (January–February 1996) wrote: "Nelson knows this style inside out and his articulate, idiomatic and exquisitely expressive approach made manifest the music's dramatic integrity."

Nelson conducts the music of Berlioz with enormous flair and an understanding for both its quirkiness and its clarity. He claims to be the composer's soulmate through a spiritual empathy that revels in extremes and a passion for communicating. His performances are convincing because he understands that Berlioz's architectural forms are based on orchestral sonorities. Bowled over by hearing Colin Davis's recording of Les Troyens, which led to the reckless mounting of his own performance in Carnegie Hall in 1972, he has continued to champion all of the composer's major works. By 1979, during his tenure in Indianapolis, he had performed all his major choral works and has subsequently performed the instrumental music countless times. His devotion is such that he designated 2003, the bicentenary of the composer's birth, to be his Berlioz year to perform all the operas.

Nelson's choral background and his spiritual awareness led to the founding of Soli Deo Gloria in 1993, an organization for promoting sacred classical music and expanding its repertoire by commissioning works from promising composers. Thus far, premieres by James MacMillan, Paul Schoenfield, Augusta Read Thomas, Christopher Rouse, and George Arasimowicz have resulted. The organization has sponsored performances of music by Górecki in Chicago and of Brahms's Requiem in Shanghai, sung in Chinese. Nelson has consistently championed new music. In addition to the premieres mentioned above, he gave the first performance of *Casa Guidi*, a song cycle composed especially for Frederica von Stade by Dominick Argento in 1986, and Takemitsu's *I Hear the Water Dreaming* in 1987. He conducted the premiere of *Galina* (based on the life of soprano Galina Vishnevskaya) by Marcel Landowski at the Opéra National de Lyon in 1996.

Nelson's stature and worth as a conductor is summed up succinctly by critic Donald Vroon in a review in the *American Record Guide* (March–April 1996): "I have known John Nelson's conducting for many years, and I can say confidently that he goes from strength to strength. He has never stagnated; he has plunged ever deeper into music like this (Berlioz) to give us a stronger understanding of it. He is not beating time; he is shaping phrases and making every entry, every sentence count."

Further Reading

Jacobson, Bernard. "Paris Tackles the Italian-Trained Saxon Londoner: A Sublime Handel 'L'Allegro.'" *Fanfare* 24 (March–April 2001): 48–52.

Lane, Chester. "A Requiem for Humanity: 'Ein Deutsches Requiem' Comes to the People's Republic of China, in the Language of the People." *Symphony* 48, no. 2 (1997): 40–42.

Moore, Tom. "A Conversation with John Nelson." *Fanfare* 14, no. 6 (1991): 62.

Scherer, Barrymore Laurence. "The Other Berlioz Man." *Gramophone* 70 (June 1992): 10–11.

Selected Recordings

Berlioz: *Benvenuto Cellini*; Gregory Kunde (*Benvenuto Cellini*); Patrizia Ciofi (*Teresa*); Joyce di Donato (*Ascanio*); Jean-François Lapointe (*Fieramosca*); Laurent Naouri (*Balducci*); Renaud Delaigue (*Pope Clement VII*); Eric Salha (*Francesco*); Marc Mauillon (*Bernardino*); Eric Huchet (*Innkeeper*); Ronan Nédélec (*Pompeo*); Natl O de France; Ch de Radio France. Virgin 7243 5 45706 2 9.

Handel: *Semele*; John Aler (t), Kathleen Battle (s), Marilyn Horne (ms), Sylvia McNair (s); Michael Chance (ct); Samuel Ramey (b); Neil Mackie (t); Mark S. Doss (b); Ambrosian Op. Ch; English CO. DGG 435782.

Loeffler: *La Mort de Tintagiles*; *Irish Fantasies*; Jennie Hansen (Viola d'amore); Neil Rosenshein (t); Indianapolis SO. New World 80332.

Mozart: *Clarinet Concerto in A, K 622*; *Horn Concerto No. 4 in Eb, K 495*; *Oboe Concerto in C, K 271k, "Ferlendis."* Mozart (L): *Trumpet Concerto in D*; Paul Meyer (cl); David Guerrier (cor, tp); Francois Leleux (ob); Paris Op Ens. Virgin 32627.

∿

Oue, Eiji
Born 3 October 1956 in Hiroshima, Japan

When Oue was appointed music director of the Minnesota Orchestra in 1995, it was a surprise. The players and the administration had been impressed by the vitality of his conducting when he had appeared as a guest. His approach must have provided a stark contrast to the dour demeanor of the incumbent music director, Edo de Waart. Nonetheless, his appointment to one of the nation's leading orchestras from the relative obscurity of the Erie (Pa.) PO was a considerable gamble. Concern was expressed in some quarters that he lacked the experience and range of repertoire needed for an orchestra of this caliber. Undeterred, and seizing upon his most appealing characteristics, the orchestra's publicity machine went into overdrive, spending a cool $500,000 to promote the appointee to the Minnesota public.

Reflecting on his seven-year tenure in this post, one has much to praise. Oue threw himself into the job with total commitment and outreach that extended far beyond the routine duties of music director. It is said he turned down prestigious guest appearances to work with previously scheduled school groups in the Minnesota hinterland. The qualities of boundless energy and enthusiasm that he brought to his performances were focused on conveying the emotional heart of the music to his listeners. For this reason his most successful repertoire was the late-romantic, extroverted scores of Richard Strauss, Mahler, and Respighi. For many this visceral impact was enough, but some found his readings superficial, even to the point of vulgarity and bombast. Critics said his performances frequently lacked structure, subtle detail, and contrast. He routinely committed all his scores to memory, even when accompanying a soloist (giving rise to performance anxieties on a number of occasions). He was also considered too deferential to his soloists at times. There is no question, though, that he made significant progress as an artist during his tenure. Comparing performances of Mahler's Second Symphony, Michael Anthony in the Minneapolis *Star Tribune* (31 May 2002) commented on "the special moments of thoughtfulness . . . that weren't there six years ago." He had maintained the orchestra's high performance standards, placing them firmly on the international map with his recordings and the various tours he made. The fourteen discs he produced included the music of Rachmaninoff, Respighi, Ravel, Strauss, Bernstein, and Copland. His CD of music by Argento won a Record of the Year award in the contemporary classical category (2004).

Oue began piano lessons at the age of four and by the time he was fifteen had been accepted by the Toho School of Music as a performance major. As a conducting student of Hideo Saito he was taken under the wing of Seiji Ozawa, who persuaded him to attend the summer school at Tanglewood. It was here that he first encountered Leonard Bernstein, who was to be his chief mentor over the succeeding decade. After obtaining his bachelor's degree in 1978, he enrolled at the New England Conservatory of Music. Winning the Koussevitzky Prize in 1980 and the Salzburg competition the following year enhanced his reputation. In 1982 he was awarded a fellowship by the Los Angeles Philharmonic Institute and briefly studied with Sergiu Celibidache. The same year he took on the directorships of the New Bedford (Mass.) SO, the Boston Mozarteum Orchestra, and the Greater Boston Youth Orchestra. In 1985 he toured with Bernstein and joined the faculty of Brown University. The following year he was appointed to conduct the Empire State (N.Y.) YSO. From 1986–90 he served as associate conductor of the Buffalo (N.Y.) PO. His career received a boost when he was invited to conduct the London SO on a tour of Japan (1990) and appointed resident conductor of the Pacific Music Festival in Sapporo. His successful tenure as music director of the Erie PO (1991–95) served as the prelude to his Minnesota appointment. Nineteen ninety-five was also the year of his debut with the Osaka PO, and in 1997 he became music director of the Grand Teton Music Festival. His first European appointment was as chief conductor to the NDR Philharmonie of Hannover in 1998, the same year that he took his Minnesota orchestra on a successful tour of Japan. He has since toured with the Hannover orchestra to Spain, Austria, Hungary, Croatia, Brazil, and Japan. Since 2000, Oue has been a conducting professor at the Music and Drama School in Hannover. After maintaining a close relationship with the Osaka PO as guest conductor over a number of years, he became music director in 2003. He made his Bayreuth Festival debut in 2005 with *Tristan und Isolde*, becoming the first Asian to conduct there.

Further Reading

Anthony, Michael. "Minnesota Orchestra, Eiji Oue." *American Record Guide* 57, no. 4 (1994): 43.

French, Gilbert G. "A Chat with Eiji Oue." *American Record Guide* 62 (March–April 1999): 20–22.

Kozinn, Allan. "The Minnesota's Unexpected Choice." *New York Times*, 29 December 1993, C11.

Oue, Eiji. *Minnesota Orchestra Tour Europe 98: February 14–March 5, 1998.* Minneapolis, Minn.: Orchestra, 1998.

Snyder, Neal. "Interview: Eiji Oue—Giving Kids a Classical Choice." *Teaching Music* 3, no. 4 (1996): 44–46.

Selected Recordings
Antheil: *Piano Concertos: No. 1, no. 2*; *A Jazz Symphony*; *Jazz Sonata*; *Can-Can*; *Sonatina*; *Death of Machines*; *Little Shimmy*; Markus Becker (pf); North German RSO. CPO 777 109.
Argento: *In Praise of Music*; *Casa Guidi*; *Capriccio for Clarinet and Orchestra* "Rossini in Paris"; Frederica von Stade (ms); Burt Hara (cl); Minnesota O. Reference RR-100CD.
Mahler: *Das Lied von der Erde*; Michelle DeYoung (ms); Jon Villars (t); Minnesota O. Reference 88.
Martinů: *Concerto for 2 Pianos*. Schnittke: *Concerto for Piano Four Hands*; *Hommage à Grieg*; *Polyphonic Tango*; Aglika Genova (pf); Liuben Dimitrov (pf); Kathrin Rabus (vn); Hannover Radio PO. CPO 999804.
Reveries; music by Satie, Debussy, Fauré, Grieg, Massenet, Wofl-Ferrari, Gounod, Tchaikovsky, Sibelius; Minnesota O. Reference RR-99CD.

∽

Ozawa, Seiji
Born 1 September 1935 in Fenytien (now Shenyang), China

In 2002, Ozawa took up his responsibilities as music director of the Vienna State Opera. He had completed twenty-seven years as director of the Boston SO, the longest tenure in the orchestra's history. His Boston years were marked by great achievements but were never without controversy. On his departure, there was a sense, shared by musicians, critics, and some sections of the public, that he had stayed too long and that his relationship with the orchestra had become jaded.

At his birth in the Manchurian city of Fenytien (at a turbulent time in Sino-Japanese history), the likelihood of this third son of a Japanese dentist becoming a superstar of Western music was pretty remote. The only Western-style music that Ozawa would have heard as a child were the hymns at the Presbyterian church his mother attended. By 1944, the family had moved to Tokyo and was able to satisfy their son's desire to take piano lessons. In due course he became a student at the newly established Toho School of Music and fell under the influence of its founder, the cellist and conductor Hideo Saito, who had studied in Leipzig and Berlin. A freak sports accident (accounts vary as to whether he was playing soccer or rugby) broke two fingers and resulted in his taking composition and conducting studies in place of piano. His talent and abilities were evident when he took first place in both subjects in his graduating class and was given the opportunity to conduct the NHK (Japanese Radio) SO and the Japan PO. On the advice of his mentor and with very few resources he journeyed to Besançon in southeastern France, the venue of a prestigious conducting competition. He so impressed the jury, especially then–music director of the Boston SO, Charles Munch, that he won first prize and an invitation to attend the Tanglewood Institute in Massachusetts the following summer. Meanwhile he continued his schooling with Eugène Bigot in Paris and won a scholarship to study with Herbert von Karajan in Berlin. At Tanglewood he won the Koussevitzky Prize, the support of Aaron Copland, and the admiration of the benefactor's widow. This brought him to the attention of Leonard Bernstein, who, while touring with the New York PO to Berlin, was so impressed by Ozawa's conducting that he invited him to become one of his assistant conductors for the 1961–62 season. His performances with the NYPO of works by Charles Ives and contemporary Japanese composers continued to make a positive impression, and he toured with the orchestra to Japan in the spring of 1961. There followed an invitation to revisit with NHK Orchestra, but it was a much more confident and experienced Ozawa who stood before them on this occasion. The orchestra resented his newfound authority, however, and refused to play the concert. This incident demonstrated stubbornness on the part of Ozawa and his willingness to resist tradition and stick to his guns. His career continued to make progress back in the U.S., however. He made his debut with the San Francisco SO in 1962 and conducted a series of outdoor summer concerts with the Lewisohn Stadium Orchestra in 1963 and 1964. As often happens with aspiring young practitioners, an important opportunity opened up for Ozawa when he was called in as a last-minute replacement for an indisposed colleague. In this instance, it was to conduct two concerts with the Chicago SO at the Ravinia Festival. Nineteen sixty-four proved a pivotal year because he began a five-year term as music director at Ravinia, debuted with both the Boston SO and the Toronto (Ontario) SO, and returned to spend another season with the NYPO as, in effect, its chief conductor while Bernstein was away on sabbatical. He renewed Japanese ties that same year as conductor of the Toho String Orchestra tour in two New York City concerts that garnered rave reviews. His first major appointment came in 1965 in Toronto, after he directed the TSO on a European tour earlier in the fall. He stayed with the orchestra for four years, demonstrating his abilities as an orchestra trainer and his particular talent for directing large-scale and complex scores. A much admired recording of Messiaen's *Turungalila-symphonie* dates from this period. In 1968, he signed on as music director of the San Francisco SO, and in 1969 made his operatic debut at the Salzburg Festival, leading performances of *Cosi fan tutte*. His links to the Boston SO had not been severed by these other activities; he became artistic director of the Tanglewood Festival in 1970 and, *gradus ad parnassum*, music director of the orchestra in 1973. Thus began the long and sometimes uneasy record-breaking tenure.

Over the years he showed an unrivaled mastery of the colorful and fiery repertoire that comes mostly from the early twentieth century—Stravinsky, Ives, Bartók, and Prokofiev—and he maintained the nonpareil reputation of the Boston SO in French music, particularly Ravel. The orchestra appreciated his clear direction and efficient rehearsing. His conducting became more authoritative with the passage of time and his interpretations of works that were judged unsatisfactory early on, such as those of Mahler, began to show a marked improvement. Nevertheless, there was a sense that his engagement with the orchestra and the musical life of the city of Boston was never as close as it ought to have been, with periods of intense activity followed by periods of absence. This was partly due to the fact that Ozawa always overextended himself, leading at one point to a serious breakdown in health due to exhaustion. At first this disengagement was explained by his other commitments to the SFSO and his newfound attachment to opera. His decision to base his family in Japan and spend necessary time with them was another contributory factor.

Similar criticism surrounded his relationship to Tanglewood, which seemed at one point to have become halfhearted. His awareness of this criticism led him to make a more positive commitment to the festival, but it was done in such an undiplomatic way that it caused one of the most bitter and public brouhahas the classical music world has seen in recent memory. Enjoying the reputation as one of the most sympathetic orchestral accompanists in the business, Ozawa would not tolerate artists with "prima donna-ish" temperaments no matter how much of a box office draw they might be, preferring to work with musicians whose integrity and dedication he respected. In fairness, it has to be said that Ozawa's intervention did produce positive effects in subsequent years.

It is generally agreed that Ozawa added power to the orchestra's sound, but another criticism that emerged in the early days was that he did not do enough to sustain the reputation the orchestra had earned in the Koussevitzky years for championing new music. Although he was very good at directing new music, he didn't seem to have much enthusiasm for it and never championed any composers. As the orchestra approached its centenary in

1981, Ozawa set about dispelling such criticism by commissioning a series of twelve works from American and European composers and embarking on a retrospective of compositions, including Bartók's *Concerto for Orchestra* and Stravinsky's *Symphony of Psalms*, that had been given their first U.S. performance in Boston. Subsequent commissions included *The Shadows of Time* from Henri Dutilleux, a longtime associate at the Tanglewood Festival.

Continuing ties with Japan, in 1984 he cofounded the Saito Kinen Orchestra with his onetime classmate and Toronto associate, Kazuyoshi Akiyama, in memory of their revered teacher; he also founded the Saito Kinen Festival in 1992.

Ozawa has been guest conductor with leading orchestras around the world: the Vienna PO, Berlin PO, Orchestre National de France, Orchestre de Paris, London SO, London PO, and Philharmonia Orchestra, among numerous others.

Ozawa's conducting style personifies his strengths. He is lithe and balletic on the podium, and his gestures are clear and communicative. Since 1994 he has given up using a baton, so his hand gestures have become even more expressive. He has a fine ear for orchestral sonorities, a mind that can decode the complex textures of many modern scores, a phenomenal memory, and an uncanny ability to accompany sympathetically—as Anne-Sophie Mutter described it, "to be like a glove to a soloist." On the other hand, many critics have found his music-making to be superficially dazzling, lacking depth of emotional feeling and inner meaning. His attempts to garner excitement through sheer sound too often result in raucousness and an obfuscation of contrapuntal and rhythmic detail. The dissatisfaction of the players led one Boston critic to quip that Ozawa looked better than the orchestra sounded. Summing up, another critic wrote that Ozawa's tenure had been one of creative growth overall, but that it hadn't always been a tidy process.

It is quite likely that his sterling qualities, coupled with the deep sense of tradition the Vienna PO carries with it, will result in an even more productive and satisfying partnership than the marathon Boston one proved to be. The Viennese must be satisfied; he is contracted to stay on at the State Opera until at least 2010.

Further Reading

Ashman, Mike. "Seiji Ozawa." *Music & Musicians* 28 (September 1979): 13–14.

Ellis, Bill. "Ozawa's Festival: Saito Kinen Gets Better." *American Record Guide* 57, no. 6 (1994): 44–45.

Hart, Philip. "Seiji Ozawa." In *Conductors: A New Generation*, 165–94. New York: Charles Scribner's Sons, 1983.

"Ozawa, Seiji." In *World Musicians*, edited by Clifford Thompson, 728–30. New York: H. W. Wilson Company, 1999.

Page, Tim. "Keeping Time at Tanglewood: Seiji Ozawa's Legacy at the Country's Most Prestigious Summer Classical Music Festival." *Opera News* 68 (June 2004): 26–29.

Scherer, Barrymore Laurence. "Seiji at the Met." *Opera News* 57 (December 1992): 8–10.

Terry, Ken. "Seiji Ozawa." *Fugue* 4 (March 1980): 33–35.

Selected Recordings

Bartók: *Music for Strings, Percussion and Celesta; Concerto for Viola;* Wolfram Christ (va); Berlin PO. DGG 437993.

Bizet: *Symphony in C; Patrie Overture; Jeux d'enfants; Carmen Suites: No. 1; No. 2;* O Natl de France. EMI 5 86089.

Ives: *Central Park in the Dark; Symphony no. 4;* Jerome Rosen (pf); Tanglewood Festival Ch; Boston SO. From DGG 423243.

Prokofiev: *Romeo and Juliet;* Boston SO. DGG 423268.

Ravel: *Daphnis et Chloé; Valses nobles et sentimentales;* Tanglewood Festival Ch (John Oliver, dir); Boston SO. DGG Eloquence 476 8429.

⌒

Perick, Christof
Born 23 October 1946 in Hamburg, Germany

One might wonder why Perick, given his classic German musical education and vast experience in some of the leading opera houses and concert halls in Europe and the U.S., would consider taking so humble an appointment as that of music director of the Charlotte (N.C.) SO. It is certainly not one of the nation's premier ensembles, being about average in the second-tier ratings. But Charlotte is a thriving and expanding city—one of the most prosperous in the country—and has a community with the will and the means to support and promote such a prestigious institution as a symphony orchestra. It was perhaps a shrewd move, then, to choose it as a means of establishing his directorial credentials and as a stepping-stone to loftier U.S. ambitions. Perick had previously expressed his admiration for American orchestras and a wish to again be a music director here. His previous experience in a permanent position was as music director of the Los Angeles CO (1991–94) where, according to some accounts, he frequently "outshone in quest and quality" the rival Los Angeles PO. (In 1988, he was appointed chief conductor of the ill-fated Chicago-based Illinois SO, which folded for lack of financial resources shortly thereafter.) His first seasons in Charlotte saw an increase in orchestra personnel and a growth in artistic accomplishment. The organization received a boost with the appointment of Jinny Leem, considered one of the most talented violinists in the country, as concert mistress. Overall, the CSO has taken on a more refined tone and achieved a sharper ensemble. The players feel they have been taken to a higher artistic level, and the conductor has considerably expanded the repertory and attracted some of the most promising of the younger generation of guest artists. Although he continues to commute into North Carolina from Nuremberg, where he serves as artistic director of the city's opera house, he remains commited to Charlotte at least until 2009.

Perick, whose father was concertmaster of the Hamburg PO, grew up in a highly musical environment. In the 1960s, for example, the teenager regularly attended the Bayreuth Festival, where he witnessed such outstanding conducting role models as Hans Knappertsbusch and Rudolf Kempe in action. He attended the Hamburg Conservatory, studied conducting with Wilhelm Brückner-Rüggeberg, and worked for a time as an assistant conductor at the Hamburg State Opera. His first appointment was at Trier (1970–72), then Darmstadt (1972–74), before becoming *Generalmusikdirektor* in Saarbrücken (1974–77), and Karlsruhe (1977–86). From 1977 to 1984 he held the appointment as first conductor at the Deutsche Oper in Berlin and led that company on tour to the U.S. in 1989, conducting a controversial production of Wagner's *Ring* cycle at the Kennedy Center. In 1986, he made his debuts at the Lyric Opera of Chicago with an uncut *Parsifal* and at the Met with *Die Meistersinger*. In 1990 he first appeared with the New York PO. He served as principal guest conductor of the Semperoper in Dresden (1992–2003) and became *Generalmusikdirektor* in Hannover (1993–96). He was appointed music director of the Nuremberg PO and State Theater in 2005.

As a guest conductor, Perick has appeared throughout North America in Los Angeles, Boston, San Francisco, Saint Louis, Cincinnati, Houston, Dallas, San Diego, Atlanta, Detroit, Seattle, Indianapolis, Milwaukee, Washington, D.C., Toronto, Calgary, and Quebec. Specializing in the German operatic repertory of Beethoven, Wagner, and Strauss, he appeared at the Met for ten consecutive seasons. In Europe he conducts regularly in Berlin, Vienna, and Paris. He has also made an outstanding contribution to the encouragement of younger musicians and frequently conducts the German National Youth Orchestra at home and on tour. He has also lent his talents to the Music Academy of the West Festival in California.

Reviewing Perick's career, one notices some surprising inconsistencies. His performances seem to range from the scintillating to the downright dull, although, in fairness, far more of the former than the latter! One frequently mentioned characteristic is his ability to allow music to flow naturally but purposefully. It leads one to speculate that he may become, like Otto Klemperer or Eugen Jochum, a master at revealing the grand architectural dimension and structure of the music. Another strength is his alertness to the inherent drama in opera and its realization in performance. He has earned admiration as a sympathetic accompanist in the theater and concert hall. Firmly rooted in the Germanic tradition, especially that of Wagner and his successors (Strauss, Schreker, Schmidt), he has left the mission of promoting American and new music to his colleagues in Charlotte. He has a particularly winning way with Haydn, whom he treats with due respect (he recorded several symphonies with the Los Angeles CO), and occasionally strays into the French and Russian repertory.

Further Reading

Kinzer, S. "Arts in America: A New Conductor Shifts an Orchestra's Mood to Allegro." *New York Times*, 9 May 2001, 2.

Rosen, Ronald S. "Stranger in Paradise: The Life and Adventures of the Los Angeles Chamber Orchestra." *Musical Quarterly* 80, no. 2 (1996): 225–26.

Vittes, Laurence. "Letter from Los Angeles." *Gramophone* 68 (April 1991): 1792.

Selected Recordings

Haydn: *Symphonies 38, 82, and 104*; Los Angeles CO. Dorian 90168.

Schmidt: *Notre Dame*; Jones; Moll; Laubenthal King, et al.; St. Hedwig's Cathedral Ch; RIAS Kammerchor; Berlin RSO. Capriccio 248/9.

Strauss (R): *Elektra*; Forrester; Vinzing; Rysanek; et al.; Ch de Radio France; O Natl de France. Rodolphe RPC 32420/21.

∾

Preu, Eckart
Born 24 August 1969 in Erfurt, GDR

Eckart Preu (rhymes with joy) began voice lessons at age three and piano at five, at the insistence of his musically inclined father. He admits that he once hated practicing the piano and cried at each lesson, but now is grateful for them. With his older brother, Hans-Peter, who is also a conductor, Preu went to the boarding school of the Dresden Boys Choir (Dresdner Kreuzchor) at age ten. He remained there for eight years, eventually becoming a soloist, rehearsal pianist, and assistant conductor. He also worked as a vocal coach with the Altenburg Opera and the Erfurt Opera House. Compulsory military service ended suddenly in 1989 with the fall of the Berlin wall, so he went back to music, earning a master's degree in conducting from the Hochschule für Musik in Weimar and studying under Jean-Sebastien Bereau at the Conservatoire National Supérieur de Musique in Paris. While still in Europe, he was music director of the Orchestre International de Paris from 1993 to 1995 and served as assistant conductor at Radio France.

When he won the National Conducting Competition of the German Academic Exchange Service (Deutscher Akademischer Austauschdienst) in 1996, Preu moved to the U.S. to attend the Hartt School of Music. There he won the Karl Böhm Conducting Scholarship and earned a graduate degree (1999) studying with Harold **Farberman**.

He began working with the Bard Music Festival in 1997 as assistant and guest conductor, and from 1999–2000 was visiting professor at Bard College. In 1998 he won third prize at the International Competition for Young Conductors of the European Union in Spoleto, Italy. Over the next several years, Preu's posts included principal conductor of the New Amsterdam (N.Y.) SO, music director of the Norwalk (Conn.) YSO (1998–2001), resident conductor of the American Russian Young Artists Orchestra (1999–2004), resident conductor of the American SO (1997–2004), and associate conductor of the Richmond (Va.) SO (2001–4).

Currently music director of the Spokane (Wash.) SO (2004–present) and the Stamford (Conn.) SO (2005–present), the energetic Preu looks for ways to make the concert experience fresh, to help audiences discover something new, and to make great music relevant, accessible, and enjoyable for all kinds of listeners, regardless of age or musical background. Presenting Vivaldi's *Four Seasons*, for example, he prefaced each concerto by quoting from the composer's descriptive sonnets. His wry sense of humor, enthusiasm, genuineness, and ability to explain music concisely contribute to his artistic and personal rapport with his orchestras and members of the community. Preu doesn't believe in "playing down," but does think there is classical music for everyone and tries to bring it to unconventional venues to reach a variety of people. He says, "The basic presentation of concerts has not changed much since the times of the late Joseph Haydn and I think it's really time to rip the wigs off our heads and get a face-lift." Preu also says that he hates a formal, stuffy atmosphere, preferring to go to a concert to have fun and feel good. That's why he left Germany, he notes, "because we took music way too seriously there." In Spokane, he started a series at a downtown nightclub in which the orchestra wore jeans and polo shirts and played shorter pieces against a backdrop of rock-concert lighting and a video screen.

On the podium Preu is expressive but exacting, with a wide range of gestures and a depth of feeling that he ably communicates to the orchestra. Off the podium, he is a frequent guest speaker for local businesses, community organizations, and schools. He also writes arts feature articles for the *Stamford-Norwalk Advocate*.

As a guest conductor, he has led the Jerusalem SO (Israel), Radio PO of Slovenia, Pecs PO (Hungary), Varna PO (Bulgaria), Nouvel Ensemble du Conservatoire Supérieur de Musique de Paris, and in Germany the Jenaer Philharmoniker, Hallesche PO, Thüringer Kammerorchester, Landessinfonieorchester Gotha, and Jugendorchester Berlin. He also served for two years on the guest faculty of the C. W. Post Chamber Music Festival (N.Y.).

⁓

Previn, André (George)
Born 6 April 1929 in Berlin, Germany

Previn was already an accomplished pianist when he enrolled at the Berlin Academy (Hochschule) of Music at the age of six. A few years later, as a teenager living in Los Angeles, his lifelong interest in jazz was sparked by hearing the piano playing of jazz great Art Tatum. A jazz transcription he notated for the pianist José Iturbi to play in the movie *Holiday in Mexico* was his entrée into the Hollywood music scene. Meanwhile, he had been receiving composition lessons from Joseph Achron, Ernst Toch, and Mario Castelnuovo-Tedesca, as well as composing for and conducting student ensembles. These accomplishments, with the addition of playing chamber music with the renowned violinist Joseph Szigeti, make up the various elements with which he was to build his diverse musical career.

His family, of Russian Jewish descent, was forced to flee Germany in 1938 and settled briefly in Paris. They arrived in the U.S. in 1939 to live in Los Angeles, where an uncle was an executive at MGM studios. André's precocious talent meant that he soon began to earn a living through music. While still a student at Beverly Hills High School, he was providing music for the annual senior show, playing and recording jazz, and directing orchestrations and arrangements for local radio stations. Moving to MGM, his work consisted of rehearsing musical numbers, synchronizing sound tracks, and arranging and composing scores (one of which, *Three Little Words*, was nominated for an Oscar). Having become a U.S. citizen in 1943, he had his career interrupted by two years of military service (1950–52). Even so, since he was stationed in San Francisco, he was able to put his musical talents to use making arrangements for the Sixth Army Band and take conducting lessons from Pierre Monteux, then music director of the San Francisco SO. When his work at MGM resumed, Previn's reputation and achievements, including creating adaptations (Kiss Me Kate, for example) and original scores for up to six films a year, began to mount up. He continued to perform with jazz combos and appeared, on occasion, as solo pianist with orchestras. His smoldering ambition to become a symphony orchestra conductor resulted in guest appearances with the Los Angeles PO and his "official" conducting debut with the Saint Louis SO in 1962.

It appears that the transition from Hollywood wunderkind to conductor of symphony orchestras, though surprising, was remarkably rapid and smooth. From 1964 he was a regular guest conductor with the Houston SO and already making recordings with the London SO. Previn's contract with RCA to record a complete cycle of Vaughan Williams's symphonies with the London SO (thereby placing his work in direct comparison with the authoritative recordings of Sir Adrian Boult) was a bold step, demonstrating his especial fondness for the music of then-contemporary English composers. He played Benjamin Britten's Sinfonia da requiem at his New York City debut and his recording of William Walton's first symphony was very warmly received. In 1967 he succeeded Sir John Barbirolli as chief conductor of the Houston (Tex.) SO and was soon making a favorable impression there with imaginative programming, community outreach through children's concerts, and open rehearsals for students. His appointment to the London SO (1968) came about at the instigation of the players, and his tenure as principal conductor, which lasted until 1979, was the longest in the orchestra's history. Previn's penchant for popularizing classical music led to a series of television programs similar to those Leonard Bernstein had pioneered a generation earlier, and thus he became a well-known "personality" in the UK. His switch to classical conducting was not a Jekyll and Hyde affair. He was still at work in the popular field, composing pop songs and the musicals Coco, in association with Jay Lerner (1969), and The Good Companions (1974). His collaboration with Tom Stoppard, Every Good Boy Deserves Favour (1976), was an innovative production that required the inclusion of a symphony orchestra. With respect to musical theater, the comparison with Bernstein is again unavoidable. And with the LSO he composed and conducted more "serious" music: concertos for cello (1968), violin (1969), and guitar (1970), Overture to a Comedy (1966), and Four Songs for Soprano and Orchestra (1968). In 1976, Previn was appointed music director of the Pittsburgh SO, a post he relinquished in 1984 after an ongoing dispute with management. Nevertheless, he left a familiar hallmark in Pittsburgh, having refined the orchestral sound, broadened its repertoire, and reached out to the general public through a television musical appreciation series similar to those he had presented in the UK. In 1985, having accepted emeritus status at the LSO, he turned his attention to the Royal PO and the Los Angeles PO. Two years later, he abdicated the musical directorship of the RPO in favor of becoming chief conductor. He was then able to devote more of his energies to Los Angeles, where he had enjoyed a much-heralded homecoming.

By 1992 he had relinquished both positions, partly out of frustration with orchestral administration but also out of a desire to indulge the other strands of his "musical bow," especially composition. His most ambitious project was an opera based on Tennessee Williams's play *A Streetcar Named Desire* (1998). He also found time to publish a memoir recalling his early years: *No Minor Chords—My Days in Hollywood*. In 1991 he renewed a close association with the LSO when he was designated conductor laureate. Although without a permanent appointment throughout much of the 1990s, his many guest appearances included numerous recording dates and regular concerts with the Vienna PO and at the Salzburg Festival, New York PO, Boston SO, Munich PO, Concertgebouw Orchestra, Dresden Staatskapelle, Philadelphia Orchestra, and Cleveland Orchestra. In the 2002–3 season, he began a four-year term as music director of the Oslo PO. The Boston SO, with Previn conducting, premiered a violin concerto written for his then wife, Anne-Sophie Mutter, in March 2002.

Previn's somewhat mincing style of conducting and his modest, deliberately underplayed personality have not always found favor with critics who crave a more full-blooded approach. However, a survey of over four hundred recordings, although proving not entirely consistent in quality, belies the charge of blandness. His series of Prokofiev recordings with the Los Angeles forces and his performance of Rachmaninoff's Second Symphony with the Royal PO, for instance, are considered the very finest renditions available. Though he has not neglected the classics, it seems rather appropriate, considering his biography, that he seems to have found a particular affinity with Russian, French, English, and American music.

Website
http://www.andre-previn.com

Further Reading
Bookspan, Martin, and Ross Yockey. *André Previn: A Biography*. Garden City, N.Y.: Doubleday, 1981.
Greenfield, Edward. *André Previn*. New York: Drake Publisher, 1973.

Hurwitz, David. "André Previn, the Maestro with That Certain Swing (interview)." *Schwann Inside Jazz & Classical* 2 (March 2001): 14–18.
"One to One: You Ask the Questions." *Gramophone* 80 (June 2002): 29.
Previn, André. *No Minor Chords: My Days in Hollywood.* Garden City, N.Y.: Doubleday, 1991.
Previn, André." In *World Musicians,* edited by Clifford Thompson, 775–78. New York: H. W. Wilson Company, 1999.
Schwarz, K. Robert. "Previn: A Man for All Seasons." *Classic CD* 59 (March 1995): 32–33.

Selected Recordings
Elgar: *Violin Concerto.* Walton: *Violin Concerto*; Daniel Müller-Schott (vn); Oslo PO. Orfeo 621061.
Previn: *Violin Concerto* "Anne-Sophie." Bernstein: *Serenade*; Anne-Sophie Mutter (vn); Boston SO; London SO. DGG B0001313-02.
Prokofiev: *Alexander Nevsky*; *Lieutenant Kijé Suite*; Christine Cairns (ms); Los Angeles Master Ch; Los Angeles PO. Telarc 80143.
Rachmaninoff: *Symphony no. 2*; Royal PO. Telarc 80113.
Vaughan Williams: *Symphony no. 3* "Pastoral"; *Symphony no. 4 in f*; Heather Harper (s); London SO. RCA GD 90503.

⁓

Prieto, Carlos Miguel
Born 14 November 1965 in Mexico City, Mexico

Born into a musical family, Carlos Miguel Prieto has played violin in the Cuarteto Prieto since he was young, along with his famous cellist father, Carlos Prieto. His paternal grandparents, earlier members of the quartet, played violin and viola. Nevertheless, when Prieto came to the United States to attend Princeton in the 1980s, he earned a degree in electrical engineering and went home to work in the sugar industry. After getting an MBA at Harvard in 1992, where he was concertmaster of the orchestra, he returned to business in Mexico for another two years before quitting to study conducting.

Prieto made his conducting debut with the National SO of Mexico in 1995 to great acclaim. From 1998 to 2002 he served as associate conductor of the Mexico City PO. In 1998 the government of Mexico and the Embassy of Austria bestowed on him the Mozart Medal of Honor. Two years later he founded the Mozart-Haydn Festival, an annual series of six concerts based in Mexico City. He remains the festival's music director. He spent a couple of years as assistant conductor of the San Antonio (Tex.) SO in the early 2000s. In 2002, Prieto became music director of the Xalapa SO, Mexico's oldest orchestra, as well as principal conductor for the Washington, D.C.–based Youth Orchestra of the Americas. The Mexican Union of Music and Theater Critics voted him Conductor of the Year in 2002. The following year Prieto accepted two more positions, associate conductor for the Houston (Tex.) SO and music director for the Huntsville (Ala.) SO. In 2006, he resigned his Houston position and began two new music directorships at the Louisiana PO and the Orquesta Sinfónica de Mineria in Mexico City.

A major proponent of twentieth-century music, Prieto has conducted more than fifty world premieres of works by Mexican and American composers. He believes contact with contemporary composers keeps an orchestra alive and that the new works cast an interesting light on the classics. One of his programs in Houston was described in the *Houston Chronicle* as "a free-wheeling mix of Old and New World music." He thinks that while going to a concert should be about surprises, the orchestra should offer not only entertainment, but also music to heal souls and satisfy a hunger.

The gregarious, engaging, and multilingual Prieto leads postconcert dialogues which sometimes include the composers in person. Popular with audiences and musicians alike, the charismatic leader has a crisp and energetic conducting style. His entrepreneurial background and interests were assets when he went to the LPO. As one member of the search committee noted, "It helps to have a maestro who knows his music and also his balance sheet" (*Times-Picayune*).

Prieto has made guest appearances with the Dallas, Phoenix, Omaha, Milwaukee, New Mexico, Indianapolis, Columbus, and Nashville symphony orchestras, the Florida PO, Calgary PO, Dayton PO, Netherlands RSO, Budapest SO, Teatro Colon in Buenos Aires, and every major orchestra in Mexico. He has also conducted festivals and other orchestras in Europe, Russia, Israel, and Latin America.

Selected Recordings

Conciertos y chôro; music by Chávez, Guarnieri, and Ibarra; Carlos Prieto (vc), Edison Quintana (pf); O of the Americas. Urtext 023.

Mozart: *Piano Concerto no. 14 in E♭ major*, K 449; *Piano Concerto no. 23 in A major*, K 488; *Piano Concerto no. 25 in C major*, K 503; Jorge Federico Osorio (pf); Mozart-Haydn Festival O. Artek 24, live.

Musica para divertirse; music by Pérez Prado, Poulenc, Zyman, Bozza, Lavista, Milhaud, Toussaint; Sinfonietta Ventus. Urtext 027.

Revueltas: *Sensemayá; Redes; Homenaje a Federico García Lorca; Janitzio; Musica para charlar; Ocho por radio*; Xalapa SO. Urtext 088.

Toussaint: *Cello Concerto no. 2.* Márquez: *Espejos en la arena.* Sierra: *Cello Concerto "Quatro versos";* Carlos Prieto (vc); O of the Americas. Urtext 047.

Rachleff, Larry
Born 25 February 1955 in New London, Connecticut

Larry Rachleff began directing wind ensembles and concert bands in college, while earning a bachelor of science degree from the University of Connecticut (1977) and two master of music degrees from the University of Michigan (1979). He successively held faculty positions at the University of Texas, Arlington (1979–81), the University of Connecticut (1981–83), and the University of Michigan. A percussionist as well as a conductor, he was drawn to the orchestral repertoire and focused his attention accordingly, accepting the position of conductor of the Opera Theatre at the University of Southern California and joining the faculty of the Oberlin Conservatory, where he was music director of orchestras and conductor of the Contemporary Ensemble. In 1988 he was music director for the American-Soviet Youth Orchestra tour.

In 1991 Rachleff joined the faculty of Rice University's Shepherd School of Music, becoming a professor of music and music director of the Shepherd School SO and CO. Colleagues and students alike say he has an amazing ability to teach and inspire, citing his talent for conveying what he wants from his musicians, his painstaking effort and intense preparation, his egalitarianism and commitment to each student, his terrific musicianship, his openness to suggestion and eagerness to keep learning, and his sense of humor. He has carried his teaching skills abroad, conducting and presenting master classes at the Fryderyk Chopin Academy in Warsaw, the Zurich Hochschule for Music and Theater, and the Sydney and Queensland Conservatorium Orchestras. He also has served as conducting teacher for the American Symphony Orchestra League, the Conductors Guild, and the International Workshop for Conductors in the Czech Republic.

Since 1992, Rachleff has also been principal conductor and music director for Chicago's Symphony II, now the Chicago PO, winning the 2002 Orchestra of the Year award from the Illinois Council of Orchestras. He added a third position to his busy slate in 1996, when he became music director of the Rhode Island PO. Rachleff recently extended his contract there through 2012. Next was the Sunflower Music Festival in Topeka (Kans.), of which he has been music director four times since 2001. In 2004, the energetic Rachleff also became music director of the San Antonio (Tex.) SO. In November 2006, however, the announcement that this relationship will cease when his current contract expires in 2008 began provoking considerable controversy.

An enthusiastic advocate of contemporary music, particularly American, Rachleff says the best way to program new music that stretches an audience is to surround it with the great masterworks. Combining the familiar with the innovative helps the audience to compare and contrast them. He believes in talking to concert audiences to prepare them for what they will hear. When he instituted postconcert discussions in Rhode Island, Rachleff was surprised by the hundreds of concertgoers who stayed, reinforcing his belief that even if classical music isn't *for* everyone, it can be made accessible *to* everyone. Rachleff sees the conductor and orchestra as teachers responsible for creating or providing musical understanding. He also champions music education in public schools, conducting all-state orchestras and festivals across the country.

Rachleff on the podium is described as intense, highly energized, graceful, precise, and facially expressive. Usually he conducts from memory so as to be freer to communicate and have unrestricted podium space. His extraordinary technical command and artistic interpretations inspire confidence and elicit electrifying and emotional concerts.

Rachleff also schedules time for guest appearances with orchestras such as the Los Angeles PO, Houston SO, Seattle SO, Indianapolis SO, Cleveland Orchestra, and Los Angeles CO, in addition to summer conducting at Aspen, Tanglewood, National Music Camp at Interlochen, and the Music Academy of the West with the National Repertory Orchestra and Breckenridge CO.

Further Reading

Barton, Gary. "On the Podium with Larry Rachleff." *Instrumentalist* 56 (October 2001): 15–19.

Harris, Fred E. *Conducting with Feeling*. Galesville, Md.: Meredith Music Publications, 2001.

Kaplan, David. "A Passion for Music." *Rice News*, 2 February 1998. http://www.media.rice.edu/media/NewsBot.asp?MODE=VIEW&ID=3973 &SnID=2.

Larsen, Catherine. "Interview with Larry Rachleff: The Heart and the Brain in Performing." In *Performing with Understanding: The Challenge of the National Standards for Music Education*, edited by Bennett Reimer, 139–52. Reston, Va.: Music Educators National Conference, 2000.

Selected Recordings

Avalon: *Piano Concerto*; *Concerto for Flute, Harp, and Strings*; Robert Avalon (pf); Megan Meisenbach (fl); Mary Golden (hp); Foundation for Modern Music O. Centaur CRC 2484.

Bach (Jan): *Gala Fanfare*; *Concerto for Horn*; *French Suite for Solo Horn*; *Four Two-Bit Contraptions for Flute and Horn*; *Helix*; Jean Berkenstock (fl); Stephen Duke (sax); Jon Boen (cor); Chicago Philharmonic. Equilibrium EQ79.

Daugherty (Michael): *Snap!*; *Blue Like an Orange*. Miller: *Beyond the Wheel*; Gregory Fulkerson (vn); Oberlin Wind Ens; Oberlin Contemporary Music Ens. From *New Music from Oberlin*, Opus One 138.

Fields: *Sages of Chelm*; Paul Ellison (cb); Houston Sinfonia. Centaur CRC 2699.

Welcher: *Concerto for Violin*; Paul Kantor (vn); Symphony II. From *Music of William Bolcom and Dan Welcher*, Equilibrium EQ60.

⌐∽

Reischl, Bridget-Michaele
Born 13 August 1963 in Lakewood, California

Bridget-Michaele Reischl has covered a lot of ground since she earned her bachelor of music degree from the Eastman School of Music in 1985. Studying there with David Effron, she continued her work with Robert **Spano** at Bowling Green (Ohio) State University and with Arthur Winograd at the Hartt School of Music. While at Hartt she won the Karl Böhm Conducting Scholarship (1988), and she received her artist diploma in conducting in 1990.

During these years she was also assistant conductor for the Hartt Opera Theater (1985–88), music director for the Jackson (Mich.) YO (1986–88), and music director for the Bowling Green New Music Ensemble (1986–88). She won conducting fellowships at the Aspen Music Festival in 1987 and Tanglewood Music Festival in 1993. From 1990 to 1992 Reischl was interim orchestra conductor at the Oberlin Conservatory of Music.

Then in 1992 she accepted appointments as music director of the Lawrence (Wisc.) SO and associate professor of conducting at the Lawrence University Conservatory of Music. In 1995 Reischl became both the first woman and the first American to win the Antonio Pedrotti International Competition for Orchestra Conductors in Trento, Italy, besting a field of sixty. She took on an additional position in 2001, becoming music director for the Green Bay (Wisc.) SO, where she has immersed herself in the community and earned a reputation as high-energy, gifted, and a good teacher. Reischl began leading a series of adult education courses and introduced informational talks before each concert. Under her leadership the orchestra has been said to combine delicacy with power and finesse with passion.

Reischl left Lawrence in 2004 to take new positions in Indiana, where she became artistic director and conductor for the Muncie SO, director of the Ball State SO, and music performance instructor at the Ball State School of Music. With the MSO she initiated "Classical Conversations" that are held an hour before each concert to discuss the upcoming pieces, composers, and special guests. She also led "Talk Back" postconcert sessions at a local restaurant, where she and players answered questions from interested audience members. After six months on the Indiana jobs, Reischl announced she would be leaving them at the end of the season to return to the Oberlin Conservatory of Music in July 2005. Here she became visiting associate professor of conducting and music director of the Oberlin Orchestra and Oberlin CO. She conducts symphony concerts and the opera, and has already led the orchestra on a concert tour of China.

As a guest conductor Reischl has appeared with the Atlanta SO, Baton Rouge SO, Brooklyn PO, Dayton PO, Orchestra Regionale Toscana, Orchestra Sinfonica Siciliana, Milwaukee SO, Thessaloniki State SO, Orchestra Haydn di Bolzano e Trento, and others, particularly throughout Italy and Greece.

Selected Recordings

Logan: *Runagate, Runagate*; Suzanne Hickman (cl); Roseanna Cannizzo (pf); Jason Roberts (perc); Barbara Piaziouros (fl); William Brown (t); Samuel Breene (vn); Lori Hamburg (vc); Lawrence Conservatory Contemporary Music Ens; From *A la par*, Composers Recordings CRI 823, live: Appleton 1/1997.

Saint-Saëns: *Introduction et rondo capriccioso*, Op. 28. Fauré: *Pavane*, Op. 50. Vieuxtemps: *Concerto no. 5 in A minor*, Op. 37; Sonig Tchakerian (vn); Orchestra di Padova e del Veneto. Velut Luna SPE014, live 3/1997.

⌒

Richman, Lucas
Born 31 January 1964 in Los Angeles, California

Lucas Richman played both the piano and the violin at a young age, composing his first real piece at age twelve. He made his conducting debut at age sixteen, leading Brahms's *Academic Festival Overture* at the Tanglewood summer festival. He went on to earn a bachelor's degree from the University of California Los Angeles (UCLA) in 1984 and a master of music degree in orchestral conducting from the University of Southern California (USC) in 1987.

Music director and conductor of the Knoxville (Tenn.) SO since 2003, Richman spent much of his early career in Los Angeles. While a student he conducted the Young Musicians Foundation (1984–87), and he cofounded and spent five years with the Lo Cal Composers Ensemble, a group of five composers known for creating music and performing it in unusual venues (1984–89). He was a member of the UCLA music and theater department faculty from 1988 to 1992, assistant conductor of the Pacific SO in Orange County from 1988 to 1991, and guest conductor of the Los Angeles PO during 1992 and 1993. In 1994 he helped found the Stephen Wise Music Academy, an academic conservatory dedicated to inspiring passion and inquiry into the study of music, offering a complete program in instrumental and vocal performance, music theory, composition, listening skills, and history. Richman's next home was Pittsburgh, where he served as assistant conductor (1998–2002) and resident conductor (2002–4) of the Pittsburgh SO under music director Mariss **Jansons**. From 2000 to 2004 he was also artistic director of Pittsburgh's City Music Center CO, composed of young musicians from the area.

Youth programs are a continuing focus for Richman, who loves to introduce music to people as young as infants and toddlers. Many of Richman's numerous compositions have been written for children, such as those on his *Day Is Done* recording, which features lullabies he wrote and arranged. He has also written a children's book to accompany the CD. He was principal conductor for the Disney Young Musicians SO (1999), has been a member of the music advisory board for the Young Musicians Foundation since 1995, and has been music director for the Young Musicians Foundation Debut Orchestra Camp since 2001. Under Richman's leadership, the KSO has begun an annual Young Composer's Competition open to Tennessee residents under the age of twenty-five. The winning scores are performed by the Knoxville Symphony CO. Richman promotes the KSO as a vital element of the Knoxville community, and says the organization cannot excel only in the concert hall but must extend programming beyond it. He advocates not only youth programs but also wellness programs that use music to promote healing.

Richman was awarded the Prix Davidoff in 1988 subsequent to his selection by Leonard Bernstein to conduct the Schleswig-Holstein Music Festival

Orchestra. He received the Dramalogue Award for musical direction of Bernstein's *Candide* in 1996. The Tennessee Music Teachers Association named Richman the 2005 Composer of the Year.

Though he favors American composers such as Bernstein, he also expresses a fondness for the music of Brahms, Dvořák, and Shostakovich. In addition, he has in recent years worked with composers to record their film scores for movies including *As Good As It Gets*, *The Manchurian Candidate*, and *The Village*.

Richman has appeared as guest conductor with various orchestras, including the New York PO, Los Angeles PO, Baltimore SO, Delaware SO, San Antonio SO, Cleveland Chamber Symphony, Omaha SO, Canada's National Arts Centre Orchestra, SWR SO of Kaiserslautern (Germany), Tiroler Kammerorchester InnStrumenti (Austria), and Zagreb PO (Croatia).

Selected Recordings

Leese: *Music for Harp, Percussion and Strings*; Cleveland CS; On *Telling Tales: Music from the Cleveland Composers Guild*. Capstone 8736.

Richman: *Day Is Done: An Album of Lullabies*; Debbie Richman; Shira Adler; Lucas Richman; North Star Kids; Pittsburgh SO. Ledor Music.

Taieb: *The Alchemist's Symphony*; Paramount Pictures Studio O. RCA 09026-63157-2.

∼

Robertson, David
Born 19 July 1958 in Santa Monica, California

Robertson's appointment to a three-year term as conductor of the troubled Saint Louis SO (announced 10 December 2003) was greeted with much enthusiasm. One of the leading conductors of his generation, he has made his reputation as a fresh and virile interpreter of the standard repertoire, with a striking affinity for contemporary music. He also brings a command of the core operatic repertoire. With his all-encompassing talent and solid track record he is clearly regarded as a very good "catch" for Saint Louis. In return, he works with an orchestra that is both very accomplished and supported by one of the best outreach and educational programs in the country. He admires the orchestra's "generosity of spirit," especially the way it was able to dig itself out of a recent financial crisis while keeping its artistic priorities intact. Robertson feels a special chemistry with the orchestra and sees it as having a crucial role to play. His first-year report card (July 2006) yielded straight

A's. He was praised for innovative programming, and for a commitment that has raised orchestra morale and engaged the community to the benefit of the institution and the City of Saint Louis. He had lived up to expectations so well that there was early speculation about how long the Saint Louis SO would be able to keep him and considerable relief when he extended his contract through 2010.

Robertson is drawn to the notion that an orchestra should be a focal point of, connect with, and enhance the community. It should also serve as a model of what can be achieved when a group works toward a common purpose. He has said, "I really like to think about place, the type of music they like—the tradition, the sort of people they are—to make something that is really special for them." Orchestras should take the audience members' tastes into account while at the same time present them with listening challenges. Live music, he believes, provides a unique experience that cannot be had from any other medium. If the music is familiar to the audience, the performance should convey the impression of a first hearing. If the audience is hearing new or difficult music, there needs to be something from previous experiences to which they can relate. One innovative strategy, for example, was to segue from Wagner's *Tristan und Isolde* prelude into Schoenberg's *Erwartung*, thus leading from the shifting chromaticism of the former into the latter's atonality. Another ploy he has used for getting music across to his audience is emphasizing the interconnectedness of repertoire and its relationship to its milieu. Thus, his programs are often an intriguing mix of the familiar and unfamiliar, for, as he himself knows, even professionals reach a saturation point if too much new music is presented all at once. Robertson likes to talk to his audience, especially before introducing unfamiliar music, but his intellect and sharp mind can make this a self-defeating strategy: he has been known to talk for too long and at too sophisticated a level.

Robertson is a gifted and technically assured practitioner with a phenomenal technique honed by extensive experience performing difficult modern scores. He has an unobtrusive podium manner and relies on precise and expressive hand gestures to draw out the best from his players and to present the audience with a lucid and powerful interpretation. He conceives the conductor's role as blending his forces into a unified conception of a work, while, at the same time, leaving space for the creative contribution of individual players. One of his greatest skills is being able to shed new light on the most familiar repertoire not for the sake of novelty but to reveal new and refreshing facets that surprise and galvanize the listener. His performances of Beethoven's Fifth Symphony, for instance, are not to be missed! He is especially admired for his handling of texture, color, and pacing. His interpretations reveal an unnerving and supple sense of rhythmic momentum, a clear grasp of formal shaping, and an expressivity that runs the gamut from full-blooded to delicate.

Robertson is both a fierce intellectual and a dedicated populist. He devised innovative interdisciplinary programs such as "Seeing Debussy, Hearing Monet," one of the "Perspectives Series" concerts he presented at Carnegie Hall, and encouraged younger patrons in Saint Louis through the "Sound Check" program which provides low-cost admissions. He is deeply concerned about the validity and future of artistic pursuits and their relationships to daily life. His approach is articulate and didactic while at the same time acknowledging those aspects of music-making which are beyond, or at least precede words: "I have the feeling of being able to grasp a thought in musical terms before I am able to articulate it." As a composer himself, he has described the creative process by using the metaphor of a butterfly plucked out of the air and fixed onto paper without losing anything of its intrinsic quality, and as a conductor, "how to recreate the composer's recognition of the material in the minds of the audience." He comes to Saint Louis as more than just a specialist in contemporary music because he does almost everything well, in part because of having worked closely with other living composers.

Robertson was born into a musical family and grew up surrounded by the showbiz culture of southern California. He took lessons in piano, trumpet, and French horn and was soon playing in local youth orchestras. He had his first conducting experience in seventh grade when a substitute orchestra teacher offered him the chance to rehearse his elementary school orchestra. Formal training took him to the Royal Academy of Music, the most staid of London's music colleges, where he studied composition as well as French horn and conducting. His first professional appointment was as resident conductor of the Jerusalem SO (1985–87). He made his Met debut with *The Makropoulos Affair* in 1991. From 1992 to 2000 he was music director of the Ensemble Intercontemporain, an organization founded by Pierre Boulez and dedicated to the performance of new music. During this period his reputation was enhanced by an increasing number of guest appearances, and in 1997 he won a Seaver/NEA Conductors Award. The same year he made his double debut in San Francisco, first at the Opera where he conducted *Rigoletto* (receiving a rare negative review) and then at the Symphony, with a program of Messiaen's *L'Ascension*, Walton's Viola Concerto, and Beethoven's Fifth Symphony (performances receiving very favorable reviews). He appeared with the Cleveland Orchestra at the Blossom Festival in 1998 and made his debuts in Houston and Saint Louis the following year. By this time he had done enough to earn *Musical America's* Conductor of the Year designation (1999). He was appointed to a four-year term as music director of the Orchestre National de Lyon in 2000 and became artistic director of the city's auditorium, the first individual to hold both positions. His debut with the Berlin PO took place in 2002. In October 2005, he was appointed principal guest conductor of the BBC SO and in 2006 he received Columbia University's Ditson Conductor's Award for "exceptional commitment to the performance of works by American composers."

As a guest conductor, Robertson has appeared extensively in Europe and the U.S. with the London SO, BBC SO, Hallé Orchestra, Bavarian RSO, NDR/Hamburg Orchestra, Berlin Staatskapelle, La Scala PO, RAI Orchestra (Turin), Rotterdam PO, Orchestre de Paris, NHK SO (Japan), Los Angeles PO, Philadelphia Orchestra, Atlanta SO, Houston SO, and San Francisco SO. He has also appeared at the following prestigious opera houses: La Scala, Bavarian State Opera, Thèatre du Chatelet, Hamburg Opera, and Opéra de Lyon.

Robertson is an enthusiastic booster of young musical talent and has led workshops associated with his ensembles in Paris and Lyon, and in the U.S. at the Juilliard School and the Tanglewood and Aspen festivals.

Further Reading

Gervasoni, P. "David Robertson et les vingt ans de l'Ensemble Intercontemporain." *Diapason* (France) 433 (January 1997): 24–27. [French]

Mancini, J. "Concert Reviews: Robertson All the Rage." *20th Century Music* 5 (March 1998): 11–12.

Matthew-Walker, R. "David Robertson." *Musical Opinion* 129 (November–December 2005): 32–33.

Ross, Alex. "The Evangelist: David Robertson Lifts Up the Saint Louis Symphony." *New Yorker* 81, no. 39 (2005): 106.

Wallace, Helen. "Music That Changed Me—David Robertson (interview)." *BBC Music* 14 (January 2006): 114.

Selected Recordings

Bartók: *Dance Suite for Orchestra; Four Pieces for Orchestra; The Miraculous Mandarin;* Lyon National Ch Soloists; Lyon Natl O. Harmonia Mundi 901777.

Chin: *XI;* Ensemble Intercontemporain. From DGG 000404402.

Dusapin: *La melancholia;* Nan Christie (s); Cécile Éloir (ms); Timothy Greacen (ct); Martyn Hill (t); Lyon Natl Ch; Lyon Natl O. From Montaigne 782073.

Dvořák: *Cello Concerto in b*; Jan Vogler (vc); New York PO. From Sony 73716.

Schmitt: *Symphonie Concertante for Piano and Orchestra*, Op. 82; *Rêves*; *Soirs*; Hüseyin Sermet (pf); Monte Carlo PO. Naïve 4908.

〜

Runnicles, Donald
Born 15 November 1964 in Edinburgh, Scotland

Runnicles emerged as a conductor on the well-trodden path of German provincial opera houses. It was because of his role as musical assistant to James **Levine**, preparing the 1982 performances of *Parsifal* at the Bayreuth Festival, that he found himself in the same role in New York City for the Met's 1988 production of Berg's *Lulu*. When Levine sustained a pinched nerve, Runnicles stepped in on five hours notice, never having conducted or even rehearsed the piece. His success at bringing this off brought him to the attention of the San Francisco Opera, and he was invited to conduct the *Ring* cycle there in 1990. He went on to conduct it at the Vienna State Opera shortly thereafter, and the same year he was appointed music director of the San Francisco company (1992). In 2000 the Atlanta (Ga.) SO made the joint appointment of Runnicles as principal guest conductor and Robert **Spano** as music director. This was to be a creative collaboration with the two of them consulting on programming and other decisions. In has proved to be a successful partnership for the entire organization, and the original contract was extended for another five-year term. The 2001–2 season saw Runnicles become principal conductor of the Orchestra of Saint Luke's in New York. He refused the offer of the music directorship, feeling that it was inappropriate for him to lead an organization known for its self-governance and protean nature.

Born in Edinburgh, Runnicles was educated at the university there and at Cambridge University before spending a year's apprenticeship at the London Opera Centre. He worked as a *repetiteur* at the opera house in Mannheim and made his conducting debut there in a performance of *The Tales of Hoffmann* in 1980. The Hannover Opera made him their principal conductor in 1987 and he made a Hamburg Opera debut the same year. In 1989 he became music director at the Freiburg Opera. After making his San Francisco Opera debut in 1990, he conducted *Don Giovanni* at Glyndebourne the following year and *Tannhäuser* at Bayreuth the year after that. He made his San Francisco SO debut with Benjamin Britten's *War Requiem* in 1995, deputizing for the indisposed André **Previn**. He scored a signal triumph on another occasion when, in 2003, the Atlanta Symphony Chorus joined forces with the Berlin PO to perform *War Requiem* under him in Berlin. At the conclusion of the performance a remarkable spectacle occurred when the members of what many consider the world's leading orchestra turned around to applaud this fine amateur chorus. He first appeared at the Salzburg Festival in 1996 conducting Mozart's *Don Giovanni*, and he also led Korngold's *Die tote Stadt* there in 2004.

Runnicles conducted over thirty-five productions during the first ten years of his directorship in San Francisco. As well as the standard fare, he introduced two new works: *The Dangerous Liaisons* by Conrad Susa (1994) and *Harvey Milk* by Stewart Wallace (1995). Both performances were videotaped for commercial distribution. A commission for a new work based on the life of atomic scientist J. Robert Oppenheimer, *Doctor Atomic* by John **Adams**, premiered in October 2005. Besides the *Ring* cycle, he has conducted Verdi, *Billy Budd*, *Peter Grimes*, *Salome*, *Don Giovanni*, and *Idomeneo* at the Vienna State Opera. He introduced two twentieth-century Russian operas, Shostakovich's *Lady Macbeth of Mtensk* and Prokofiev's *Fiery Angel*, at the Volksoper across town. He has appeared at opera houses in Paris, Milan, Berlin, Munich, Cologne, Copenhagen, Zurich, and Amsterdam. In his hometown of Edinburgh he appears regularly at the Festival, having opened it in 1994 with a performance of Mahler's Eighth Symphony.

He received a 1997 Grammy nomination for his recording of Gluck's *Orphée et Eurydice*, and his recording roster also includes *Hänsel und Gretel*, *Capuleti e i Montecchi*, and highlights from the *Ring* cycle with the Dresden Staatskapelle. He has recorded a well-received performance of Orff's *Carmina Burana* and Beethoven's Ninth Symphony with the Atlanta forces, and a set of Mozart symphonies with the Orchestra of St. Luke's.

Runnicles's approach to conducting was influenced by his training in German opera houses, where he often had to conduct without orchestral rehearsals and where success depended upon creating a spontaneous rapport with singers and audiences. He rejects the notion of conductor as dictator and feels his role is that of facilitator, imparting energy to the orchestra and realizing the composer's intentions faithfully, along with making any modifications needed for specific venues. This attitude should make his refusal to become artistic director of the Orchestra of Saint Luke's less surprising.

Website
http://www.donaldrunnicles.com/

Further Reading

Buchau, S. von. "Baywatch." *Opera News* 59 (September 1994): 18.

Clark, Andrew. "Donald Runnicles." *Opera* 44 (August 1993): 893–98.

Pfaff, T. "The Flying Scotsman." *San Francisco Opera Magazine* 71, no. 3 (1993): 22.

Power, Matthew. "Interview: Donald Runnicles." *Gramophone* 83 (October 2005): 12.

Rowe, Georgia. "Steadfast: Conductor Donald Runnicles Has Survived Two Regime Changes and Paved the Way for a New Era at San Francisco Opera." *Opera News* 70 (September 2005): 44–47.

Ruhe, Pierre, and Tom Sabulis. "Symphony Conductor Out on a Limb Politically." *Atlanta Journal-Consitution*, 19 August 2004, B1.

Sabulis, Tom. "Donald Runnicles: ASO's No. 1 Guest." *Atlanta Journal-Consitution*, 8 October 2000, L1.

Selected Recordings

Gluck: *Orphée et Eurydice*; Dawn Upshaw (s), Jennifer Larmore (ms), Alison Hagley (s); San Francisco Op Ch; San Francisco Op O. Teldec 98418.

Korngold: *Die tote Stadt*; soloists; Vienna State Op Ch; Vienna PO. Orfeo d'Or 634042.

Mozart: *Requiem* (Ed. Levin); Christine Brewer (s); Ruxandra Donose (a); John Tessier (t); Eric Owens (b); Atlanta SO and Ch. Telarc CD-80636.

Strauss (R): *Death and Transfiguration*; *4 Last Songs*. Wagner: *Tristan und Isolde: Prelude and Liebestod*; Christine Brewer (s); Atlanta SO. Telarc CD-80661.

Wagner: *Tristan und Isolde*; Christine Brewer (s); John Treleaven (t); Dagmar Pecková (s); Boaz Daniel (br); Jared Holt (t); Jonathan Lemalu (br); Eugene Ginty (t); Mark Le Brocq (t); Peter Rose (b); Apollo Voices; BBC SO. Warner Classics 62964.

∿

Salonen, Esa-Pekka
Born 30 June 1958 in Helsinki, Finland

Salonen is not the first musician to juggle the demands of being both conductor and composer. Unlike many conductors, he did not cherish the ambition to become one from an early age, or experience a defining moment when the realization "this is what I want to do" struck. For Salonen, conducting came about almost casually as part of the shared duties of a performing group of young composers. At that time he was established as a horn player and composer, and conducting formed the third and least important facet of his musical activities. However, as he himself says, "I realized I was quite good at it," which persuaded him to take some conducting lessons. His subsequent success and meteoric rise as a conductor have tended to over-shadow his activities as a composer, and he has been obliged to give up horn playing altogether. Composing and conducting are both complementary and conflicting, and trying to reconcile them has been a constant dilemma.

Salonen comes from a musical family and was given the opportunity to learn the piano at an early age. This did not much appeal to him, however, and it wasn't until he learned the recorder in school and switched to the trumpet shortly thereafter that his musical education really began. After playing trumpet for a number of years he was persuaded, at the age of eleven, to switch to the French horn. He became a dedicated student and made rapid progress. His interest in composition developed gradually, and when he entered the Sibelius Academy in Helsinki in 1973 it was to study horn with Holgar Fransman and composition with Einojuhani Rautavaara. As a student, he was already freelancing as a horn player in the leading Helsinki orchestras and was part of a group of young composers that included Kaija Saariaho and Magnus Lindberg. They modeled themselves on the Darmstadt School, espousing the experimental modernism of Stockhausen, Boulez, and Cage. Hence the foundation of the performance ensemble Ears Open! and a subsequent group called the Tomeii Ensemble. After graduation in 1977, Salonen pursued further studies in composition with Franco Donatoni in Siena and Niccolo Castiglioni in Milan. He had also taken some classes in Bayreuth and Darmstadt. He made his orchestral conducting debut with the Finnish RSO and recorded an operatic double bill of *Schauspieldirektor* and *Hänsel und Gretel* for Finnish Television. His guest appearances throughout Scandinavia and beyond included a production of *Wozzeck* at the Swedish Royal Opera. His big break came, as it so often does, when he was called in on short notice to direct a performance of Mahler's Symphony no. 3 with the Philharmonia Orchestra in London to much acclaim. His first appointment followed in 1984 when he became principal conductor of the Swedish RSO (1984–94) and principal guest conductor of the Oslo PO. This was also the year he debuted with the Los Angeles PO. A year later he became principal guest conductor of the Philharmonia Orchestra, which he remained until 1995. His achievements with the Swedish RSO included a tour of the U.S. in 1987.

The Los Angeles PO was in somewhat of a predicament in 1989. After a dozen or so years with the two elder statesmen Giulini and **Previn** at the helm, the orchestra needed to counter the impression that it had become dull, homely, and irrelevant. The orchestra's general manager, Ernest Fleisch-mann, had earmarked Salonen for guest appearances soon after his now fa-mous Mahler debut and had a strong feeling that he was the right choice to nudge the orchestra into America's premier league. Salonen had looks and charisma that the Los Angeles publicity machine could really get its teeth into! Through his guest appearances he was well known to the players, and the majority of them approved his appointment. (The "wrong note test"— when players deliberately play wrong notes to test out a new conductor—had been successfully negotiated at his very first rehearsal, when preparing a Lu-tosławski symphony.) He knew that there would be no galvanizing of the Los Angeles public if he could not first inspire the players. Salonen commands an unusually clear and graceful beat to achieve his musical aims. His gestures can become effectively athletic in performance, leading to lucid and dynamic interpretations. He assumes a laid-back, non-domineering, and coaxing ap-proach in rehearsals, which, at the same time, conveys an air of command and control. Coming from a strong European tradition, he had definite ideas about how he wanted to modify the orchestra's romantically centered, extro-verted sound by adding more sensitivity and range. As he commented later, the LAPO is not a particularly mean orchestra and it responded positively to his intentions. The right chemistry to produce a sustained level of excite-ment and commitment was soon in evidence. His ambition to program more challenging material may have caused some raised eyebrows at first, but in general the orchestra was willing to follow him along innovative paths. To plan an effective strategy for leading the orchestra into the next century, it was necessary to understand the context within which it operated. The irony is that Los Angeles is a diverse ethnic community, and what passes for estab-lishment culture stems from Hollywood. Thus, the ethos of symphonic mu-sic helps support the counterculture of a vibrant contemporary arts scene. It is in this sense that Salonen's promise to program a majority of twentieth-century music makes sense. He aims to expand audiences by encouraging younger adherents, and the music of Bartók, Stravinsky, and Sibelius is ini-tially easier to relate to than that of Mozart or Beethoven. Later twentieth-century music by the likes of Lutosławski and Ligeti works better juxtaposed with the acknowledged masterpieces of the earlier twentieth century. A prag-matic approach also ensures that new music will speak for itself when placed in a thematic and stylistic context. Salonen's inclination is to de-emphasize the high Romantic repertoire in favor of searching out the best of contem-porary music and revisiting the classical repertoire—he has a special affinity with the "wacky" world of Haydn's symphonies. True to his promise, two-thirds of the works programmed have been of twentieth-century music, with premieres and performances of works by leading contemporary composers such as Henri Dutilleux, Luciano Berio, Elliot Carter, Bernard Rands, John **Adams**, Steven Stuky, and Kaija Saariaho. In the 2002–3 season, for example, there were premieres of works by William Kraft, Gabriela Ortiz, Augusta Read Thomas, and by Salonen himself.

As well as new music, he has introduced a number of innovations designed to broaden the scope and appeal of the orchestra, including neighborhood residency programs often profiling ethnic music, youth concerts, school visits, preconcert lectures, and chamber ensemble presentations. As Salonen sees himself as having a conductor/composer duality, a complementary notion is for the orchestra to see itself as a "community of musicians," a term coined by Fleischmann. He staged "Casual Friday Concerts" in an informal setting to appeal to audiences not familiar with the ritual or fare of classical concerts, followed by postconcert schmoozing with the conductor and players. The "Sounds about Town" series gave other local classical and crossover ensembles a performance platform. The "Filmharmonic" series linked up with Hollywood for a series of newly commissioned multimedia works and performances of silent films with new or specially arranged scores played by the orchestra. Participants included film composers Jerry Goldsmith, Danny Elfman, and Alan Silvestri, and directors Perry Harlan, Tim Burton, and Paul Verhoeven. Another outlet for contemporary music was the "Green Umbrella New Music" series.

A crowning moment in this LAPO/Salonen partnership was the move into the $274 million purpose-built Walt Disney Hall in 2003. The orchestra required a period of adjustment because, as expected, the ambience in the new building was unlike that which it had been used to. From the outset it was clear that the auditorium could accommodate a warmer, less strident approach across the whole dynamic range from *very* soft to *very* loud. Salonen claimed that the tremendous acoustics would reflect "the energy and exuberance of the orchestra" and bring back the intimacy of classical music.

Immediately prior to his taking over as music director, Salonen and the orchestra spent a month in residence at the 1992 Salzburg Festival. Their major assignment was a series of performances of Messiaen's five-hour opera *St. Francis of Assisi*. Although the staging was controversial, the contribution of orchestra and conductor was highly praised. Eight critically acclaimed international tours through Europe, the Americas, and Asia followed during the next ten years. One highlight was the month-long residency at the Stravinsky Festival in Paris in the fall of 1996, which included performances of *The Rake's Progress*.

In addition to his work with the LAPO, Salonen conducted *Mathis der Maler* at Covent Garden in 1995. A memorable *Pelleas et Melisande* in Los Angeles the same year was praised for its "taut, psychologically precise reading of the score without sacrificing the sensuousness of Debussy's ever-astonishing orchestration." He was music director of the 1995–96 Helsinki Festival; unfortunately, its artistic success was not matched financially. Together with Ernest Fleischmann, he became music director of the well-established festival of contemporary music in Ojai (1999). In 2001 he participated in the Related Rocks Festival on London's South Bank. He accepted the post of principal conductor of the Phiharmonia Orchestra beginning in 2008, an ensemble with which he has enjoyed a fruitful relationship since his dramatic debut in 1983.

Salonen's extensive discography includes a number of award-winning recordings. He received a 1996 Grammy for performances of the Bartók piano concertos with soloist Yefim Bronfman, and his recording of film scores by Bernard Hermann was nominated the following year. Some of his earliest recordings were with the Swedish RSO and include a Nielsen symphony cycle and a disc of music by Dallapiccola. With the Philharmonia Orchestra he has recorded *The Rite of Spring* and Messiaen's *Turungalila-symphonie*. Recordings by the Los Angeles PO include: Bartók, *Concerto for Orchestra*; Bruckner, *Symphony no. 4*; Debussy, *Images*, *La Mer*, etc.; Lutosławski, *Symphonies nos. 3 and 4*; Mahler, *Das Lied von der Erde* and *Symphony no. 3*; Sibelius, *Kullervo* and *Lemmikäinen Legends*; Ligeti's opera *Le Grand Macabre*, and music of Kaija Saariaho.

Salonen's interpretations are praised for their youthful energy and enthusiasm. He understands his scores from a composer's point of view and directs with an assurance and clarity that musicians and audiences alike find compelling. If there is criticism, it is that he sometimes misses the forest for the trees; his approach is too left-brained and detailed, to the detriment of the atmosphere and characterization of the music.

We may surmise that it comes as no surprise to Salonen that Bernstein and Boulez both had problems balancing the creative and performing aspects of their lives. Salonen started out with strong composing aspirations, but circumstances conspired to turn him from a composer-conductor into a conductor-composer. He admits that his ability to compose is restricted ("There are moments when there is too much music around me to be able to compose") and he uses odd moments to jot down ideas as material to work with later. At this time in his life he cannot imagine *not* conducting; however, he is willing to do less of it if that is what is necessary to compose more. He has completed several major composing projects since 1992, not least the *LA Variations* of 1996, written for the Los Angeles orchestra. He took off most of 2000 to concentrate on a commission from the Aix-en-Provence Festival to compose an opera based on Hoeg's novel *The Woman and the Ape*. Unfortunately, this project did not materialize, as he spent much of his sabbatical year finishing projects already begun and a new work for cellist Ansi Kartunnen titled *Mania*, in addition to supervising a CD of his own music. A volte-face occurred when he realized that other conductors were capable of conducting his music (he had previously joked that he got into conducting to ensure good performances of his pieces), but that he alone could compose it, "so from now on I will only spend half of the year conducting, and the rest composing." It came as no surprise, therefore, when he announced his intention of relinquishing the LAPO directorship at the end of the 2008–9 season (to be succeeded by Gustavo Dudamel).

Salonen is a very dedicated musician who really cares about the viability of orchestral music over the next twenty or thirty years. His commitment to the LAPO provided an ideal opportunity to realize his ideas and ambitions for keeping the great tradition of orchestral music-making vibrant and relevant.

Website
http://www.esapekkasalonen.com

Further Reading

Glass, Herbert. "A Passion for Clarity." *Gramophone* 70 (August 1992): 26–27.

Haeyrynen, A. "Esa-Pekka Salonen: The Composer behind the Conductor." *Finnish Music Quarterly*, no. 3 (1998): 18–24.

Mangan, Timothy. "Becoming Esa-Pekka: How Salonen Made Himself a Vital Part of Los Angeles's Cultural Life." *Opera News* 70 (July 2005): 30–33.

Marum, Lisa. "Esa-Pekka Salonen, Conductor." *Ovation* 6 (December 1985): 50.

Rosen, Jesse. "Holistic Approach: Esa-Pekka Salonen on Training Composers and Conductors to Speak the Same Language." *Symphony* 54 (March–April 2003): 15–20.

Stearns, David Patrick. "20/20 Revision: Esa-Pekka Salonen Has a Progressive View of the Opera Scores He Conducts (interview)." *Opera News* 63 (December 1998): 38–41.

Selected Recordings
Haydn: *Symphonies 22, 78, and 82*; Stockholm CO. Sony 45972.
Lutosławski: *Symphonies 3 and 4*; *Les espaces du sommeil*; John Shirley-Quirk (br); Los Angeles PO. Sony 66280.
Messiaen: *Couleurs de la cité céleste*; *Oiseaux exotiques*; *Des canyons aux étoiles*; Paul Crossley (pf); London Sinfonietta. CBS 44762.
Saariaho: *L'Amour de loin*; Gerald Finley (*Jaufré Rudel*); Dawn Upshaw (*Clémence*); Monica Groop (*Le Pelerin*); Finnish Natl Op O and Ch. DGG 0004721-09 DVD.
Sibelius: *Violin Concerto*. Nielsen: *Violin Concerto*; Lin Cho-Liang (vn); Philharmonia O; Swedish RSO. Sony 92613.

∿
Sanderling, Stefan
Born 8 February 1964 in East Berlin, GDR

Sanderling's ties to the U.S. go back to 1988 when he arrived in southern California seeking political asylum. He attended the University of Southern California, where he received conducting tuition from Daniel Lewis, and the Los Angeles Philharmonic Institute. During the summer of 1989 he attended Tanglewood, working with Bernstein, **Ozawa**, **Slatkin**, and **Temirkanov**. After laying the foundation of a successful career in Europe, he has made the U.S. the focus of his professional activities in recent years and has become a sought-after guest conductor, with appointments in Toledo (Ohio) and Tampa (Fla.).

Sanderling has built a considerable reputation for music-making that veers toward interpretations that are, for the most part, expansive, well formulated, and deeply felt. This contrasts significantly with many conductors of his generation who tend toward podium histrionics. His baton technique of contained, economical gestures is nevertheless highly effective. He tends to adopt slowish base tempi that allow scope for subtle variation, phrasing, and voicing, all the while creating momentum for carefully graded crescendos and thrilling climaxes. He has the singular ability to make his performances seem fresh, unique, and revealing; no two performances of a score are ever the same, a quality that particularly sets him apart from his run-of-the-mill colleagues. And yet his rehearsal approach is collegial and his personality is congenial. He seems to combine the three roles demanded of a modern music director: musician, administrator, and figurehead publicist.

Sanderling is the son of the distinguished German conductor Kurt Sanderling, a Jewish musician who fled to Russia to escape the Nazis. After spending twenty years as associate conductor of the Leningrad PO, he returned to Berlin in 1960 to become one of the leading cultural icons of the GDR. Stefan's first inclination was to become a scholar, but, as a musicology student at the University of Halle, he got into hot water with the authorities by writing a politically subversive program note for a performance of Shostakovich's Sixth Symphony, to be performed in the presence of the Russian ambassador. The consequences of this were somewhat mitigated by his father's eminence and by the intervention of Kurt **Masur**, who suggested he come study conducting with him at the conservatory in Leipzig. His rebellious nature sat ill with the authoritarian state (he had previously served jail time for avoiding compulsory military service) and this fueled his ambition to get out of East Germany. However, the precipitate fall of the Iron Curtain proved auspicious for Sanderling's career, as the wholesale upheaval that ensued provided the opportunity for him to be appointed *Generalmusikdirektor* in the city of Potsdam (1990) as a relatively inexperienced conductor. Five years of on-the-job training led to his to his progression to *Generalmusikdirektor* of the Staatstheater in Mainz (1996–2000). He had further opportunity to demonstrate his mettle as music director with the newly formed Orchestre de Bretagne, where his tenure saw not only exponential growth in the list of subscribers and a number of favorably reviewed recordings, but also, after five years of work, the development of an ensemble capable of making a successful tour to the U.S. (2002). Meanwhile, he had been making quite a reputation for himself as a guest conductor appearing with, among others, the Los Angeles PO, Saint Louis SO, Detroit SO, Baltimore SO, Houston SO, and Saint Paul CO. He served as principle conductor and artistic advisor of the Toledo SO during its interregnum (2002–4) before committing himself to a five-year contract with the Florida Orchestra in Tampa.

His commitment to the Florida Orchestra offered a challenge since, although it is a very fine group of players, it has been on a rather shaky fiscal footing for a number of years and lacks a permanent home. During Sanderling's first year in charge he was faced with the loss of a number of key players and a 10 percent reduction of support staff due to financial constraints. He established a rapport with the orchestra from the first and was impressed with how good they were. He "cased" the Tampa Bay area prior to his audition performance and subsequently gave a commitment to set up his base there so that he would be able to do all that was asked of him with regard to fund-raising and community support. His exuberance and commitment made him the unanimous choice of the orchestra's search committee. John Mc-Kelvey, writing in the *American Record Guide* in 2003, claimed that the orchestra's performance of Sibelius's Fifth Symphony was the finest he had ever heard, comparing it to those of Krauss, Szell, **Temirkanov**, and Colin Davis. For the 2005–6 season, Sanderling devised a rather gimmicky, if intriguing, schedule pairing all nine Beethoven symphonies with works referring to the equivalent number, for example, Beethoven's Symphony no. Seven with Kurt Weill's theater piece *The Seven Deadly Sins*.

Sanderling's repertoire encompasses a broad swath from Mozart to Webern and Prokofiev. He claims a special affinity with Shostakovich, who was a frequent visitor to the family home in Leningrad. He conducted the first performance of Kirchner's opera *Gilgamesh* in Hannover in 2000 and frequently programs contemporary music: George Rochberg and Mark Antony Turnage, among others. He opened his recording account in 1992 with the London SO for Sony Classical. Subsequently, he has recorded with the National SO of Ireland, Royal PO, and Texas Festival Orchestra. With the Orchestre de Bretagne he has explored neglected repertoire of the French classicists Grétry, Gossec, and Méhul.

Further Reading

Fleming, John. "Tearing Down the Walls." *St. Petersburg Times* (Fla.), 21 September 2003, 1F.

McKelvey, John P. "Musical Gold in Tampa Bay: Sanderling a Powerful Presence at Florida Orchestra." *American Record Guide* 66 (July–August 2003): 14–15.

Selected Recordings

Gossec: *Symphonies: In G, E♭, and E♭; Grande Symphonie in F; Gavotte in D; Suite of Dances* (orch. Calmel); O de Bretagne. ASV 1124.

Tchaikovsky: *Suites for Orchestra, 1–4*; National SO of Ireland. Naxos 550644; 550728.

Stravinsky: *Pulcinella; Danses concertantes*; Ian Bostridge (t); Fiona James (s); Henry Herford (br); Bournemouth Sinfonietta. Naxos 553181.

∿

Sawallisch, Wolfgang
Born 26 August 1923 in Munich, Germany

An experienced and highly regarded conductor of concerts and opera, and a piano-accompanist of note, Sawallisch accepted his first U.S. appointment to lead the Philadelphia Orchestra in 1993 at the age of seventy—an appointment which was to last for ten years. This was, in fact, his first appointment outside German-speaking lands. Although he had appeared regularly as a guest conductor in Europe and Japan, his international reputation was largely confined to his dependable work in the opera house, a famous early recording of Strauss's opera *Capriccio* with Elisabeth Schwarzkopf and the Philharmonia Orchestra, and recordings of several of the composer's other lesser-known operas in more recent times. His exposure in the U.S. had been almost exclusively with the Philadelphia Orchestra, which he first conducted in 1966 and then more frequently after 1984. The announcement that he was to be music director took many in the music world by surprise.

Sawallisch is perhaps the last of the illustrious line of conductors in the German Kapellmeister tradition that stretches back at least as far as Carl Maria von Weber in the nineteenth century. As an elder statesman and a thorough conservative, musically speaking, was he the right choice to rejuvenate the Philadelphia Orchestra's image and attract a wider audience at home and abroad? His appointment seemed to follow the trend previously set by the Cleveland and New York orchestras in selecting leaders for their ability to restore high art and tradition following the tenures of their somewhat wayward predecessors. In this respect, Sawallisch was an excellent choice: the complete musician with prodigious skills, an inherent musicality, and a concern to serve music before any notions of personal power or publicity. This integrity and competence were qualities that the players, and the audience, too, in a less direct way, were to appreciate increasingly over the duration of his term, and their depth helps explain why his performances were constantly satisfying. With his spry and dapper appearance he carried his seventy-plus years well, and it was only at the very end of his tenure that the physical strain associated with the role of an orchestral CEO began to tell. The requisite chemistry between orchestra and conductor was soon established, and the players, appreciating a conducting style both restrained and expressive, were able to pick up easily on his gestures to produce the desired effect. Over time he was able to temper the orchestra's unforced, opulent sound so appropriate for Tchaikovsky and Strauss to a leaner, focused, and more elegant one for Haydn, Mozart, and Beethoven. In general, his tempi tended to be brisk but always controlled without sounding hurried; his inbred sense of phrasing and musical architecture was omnipresent and his attention to texture, especially in the inner parts, gave his performances an unequalled transparency.

His forte in Richard Strauss and the classics, Sawallisch did not bring with him a reputation as a trailblazer in new or adventurous programming, although he had performed music by a number of contemporary West German composers working in an idiom he described as susceptible to "traditional influences." Admitting to extremely conservative taste in contemporary music, he did, however, make a commitment to play music not ordinarily heard in Philadelphia. This turned out to be music by Hindemith, Weill, Werner Egk, Karl Amadeus Hartmann, and Hans Werner Henze. He expressed the intention to look into the works of American composers and gave Howard Hanson's *Romantic Symphony* and Ned Rorem's *Eagles* an airing. He also gave first performances of works by Wolfgang Rihm (*First Song*, 1997), Einojuhani Rautavaara (*Symphony no. 8*, 2000), Kristopf Penderecki (*"Resurrection" Piano Concerto*, 2002), and, to celebrate the opening of the orchestra's new concert auditorium, Kimmel Center, in 2001, Aaron Jay Kernis's *Color Wheel*. The music world was startled to learn that the repertoire for the orchestra's centenary season (1999–2000) was to be devoted exclusively to works composed during the orchestra's existence! Programs composed entirely of twentieth-century compositions turned out not to be as daunting as first feared. Another notable feature of Sawallisch's programming was the resurgence of Bach transcriptions for full orchestra, included to highlight the orchestra's lavish sound and as a gesture of homage to the former music director and arranger, Leopold Stokowski. During his tenure, Sawallisch led the orchestra annually in concerts at Carnegie Hall and accompanied them on eight international tours. As well as appearances in Japan, the Asian tour of 1999 included debut concerts in Malaysia and Taiwan, and a week's residency in Vietnam was the first by a U.S. orchestra. Sawallisch showed commitment to Philadelphia and the orchestra's outreach programs through children's concerts and active support of the Curtis Institute. One remarkable innovation that occurred on his watch was the first cyber-cast by a major orchestra, offering worldwide computer access. In addition to the broadcast concert of 29 April 1997, an online chat session with the conductor followed the performance. His recordings with the Philadelphia Orchestra include the orchestral works of Richard Strauss and works by Bruckner, Dvořák, Hindemith, Tchaikovsky, and Wagner, and orchestral transcriptions by Stokowski. Sawallisch has been a regular guest conductor in Vienna and Tokyo and has conducted the world's leading orchestras in Berlin, Paris, London, Prague, and Tel Aviv. Over the course of ten years his new hires accounted for one-third of the Philadelphia Orchestra's personnel. Having inherited an ensemble as fine as any in the world, he bequeathed to his successor one whose prowess had been further enhanced by his careful stewardship.

Further Reading
Blyth, Alan. "Wolfgang Sawallisch." *Opera* 40 (Annual Festival Issue 1989): 16–20.
Jacobson, Bernard. "Sawallisch on Strauss (interview)." *Opera News* 64 (August 1999): 22–25.
Rodríguez-Peralta, Phyllis W. *Philadelphia Maestros: Ormandy, Muti, Sawallisch.* Philadelphia: Temple University Press, 2006.
Sawallisch, Wolfgang. *Im Interesse der Deutlichkeit: Mein Leben mit der Musik.* Hamburg, Ger.: Hoffmann und Campe, 1993. (Autobiography) [German]
Schumann, Karl. "A Life with Music." *Gramophone* 68 (December 1990): 1161–62.

Selected Recordings
Barber: *Symphony no. 1*. Schumann: *Symphony no. 4*; Bavarian State O. Farao S108109.
Hindemith: *Symphonic Metamorphosis on Themes of Carl Maria von Weber*; *Nobilissima Visione*; *Symphony "Mathis der Maler"*; Jeffrey Khaner (fl); Philadelphia O. EMI 55230.
Schubert: *Symphonies 5, 6, 8, and 9*; Dresden Staatskapelle. Phillips 446539.
Strauss (R): *Capriccio*; Schwartzkopf; Moffo; Gedda; Hotter; Wächter; et al.; Philharmonia O. EMI 67391.
Weber: *Overtures: Euryanthe, Ruler of the Spirits, Abu Hassan, Jubel, Der Freischütz, Preciosa, Oberon*; Philharmonia O. EMI 5 75645.

⌒

Schermerhorn, Kenneth (de Witt)
Born 20 November 1929 in Schenectady, New York
Died 18 April 2005 in Nashville, Tennessee

Schermerhorn had a long and distinguished conducting career, most notably his twenty-three-year tenure as music director of the Nashville (Tenn.) SO, interrupted only by the onset of his fatal illness in 2005. He was held in such regard in this city that the new $20 million purpose-built concert hall has been named for him—Schermerhorn Symphony Hall opened in 2006. Such longevity of tenure could not have been foreseen in 1988 when the orchestra and its board parted company, resulting in a bankruptcy filing. New management heralded a remarkable recovery culminating in a prestigious and well-received appearance at Carnegie Hall in 2000. But the orchestra had been a presence on the musical scene for several years previously. Once the financial side was on an even keel, the credit for its artistic progress was primarily the conductor's. After its New York appearance the orchestra went on to produce a series of generally admired recordings for the *Naxos American Classics* series. These include symphonies by Hanson, Ives, Carter, and Amy Beach, the last being coupled with her Piano Concerto in C♯ Minor, which critics hailed as a major rediscovery. The Carter symphony was paired with his fiendishly difficult Piano Concerto of 1964–65. For their efforts, Schermerhorn and the orchestra received two Grammy nominations in 2005. The previous year they had received an ASCAP adventurous programming award. As a tribute to the conductor's standing, Naxos also laid down a Nashville performance of Beethoven's *Missa solemnis* in 2004, which, despite some criticism of the soloists and chorus, was praised for the conductor's unforced and sensitive reading of the score.

Previous to his work with Naxos, Schermerhorn had recorded with the Hong Kong PO and the Bratislava SO. His recording roster, which includes music by Villa-Lobos, Glazunov, Cui, and David Amram, together with some unfamiliar Richard Strauss and familiar Beethoven, Dvořák, and Sibelius, is indicative of the eclectic and wide-ranging repertoire that was a feature of his programming throughout his career. Take the program for the 2000 Carnegie Hall concert as an example: Beethoven, Richard Strauss, Charles Ives, and the New York debut of a concerto by Mark O'Connor. As a composer of merit himself, Schermerhorn felt an obligation to support contemporary composers, and performed and commissioned works by Roger Sessions, Ulysses Kay, Robert Starer, George Rochberg, and John Downey.

Schermerhorn began his career as a trumpet player but undertook conducting studies with Richard Burgin upon entering the New England Conservatory of Music. He attended the Berkshire Music School at Tanglewood, where he worked under Bernstein and went on to win the Koussevitzky Conducting Prize. After graduating from the conservatory in 1950 he began his conducting career with the Seventh Army SO (1954–55), including an appearance at London's Royal Albert Hall. He made a special point of presenting contemporary American composers to European audiences. He spent eleven years (1957–68) as conductor of the American Ballet Theatre, a post to which he would return for two additional years in 1982. After a season spent as assistant conductor of the New York PO (1959–60), his first directorship was across the river in Newark (N.J.) with the New Jersey SO (1963–68), which made significant strides forward under his leadership. For his next appointment he moved west to the Milwaukee (Wisc.) SO for a twelve-year stay (1968–80). Here he certainly made his mark, taking the MSO on eight national tours with six Carnegie Hall appearances, and leading it to the forefront of that tier of orchestras just below the top. From 1984 to 1988 he led the Hong Kong PO, an interesting mix of Chinese, European, and American players. As well as recording successfully, he led them on a groundbreaking tour to mainland China in 1986, with concerts in Hangzhou, Shanghai, and Beijing. Other career highlights from this period include conducting Baryshnikov's Kennedy Center *Nutcracker* (1977) and the Met's Centennial Gala (1983). Schermerhorn considered himself equally a theater and concert conductor. As well as conducting ballet, he appeared in the opera houses of San Francisco, San Diego, Edmonton, Baltimore, Pittsburgh, San Antonio, Milwaukee, and at home in Nashville. He was guest conductor of the New York PO, Philadelphia Orchestra, Boston SO, Cleveland Orchestra, and the orchestras of Baltimore, Chattanooga, Cincinnati, Columbus, Delaware, Detroit, Richmond, San Antonio, and Seattle, among others. He visited Taiwan, Mexico, and Croatia as guest conductor, and toured abroad to Australia and Japan as well as China.

Throughout his career, Schermerhorn demonstrated great versatility. He invested fully in the music's passion and expressiveness wherever appropriate. His particular strengths were rhythmic flexibility and the ability to find just the right pacing while, at the same time, allowing the music to breathe. In working with orchestras he was always responsive to their needs and suggestions without ever sparing his considerable ego. As a composer he occasionally programmed one of his own short works. He delighted in writing music for special occasions. The concert for the opening of the new Nashville Public Library in 2001, for example, included a fanfare he wrote for the occasion.

Further Reading

Bostick, Alan. "Kenneth Schermerhorn—1929–2005." *Tennessean*, 19 April 2005, 1A.

Fleming, Shirley. "The Hong Kong Philharmonic Goes to China." *High Fidelity/Musical America Edition* 36 (August 1986): 34–40.

Freedman, G. "Speaking with Schermerhorn (interview)." *Music Journal* 36 (July 1978): 14–17.

Ingram, Martha Rivers, and D. B. Kellogg. *Kenneth Schermerhorn: He Will Always Be the Music*. Nashville, Tenn.: Nashville Symphony Association, 2006.

Selected Recordings
Beach (Amy): *Concerto for Piano*; *Gaelic Symphony*; Alan Feinberg (pf); Nashville SO. Naxos 8559139.
Beethoven: *Missa solemnis*, Op. 123; Lori Phillips (s); Robynne Redmon (ms); James Taylor (t); Jay Baylon (b-b); Nashville SO and Ch. Naxos 8.557060.
Carter: *Holiday Overture*; *Symphony no. 1*; *Piano Concerto*; Mark Wait (pf); Nashville SO. Naxos 8.559151.
First Contemporary Chinese Composers Festival, 1986; music by Tan Dun, Wing Wah Chan, Xiao-Song Qu, Xiao-Gang Ye, Huang An-Lun; Joseph Banowetz (pf); Michael Rippon (br); Hong Kong PO. From Marco Polo 223915.
Liberty; music by O'Connor, Shield, Law, Einhorn; Mark O'Connor (vn); Yo-Yo Ma (vc); John Jarvis (pf); John Mock (pennywhistle); James Taylor (voice); Studio O. Sony 63216.

∿

Schwarz, Gerard
Born 19 August 1947 in Weehawken, New Jersey

Is Gerard Schwarz a provincial conductor and, if he is, has the stigma attached to that designation inhibited his progress to the top flight of world conductors? Certainly, the two places where he has been most active at the start of the twenty-first century, Seattle and Liverpool, may be regarded as provincial. But both cities support first-rate orchestras, the former of Schwarz's making. Does the fact that his early promise, identified by *New York Times* critic Harold C. Schonberg back in 1980, has not blossomed into an appointment with one of the so-called top-flight orchestras in the U.S. or Europe mean that his promise remains unfulfilled? To concentrate on his current endeavors, Schwarz gave up his New York City connections as music director of the Mostly Mozart Festival and the New York Chamber Symphony, which, together with his earlier tenure with the Los Angeles CO, identified him as a conductor of smaller forces. If his achievements in Seattle over the past twenty years are viewed objectively, there can be little doubt that he has been a major and dynamic force in American music-making. The Seattle orchestra is now one of the finest in the country, with an extensive catalogue of recordings, albeit of repertoire concentrating on twentieth-century American music. It plays in one of the finest auditoriums in the country; it has a loyal following and community recognition in one of the most dynamic cities in the nation. Snobbery and prejudice aside, Schwarz, along with such colleagues as Michael Tilson **Thomas**, Leonard **Slatkin**, David **Zinman**, and Dennis Russell **Davies**, has proved that one can follow one's own path to success. The Schwarz parents were émigré physicians and music lovers who both played the piano. Gerard, their youngest son, began taking piano lessons when he was five, but after attending a performance of *Aida* at the Met a few years later, he fell in love with the trumpet. Since his parents were somewhat dubious, he demonstrated his determination by earning money through odd jobs to pay for lessons and buy sheet music. Making rapid progress, he attended the National Music Camp at Interlochen during the summers from 1958 to 1960. In 1961 he moved to New York City to attend the School of Performing Arts High School, and the following year began lessons with the New York PO's principal trumpet player, William Vacchiano. From high school he entered the Juilliard School but was already much in demand as a player. He became a member of the American Brass Quintet and third trumpet of the American SO. From 1967 through 1975 he attended the Aspen Festival. In 1971 he was awarded a Ford Foundation award for concert artists, being the first wind player to receive the honor. With the proceeds, he commissioned a trumpet concerto from Gunther Schuller. His reputation as a trumpet soloist in mainstream and avant-garde repertoires grew and he was praised both for his technical brilliance (which he attributes in large part to the influence of such jazz greats as Miles Davis, Dizzy Gillespie, and Maynard Ferguson) and for his musicality. In 1975, on the retirement of his teacher, he succeeded to the post of co-principal trumpet of the New York PO without an audition.

All this time he had been gaining experience on the podium, beginning as conductor and music director of the Erick Hawkins Dance Company. He also worked with the Soho Ensemble, Da Capo Chamber Players, Chamber Music Society of Lincoln Center, Speculum Musicae, and Casals Festival Orchestra, performing traditional and avant-garde music. While teaching trumpet at the Aspen Festival in 1973, he was called in as a last-minute substitute to conduct Elliot Carter's Piano Concerto, a prodigiously complex score. His increasing commitment to conducting and a need to juggle his career as a top-flight instrumentalist led him, in 1975, to resign from the New York PO. He then took on the music directorships of the Eliot Feld Dance Company and the Waterloo Festival in Stanhope (N.J.), joining the faculty of Fairleigh Dickinson University. It was at Waterloo that Schwarz began to specialize in presenting the works of the mid-century generation of American composers such as Howard Hanson, William Schuman, David Diamond, and Walter Piston. Through a contact there he was invited to direct a performance of the

Bach Brandenburg Concertos at the 92nd Street Y. This ensemble became established as the Y Chamber Symphony, which eventually became the New York Chamber Symphony with which Schwarz worked from 1977 to 2001. The orchestra became noted for its blend of old and new programming and laid down a classic recording of the Haydn and Hummel trumpet concertos with Schwarz as director and soloist. Among his guest-conducting invitations were appearances with the Los Angeles CO, and when music director Neville Marriner departed, Schwarz was appointed his successor. During his seven-year tenure (1977–85) he increased audience size and embarked on a successful recording contract. In 1981, he inaugurated "Music Today," a contemporary music series based at Merkin Concert Hall, and was its director until 1989. In 1980 he began his association with the Mostly Mozart Festival, which, at the time, had become a somewhat lackluster affair based at Lincoln Center. Schwarz's mission was to rejuvenate it by programming less familiar Mozart works and including music by the composer's contemporaries and successors. After receiving critical acclaim as the organization's advisor, he was appointed its music director in 1984.

Schwarz's association with the Seattle (Wash.) SO began in 1983 when he became its music advisor. His initial refusal to take on the directorship reflected a reluctance to move the center of his activities away from New York City, together with an awareness that the financial base of the orchestra was a little shaky. If he regarded the orchestra as a stepping-stone to better things at first, its potential and the opportunity it afforded to develop as a full-scale symphonic conductor were too tempting to pass up, and so he became principal conductor in 1984 and music director in 1985. Meanwhile, he had been flirting with opera. He led a performance of Die Entfürung with the Washington National Opera at the Kennedy Center, followed by Salome and Fidelio. He also conducted the American premiere of Wagner's early opera Das Liebesverbot and the same composer's version of Gluck's Iphigenia in Aulis in concert at the Waterloo Festival. He made his Seattle Opera debut with Cosi fan tutte in 1986.

Schwarz has remained with the Seattle SO for over twenty years, including the symphony's centennial season, 2003–4. Over the years he has been at pains to keep up the momentum of artistic growth, avoiding stale and routine performances. He has achieved this by imaginative program planning, by sharing the orchestra with the Seattle Opera, and by extracting players to form smaller ensembles for short seasons of classic and late Baroque repertoire. Schwarz has certainly devoted himself to the orchestra, having his principal home in Seattle and spending the bulk of his time there—a contrast to his younger days in New York and Los Angeles when he was accused of having too many commitments to do any of them really well. To create a first-class orchestra—which many critics in the first decade of the new century consider it to be—Schwarz has defined three leadership requirements: an active board of trustees, an efficient management team, and artistic vision. Seattle's achievements are due as much to Schwarz's administrative talents in planning seasons, inviting soloists, touring, fund-raising, and interacting with the community as to his performance on the podium. He was largely the driving force behind the building of the new Benaroya Hall, a purpose-built facility that opened in 1998. After the necessary adjustment to the hall's acoustics, the orchestra transformed its sound with added clarity and a color that strives to be "warm, dark, and blended." The orchestra has a very loyal following, usually plays to a sold-out crowd, and has weathered the economic doldrums of post–9/11 better than most.

Two thousand one was a watershed year for Schwarz because he cut his musical ties to New York City (although he remains conductor emeritus of the Mostly Mozart Festival) to take on the director's mantle of the Royal Liverpool PO, where he made an immediate and positive impression. Not all of the programming strategies borrowed from Seattle worked there, and he needed to accommodate the more staid British audiences to maintain the necessary level of support.

Schwarz's career has seldom been free of controversy. He felt that his formulaic success with the Mostly Mozart Festival was underappreciated by the Lincoln Center administration, resulting over time in a gradual decrease of his involvement, and he had a dispute with the Seattle players over the appointment of a first horn chair. Nonetheless, he has striven to remain focused on his musical priority of putting in place the building blocks of fine orchestras and planning his artistic goals rather than worrying too much about his own career path. His rehearsal technique is economical, pinpointing specific problems. One player likened his rehearsal manner more to that of a baseball coach than a "stuck-up maestro." His baton technique is not considered one of the more elegant, and his interpretations of the mainstream classics have occasionally been accused of being a little stiff.

The Liverpool connection ended abruptly when Schwarz declined either to renew his initial contract or accept a less-exalted role as an emeritus conductor. Grumblings had recently surfaced from a poll taken by the players, which may or may not be interpreted as a vote of no-confidence in the conductor, but certainly reflected some dissatisfaction. Despite the artistic achievement attributable to Schwarz and reflected in recordings released on its own label, the size of the orchestra had been reduced significantly as part of financial woes that left it carrying a sizeable deficit. As Liverpool approached a year of celebration as the European Capital of Culture in 2008, the prospects for the orchestra were far from rosy. Meanwhile considerable rumblings of discontent had been apparent for sometime in Seattle, and shortly after his return to the U.S. from his final concert in Liverpool, the conductor was faced with a similar display of frustration in the departure of the executive director and the results of a player-conducted survey that the Seattle orchestra's board was anxious to keep under wraps. Although there is substantial support remaining in Seattle, there is an equally strong feeling there that, after an association of almost twenty-five years, it is time for the conductor to move on to new pastures.

Schwarz and the Seattle orchestra have enjoyed an extensive recording schedule of over one hundred CDs and received a number of nominations and awards, including Best Classical Album and ten Grammy nominations. As well as specializing in recording of American composers—many of the recordings will feature in Naxos's retrospective *American Classics Series*— they have also laid down performances of Prokofiev, Shostakovich, Stravinsky, Bartók, Strauss, Ravel, and Wagner. In 1996 the orchestra was awarded first place by ASCAP for the performance of contemporary music, and Schwarz was the 1994 recipient of *Musical America's* Conductor of the Year award. His appearances as guest conductor include the Philadelphia Orchestra, Los Angeles PO, Baltimore SO, London SO, Berlin RSO, and Orchestre National de France. He has also built an especially close relationship with the Czech PO. From 1994 through 1997 he was artistic advisor to the Tokyu Bunkanura Cultural Center in Tokyo, in association with the Tokyo PO.

Further Reading

Bargreen, Melinda. "Midpoint for the Maestro." *Seattle Post-Intelligencer*, 9 April 2000, M1.

Caldwell, Michael. "Gerard Schwarz: From Virtuosic Trumpet Artist to World-Class Conductor." *ITG Journal* 24 (March 2000): 24–32.

Campbell, R. M. "High and Low Notes—The Symphony Celebrates Gerard Schwarz's 20th Season." *Seattle Post-Intelligencer*, 10 September 2004, E1.

"Schwarz, Gerard." In *World Musicians*, edited by Clifford Thompson, 883–87. New York: H. W. Wilson Company, 1999.

Selected Recordings

Brouwer (Margaret): *Aurolucent Circles*; *Mandala*; *Pulse*; *Remembrance*; *SIZZLE*; Evelyn Glennie (perc); Royal Liverpool PO. Naxos 8.559250.

Mozart: *Symphonies 40 and 41*; Los Angeles CO. Delos 3012.

Music of Howard Hanson, vol. 1; Carol Rosenberger (pf); Seattle SO; Seattle Chorale; New York CO. Delos 3705.

Strauss (R): *An Alpine Symphony*, Op. 64; *Suite in B♭*, Op. 4; Royal Liverpool PO. RLPO 1401.

Wagner Collection; Alessandra Marc (s), Seattle SO. Delos 3701.

⌒

Seaman, Christopher

Born 7 March 1942 in Faversham, Kent, England

Christopher Seaman attended Canterbury Cathedral Choir School (1950–55), the King's School in Canterbury (1955–60), and King's College in Cambridge, where he earned a master's degree in 1963. Along the way he also earned associate diplomas from the Royal College of Organists and the Royal College of Music. Seaman received conducting training at the Guildhall School of Music and Drama in London, winning a fellowship for 1972. (Later he returned to Guildhall as chief guest conductor.) He began his professional career as principal timpanist for the London PO, from 1964 to 1968. Then he moved to the podium, becoming assistant conductor for the BBC Scottish SO in Glasgow from 1968 to 1970 and its principal conductor from 1971 to 1977. He also was principal conductor for the Northern Sinfonia in Newcastle upon Tyne from 1973 to 1979. He accepted another principal conductorship in 1978, this one for the Robert Mayer Children's Concerts in London. From 1979 to 1983 Seaman was chief guest conductor for the Utrecht SO (Netherlands).

In 1987, he came to the U.S. to become conductor-in-residence of the Baltimore SO, where he stayed until 1998. Seaman took his first music director position with the Naples (Fla.) PO in 1993, remaining until 2004. In 1998 he became music director for the Rochester (N.Y.) PO, where he has broadened the audience base and raised the artistic level. Since 2003 he has also been course director for the Symphony Services Australia Conductor Development Program, which provides training and opportunities for young conductors.

On the podium, Seaman is said to radiate energy and have an intense but non-dictatorial demeanor. Reviewers of his work use words and phrases such as depth, stylish readings, emotional spectrum, subtlety, nuance, gripping, and highly charged. He pays meticulous attention to balance, sonority, and texture. The length of his stays with orchestras has allowed him to mold and refine their sounds. Seaman and the RPO won ASCAP awards for programming of contemporary music in both 2005 and 2006. He holds preconcert "Conductor's Prelude" talks, a combination of humorous lecture, demonstration, and question-and-answer period. He describes these popular events as a means of preparing people to have a richer musical experience. Seaman also talks to people through the media, having appeared on local radio and television call-in programs to answer questions and discuss the RPO season. He also hosted *The Concert Companion with Christopher Seaman*, a weekly radio program exploring orchestral music, which in its debut season won both the Silver Reel Award from the National Federation of Community Broadcasters and the Gabriel Award from the Catholic Academy for Communication Arts Professionals.

Seaman has made guest appearances around the world, leading the symphony orchestras of Pittsburgh, Detroit, Houston, San Francisco, Aalborg, Sydney, Trondheim, Prague Radio, Melbourne, Singapore, Bournemouth, and Birmingham, in addition to numerous others, as well as the Minnesota Orchestra, Aspen Music Festival, Het Gelders Orkest (Arnhem PO), Philharmonia Orchestra, Ulster Orchestra, New Queen's Hall Orchestra, Tonhalle Orchestra Zurich, Australian Youth Orchestra, Chicago Youth Orchestra, National Youth Orchestra of Great Britain, Queensland SO, and the philharmonic orchestras of Buffalo, Rotterdam, Netherlands Radio, Brno, Bergen, Hong Kong, Royal Liverpool, and the Czech Republic.

Selected Recordings
Orchestral Suites: Bizet: *Carmen*. Grieg: *Peer Gynt*; Philharmonia O. St. Clair 7364.
Rachmaninoff: *Piano Concerto no. 3*; *Rhapsody on a Theme of Paganini*; Jon Nakamatsu (pf); Rochester PO. Harmonia Mundi 907286.
Stravinsky: *Firebird*. Dukas: *L'apprenti sorcier*; National Youth O of Great Britain. IMP Classics 2041.
Tchaikovsky: *Piano Concerto no. 1*; *Francesca da Rimini*; Olga Kern (pf); Rochester PO; Harmonia Mundi HMU 907323.
Vaughan Williams: *Tallis Fantasia*; *The Wasps Overture and excerpts*; *Lark Ascending*; *Greensleeves Fantasia*; *English Folk Song Suite*; Jonathan Carney (vn); Royal PO. MSI Music 204431.

∿
Segal, Uriel (Uri)
Born 7 March 1944 in Jerusalem, Israel

After musical studies in Israel, London, and Siena, Segal burst upon the U.S. musical scene as winner of the 1969 Mitropoulos Conducting Competition at the age of twenty-five. The same year he made his "official" debut with the

Zeeland Orchestra in Copenhagen and shortly thereafter first appeared with the Israel PO. As prizewinner he spent a year as an assistant conductor with the New York PO, where he worked under Szell and Bernstein. He made further progress in the UK appearing with the BBC Welsh SO and the English CO. In 1972 he conducted the Chicago SO at the Ravinia Festival, and made his opera debut in Santa Fe (N.Mex.) with *Der Fliegende Holländer* in 1973. Domiciled in Europe, he was a frequent guest conductor of the South German RSO in Stuttgart and led them on tour. His appointment as principal conductor of the Bournemouth SO in 1980 lasted for only two seasons, but he enjoyed a longer tenure as chief conductor of the Philharmonia Hungarica (1981–85). He was appointed music director of the Israel CO in 1982. In 1986 he conducted the Chautauqua (N.Y.) SO, a festival orchestra associated with the Chautauqua Summer Institute, for the first time. Further appearances led to his appointment as the orchestra's music director, an appointment that he continues to hold. From 1989 to 1998 he served as principal conductor of the Century Orchestra in Osaka, Japan. During the 1980s and 1990s he regularly appeared in Israel leading the Israel PO and the fledgling Israel SO Rishon LeZion (founded in 1988). In 1995 he began a close association with the Louisville (Ky.) Orchestra, serving first as principal conductor, then as music director from 1998 to 2004, when his contract expired. He was "let go" not because of substandard performances, but because he didn't fit the bill of the modern maestro who is expected to spend much of his time working to stem the tide of fiscal insecurity and falling box office returns—a curiously American phenomenon! He was then appointed to the faculty at Indiana University.

Following his victory in the Mitropoulos competition, Segal's progress in the musical sphere was propulsive. He was soon making guest appearances with some of the most prestigious orchestras on the globe: the Berlin PO, Concertgebouw Orchestra, London SO, Orchestre de Paris, and the Orchestre de la Suisse Romande, as well as recording with the Vienna SO, London PO, English CO, and the Bournemouth SO on the premier Decca and EMI labels. His interpretations in those early years were noted for their fiery intensity. Even though he remains a very accomplished practitioner, his career has not been able to sustain its early momentum, it seems. He continued to procure performances of singular commitment, especially with Israeli orchestras, throughout the 1990s, often with repertoire slightly off the beaten track (e.g., Walton and Zemlinsky) and as a champion of contemporary Israeli composers. Reflecting on 9/11 in a recent interview with Sheila Steinman Wallace in *Community*, Louisville's Jewish newspaper, he espoused the importance of traditional cultural values for overcoming fear and uncertainty in a conflicted world.

Further Reading
Richards, D. "Uri Segal." *Music & Musicians* 29 (September 1980): 12.

Selected Recordings
Mozart: *Piano Concertos 12 and 21*; Radu Lupu (pf); English CO. Decca 417773.
Rossini: Overtures: *Tancredi; L'Italiana in Algeri; Il Turco in Italia; William Tell*; Stuttgart RSO. From Arthaus 100 721 DVD.
Schumann: *Works for Piano and Orchestra*; Vladimir Ashkenazy (pf), London SO (from *Vladimir Ashkenazy: Great Piano Concertos*). Decca 000122002.

～

Sheffer, Jonathan
Born 19 October 1953 in New York, New York

As a boy Jonathan Sheffer studied at the Westport School of Music. A graduate of Harvard, where he studied with Leonard Bernstein, he also attended Juilliard and the Aspen School of Music. Yet his career path since has been decidedly unconventional. A prolific composer of music for film and theater, Sheffer's canon includes orchestral works, musicals, operas, film scores, concertos, song cycles, and solo piano pieces. His opera, *Blood on the Dining Room Floor*, enjoyed a critically acclaimed off-Broadway run in 2000 and received the Richard Rodgers Production Award from the American Academy of Arts and Letters. After conducting three film score recordings (the first of many) with the Seattle (Wash.) SO, he finally made his conducting debut on the concert stage in 1991 with the San Diego (Calif.) SO. He spent 1992 as assistant to Michael Tilson **Thomas** at the London SO and L'Orchestre National de France. Sheffer says he learned from him how to be a conductor off the podium—ways to study the score, how to prepare to rehearse, how to be articulate about music.

After nearly a decade scoring and conducting films, Sheffer returned to New York and in 1995 founded the Eos Orchestra, named after the Greek goddess of the dawn to signify the new approaches to music. During the innovative orchestra's ten-year existence, Sheffer's programming earned the reputation of breaking down musical barriers and opening the doors of classical music and opera to the unfamiliar by juxtaposing thematic programming and visual and theatrical elements with excellent music. He used as much American music as possible and specialized in finding little-known music. Some accuse him of allowing the idea to become more important than the program itself. The energetic Sheffer says he considers the needs of the audience first and foremost, and that his goal is to glorify tradition and tra-ditional music while combating the image of stuffiness. Sheffer and Eos re-leased four recordings, one of which, *Celluloid Copland*, was nominated for a 2001 Grammy for Best Classical Crossover Album.

In 2001 Sheffer accepted the position of artistic director and conductor for Red {an orchestra} in Cleveland. Red, for *redefine*, *redesign*, and *rediscover*, strives to make music exciting to a diverse community by shaking concerts loose from old formats. Sheffer's skill at blending both well-known and neg-lected music with elements of film, dance, theater, and other arts to create interesting concerts without dumbing down the music has helped Red {an or-chestra} succeed in its mission. Critics don't always agree with his concert concepts, but typically they find little fault with the musical execution, de-scribing Red's performances and Sheffer's direction as passionate, precise, vi-brant, sensitive, intense, and eloquent.

As a guest, Sheffer has conducted opera, concerts, and dance for New York City Opera, Juilliard Orchestra at the Spoleto Festival (Italy), Ravinia Festi-val, New World Symphony, American Ballet Theatre at the Metropolitan Opera, Mark Morris Dance Company at BAM, Scottish CO at the Edin-burgh Festival, Sapporo SO, United World Philharmonic Youth Orchestra in Bonn, Brooklyn PO, and Filharmonica di Roma. In 2003 he was a visiting artist at the American Academy in Rome.

Website
http://jonathansheffer.com

Further Reading
Ivry, Benjamin. "A Chat with Jonathan Sheffer." *American Record Guide* 67 (July–August 2004): 8–10.
Sheffer, Jonathan. "The Last of Eos." *NewMusicBox*, 2 June 2005. http://www.newmusicbox.org/
Wright, David. "An Orchestra's Success Breeds a Sequel." *New York Times*, 30 April 2000, II-15, 24.

Selected Recordings
Bowles: *Music of Paul Bowles*; Eos Ensemble. BMG Catalyst 09026-68409.
Celluloid Copland: Copland: *From Sorcery to Science*; *The City*; *Cummington Story*; *North Star*; Eos Orchestra. Telarc CD-80583.
Gershwin: *Complete Works for Piano and Orchestra*; Michael Boriskin (pf), Todd Levy (cl); Eos Orchestra. Conifer 51342.

Music for Merce; Eos Ensemble. BMG Catalyst 09026-68751.
Sheffer: *The Omen IV: The Awakening* (film score/soundtrack); Seattle SO. Varese Sarabande.

〜

Shimada, Toshiyuki
Born 23 December 1951 in Tokyo, Japan

Toshiyuki Shimada made his conducting debut with the Tokyo Boys Choir at age eleven. When he was fifteen, his family moved to the U.S. Shimada holds a BM degree in conducting and clarinet from California State University at Northridge (1977). He began his career immediately upon graduation, as director of music and conductor of the Young Musicians Foundation's Debut Orchestra in Los Angeles (1978–81), and in 1981 was chosen as Exxon/National Endowment for the Arts conductor. The same year he accepted an assistant conductor position with the Houston (Tex.) SO. During his six years in Houston, he rose to associate conductor of the HSO in 1985, and he also became music director for the Shepherd School of Music SO at Rice University, the Cambiata Soloists, and the Nassau (N.Y.) SO.

In 1986 Shimada began a long tenure as music director and conductor of the Portland (Maine) SO. There he became known particularly for his efforts to couple masterworks with new American pieces. He championed the work of contemporary female composers, tried to do at least one piece by Bartók each season, and strove for balance and unity both within each concert and within concert seasons. The PSO received an ASCAP award for adventuresome programming of contemporary music in 1989. Shimada is credited not only with improving the PSO, but also with making its output more approachable and appealing without compromising artistic integrity. Gregarious and dynamic yet patient and polite, he believes strongly in the emotional experience of the concert hall and inspires passion in his musicians.

After twenty years in Portland, Shimada left to become music director of the Yale SO and associate professor at the Yale School of Music in 2006. The PSO has named him music director laureate. He is also music director and chief creative officer of Trinity Music Partners, LLC, which in 2005 received worldwide rights to produce recordings from the Vatican Library Collection. Shimada is principal conductor for Vienna Modern Masters, for which he records with the Moravian PO (Czech Republic).

Shimada is a frequent guest conductor throughout the U.S. and Europe, leading the Moravian PO, Prague CO, Slovak PO, Karlsbad SO, L'Orchestre

National de Lille, Royal Scottish National Orchestra, Tonkünstler Orchestra (Austria), Symphonisches Orchester Berlin, Saas Fee Music Festival (Switzerland), and Vienna Modern Masters International Music Festival; the symphony orchestras of Honolulu, Edmonton, Green Bay, Youngstown, Houston, San Jose, and Springfield (Mass.); and the Pacific SO, Colonial SO, Boston Pops, Chautauqua SO, and Western New York CO.

Website
http://hometown.aol.com/mdpso/index.html

Further Reading
Sharp, David. "Maestro Hopes to Tap Musical Treasures at Vatican Library." Associated Press State and Local Wire, 22 May 2005. http://web.lexis-nexis.com/universe
Shimada, Toshiyuki. "Emotion!" *World Association for Symphonic Bands and Ensembles (WASBE) Journal* 5 (1998): 68–70.

Selected Recordings
Brings: *Holy Sonnets*; From *Psalterium Davidicum*; Moravian PO; From *Music for Voices*, Capstone CPS-8731.
Jacob: *Winter Lightning*; *Carol of the Bells*; Jeffrey Jacob (pf); Moravian PO. From *Orchestra Music of Jeffrey Jacob*, Vienna Modern Masters VMM 3057.
Music from Six Continents, 2001 Series; Jiri Vydra (tb); Moravian PO. Vienna Modern Masters VMM 3052.
Schwartz: *Voyager for Orchestra*; *Timepiece 1794 for Chamber Orchestra*; Moravian PO; From *Voyager: Five Works for Orchestra*, Albany Records TROY646.
Van de Vate: *All Quiet on the Western Front*; Michael Polscer (t); Dominic Natoli (t); Steven Scheschareg (br); Marek Olbrzymek (t); Linda Healy-Steck (s); Martha Jane Howe (c); Josef Krenmair (b-b); Evelyn Petros (s); Moravian PO. Vienna Modern Masters VMM 4004.

⌒

Slatkin, Leonard
Born 1 September 1944 in Los Angeles, California

Slatkin's unassuming, regular-guy image is transformed into something significantly more animated when he steps up to a podium. He is the success story for the modern American conductor, someone who has the cool workmanlike rehearsal manner that orchestras like, but who can also turn on electrifying performances that leave audiences awestruck and breathless. Not only does he conduct well, but his ability to fill seats and raise money makes him the *compleat* music director, which his stints in Saint Louis and Washington, D.C., have proved. He is an activist musician who concerns himself with the state of education in public schools, with training youth orchestras, and with taking his orchestra out into the field. He has a way of talking to people about music rivaling that of the redoubtable Leonard Bernstein. Slatkin's apprenticeship with, development of, and commitment to the Saint Louis SO have been his chief means of honing his skills to create a conducting *persona* that is noted for its grasp of balance, form, and clarity. This provincial base allowed him to devote time to intensive preparation of scores and, as an orchestra builder, to gain the added reputation as a leading champion of new music such that Michael Walsch in *Time Magazine* determined the Saint Louis SO as second in the nation. He was well set to do for the National SO in Washington what he had previously done in Saint Louis.

Contradictions within Slatkin are hardly surprising considering his upbringing. What might at first have seemed a perfect milieu for a musician to be born into proved to be a mixed blessing. His parents were professional musicians of a high order, both living and working in Hollywood. His father, Felix, was concertmaster of the Twentieth Century Fox studio orchestra, and, in the evenings, leader of the famed Hollywood Quartet. He also conducted the Hollywood Bowl SO and the Concert Arts CO. His mother was Eleanor Aller, who played in studios by day and was the cellist of the quartet. The home was full of musical talk and music-making from dawn till dusk, and when Leonard and his younger brother Frederick showed musical aptitude, they were set to learn the violin from an early age. (Frederick later became a distinguished cellist.) One may wonder, with all the musical activities going on, when there was time for any parenting. In fact, the boys' upbringing was largely left to a series of housekeepers. Just as Mozart's relationship with his father was famously conflicted, so Leonard's relationship with Felix, who was an alcoholic and a gambler, was fraught with tension. He has described their relationship as fiercely competitive and, although his father gave him conducting lessons, declares that he could never have considered a conducting career so long as his father was alive. He felt his inferiority as a violinist to the extent that he switched to viola at the age of fourteen because no one else in the family played it. There was even a time in his late teens when he had decided not to pursue a musical career and enrolled at the Los Angeles City College as an English major. Less than a month later, his father unexpectedly died of a heart attack; this event, however tragic, was liberating for the young man who now had the option of deciding for himself what he wanted to be. An opportunity to conduct during the 1963 Aspen Festival was enough to convince Leonard that he had the wherewithal to become a conductor. More importantly, he came to the notice of the eminent Czech conductor Walter Susskind, who was teaching there that year and persuaded him to enroll at Juilliard and study with Jean Morel. He made his Carnegie Hall debut in 1966 conducting the YSO of New York. After graduating, he was invited to become Susskind's assistant with the Saint Louis SO, where he received generous conducting opportunities, including one to record Gershwin for the Vox company. He steadily progressed to become associate conductor in 1971, associate principal conductor in 1974, and principal guest conductor in 1975. His interest in encouraging young musicians resulted in the formation of the Saint Louis Symphony Youth Orchestra in 1969. So much had his reputation grown that he began to be in demand as a guest conductor, making his debuts with the New York PO, the Chicago SO, and the Royal PO, and being named principal guest conductor by the Minnesota Orchestra (1974–80). His apprenticeship served, Slatkin was ready to take on the mantle of music director, and when the opportunity arose with the New Orleans (La.) SO, he accepted it. He was in the position for less than two years and beginning to make an impression with the orchestra and the New Orleans public when a serious financial crisis and the offer of the vacant directorship in Saint Louis persuaded him to return there.

Slatkin's term as musical director of the Saint Louis SO is legendary. If *Time's* correspondent quoted above exaggerated the orchestra's ranking, it was not by very much. With an extensive catalogue of recording to its credit, the orchestra's prestige rivaled that of the "Big Five" (New York, Boston, Chicago, Philadelphia, and Cleveland). Such was the partnership that some commentators felt that without Slatkin, the orchestra would quickly slip back into mediocrity. What accounted for this success was his patient ensemble building, knowing exactly what his goals were, and exploiting his particular musical instincts for rhythmic vitality, formal cohesiveness, and orchestral color and texture. The fact that Saint Louis is viewed as a provincial city allowed its orchestra the freedom to develop a distinctive identity without fear of close comparison. Although Slatkin's readings of the mainstream classical and romantic repertoire were admired for their balance and straightforwardness, it was in the realm of romantic showpieces by Tchaikovsky, Stravinsky, Rachmaninoff, Bartók, Sibelius, Nielsen, and Strauss, along with specialties in English and American music, that he excelled; these pieces make up the bulk of his recorded opus. In the off-seasons he conducted the Minnesota Orchestra's Sommerfest and appeared at New York City's Mostly

Mozart Festival. He continued to be in demand as a guest conductor in the U.S. and Europe and made his Berlin PO debut in 1985. In 1992, he became the artistic director of the Blossom Music Festival, the Cleveland Orchestra's summer home. He led a two-week festival of American music with the London PO at London's South Bank Centre in 1994. After an association of nearly thirty years, the Saint Louis orchestra conferred on him the title of conductor laureate when he moved to Washington, D.C., to take up the reins of the National SO in 1996.

Throughout its history, the National SO had never achieved the distinction its name implies. With falling revenues, shrinking audiences, and lowered prestige, it was in need of a salvage operation, and, based on his record in Saint Louis, Slatkin was considered a perfect fit for the task of rebuilding. Here was someone willing to commit wholeheartedly to the orchestra and work to build its standing within its constituency and beyond. For Slatkin the position conferred more prestige and influence; an arts institution in the nation's capital could serve as bully pulpit for the arts and music education on behalf of the entire nation. In revitalizing the orchestra he hoped to set an example for other orchestras around the country, many of which were experiencing difficult times. There were personal reasons, also: he could spend more time with his family and travel less. His game plan included a willingness to blur the distinction between art and entertainment in order to capture the target audience—people who would be attracted by a certain amount of razzmatazz but come to value the concert-going experience as unique and life-enhancing. Five or six years into his tenure, his unique blend of music-making, with its attention to detail and creative programming, had brought in favorable results.

Perhaps the stiffest test an orchestra undergoes is subjecting itself to foreign critics while on tour. During a three-week European tour in the spring of 2002, the orchestra garnered largely favorable responses that highlighted its strengths. The *Irish Times* critic Martin Adams noted the "American-style discipline" of the playing: the brass "weighty and firm toned," the woodwinds "rugged and unanimous," and the strings "a multi-faceted single personality." A more grudging English critic, Richard Morrison, wrote, "but what it lacks in individual flair, it makes up in surging collective spirit." In Germany the orchestra was praised for its "fine-tuned brilliance" and the Berlin critic Wolfgang Fuhrmann concluded, "The National SO does its name justice." The conductor's direction was praised for being "prudent and detail specific," which "drives his musicians to grand achievements with economical gestures." If the orchestra had not yet reached the echelons of the elite, it had certainly made demonstrable and rapid progress under Slatkin.

The situation Slatkin faced on his appointment as chief conductor of the BBC SO (2000) was entirely different from his previous experiences. The orchestra's high technical standards were already established, and it had a tradition of playing a broad repertoire of the new and the old, the familiar and the unfamiliar. Also, as part of the BBC, it did not have the financial insecurity that so many orchestras experience. It was thought that the orchestra would respond positively to Slatkin's communication skills, efficient rehearsals, and "down-to-earth" personality that would not alienate hard-bitten professional players. One of the duties of the BBC chief is to take the lion's share of the summer festival Promenade concerts, including the festive first and last nights (he was the first non-Brit to do so). His first "last-night" program (2001) was disrupted by the events of 9/11 just a few days earlier, and Slatkin was much admired for his sensitivity in replacing the traditional jingoistic items with the Barber *Adagio* and the last movement of Beethoven's Ninth Symphony. The equivalent concert the following year created a great deal of controversy after he decided to drop the traditionally sung version of "Rule Britannia," citing his pacifist sensibilities (which, entirely consistently, date back to when he left Indiana University for refusing to join the compulsory ROTC). However sincerely made, though, the decision was a PR blunder and alienated both the traditionalists and those who thought he was taking the affair far too seriously. In retrospect, his four-year span with the orchestra does not seem to have been an unqualified success, and his announcement that he would not be renewing his contract was not particularly surprising. Although an unparalleled advocate for contemporary music, he sometimes found himself obliged to conduct works for which he felt little affinity. Critics had complained about a lack of artistic insight and lackluster music-making. One suspects that it was simply not a good fit, after all.

However, during a dearth in the recording industry, Slatkin and the BBC SO proved a very fruitful partnership in the recording studio. In all, he has over one hundred recordings to his name, including five that won Grammy awards and more than fifty that received Grammy nominations. David Patrick Stearns dubbed Slatkin's recording of Shostakovich's Fourth Symphony "the best-ever." He has recorded with the National SO, Saint Louis SO, Philharmonia Orchestra, London PO, BBC SO, London SO, and Bayerischer RSO.

Slatkin is not just an advocate for the National SO, but for music and the arts in general. In September 2002 he was inducted into the American Classical Music Hall of Fame with a citation for "his championing and his advocacy of arts education in public schools." He has strengthened the National

SO's commitment to arts education through its National Conductors Institute, its annual state residences (the orchestra spends ten days giving performances and workshops in a different state each year), and a host of other educational events in the D.C. area. He has testified at Senate hearings on arts funding and has continued to program and record works by modern and American composers.

As all good things must come to an end, so Slatkin and the NSO have agreed to part company in 2008. In planning his future career he appears to be less than eager to tie himself down to another directorship in the immediate future (although he is said to be under consideration for the Chicago SO position). Rather he has opted for two less demanding posts as chief guest conductor of both the Los Angeles PO at the Hollywood Bowl and the Royal PO in London. Additionally, he has taken the leadership role at the Nashville (Tenn.) SO as artistic advisor for a three-year period during its protracted search for a permanent leader. This has involved conducting the inaugural concerts at the newly completed Schermerhorn Symphony Center and planning future seasons. In keeping with his pansophic imperative, he has made a long-term commitment to several weeks of residency at the Jacobs School of Music at Indiana University.

Slatkin is not a highbrow intellectual: he enjoys jazz, popular shows on television, best sellers, and is a rabid baseball fan. He shamelessly seeks to broaden the symphony orchestra paradigm; "I have no problem integrating elements of pop into high culture," he told Mathew Gurewitsch in an interview in *Civilization*.

Website
http://www.leonardslatkin.com

Further Reading

Gurewitsch, Mathew. "The Music Man." *Civilization* 3, no. 5 (1996): 62–68.
Oestreich, James. "Too Few American Maestros? Try Making Them." *New York Times*, 24 June 2001, II-27.
Saint Louis SO. *The Slatkin Years: Saint Louis Symphony Orchestra*. St. Louis, Mo.: Saint Louis Symphony Orchestra, 1996.
"Slatkin, Leonard." *Current Biography Yearbook*, 526–29. New York: H. W. Wilson, 1986.
Whiting, Melinda. "Slatkin Speaks: Straight Talk from a Statesman of American Music." *Symphony* 48, no. 4 (1997): 48–50.

Selected Recordings

Barber: *Adagio for Strings*; *The School for Scandal: Overture*; *Violin Concerto*; *Essay for Orchestra*; *Second Essay for Orchestra*; *Medea's Dance of Vengeance*; *Cello Sonata*; *Canzone for Flute and Piano*; *Excursions*; *Nocturne* "Homage to John Field"; *Summer Music*; *Souvenirs*; *Third Essay for Orchestra*; Elmar Oliveira (vn); Alan Stepansky (vc); Israela Margalit (pf); Jeanne Baxtresser (fl); Judith Le Clair (bn); Joseph Robinson (ob); Stanley Drucker (cl); Philip Myers (cor); Saint Louis SO. EMI 86561.

Bernstein: *Symphony no. 3* "Kaddish"; *Chichester Psalms*; *Missa brevis*; Jamie Bernstein (speaker); Ann Murray (ms); Pablo Strong (tb); BBC S Ch; BBC Singers; BBC SO. Chandos CHSA 5028.

Bizet: *Carmen: Suites nos. 1, 2* (excpts). Grieg: *Peer Gynt: Suites nos. 1, 2* (excpts). Rimsky-Korsakov: *Russian Easter Overture*. Satie: *Gynmopédies: Nos. 1, 3*. Borodin: *In the Steppes of Central Asia*; *Nocturne*; Saint Louis SO. Telarc 60655.

Corigliano: *Of Rage and Remembrance*; *Symphony no. 1*; National SO. RCA 168450.

Vaughan Williams: *A Sea Symphony*; Joan Rodgers (s); Simon Keenlyside (br); Trinity College Chamber Choir; BBC Symphony Ch; Philharmonia Ch; BBC SO. BBC Music Magazine Vol. 12 No. 12.

⁓

Sloane, Steven
Born 19 July 1958 in Los Angeles, California

Sloane is one of a group of young conductors whose "turf" straddles the Atlantic. Firmly established on the operatic and concert circuit in Europe, he is beginning to be noticed in U.S. opera houses and as a champion of new music. Born into an intensely musical family in Los Angeles (his father had been a student of Arnold Schoenberg), he evinced conducting aspirations when he was sixteen and later pursued studies in conducting, musicology, and viola at the University of California Los Angeles. During the summers he attended the Saratoga Performing Arts Center, summer home of the Philadelphia Orchestra, where he took private conducting lessons from Eugene Ormandy. He later spent time working with Franco Ferrara in Siena.

Of Jewish heritage, he visited Israel to pursue Jewish studies, settled there in 1981, and was taken up by the eminent Jewish maestro Gary Bertini. Over the next few years he conducted all the leading Israeli orchestras and made a name for himself as a talented choir trainer with the Tel Aviv Choir and the Tel Aviv Festival Chorus. He worked in association with Bertini at the Frankfurt Opera, where he was principal conductor from 1988 to 1992. In 1992, he returned to the U.S. for three seasons as music director of the Long Beach (Calif.) Opera.

An important and long-lived opportunity opened up when he became artistic director of the Bochum SO in 1994. Here he has been noted for expanding the scope of the repertory and for imaginative programming, which introduces thematic concepts such as "1945" (a fifty-year commemoration of the end of World War II) and "Trans-Atlantik" (an exploration of twentieth-century connections between Germany and America). In 1999 he became music director of Britain's Opera North, based in Leeds. He embarked on adventurous programming—a new production of Shostakovich's operetta *Paradise Moscow (Cheryomushki)*, for example—and performances that received very favorable reviews. Unfortunately, this approach was less successful at attracting audiences to a company that, at the best of times, exists on a shoestring. He relinquished the position in June of 2003.

His record in Europe of performing new and challenging repertory (he has embarked on a project to record the complete works of twentieth-century Austrian composer Joseph Marx) led to his being invited to succeed Dennis Russell **Davies** as conductor of the American Composers Orchestra, a New York City–based organization which gives polished and committed performances of new and neglected compositions. Surprisingly, he had never appeared with it prior to his appointment. His initial work with the orchestra gave some indication of the programming policies he was planning to pursue, from a concert staging of Samuel Barber's unfairly maligned opera, *Anthony and Cleopatra*, via the music of Frank Zappa to the music of Charles Wuorinen and a host of other composers from the younger generation. Although he relinquished the title of music director in 2006, he continues his association with the group as principal guest conductor.

He has guest conducted extensively in the opera house and concert hall. His résumé includes appearances with, among others, the Bavarian RSO, Philharmonia Orchestra, City of Birmingham SO, Orchestre National de Lyon, Prague CO, and the Teatro San Carlo Orchestra, and appearances at the Royal Opera House Covent Garden, Deutsche Oper am Rhein, Lausanne Opera, Welsh National Opera, and New Israeli Opera. His operatic roster includes: Britten's *Midsummer Night's Dream*, Weill's *Rise and Fall of the City of Mahagonny*, Janáček's *Jenufa* and *Katya Kabánova*, as well as *Tristan*, *Falstaff*, *Nozze di Figaro*, *Eugene Onegin*, and *La Traviata*.

In a profile in London's *Daily Telegraph*, Rupert Christiansen described Sloane as "a highly-motivated, earnest and focused American, with a hard competitive edge and some unnervingly big ideas." He has achieved a great deal in his career so far and is clearly a dedicated and accomplished conductor. His European reputation is well established, whereas, despite the fact that he has appeared at the New York City Opera, Seattle (Wash.) Opera, Wolftrap, and was the music director of the Spoleto USA Festival from 1998 to 2000, he is still regarded as somewhat of a fringe figure in the U.S. It is more than likely that a prestigious appointment to one of the U.S. orchestras will remedy this situation at some time in the not-too-distant future.

Further Reading

Christiansen, Rupert. "Fighting Talk and Big Ideas . . ." *Daily Telegraph*, 25 January 2001, 25.
Kozinn, Allan. "New Man for New Music: A Debut for an International Commuter." *New York Times*, 1 November 2002, E4.
Milnes, Rodney: "Come North, Young Man." *Times* (London), 21 April 1998, 36.

Selected Recordings

Bloch: *Hiver-Printemps*; *Poemes d'automne*; *Proclamation*; *Suite for Viola and Orchestra*; Reinhold Friedrich (tp); Tabea Zimmermann (va); Sophie Koch (ms); Deutsches SO Berlin. Capriccio 67076.
Marx (Joseph): *Eine Symphonische Nachtmusik*; *Idylle*; *Eine Frühlingsmusik*; Bochum SO. ASV DDD CD DCA 1137.
Shostakovich: *Suite for Jazz Orchestra*; *Moskva*; *Cherymushki*; *Tahiti Trot*; Berlin RSO. Capriccio 71096.

⌣

Smith, Mark Russell
Born 4 June 1962 in Phoenix, Arizona

The son of two musicians, Mark Russell Smith began piano lessons at five, cello lessons at eight, and was a boy chorister until adolescence. His father directed the Phoenix (Ariz.) Boys Choir for decades, while his mother accompanied the ensemble. Smith got his own start conducting by leading his friends in neighborhood Christmas caroling. After earning a BM degree in cello performance from Juilliard in 1984, Smith continued his education at the Curtis Institute of Music, where he studied with Max Rudolf and

Otto-Werner Mueller and earned a degree in conducting (1987). While a Curtis student, Smith won first prize in the National Repertory Orchestra Conductors Competition.

Upon graduation he became assistant conductor of the Opera Company of Philadelphia and the Philadelphia Singers, until in 1989 he moved back to his native Phoenix as associate conductor of the Phoenix SO. There Smith was known for innovative youth programming such as "Classical MTV" and "Symphony for the Schools." He kept the position in Phoenix until 1994, but in 1992 became music director of the Cheyenne (Wyo.) SO. Then in 1995, Smith accepted the same position for the Springfield (Mass.) SO. While there, he taught and conducted at the University of Massachusetts, always on the lookout for new partnership opportunities and additional concertgoers. The energetic conductor stepped down from both orchestras in 2000 to concentrate on his remaining job as music director for the Richmond (Va.) SO, a position he accepted in 1999. There he has been praised for his innovative programming and for the orchestra's renewed vigor, depth of sound, and expression.

Smith has continued to focus on educational programs and community outreach, initiating and promoting projects such as "Kid Vids," "Music Matters," "Musical Petting Zoo," "Classical Conversations," lunchtime concerts, and holding concerts in different venues such as schools, churches, and temples. In Springfield he did television commercials for the SSO while wearing in-line skates. He says his experience on the other side of the baton, as both a cellist and a singer, influences how he conducts. Smith is known for his passion and enthusiasm, his ability to clearly articulate ideas, his somewhat unorthodox style of conducting with his entire upper body, his casual conversational style, and his talent for connecting with and building varied audiences. He schedules thematic, demanding programs and champions current music, though the music of Brahms is one of his specialties. Smith collaborated with Yo-Yo Ma and members of the Chamber Music Society of Minnesota in Hún Qiáo (Bridge of Souls), a concert featuring world premieres by Korean, Japanese, Chinese, and American composers.

With the Winnipeg (Manitoba) SO in 2002, he conducted the final round of the first Piano E-Competition, leading six concerto performances that were streamed live over the Internet. Believing in the importance of capitalizing on technical innovation to reach worldwide audiences, he returned with the Minnesota Orchestra to lead the competition's final rounds in 2004 and again in 2006. Smith has made numerous other guest appearances, conducting orchestras such as the Minnesota Orchestra, Saint Louis SO, Houston SO, Saint Paul CO, SO of The Curtis Institute of Music, Nomus Music Festival in Novi Sad (Serbia), Hartford SO, Orquesta Sinfónica de Xalapa, Colorado SO, Eugene SO, Curtis Opera Theatre, Jacksonville SO, Berkshire Choral Festival, Eastern Music Festival, Tulsa PO, Orchestra London (Ontario), and the European Center for Opera and Vocal Art in Ghent, Belgium.

Further Reading
Deming, Larry, and Jim Gustafson. "When Worlds Collide." *Film Score Monthly* 5 (March 2000): 32, 44.

Selected Recording
Copland: *Suite from the Tender Land; 3 Latin American Sketches; Suite from the Red Pony;* Phoenix SO. Koch International Classics 3-7092-2 H1.

⌣

Solzhenitsyn, Ignat
Born 23 September 1972 in Moscow, Soviet Union

Ignat Solzhenitsyn is indeed the son of dissident author and Nobel Prize Laureate, Aleksandr Isaevich Solzhenitsyn. The family moved to Vermont in 1976, and Ignat became a U.S. citizen when his parents were naturalized in 1985. His formal piano lessons began when he was nine, and in 1987 he moved to London to study with Maria Curcio, whom he credits as his principal mentor. Solzhenitsyn returned to the U.S. in 1990 to enroll at the Curtis Institute of Music, became a piano student of Gary Graffman and a conducting student of Otto-Werner Mueller, and graduated with a BM degree in 1995. In 1994 he won an Avery Fisher Career Grant and began a lengthy tenure with the Concerto Soloists CO of Philadelphia (which dropped "Concerto Soloists" from its name in 2001), first as assistant conductor (1994–95), then as associate conductor (1995–97), principal conductor (1997–2004), and finally music director in 2004.

Solzhenitsyn, said to have chafed under the CO of Philadelphia's traditional programming, likes to try new approaches and experiment with varied repertoire. He has led the orchestra in special projects, including Bach's *Saint John Passion* and the complete *Brandenburg Concerti,* Haydn's *The Creation* and *Seven Last Words,* and a rare complete performance of Gluck's *Don Juan.* He is known not only for his "revisionist sensibility" and atypical interpretations, however, but also for his musical sensitivity and his ability to elicit a clean ensemble sound and great expression from the orchestra. Solzhenitsyn continues to tour regularly as a pianist and in 2004 was appointed to the piano faculty of the Curtis Institute. His first love, he says, is chamber music, particularly German and Austrian. Conducting, however, allows him the opportunity to perform the Russian symphonic repertory he also enjoys.

As guest conductor, Solzhenitsyn has led the symphonies of Dallas, Seattle, Indianapolis, North Carolina, Virginia, New Jersey, Nashville, Toledo, Lexington, Delaware, Anchorage, Charleston, Flagstaff, and Vermont, as well as many of the major orchestras in Russia, including the St. Petersburg PO, Moscow PO, Moscow SO, Urals PO, and Kremlin PO.

Further Reading
Kozinn, Allan. "Solzhenitsyn, the Son, in a Spotlight All His Own as Pianist and Conductor." *New York Times*, 16 April 1999, E8.

∽

Spano, Robert
Born 7 May 1961 in Conneaup, Ohio

For the soprano Heidi Grant Murphy to describe singing a performance of excerpts from Olivier Messiaen's fiendishly difficult opera *St. Francis of Assisi* as "just an ordinary experience" speaks volumes for the performance's conductor. Spano is a musicians' musician. What this means is that players appreciate his knowledge, preparation, and efficiency—in short, his professionalism. They instinctively feel that he is someone they can respect and get along with, someone who is democratic and open to constructive suggestions, and someone who never wastes their time in rehearsal. Spano has built a reputation for creative programming. He is of a generation of conductors who are seeking to break away from the moribund bill of fare that most orchestras present to their aging and shrinking audiences; he strives instead to introduce new and less familiar repertory that will attract and not repel. But he is pragmatic enough to realize that what works in New York City will not necessarily have the same effect in Atlanta. He has borrowed and amplified the concept of thematic programming as a way to dovetail old and new music meaningfully, and is not averse to technological trappings—video and lighting effects—to captivate his audience. He also appreciates that a music director has to be involved in the nuts and bolts of sustaining an orchestra: auditioning new players, fund-raising, publicity, etc. He is not gregarious by nature but is willing to do the necessary socializing to keep the orchestra in sharp focus within the community.

Spano was born into a musical family and grew up in Elkhart (Ind.). He set out to learn the flute, violin, and piano, and by the age of ten was composing quite ambitious pieces. At the age of fourteen he was invited to conduct one of his prizewinning compositions with the Elkhart SO. He later attended Oberlin College, where he initially planned to major in composition but switched to conducting under the tutelage of Robert Baustian. For graduate school he transferred to the Curtis Institute to continue his studies under Max Rudolf. As a conducting career was by no means assured, he took the post of assistant professor of conducting at Bowling Green State University, where he also directed the new music program. After three years he returned to Oberlin as a faculty member and director of the opera theater. Although rejected for a conducting fellowship at Tanglewood, he managed to secure an audition for one of the conducting assistantships with the Boston SO under Seiji **Ozawa** and was successful. He made his debut with the orchestra in 1991 with a program that included Sibelius's First Symphony, the Grieg Piano Concerto, and *Haunted Landscapes* by George Crumb. The assistantship was for three years, but he was already in demand as a guest conductor and emergency fill-in both in the concert hall and opera house. Among his appearances was a fateful one with the Atlanta SO in 1993, the same year he was awarded the Seaver/NEA Conductors Award. He made his Covent Garden debut with *Billy Budd* (1994) and his first appearances at the Chicago, Houston (Tex.), and Santa Fe (N.Mex.) opera houses in 1997. His first permanent appointment was one to which he was ideally suited, that of music director of the Brooklyn (N.Y.) PO (1996–2004). This part-time professional orchestra was associated with the Brooklyn Academy of Music and noted for its innovative programming and championing of new music under its two previous directors, Lukas Foss and Dennis Russell **Davies**. What appealed to the orchestra was Spano's proven track record of contemporary music performances and ability to achieve results on limited rehearsal as well as produce exceptionally good performances of traditional repertoire. At this time the orchestra was in dire straits financially, however, and was reduced to a five-concert series. Within three years Spano was able to turn this around without compromising the orchestra's mission. He expanded the concept of thematic concerts, which in his first season included such tags as *Beyond Good and Evil* and *Nietzsche and Music*, to that of thematic seasons: 1999–2000's theme was *The Century*; 2001–2's was *Liebstod*. During a six-concert *Song of the Earth* series (2002–3) the choices included Mahler's song cycle of the same name, Stravinsky's *Rite of Spring*, Milhaud's *La création du monde*, Copland's *El salon Mexico*, and new works by Ramon Zupko and Bright Sheng. The idea worked because it appealed to a niche audience and it distinguished the orchestra from its close rivals. Spano has a preference for seeking links from within the vast range of his musical knowledge. The musicians found the programs stimulating, which kept their performances fresh and enthusiastic, and such infectiousness always rubs off on an audience. It was hardly surprising that Spano, with his growing reputation for success, should come to the attention of headhunters from more prestigious orchestras. And so it was that in 2001 he began his first season as the music director of the Atlanta SO.

Spano's attraction for Atlanta was his reputation as a diplomat, communicator, and problem solver. The orchestra had recently been going through a difficult time with a musicians' strike, a five-year tug-of-war over the fate of Yoel Levi, the previous conductor, and a deficit of almost a million dollars. The advantage for Spano was that he had the prospect of a full season with a first-rate orchestra, but could keep Brooklyn for the kind of radical programming that wouldn't necessarily go over well in a thriving though conservative town like Atlanta. Another helpful factor was the simultaneous appointment of Donald **Runnicles** as chief guest conductor on the understanding that he, along with the orchestra's administrative staff, would collaborate on program planning. Any additional suggestions from players or public would also be welcomed. But for the orchestra to prosper, the same strategies that had worked so well in Brooklyn had to be tailored to suit Atlanta. New music of a more accessible kind could be introduced gradually, together with techniques such as showing video interviews with composers before performing their work. Music by **Adams**, Schwantner, Theofanidis, Danielpour, and Higdon worked their way into the programs. For the institution to flourish, Spano understood that it must occupy a meaningful place in the life of the community, which is why he was willing to conduct "ASO-to-Go" (family-style concerts in the suburbs) and subject himself to media hype such as being a poster-boy on the sides of buses and conducting in a Braves shirt!

With so much continuing success and being in high demand as a guest conductor, he decided to relinquish the Brooklyn position at the end of the 2003–4 season, realizing that he was not able to fulfill for them the extracurricular activities with which he was becoming so involved in Atlanta. In 2002 he appeared with the Santa Fe Opera, directing Kaija Saariaho's *L'Amour de loin*. He accepted the directorship of the Festival of Contemporary Music at Tanglewood and, in 2003, made a belated and much lauded debut with the New York PO in a program of Sibelius, Rachmaninoff, and Saariaho's *Chateau de l'ame*. In recent years he has appeared with most of the major orchestras in the U.S., including those in Chicago, Boston, Cleveland, Houston, Los Angeles, Philadelphia, Minneapolis, Washington, D.C., San Francisco, and

Toronto, and is increasingly in demand for both concerts and operas abroad. He gave his debut performance of Wagner's *Ring* cycle with the Seattle (Wash.) Opera in 2005. His recordings with Atlanta forces of Vaughan Williams's *A Sea Symphony* and of Berlioz's *Requiem* won Grammy awards. Other nominations were received for recordings of music by Jennifer Higdon and Golijov's opera, *Ainadamar*. He is an accomplished pianist and regularly performs chamber music with colleagues from the orchestras he has led.

The thematic programming that Spano pioneered in Brooklyn is only one aspect of what is needed for classical music organizations to survive and thrive in the twenty-first century, but his continuing success in Atlanta will be a beacon for similar efforts elsewhere.

Further Reading

Chastain, K. "Trading Flute for a Baton." *Flute Talk* 13 (1993): 12–14.

Davidson, Justin. "Measure for Measure: Exploring the Mysteries of Conducting." *New Yorker* 82, no. 25 (2006): 60.

Dyer, Richard. "Cleared for Takeoff." *Symphony* 51 (May–June 2000): 20–23.

Pincus, Andrew L. "Robert Spano: Turning Babel into Buzz." In *Musicians with a Mission: Keeping the Classical Tradition Alive*, 137–83. Boston: Northeastern University Press, 2002.

Selected Recordings

Berlioz: *Requiem*, Op. 5; Frank Lopardo (t); Atlanta SO and Ch. Telarc CD-80627.

Golijov: *Ainadamar*; soloists; Atlanta SO. DG 00642902.

Higdon: *City Scape*; *Concerto for Orchestra*; Atlanta SO. Telarc 60620.

Theofanidis: *The Here and Now*. Del Tredici: *Paul Revere's Ride*. Bernstein: *Symphony no. 1* "Jeremiah: Lamentation"; Hila Plitmann (s); Richard Clement (t); Brett Polegato (br); Nancy Maultsby (ms); Atlanta SO and Ch. Telarc CD 80638.

Vaughan Williams: *Symphony no. 1* "A Sea Symphony"; Christine Goerke (s); Brett Polegato (br); Atlanta SO and Ch. Telarc SACD-60588.

St. Clair, Carl
Born 5 June 1952 in Hochheim, Texas

Calmed as a baby by his aunt's piano playing, Carl St. Clair began his own lessons at age six, and by age ten he was earning superior marks in state competitions. Then he moved on to the trumpet, making all-state band and all-state orchestra in high school. Music became more important than football, so quarterback St. Clair quit the team. He went to the University of Texas at Austin, where he won a job as assistant to the head of the conducting program, Walter Ducloux. Winning a mentor as well as a job, he earned a bachelor's degree in music and a master's degree in operatic and orchestral conducting. St. Clair joined the music faculty at Southern Illinois University at Carbondale and, two years later, at the University of Michigan before his career shifted out of academia. In 1985 he won a conducting fellowship at the Tanglewood Music Center, where he studied with Leonard Bernstein. That same year he became music director of the Ann Arbor (Mich.) SO. The following year he accepted positions as assistant conductor at the Boston SO under Seiji **Ozawa** and as music director of the Cayuga CO in Ithaca (N.Y.). In 1990 St. Clair had another eventful year: He won the Seaver/NEA Conductors Award, left the BSO, and accepted the position of music director of the Pacific SO in Santa Ana (Calif.). To focus his attention on the PSO, he moved to California and resigned his positions at both the AASO (1992) and the CCO (1991).

During St. Clair's lengthy tenure, the PSO has not only grown into the third largest in the state, but has progressed in many other ways as well, resulting in increased subscriptions, balanced and much larger budgets, recording projects, an endowment, American and world premieres, expanded seasons and educational programs, and a first European tour in 2006. St. Clair's interest in the music of living composers is evidenced by regular commissioning of works, two composers-in-residence, and the annual American Composers Festival, which has been gaining national attention since it began in 2001. In 2005 St. Clair and the PSO won an ASCAP award for programming of contemporary music. He initiated an instrument-purchase program and another program offering string players low-interest loans to buy better instruments. A huge milestone was the opening of the orchestra's new home in September 2006, the Renée and Henry Segerstrom Concert Hall in Costa Mesa. Maturing along with the orchestra, St. Clair has become known not only for his interpretations of twentieth-century music, but also for his special feel for pieces in large forms requiring large forces (e.g., Mahler's Eighth Symphony) and his deep appreciation for the underlying rhythmic structures of Mozart.

Since arriving in Orange County, St. Clair has plunged into local affairs, using every opportunity to meet people and draw attention to the orchestra, which he says he "wants to become a necessity in our community." Always personable, he leads concerts in the park, holds conducting clinics with kids, and accepts numerous speaking engagements. In memory of their infant son, St. Clair and his wife Susan launched "arts-X-press," a summer program that offers arts education to middle school students. His contract with the PSO extends through 2009.

From 1998 to 2004 St. Clair was principal guest conductor for the Stuttgart RSO, and together they recorded a complete series of the twelve symphonies of Villa-Lobos. In 2005 he was appointed *Generalmusikdirektor und Chefdirigent des Deutschen Nationaltheaters und der Staatskapelle Weimar* (chief musical director of the German National Theater in Weimar and chief conductor of the Weimar State Orchestra). As such he conducts not only symphonic music, but operas. Berlin's Komische Oper announced in February 2007 that St. Clair is to take up the post of *Generalmusikdirektor* when Kirill Petrenko's contract expires at the end of the season. He is a frequent guest conductor elsewhere in Germany, but has also conducted the Atlanta SO, Boston SO, Detroit SO, Houston SO, Indianapolis SO, Los Angeles PO, New York PO, San Francisco SO, Philadelphia Orchestra, Seattle SO, and orchestras in Australia, Israel, Hong Kong, Japan, New Zealand, and South America. St. Clair also frequents summer festivals, including the Schleswig-Holstein Festival, Pacific Music Festival in Japan, Round Top Festival, Breckinridge, Tanglewood, and Texas Music Festival.

Further Reading
Boston, Bruce O., and Louis Spisto. "How Valuable Are School Music Programs? Ask PSO Conductor Carl St. Clair." *Triangle of Mu Phi Epsilon* 87, no. 1 (1993): 19–20.
Favorito, Barbara Ann. "Seeking Musical Solutions: An Interview with Carl St. Clair." *Instrumentalist* 45 (March 1991): 12–15.
Mangan, Timothy. "Hometown Maestro." *Orange County Register*, 3 September 2006, 2A.
St. Clair, Carl. "The Beat Goes On: A Former Texas Student Musician Credits His Professional Success to His Texas All-State Experience." *Southwestern Musician* 72 (May 2003): 18–19.

Selected Recordings
Danielpour: *An American Requiem*; Stephanie Blythe (ms); Marc Oswald (br); Hugh Smith (t); Pacific SO; Pacific Chorale. Reference Recordings 97.
Foss: *Concerto for Piano no. 1*; *Concerto for Piano no. 2*; *Elegy for Anne Frank*; Lukas Foss (pf); Jon Nakamatsu (pf); Yakov Kasman (pf); Eliza Foss (spoken vocals); Pacific SO. Harmonia Mundi 907243.

Goldenthal: *Fire Water Paper* "A Vietnam Oratorio"; James Maddalena (br); Ana Panagulias (s); Yo-Yo Ma (vc); Pacific SO; Pacific Chorale; Pacific Chorale Children's Choir; Ngah-Khoe Vietnamese Children's Ch. Sony 68368.
Mozart: *Sinfonia Concertante for Violin and Viola in E♭ major*, K 364. McKinley: *Concert Variations for Violin, Viola and Orchestra*; Glenn Dicterow (vn); Karen Dreyfus (va); Warsaw National PO. Master Musicians C 2122.
Villa-Lobos: *Symphony no. 6, W 447* "Sobre a linha das montanhas do Brasil"; *Symphony no. 8*; *Suite for Strings*; Stuttgart RSO. CPO 999517.

∿

Stern, Michael
Born 12 December 1959 in New York, New York

Stern, son of celebrated violinist Isaac Stern, is himself an accomplished string player who began playing the violin at the age of three and a half. His first teacher was Hiao-Tsiun Ma (father of cellist Yo-Yo Ma), and he eventually went on to study with Dorothy DeLay at Juilliard. After receiving a BA in American history from Harvard, he enrolled at the Peabody Institute to study viola under Joseph de Pasquale and to begin serious conducting studies under Max Rudolf. He attended the annual Pierre Monteux Summer School in Maine on two occasions, working under the tutelage of its director, Charles Bruck. In 1986 he was one of three young conductors chosen to take part in an intensive week's workshop with Leonard Bernstein, culminating in a joint concert with the New York PO in Avery Fisher Hall. Shortly thereafter, he received an Exxon/Arts Endowment residency as assistant conductor of the Cleveland Orchestra under Christoph von **Dohnanyi** (1986–91). After making a number of guest appearances in Europe, he was appointed permanent guest conductor of the Orchestre de Lyon, a post he held for four years (1991–95). After a single appearance with the Saarbrücken RSO he was invited to become its chief conductor, in which post he remained from 1996 to 2000. During his tenure, he led the orchestra on critically acclaimed tours to Spain, Portugal, Switzerland, and China. As a committed proponent of American music, he made recordings with the orchestra of music by Henry Cowell and Charles Ives.

Arts administrator Albert Pertalion was so impressed hearing Stern perform with the Memphis (Tenn.) SO in the fall of 1998 that he decided to form a professional-level chamber orchestra based at the Germantown

(Tenn.) Performing Arts Center, named the IRIS CO, with Stern as music director. He auditioned players from a wide area to obtain the best available and immediately booked a number of highly sought-after soloists. The mission of the organization was no less than "revitalizing the chamber orchestra repertoire with special support for American music," with the intention of commissioning and recording works by some of the brightest talent in the nation. From the first, Stern exercised considerable ingenuity in devising imaginative program mixes of new and traditional repertoire.

Stern definitely shone as one of the three finalists auditioning for the position of music director of the Kansas City (Mo.) SO, which led to his appointment in 2005. In a competitive field he impressed the search committee with his all-around skills: "his ability to rehearse . . . lead compelling performances, and to articulate his passion for the music to the audience and to the players." The feeling that this was a good match was reinforced on subsequent occasions when he led the orchestra prior to taking up his post officially in September 2005. Mickey Coalwell, writing in the *Kansas City Star* about a May 2005 concert, found the partnership had given the orchestra "a fresh, palpable energy . . . along with a new-found polish and confidence." He praised the conductor's sympathetic and creative partnering of Jion Wang in Dvořák's Cello Concerto and described the succeeding performance of Brahms's First Symphony as "a revelation." Noting the demands this score places on players and conductor alike, he found their joint achievement exceptional and thought this augured well for the future. Fan mail posted on the KCSO website includes comments such as: "Michael Stern is stunning, breathtaking, truly electrifying—he has it all," "Michael is exceptional—a privilege to see and hear. Kansas City is fortunate to have him," and "he's the greatest—best playing from the orchestra I've ever heard."

It has to be noted, however, that critics over the years have sometimes expressed reservations about Stern's abilities. They have commented on performances of his as dull, routine, and worse. As long ago as his appearance with the NYPO at the conclusion of the Bernstein workshop, his performance was by far the most cautious of the three participants. In New Jersey in 1992, *New York Times* critic Allan Kozinn, in a generally favorable review, heard "stretches . . . in which his phrasing seemed unusually tight and unyielding." A Houston critic in 1994, acknowledging his command of both score and ensemble, commented on the need for him to "become free with the music and infuse it with his individual personality." In Atlanta in 1999 his performance of Schumann's *Rhenish* Symphony was found to be "a tad ponderous." As a late replacement for an indisposed Mariss **Jansons** in Pittsburgh in 2001, a critic reported "the ensemble exhibited scant desire to dig

into the music and Stern offered little direction." A student performance of
Berlioz's *Beatrice et Benedict* during the Aspen Festival of 2003 "was a stretch
for the students . . . and conductor Michael Stern did little to help them over
the hurdles." Cruelest of all was a remark by critic Sarah Bryan Miller in the
St. Louis Post-Dispatch (4 May 2005) recalling a performance of Strauss's *Four
Last Songs* with soprano Christine Brewer, led by Stern "with all the sensitivity of a rhinoceros with a toothache."

As noted above, Stern has been a fervent champion of contemporary
American composers. Those commissioned to write works for the IRIS CO
include Lera Auerbach, Richard Danielpour, Marshall Fine, Stephen Hartke,
Jennifer Higdon, Jonathan Leshnoff, Edgar Meyer, Robert Patterson, and
Ellen Taaffe Zwilich. In addition, during its brief existence, the orchestra has
performed music by Barber, Bernstein, Copland, Foss, Glass, Harrison, Ives,
Riley, and Rorem. Stern's debut with the Kansas City orchestra included the
premiere of Ned Rorem's Cello Concerto in March 2003. Recordings with
IRIS have been made of Hartke's Clarinet Concerto, *Landscape with Blues*,
with Richard Stoltzman as soloist; Zwilich's *Rituals*; Rorem's Double Concerto; and Leshnoff's First Symphony, *Forgotten Chants and Refrains*, all issued
by Naxos in its *American Classics* series. Another double concerto, this one
released on the Arabesque label, is Danielpour's *In the Arms of the Beloved*,
performed by Jaime Laredo and Sharon Robinson. Three concertos by
Zwilich with the Florida State University Orchestra and members of the
Kalichstein-Laredo-Robinson Trio each taking solo roles are on a Koch International release. Recordings with the Saarbrücken RSO, mentioned
above, include Henry Cowell's Piano Concerto, a reconstruction of Charles
Ives's *Emerson* Piano Concerto, and his *Universe Symphony* issued on the Col
Legno label. A frequent guest conductor of the Zurich Tonhalle Orchestra,
he has recorded a disc of Stravinsky ballet scores and Prokofiev's First and
Second Violin Concertos, with Boris Belkin as soloist, on the Denon label.
He has recorded works by Tchaikovsky and Dvořák, also with Belkin as
soloist, in partnership with the London PO. A recent release (2005) from Al-
bany Records features horn player Eric Ruske and IRIS in concertos by the
Strausses, father and son (Franz and Richard in this case), and Reinhold
Glière.

Stern's list of guest appearances is singularly impressive. In the Far East he
has appeared before the leading orchestras of China, Taiwan, Japan and Singapore. In the U.S. he has led all of the principal regional orchestras, as well
as the Chicago SO and the Philadelphia Orchestra. His roster in Europe includes the Orchestre Nationales of Paris, Bordeaux, Lille, Strasbourg, and
Toulouse, orchestras in Scandinavia (Oslo, Bergen, Stockholm, Helsinki),

Russia (Moscow), Germany (Berlin, Munich, Cologne), Switzerland (Zurich and Lausanne), Hungary (Budapest), and Israel. In Britain he has conducted the London SO, London PO, BBC SO, and English CO.

Clearly there have been conflicting views of Stern's career thus far. A tendency toward restraint was noticed as long ago as 1986, when Bernstein urged him to "go crazy, Michael!" After a Kansas City concert in January 2005, critic Paul Horsley wrote that he was "still waiting to be grabbed by the lapels and shaken." There is ample evidence of another side to Stern, as when his performances have been described as "electrifying" and eliciting "bravado." Perhaps his Kansas City tenure will prove the opportunity to finally reconcile these inconsistencies.

Further Reading

Blank, Christopher. "IRIS Again in Bloom at GPAC." *Commercial Appeal* (Memphis, Tenn.), 27 October 2006, G36–37.

Blank, Christopher. "IRIS Strives to Make Art Accessible by Making It Affordable for Patrons." *Commercial Appeal* (Memphis, Tenn.), 13 September 2002, E1.

Selected Recordings

Danielpour: *A Child's Reliquary*; *In the Arms of the Beloved*; Kalichstein-Laredo-Robinson Trio; IRIS CO. Arabesque Z6767.

Hartke: *Clarinet Concerto*; *The Rose of the Winds*; *Gradūs*; *Pacific Rim*; Richard Stoltzman (cl); IRIS CO. Naxos 8.559201.

Ives: *Symphony no. 2*; *Universe Symphony* (arr. Austin); Saarbrücken RSO. Col Legno 20074.

Rubinstein: *Piano Concerto no. 4*. Scharwenka: *Piano Concerto no. 1*; Marc-André Hamelin (pf); BBC Scottish SO. Hyperion 67508.

Zwilich: *Violin Concerto*; *Rituals*; Pamela Frank (vn); Saarbrücken RSO; Nexus; IRIS CO. Naxos 8.559268.

⌒

Summers, Patrick
Born 14 August 1963 in Washington, Indiana

Summers built his career in the opera house. His active involvement with singers began at the age of thirteen when he first worked as a voice studio accompanist at Indiana University. It was the distinguished soprano Margaret Harshaw who first spotted his potential to become a conductor. Curiously enough, although neither of his parents was musical, he was attracted to the piano at the home of an eccentric aunt at the tender age of three and a half, and could read music before he learned to read words. His kindergarten teacher played recordings of Caruso and Tetrazzini to her class, and a competent local piano teacher, recognizing her student's potential, encouraged him to transfer to Indiana University in his early teens. At fifteen he appeared for a time at a seedy local piano bar playing "an extensive repertory" of show tunes. He quickly became involved in operatic activities at IU and, in 1986, successfully auditioned as an apprentice coach for the Merola Program, San Francisco Opera's summer training program. He succeeded to the directorship of the Western Opera Theater, the touring arm of the San Francisco Opera Center, and he made his debut with the San Francisco parent company conducting *Die Fledermaus* in 1990. He served as music director of the Opera Center from 1990 to 1994. From 1994 to 1999 he worked extensively as a guest conductor in Australia, at the Dallas (Tex.) Grand Opera (1996), and elsewhere, making his Met debut (with *Die Fledermaus*) in 1998. Still in his mid-thirties, Summers's considerable operatic knowledge and experience, together with an avowed enthusiasm for mounting new works, had served to make him the candidate of choice for the position of music director of the Houston Grand Opera (1999), without his ever having appeared with the company. His tenure there, in conjunction with that of David Gockley, the company's general manager, has been a highly effective mix of new and traditional repertoire. He also served as principal guest conductor of the San Francisco Opera for the 1999–2000 season.

Summers's efforts to champion new stage works go back to 1990, when he gave the American premiere of Aribert Reimann's chamber opera *The Ghost Sonata* at the Opera Center. His 1996 Dallas debut was with Lee Hoiby's *The Tempest*. For San Francisco Opera he shared conducting duties with the composer for a run of performances of André **Previn**'s *A Streetcar Named Desire* (1998), and premiered Jake Heggie's *Dead Man Walking* (2000). At Houston Grand Opera his list of first performances includes Tod Machover's *Resurrection* (1999), Carlisle Floyd's *Cold Sassy Tree* (2000), Mark Adamo's *Little Women* (revived 2000, following a studio production in 1998), Daniel Catán's *Florencia en el Amazonas* (2001), Rachel Portman's *The Little Prince* (2003), and Jake Heggie's *The End of the Affair* (2003). He also revived Floyd's 1970 opus, *Of Mice and Men* (2001). In the early 1990s he made something of a reputation as a Rossini specialist, bringing out the composer's richness of orchestration and emotional expressiveness, but his standard operatic repertory ranges from his own realization of Monteverdi's *L'Incorarione di Poppea* to Charpentier's *Louise*, encompassing Handel, Mozart, Bellini, Verdi, Bizet, Gounod, and Puccini along the way.

Summers's approach to music-making is to attempt to get to the emotional heart of a work and, being moved by it himself, evoke an equivalent response in his players and audience. This does not always suit some critics who claim to hear a vapid sheen to his work. With an impeccable technique, he aims to be as conscientious as possible in order to realize the composer's intentions in operatic performances—as far as the suppression of egos for the collective good will allow! His passion for new music comes from the conviction that the health of operatic culture as a whole depends on the infusion of new "complex, skillful, emotional music that people can relate to." He backs this up by keeping new works in the repertory and recording their revivals, a luxury seldom enjoyed by composers. After years of coaching and accompanying singers, his sympathetic treatment of them, based on a deep understanding of phrasing and breath control, pairs with a control of orchestral balance to achieve a remarkable degree of vocal and orchestral clarity. He recently estimated that he spends 70 percent of his working life in opera houses in the U.S., Europe, Australia, and as far afield as China and Japan. He is starting to build a reputation in the concert hall conducting choral and instrumental music and, he says, relishing the opportunity to make music purely for the sake of it.

A successful tour with the English CO and soloists Olga Borodina and Dimitri Hvorostovsky in 1997 led to Summers's first CD release on the Phillips label. This was followed by his direction of a Grammy-winning *Bel Canto* recital featuring Renée Fleming, the Orchestra of Saint Luke's, and the Coro de Maggio Musicale Fiorentino on Decca. Original cast recordings of *Little Women* and *Dead Man Walking* were released in 2002, and of *Florencia* and *Of Mice and Men* in 2003.

Further Reading

Johnson, Chelsey. "Backtalk." *Opera News* 63 (July 1998): 29.
Necula, Cristina. "No Artifice: Patrick Summers (interview)." *Classical Singer* 18 (November 2005): 22–27.
Thomason, Paul. "Summers Time (interview with Patrick Summers)." *Opera News* 63 (November 1998): 46–49.
Ward, Charles. "A Man of Many Talents." *Houston Chronicle*, 28 January 2005, Star 5.

Selected Recordings

Arias and Duets: Olga Borodina and Dmitri Hvorostovsky; English CO. Phillips 454439.
Catán: *Florencia en el Amazonas*; Mark S. Doss (*Riolobo*); Ana Maria Martinez (*Rosalba*); Suzanna Guzman (*Paula*); Hector Vasquez (*Alvaro*); Oren

Gradus (*Capitán*); Patricia Schumann (*Florencia*); Chad Shelton (*Arcadio*); Houston Grand Opera O and Ch. Albany 531/32.

Floyd: *Cold Sassy Tree*; soloists; Houston Grand Op Ch; Houston Grand Op O. Albany 758/59.

Heggie: *Dead Man Walking*; Susan Graham (ms); John Packard (br); Frederica von Stade (ms); San Francisco Girls Ch; San Francisco Boys Ch; Golden Gate Boys' Ch; San Francisco Op Ch; San Francisco Op O. Erato 86238.

～

Tchivzhel, Edvard
Born 29 January 1944 in Leningrad, Soviet Union

Edvard Tchivzhel, son of professional musicians with the Kirov Theater of Opera and Ballet, showed early talent and began his musical training at age five, eventually entering the Leningrad Conservatoire. He studied piano and conducting, graduating with distinction in both areas, and completed three years of postgraduate study at the Conservatoire's Higher Academie of Music under Arvid Jansons. In 1971 Tchivzhel accomplished a rare feat by winning the third Soviet Conductors Competition in Moscow a year before graduating from the Conservatoire.

Tchivzhel began his career in 1973 as music director and principal conductor of the Karelian SO of National Television and Radio, a position he would hold until his defection to the U.S. in 1991. From 1974 to 1977 he was assistant conductor to the legendary Yevgeni Mravinsky at the Leningrad PO. In years following, he became permanent guest conductor with the LPO and guest conducted many other Soviet and European orchestras. In 1986 he was named chief conductor of the Umea Sinfonietta (Sweden), yet was passed over for major posts in the Soviet Union. Tchivzhel believes he wasn't considered to lead an important orchestra because of his Latvian ancestry. While touring the U.S. as associate conductor with the USSR State SO in 1991, Tchivzhel and his wife and son were given political asylum.

He was artist-in-residence at the Governor's School for the Arts at Furman University (Greenville, S.C.) during 1991 and 1992. From 1992 to 1994 Tchivzhel was music director for the Atlantic Sinfonietta in New York. He accepted the position of music director at the Fort Wayne (Ind.) PO in 1993 and has enjoyed an extended tenure there. Tchivzhel is credited with having invigorated both the orchestra and the city. His first goal, he says, is to bring musical excitement to the community, and indeed he makes people eager to come to concerts. He also brings excitement and energy to rehearsals and has inspired his musicians to raise their levels of performance. On the podium he is known for sensitivity, sometimes putting down the baton to use his hands instead. After performing Dvořák's Cello Concerto under Tchivzhel's leadership, cellist Yo-Yo Ma called him a master and said, "I was stunned to hear Maestro Tchivzhel's music-making that is indisputably commanding and communicative." In January 2007, Tchivzhel announced he would be leaving the Fort Wayne PO at the expiration of his contract in 2008.

Since 1994 Tchivzhel has also been permanent guest conductor with the Auckland PO in New Zealand. Nineteen ninety-nine was a notable year for Tchivzhel: He and his family became U.S. citizens, and he accepted a second position, music director and conductor for the Greenville (S.C.) SO. There he also teaches master classes in conducting as a distinguished visiting professor at Furman University. In 2004, Indiana Congressman Mark Souder presented Tchivzhel with the Congressional Johnny Appleseed Award in recognition of his contribution and commitment to the public in planting seeds of goodwill for generations to come. Tchivzhel says it is important for young people to understand the language of classical music so they will become adults who can enjoy the richness of human culture.

Tchivzhel guest conducts around the world, having appeared in England, Germany, the Czech Republic, Poland, Romania, Scandinavia, Japan, Australia, and New Zealand. He has led the symphony orchestras of Helsinborg, Malmö, and Norrköpping, the Stockholm PO, Baltimore SO, Indianapolis SO, Grand Rapids SO, and Orquestra Sinfônica Brasileira in Rio de Janeiro. Tchivzhel returned to Russia in 2003 (for the first time since his defection) to conduct his former Leningrad orchestra, the renamed St. Petersburg PO.

Further Reading

Penhallow, Steve. "Edvard Tchivzhel's New World Symphony: From Assigned Posts and Limited Repertoire to Freedom and Fort Wayne's Classical Talent." *Journal Gazette*, 15 December 1996, 1E.

Selected Recordings

Music for Martha Graham III: Dello Joio: *Seraphic Dialogues; Exaltation of Larks; Diversion of Angels*; Atlantic Sinfonietta. Koch International Classics 3-7167-2H1.

Prokofiev: *Piano Concerto no. 3 in C*. Liszt: *Piano Concerto no. 1 in E♭ major*. Rachmaninoff: *Rhapsody on a Theme of Paganini*, Op. 43; Olivier Cazal (pf); Duncan Gifford (pf); Vitaly Samoshko (pf); Sydney SO. From Sydney International Piano Competition of Australia 1992, ABC Classics 476 227-4.

Rachmaninoff: *Rhapsody on a Theme of Paganini*; *Piano Concerto no. 3 in D minor*, Op. 30. Tchaikovsky: *Piano Concerto no. 1 in B♭ minor*, Op. 23; Ayako Uehara (pf); Evgeny Ukhanov (pf); Marino Kolomiitseva (pf); Sydney SO. From Sydney International Piano Competition of Australia 2000, ABC Classics 461 654-2.
Tchaikovsky: *Symphony no. 6*. Strauss (R): *Don Juan*; Fort Wayne PO. Sweetwater Sound FWP 012345.

⌒

Temirkanov, Yuri
Born 10 December 1938 in Nal'chik, Soviet Union

Temirkanov's unconventional conducting style leaves players, audiences, and critics bemused as to what his performances achieve and how he achieves it! His fascinating wheedling and cajoling gestures (he conducts without a baton) seem to dispense with the customary role of beating time and cueing-in players. Yet his bending and arm-sweeping usually do produce something remarkable. His fluid conducting style encourages expression by players who seem to play with care and abandon at the same time. In rehearsal he is known to guide with a minimum of words and gestures, resulting in emotional and deeply musical performances. His Slavic training has given him the ability to create an orchestral palette that is particularly appropriate to the Russian and Central European repertoire that is his specialty: typically a warmth of string tone built up from the basses, lithe woodwinds, and rasping brass. As a guest conductor, he is able to work with members of any orchestra on both his and their terms: he gets them to do what he wants without asking them to change anything! He has that uncanny ability to make even the most familiar works sound fresh and invigorated, or as one player put it: "He transcends the score."

The Baltimore SO Board, convinced that Temirkanov was the right fit to succeed David **Zinman**, courted him assiduously. The positive response from all sides that his previous guest appearances had received was the primary stimulus. But a particular successor is frequently appealing because of the contrast he or she provides to the previous music director, and that may have been a factor in this instance. For Temirkanov the attraction was that this fine orchestra had the scope and the will to grow. He found the Baltimore milieu to his liking (an estuary city like his hometown, St. Petersburg), and was intrigued by the plan to build the orchestra another concert hall, the Music Center at Strathmore, in the Washington, D.C., suburbs.

A new music director, aside from producing excellent performances, is expected to make his mark on two aspects of the orchestra: its essential sound and its repertoire. Regarding the first, it was soon evident that the orchestra's precision was infused by a warmer, richer string tone and a burnished sheen overall. This observation ties into the second, since this sound is ideal for the full-bodied, deeply expressive Russian and German works that became the mainstay of the repertoire. Where he expanded his programs it was toward the mainstream Soviet-era composers, Shostakovich and Prokofiev, especially those works less familiar in the West and for whom he feels a special affinity. Rather than playing the Americans, whose music had been the orchestra's standard pieces under **Zinman**, Temirkanov preferred to add more Teutonic repertoire, particularly Brahms, Mahler, Haydn, and Mozart. However, it should not be forgotten that he did provide committed performances of music by Charles Ives, Samuel Barber, George Gershwin, and the intriguing Giya Kancheli. This shift to the "center" may also have been what the orchestra's board had in mind, considering the always-needy state of orchestra financing in the U.S. In this regard Temirkanov showed remarkable acuity. His congenial personality and willingness to mingle with the prominent and wealthy proved a great asset.

The fact that he has presided over a significant turnover of players reveals a tougher side to his character. His desire to develop the orchestra's sound through a cooperative learning process had its limitations. In fact, Baltimore did not escape the financial downturn experienced by most other arts organizations as a result of the events of 9/11. Despite the successful opening of the new concert hall at Strathmore (February 2005), Temirkanov's commitment to Baltimore was tempered by a number of factors, and he announced his intention to step down as music director when his contract expired at the end of the 2005–6 season. This decision, much regretted by players, critics, and public alike, was no doubt influenced by the organization's stated aim of "reinventing itself," the appointment of a controversial board president, and the continuing slide deeper into debt.

To provide context for his Baltimore tenure it helps to examine the situation that has been the mainstay of Temirkanov's career: his conductorship of the then Leningrad, now St. Petersburg PO. Once again, basic contradictions emerge. Although the recent era has witnessed many changes in Russia, many things have stayed the same. A love-hate relationship with his native country led him to a sense of great responsibility toward the orchestra. When he took over from the legendary Mravinsky, he inherited an orchestra with serious musical and morale problems, exacerbated by defections to the West throughout the 1970s and 1980s and a work ethic and discipline further eroded during the Brezhnev era. As the Soviet Union collapsed, he presided over a transition that displayed his sterling ability to engender trust and faith in his players. As government subsidies dried up, the orchestra was left to shift for itself and, despite a loyal following at home, was obliged to tour abroad for large portions of the year. Touring led to a narrowing of the repertoire, as foreign audiences expected to hear Russian music. What surprised critics was that even though the orchestra could be decidedly slipshod at times, other musical qualities, such as the hefty punches of emotional power in Temirkanov's interpretations, were always in evidence.

Temirkanov's childhood was spent during the grim days of World War II. His musical propensities ensured him a place, at age thirteen, at the Leningrad School for Talented Children. He went on to study violin and viola at the Conservatory and, after graduating in 1962, to postgraduate work in the conducting class of Ilya Musin. He spent a year as assistant to Mravinsky and took up his first appointment as conductor of the Malïy Opera Theater, Leningrad. As winner of the 1967 USSR Contest for Conductors in Moscow, he served as assistant to Kondrashin on an international tour of the Moscow PO with David Oistrakh as soloist. In 1968 he was appointed chief conductor of the Leningrad SO. During his tenure (1968–76) he made his debut with the Vienna PO at the Salzburg Festival and his U.S. debut with the Philadelphia Orchestra in 1975. He became director of the Kirov Opera and Ballet Theater (1976–88), where he displayed his talents not only in the pit but also as stage director. He led the company in his own productions of the Russian classics *The Queen of Spades*, *Eugene Onegin*, and *Boris Godunov* in residency at Covent Garden in 1987. During his long tenure with the Leningrad PO he was appointed principal guest conductor of the Royal PO (1979) and then its principal conductor (1982–88). In addition, he served as chief guest conductor of the Dresden PO (1994) and the Danish RSO (1997). He made his U.S. opera debut in San Francisco in 1998.

Temirkanov has recorded extensively since 1988, chiefly on the BMG/RCA label. With the Royal PO he has recorded the complete ballets of Stravinsky, the complete symphonies of Tchaikovsky, and music by Rachmaninoff, Mussorgsky, and Brahms. His version of Rachmaninoff's Second Symphony was considered "arguably the most stunning account available." With the Leningrad/St. Petersburg PO he has laid down an extensive catalog of Russian music, including Shostakovich, Prokofiev, Rachmaninoff, Berlioz, Ravel, and Sibelius. He has also recorded with the New York PO, Moscow PO, USSR State SO, and RSO of Berlin, among others. As a guest conductor he frequently appears with the Vienna PO, Dresden Staatskapelle, London PO, Concertgebouw Orchestra, and L'Orchestra di Santa Cecilia,

Rome. In the U.S. he regularly conducts the orchestras of New York, Philadelphia, Boston, Chicago, Los Angeles, and San Francisco.

Website
http://www.temirkanov.com

Further Reading

Goodwin, Noël. "Temirkanov and the Kirov Opera." *Opera* 38 (July 1987): 751–54.
Pountney, David Willoughby. "Words, Music and Tradition." *Opera* 38 (December 1987): 1375–79.
Robinson, Harlow Loomis. "Yuri Temirkanov: A Russian Conductor Copes with Change." *American Record Guide* 59, no. 1 (1996): 12–14.
Selby, Holly. "A Measure of the BSO's New Maestro." *Baltimore Sun*, 20 January 2000, 1E.
Smith, Tim. "A Natural Flow (Baltimore Symphony Orchestra's New Music Director, Yuri Temirkanov)." *Symphony* 52 (March–April 2001): 30–35.
"Temirkanov to Take the Helm in Baltimore." *Symphony* 49, no. 1 (1998): 9–10.

Selected Recordings

Mussorgsky: *Pictures at an Exhibition* (orch. Ravel); *Khovanshchina: Act 1 Prelude*; *Songs and Dances of Death*; Sergei Leiferkus (br), Royal PO. RCA 59423.
Ravel: *Ma mère l'oye*; *La Valse*. Gade (Jacob): *Jalousie*. Tchaikovsky: *Nutcracker Suite*; Johannes Soe Hansen (vn); Danish RSO. Chandos 9799.
Rimsky-Korsakov: *Scheherazade*; *Russian Easter Festival Overture*; Glenn Dicterow (vn); New York PO. RCA 61173.
Shostakovich: *Symphonies 5 and 6*; St. Petersburg PO. Warner 62354.
Tchaikovsky: *Eugene Onegin*; Sergei Leiferkus (br); Yuri Marusin (t); Larissa Dyadkova (ms); Tatiana Novikova (s); Kirov O. Kultur Video 1165 DVD.

~

Thomas, Michael Tilson
Born 21 December 1944 in Los Angeles, California

Although not quite unique, Michael Tilson Thomas is one of a new breed of conductors who don't merely pay lip service to contemporary music but regularly make it an integral part of their programming and attract enthusiastic audiences for it. Shaking off his image as a "difficult customer," he has enjoyed two of the most successful musical partnerships in recent years. As music director of the London SO from 1988 to 1995, he was able to turn around an organization experiencing significant financial and artistic difficulties. After four years under him the orchestra had erased its deficit, increased its box office, and quadrupled its sponsorship. It prospered artistically as well, thanks to Thomas's adventurous programming, appealing presence on the podium, and magnetic personality. If London was artistically vibrant in the last two decades of the century, San Francisco has been even more fertile ground for the kind of artistic adventurousness that is one of Thomas's hallmarks. With a repertory that includes a high proportion of twentieth-century works and features compositions by Americans on nearly every program, his partnership with the San Francisco SO has been a success story with audiences and critics alike, at home, on tour, and in the recording studio. Unlike many of his contemporaries, Thomas has ignored mainland Europe and taken some of the spotlight away from the traditional East Coast focus of orchestral musicmaking in the U.S.

Michael Tilson Thomas was born into a "showbiz" family in Hollywood. He demonstrated an early precocity and musical talent. In his teens he also developed an interest in science, and it wasn't until he had completed his undergraduate education that he resolved on music as a career. He was able to play the piano by ear at an early age, was reading music at the age of eight, and considered himself a potential conductor at the age of thirteen. He took keyboard lessons from a number of excellent teachers in the Los Angeles area, and came under the tutelage of composer Ingolph Dahl for a thorough grounding in music theory while an undergraduate at the University of Southern California. His experience accompanying students in the master classes of Jascha Heifetz and Gregor Piatigorsky was also significant, as was his meeting with Igor Stravinsky at about the same time. On his own account he became associated with the Young Musicians Foundation Debut Orchestra as its conductor and occasional solo pianist. This gave him valuable experience performing works by Stravinsky and the leading avantgarde composers of the day: Boulez, Stockhausen, Foss, and Cage. He attended the Bayreuth Festival in 1966 and 1967 working as assistant to Pierre Boulez, who was conducting *Parsifal*, and he attended classes given by Wagner's granddaughter Friedelind. The association with Boulez was extended when he assisted him at the Ojai Festival in California and became its chief conductor in 1968. A major achievement while attending Tanglewood on a conducting fellowship was to win the Koussevitzky Prize that enabled him to become associate conductor of the Boston SO in 1969. He made a remarkable New York City debut with the orchestra, taking over mid-concert when the conductor William Steinberg became unwell. Thomas went on to conduct thirty-seven more concerts that year and was appointed the orchestra's associate conductor the next year. In 1970 other career opportunities opened up when he made his debut with the London SO and appeared at the Ravinia and Mostly Mozart festivals. His recording that year of Carl Ruggles's *Sun-treader* received two Grammy nominations, and the trade publication *Musical America* named him Musician of the Year (1971). The Boston SO upped his status to principal guest conductor, a post he held until 1974. His first directorship lasted from 1971 to 1979 and was with the Buffalo (N.Y.) PO, which under a previous director, Lukas Foss, had already established a reputation for adventurous programming. Thomas's reputation as a music proselytizer blossomed during the six years (1971–77) he spent as music director of the New York PO's Young People's Concerts, many of which were televised.

Thomas's close association with Leonard Bernstein dates from his years at Tanglewood and was to last until the latter's death in 1990. To portray him as a Bernstein clone is grossly unjust, although the similarities between the two are striking: eclectic composers, flamboyant conductors, accomplished pianists, Jewish, gay, educators, and iconoclasts. Bernstein's mentoring must have been beneficial in many ways, although the constant harping on it has also been a burden to someone seeking to establish his own persona.

Thomas's tenure at Buffalo has been described as controversial, but guest conducting and recording helped consolidate his reputation. The recording of *Carmina Burana* with the Cleveland Orchestra won a Grammy in 1974, the same year he made a fateful debut with the San Francisco SO. A humiliating arrest for drug possession in 1978 effectively ended his period as an *enfant terrible* and forced him to indulge in some soul-searching. In 1979 he made one of his rare forays into the opera house to conduct the reconstructed three-act version of Alban Berg's *Lulu* in Santa Fe (another was the production of Janáček's *Cunning Little Vixen* for New York City Opera in 1981). His tenure as principal guest conductor of the Los Angeles PO (1981–85) was not without its problems. There was friction between him and the orchestra's general manager, although his musical achievements were never in doubt. In 1985 he began a three-year term as principal conductor of the Great Worlds Music Festival in Massachusetts. A significant career move occurred in 1987 when he became conductor and mentor of the New World Symphony, a Miami-based (Fla.) organization that serves as a training vehicle for instrumentalists recently graduated from schools and colleges. The purpose was to create a staging post where talented young players receive a solid grounding so that, after a year or two, they can successfully adjust to the arduous life of a professional symphony orchestra musician. This was just the thing to give ample scope to his educational zeal and his abilities as communicator and orchestra builder.

Thomas's appointment as principal conductor of the London SO got off to an auspicious start by his being the players' choice. This provided all the more incentive to create a close working relationship based on mutual respect. The success of this partnership suggests that, in midlife, Thomas had reached an appropriate level of maturity, both musically and emotionally. His endeavors during this period were notable, including the establishment of London's Barbican Centre as a leading venue for the kind of varied, catholic, and imaginative programming for which he is best known, and a series of outstanding recordings that captured the orchestra in top form.

Michael Tilson Thomas's close association with the San Francisco SO (appointed music director and principal conductor in 1995) also seems to have been a marriage made in heaven. He is clearly at home in the cultural and social ambience of the city and its rich ethnic, multicultural, and experimental heritage. It is a place where he can play to his strengths: imagination, innovation, and crowd-pleasing podium theatrics. With his integrated programming he is attempting a kind of double conjuring trick: persuading the traditional older audience that new music has something to offer them, and attracting a younger and newer audience who can relate to the sonic world of contemporary music but who find the language of traditional classical music forbidding. There is no question but that his music-making is exciting; he imposes his personality on the orchestra in order to bring out theirs. Whenever his fertile imagination takes him in one direction, his instinct tells him to seek out a different path next time so as not to get stuck in a rut—however successful that rut may have been. His concerts are challenging, balanced, and never complaisant, because he wants the concert hall to be a place of musical inquiry. His concepts are more than salesmanship, for in reaching out, he is helping the community define itself. Success is measured by the quality of performances that depend on the chemistry between conductor, players, and audience. Thomas never stints himself. In an interview with Edward Seckerson, he explains his approach with the remark that "music is a very elevated form of show business." When judged by the standards achieved in the recording studio, the San Francisco SO can compete on equal terms with more illustrious orchestras back east. This clearly indicates Thomas's mettle as an orchestral trainer. His appealing persona and flamboyant conducting style should not blind us to the solid musicianship that informs them. About a recent performance of Rimsky-Korsakov's rarely performed opera *Mlada*, one critic wrote that the performance exhibited an "understanding that was as disciplined as it was energetic and gleeful." Thomas does not conform to the traditional image of the maestro as martinet. He himself has said that he hopes to see orchestral playing become "much more soloistic and much more personal." Reviewing a performance of Schoenberg's *Five Orchestral Pieces*, one critic observed: "The playing of the individual sections, so important to the piece, was nothing short of brilliant." Perhaps Marilyn Tucker summed up his achievement best when she wrote that a performance of *The Rite of Spring* had "such flawless precision that one actually heard things in the masterpiece that had never come through before" (*American Record Guide*, September–October 1999). Thomas does not program modern works out of a sense of duty, but because he is genuinely excited by them and is constantly seeking to extend the boundaries of music. He admits that he finds playing the classics more of a challenge, wishing to make them sound fresh and spontaneous and free from distortion or gimmicks. Throughout his career he has understood that the role of musical director extends beyond programming, rehearsing, and podium antics to evangelizing and outreach. His ability to speak about music (always a hazardous business) in a way that helps audiences relate to it better, that is, to make the experience of listening more meaningful in an emotional and responsive rather than merely intellectual way, has been a great asset and is largely responsible for his success in attracting audiences, whom he frequently addresses from the podium during concerts. This affable and unsophisticated way of expressing himself has also worked well on television, where he has had a string of successes beginning with the New York Young People's Concerts in 1971 and followed by the "Discovery Concerts" for the BBC and "Celebrating Gershwin," a joint U.S.-European production marking the fiftieth anniversary of the composer's death.

His recording catalog is extensive and ranges from Adolphe Adam to John **Adams**. It reflects his preference for late romantic and twentieth-century repertory, particularly the Russians, Mahler, Schoenberg, Stravinsky, Gershwin, Ives, Cage, Boulez, and Reich, but includes some Bach and Beethoven as well. He has received numerous awards, including half a dozen Grammy awards, the two most recent being for Mahler's Sixth Symphony in 2002 and his Third Symphony in 2004. He also has one in the Best Jazz Vocalist category for *Gershwin Live!*, a collaboration with singer Sarah Vaughan. In establishing his own label for the San Francisco SO (SFS Media) he is seeking to take full advantage of cutting-edge technology so that recorded sound can be as close as possible to the concert hall experience. Other labels he has recorded for include: Decca, Delos, DGG, EMI, Nonesuch, and RCA.

As noted previously, he has mostly shunned the opera house, which he finds unsatisfying, preferring rather to mount semi-staged performances in the concert hall, which he did successfully with Mlada in 2002 and The Flying Dutchman in 2003, among others.

Michael Tilson Thomas is also a composer of repute. His composition From the Diary of Anne Frank, whose premiere featured Audrey Hepburn as narrator, has been performed worldwide.

Further Reading

Abbot, Christopher. "Mahler at Midpoint: A Conversation with Michael Tilson Thomas." Fanfare 28 (March–April 2005): 39–44.

Cott, Jonathan, and Julian Broad. "Michael Tilson Thomas: America's Most Innovative Maestro Talks about James Brown, Nirvana and the Future of Music." Rolling Stone (16 December 1999): 71.

Darter, Tom. "Michael Tilson Thomas: Conductor, Pianist, Composer." Keyboard 22 (July 1996): 62–68.

James, Jamie. "Michael Tilson Thomas." Gramophone 68 (February 1991): 1493.

Keener, Andrew D. "Walking the Dog with Uncle Harry." Gramophone 63 (June 1985): 20–21.

"MTT, Music Dynamo (interview)." Music Journal 34 (May 1976): 10–11.

Thomas, Michael Tilson, and Edward Seckerson. Michael Tilson Thomas, Viva Voce: Conversations with Edward Seckerson. Boston: Faber and Faber, 1994.

Selected Recordings

Gershwin: Overtures: Oh Kay!; Funny Face; Girl Crazy; Strike Up the Band; Of Thee I Sing; Let 'em Eat Cake; Rhapsody in Blue; An American in Paris; Promenade: Walking the Dog; Fascinating Rhythm; George Gershwin (pf); Sarah Vaughan (vocal); et al. Buffalo PO; Los Angeles PO; New York PO. Sony 93018.

Ives: Three Places in New England. Ruggles: Sun-treader. Piston: Symphony no. 2; Boston SO. DGG 463 633–2.

Mahler: Symphony no. 9; San Francisco SO. SFS Media 821936-0007-2.

New World Jazz: music by Adams, Bernstein, Gershwin, Milhaud, Stravinsky, Hindemith, Antheil, Raskin; New World Symphony. RCA 68798.

Stravinsky: Symphony of Psalms; Symphony in 3 Movements; Symphony in C; London S Ch; London SO. Sony 53275.

Vänskä, Osmo
Born 28 February 1953 in Sääminki, Finland

In midlife Vänskä has acquired a reputation as one of the most distinguished and admired conductors of his generation. As he developed skills through experience, hard work, and musical integrity, his career progressed at a steady pace, leaving him feeling mostly sanguine as two of his classmates (see below) raced ahead. Nonetheless, his achievements have been remarkable—spectacular, even—forcing themselves onto classical music's consciousness from obscure and faraway places. He transformed a provincial Finnish orchestra into a most accomplished ensemble with flagship performances of Sibelius that have redefined that composer's music for generations to come! He brought the Icelandic SO to Carnegie Hall to present a program that made the New York critics, hardly believing their ears, sit up and take note! His tenure with the BBC Scottish SO raised it from mediocrity to a level where cycles of Beethoven and Nielsen symphonies held their own with the best. It is likely that his infectious enthusiasm will inspire his latest ensemble, the Minnesota Orchestra, to achieve its ambition of becoming one of the top three in the U.S.

Vänskä's dour and modest persona on the podium fits in well with Minnesota's Nordic culture and its disdain of showmanship. His reputation for having a communal, collegial approach to music-making, in addition to absolute conviction of conception and determination to see it realized, made an immediate impression on the talented and ambitious players of the Minnesota Orchestra. In pursuit of high goals, he brought with him a recording contract and the commitment to tour during his first season as music director (which coincided with the orchestra's centenary). His musical strength (his weaknesses are much harder to identify!) is his mastery of orchestral drama, achieved through well-judged and flexible tempi, control of dynamic gradations, and powerful, non-bombastic climaxes. He strives to integrate fidelity to the score with vital and spiritually charged interpretations, revealing an ability that one critic characterized as "real imagination, real understanding." Perhaps it is a Baltic trait (shared by Mariss **Jansons**) to admit to a belief, as he does, that music has the power to transform lives. He rehearses relentlessly and conducts with abandon, seeking to convey all that he has absorbed from his musical experiences as player, conductor, and "unrelentingly detailed thinker about music." Thus his unsentimental, hard-edged, and deeply passionate interpretations of Sibelius and his brisk, lithe, and revealing Beethoven readings are two of the hallmarks of his career so far. But he is determined to avoid being pigeonholed as a specialist. Apart from the Baltic composers, he excels in the Slavic repertory from Tchaikovsky to Lutosławski by way of Rachmaninoff, Stravinsky, Shostakovich, Prokofiev, and Szymanowski, but he has also included the music of Bartók, Berlioz, and, of course, Mozart in his recent programs. He has championed contemporary music, particularly that of his compatriots Aho and Rautavaara, but also the Scot James MacMillan. Having performed some Hanson, Ives, and Copland, he intends to explore contemporary American composers, beginning with Aaron Jay Kernis, the MO's composer-in-residence, and others such as John **Adams**, Steven Paulus, and the Argentinian Osvaldo Golijov. His own composition *Here! . . . Beyond?*, from 2003, received its American premiere at an MO concert in October 2006, to critical acclaim.

Born in a small town in the Mikkeli province, Vänskä was the son of a grocer and folk-fiddler who encouraged all his children to learn a musical instrument. Vänskä's lot, at the age of eight, was the clarinet. Ten years later he was so accomplished on the instrument that he was appointed principal clarinetist of the Turku PO (1971–76), and in order to improve still more, received lessons from the Berlin PO's Karl Leister in 1973. He went on to occupy the co-principal chair of the Helsinki PO (1977–82). In the meantime he had been taking conducting lessons with the country's leading teacher, Jorma Panula, at the Sibelius Academy in a class that included Esa-Pekka **Salonen**, Jukka-Pekka Saraste, and Sakari Oramo, all of whom went on to achieve world renown. He achieved recognition as a conductor by winning the Besançon International Young Conductor's Competition in 1982. He served as principal guest conductor of the Lahti (Finland) SO from 1985 to 1988 before becoming its music director, a post he continues to hold (as of 2007). He was chief conductor of the Tapiola Sinfonietta (1990–92) and then music director of the Icelandic SO, which tenure culminated in the remarkable tour of the U.S. in 1996. Having acquired a reputation as a formidable orchestral trainer, he next moved to Glasgow for six years of accomplishment as chief conductor of the BBC Scottish SO (1996–2002) before taking up his post as the tenth music director of the Minnesota Orchestra at the beginning of the 2003 season.

He has recorded over fifty CDs on the BIS label, mostly with the Lahti orchestra, featuring several of Finnish composer Kalevi Aho's massive symphonies and orchestral works. Most significant, though, has been his series of Sibelius symphonies and orchestral works, including an earlier, unknown four-movement version of the Fifth Symphony. His tally with this company includes recordings by other Finnish composers: Rautavaara, Sallinen, Klani,

Kokkonen, Martinnen, and Kajanus. He has also recorded with the Tapiola Sinfonietta, Stockholm PO, and Oslo PO and produced a complete cycle of Nielsen symphonies with the BBC Scottish SO. He has embarked on recording a complete cycle of Beethoven symphonies with the Minnesota Orchestra. His guest appearances include the Chicago, Boston, Cleveland, Philadelphia, San Francisco, Saint Louis, and National orchestras in the U.S., and the Helsinki PO, Concertgebouw Orchestra, Munich PO, Deutsches SO Berlin, and Orchestre National de France in Europe. He has expressed some reservations about what can be achieved with the few rehearsals he gets when appearing before a new orchestra, but he clearly enjoys showing off his own orchestras on tour, including a Lahti SO visit to Japan in 2003.

Further Reading

Clark, Andrew. "Sibelius Rediscovered." *Financial Times*, 7 March 1997, 19.
Peiken, Matt. "Conducting Business: Osmo Vanska, the Minnesota Orchestra's New Music Director, Is a Taskmaster . . ." *Saint Paul Pioneer Press*, 31 August 2003, E1.
Pennanen, Ainomaija. "Osmo Vaenskae [sic] Mounts the Podium." *Finnish Music Quarterly* no. 3 (1991): 17–19.
Quinn, Michael. "Interview." *Gramophone* 82 (March 2005): 12.
Quint, Andrew. "Osmo Vänskä, the Minnesota Orchestra, and BIS Begin a New Beethoven Symphony Cycle on Multichannel SACD." *Fanfare* 28 (March–April 2005): 50–52.
Tuomisto, Matti. "Not by Sibelius Alone . . ." *Finnish Music Quarterly* no. 4 (1999): 52–57.

Selected Recordings

Aho: *Symphony no. 3*. Mussorgsky: *Songs and Dances of Death* (arr. and orch. Aho); Jaakko Kuusisto (vn); Matti Salminen (b); Lahti SO. BIS CD-1186.
Beethoven: *Symphonies: No. 3 "Eroica"; No. 8*; Minnesota O. BIS 1516.
Britten: *Sinfonietta; Serenade for Tenor, Horn and Strings; Now Sleeps the Crimson Petal; Nocturne*; Christoph Prégardien (t); Ib Lanzky-Otto (cor); Tapiola Sinfonietta. BIS 540.
Leifs: *Symphony no. 1 "Saga"*; Iceland SO. BIS 730.
Nielsen: *Symphonies: No. 2, Op. 16, "The Four Temperaments"; No. 5, Op. 50*; BBC Scottish SO. BIS 1289.

∿

Venzago, Mario
Born 1 July 1948 in Zurich, Switzerland

The appointment of the Swiss Venzago to be the sixth music director of the Indianapolis (Ind.) SO came as a surprise, not least to himself! It is, after all, in the top tier of American orchestras, one of only eighteen that provide full-time employment. Having spent most of his conducting career, beginning in the 1970s, in Europe, he was not a familiar name, although he had established close ties with the Baltimore SO and the New Jersey SO as a guest conductor. In fact, he made his American debut as long ago as 1988 at the Hollywood Bowl when attending the Los Angeles Philharmonic Institute under Leonard Bernstein. Having begun to whittle down a fifty-strong pool of candidates, the ISO board invited Venzago for two audition concerts in 2001. He naturally chose to conduct programs that reflected his strengths: one of French music including Debussy's *La Mer* and Ravel's *La Valse*, and one that was all Schumann. In the selection process following the auditions, he obtained the support of the majority in a players' ballot and the unanimous endorsement of the search committee. He signed up for four years in the spring of 2002, to be extended on a mutually agreed yearly basis. Previous commitments limited his first-year appearances to three concerts; his first full schedule was the 2003–4 season.

A lively mind and his experience working in the U.S. have made Venzago savvy of the American musical scene. He is mindful of the difference between the aloof, dictatorial maestro image in Europe and the more collegial approach now common in the U.S. He also realizes and accepts the extra-musical activities that a music director is expected to take on as a cultural icon in American communities. He has shown his willingness to support outreach projects by participating in the "Indiana Series" of concerts that play at venues in the Indiana hinterland. He is also able to wear the mantle of a populist, discussing Indianapolis's diverse musical scene—jazz, blues, folk, and pop—while trumpeting all his orchestra has to offer, and expressing his newfound interest in the Hoosier passion for basketball. Considering his reputation in Europe as somewhat of a specialist in new music, it is hardly surprising that a generous number of works by contemporary American composers have appeared on his programs. This programming is supported by a solid base of works drawn from the traditional nineteenth-century repertoire. His first full season of offerings was a tad self-indulgent; he described the works in his appealingly idiosyncratic English as, "a little bit of things I want to do with the orchestra."

Venzago began his musical career as a pianist and accompanist (his recording of Janáček's *The Diary of One Who Disappeared* with tenor Peter Keller won both a Grand Prix du Disque and a Diapason d'Or award), and one could argue that the strengths of his conducting reflect a pianist's sensibilities rather than those of someone who has been an orchestral player. In this respect he seeks textural and instrumental clarity with clear articulation, exploiting a subtle range of dynamics and a pronounced sense of flow. His performances are intense and meticulous, brilliant and full of character. This pianistic approach occasionally comes to grief, however, when his use of rubato and dynamic shading is carried to excess and as a result sounds affected and self-indulgent. In a brief *Indianapolis Monthly* (2002) interview, he articulated the nub of his approach. It stems from a fear that concert music-making will become a museum art; to counteract this he approaches the great masterworks of Beethoven, Schubert, Brahms, and others "like new pieces every time." But what exactly does this mean? Is it the ability, as Sir Edward Elgar once famously remarked when recording his *Pomp and Circumstance March Number One*, to "play this [tune] as though you have never heard it before," or does it mean to set out deliberately to make performances sound unlike anyone else's? By choosing the title *A Different Schumann* for his recorded cycle of the composer's orchestral works with the Basel SO, he seemed to be tending toward the latter, and the critics were not impressed with the quality of the work. Steven Haller in the *American Record Guide* found this "herky-jerky" approach "too coy for words"—a case of the expressive becoming excessive. Venzago accounts for this in the same interview quoted above: "Perhaps I like to be extreme, but at least the music is alive."

Performances with the ISO have, in general, been free of eccentricities and well received. Venzago's philosophy at the beginning was to establish a creative relationship with the orchestra and experiment "to find works suited to our musical personality." The warm orchestral sound heard on recordings of German orchestras from the interwar years is the model that he hoped to emulate with his Indianapolis forces. As a figurehead, he planned to achieve artistic success by triggering an emotional commitment to the music from the players. His unusually wide repertoire has resulted in some imaginative programming: Schoenberg's *A Survivor from Warsaw* paired with Beethoven's Ninth Symphony, for example. A retired musicology professor at Indiana University, Malcolm H. Brown, found the performance of Shostakovich's Fourth Symphony "unbelievably profound."

Having begun learning to play the piano at the age of five, Venzago pursued his musical studies at the Zurich Conservatory while attending university there. For further study he entered the Vienna Conservatory and participated in the conducting class of Hans Swarowsky. He began his conducting career with Swiss Radio in Lugano and as principal conductor for the broadcasts of the Suisse Romande Orchestra in Geneva. In 1978 he was appointed principal conductor of the Winterthur City Orchestra and later became music director of the Heidelberg Opera (1986–89). He moved to Frankfurt in 1989 for a three-year stint as director of the German Chamber PO (Deutsche Kammerphilharmonie). His next stay was in Graz, where he presided at the opera (1990–95). Nineteen ninety-five was the year of his debut with the Baltimore SO, which initiated regular return appearances, and he eventually became director of the orchestra's Summer Festival (2000–3). Meanwhile, in Switzerland he served as music director of the Basel SO, and in the Basque region of Spain as conductor of the Euskadi National Orchestra (1998–2001). In 2001 he shifted his activities to Sweden, becoming principal guest conductor of the Malmö SO and then, in 2003, musical director of the Göteburg SO, where he had been a regular and popular guest conductor.

As a guest conductor, Venzago has appeared extensively throughout Europe and in North America and Japan. Appearances include the Berlin PO, Vienna SO, Leipzig Gewandhaus Orchestra, Bavarian RSO, Munich PO, Tonhalle Orchestra, Copenhagen PO, London PO, City of Birmingham SO, Philadelphia Orchestra, Florida PO, and the NHK Orchestra in Tokyo. He has also conducted at the Komische Oper in Berlin, the Lucerne Opera, and the festivals of Salzburg and Lucerne.

As mentioned above, Venzago's wide repertoire ranges from Bach and Handel to Stockhausen and Nono. He has served twentieth-century music well alongside the core of nineteenth-century repertoire, with particular emphasis on Schubert, Schumann, Brahms, and Bruckner. In the U.S. he has performed a number of works by contemporary American composers including Eric Stokes, Jennifer Higdon, James Beckel, Brian Current, and John Corigliano. His recorded output is extensive, principally with the Basel SO, the Swiss Philharmonic Studio Orchestra, and the Swiss Workplace (Werkstatt) Philarmonic. He has been a champion of music by Swiss composers, including the operas *Venus* and *Penthesilea* by Othmar Schoeck, Honegger's operetta *Les aventures du Roi Pausole*, Raff's posthumous Symphony Number Eleven, Raffaele d'Allesandro's Symphony Number One and Third Piano Concerto, and instrumental music by Willy Burkhard. Other rarities committed to disc include Schoenberg's *Suite in G*, Gubaidulina's *Seven Words for Cello, Bayan and Strings* (1982), and a version for piano and orchestra of Schumann's *Konzertstück* originally for four horns and orchestra.

Website

http://www.mariovenzago.com

Further Reading
"At Home in Indiana." *Symphony* 54 (January–February 2003): 12.
Smith, Whitney. "Visible Venzago." *Indianapolis Star*, 9 March 2003, IO 1.

Selected Recordings
Gubaidulina: ". . . *The deceitful face of hope and of despair*"; *Sieben Worte*; Sharon Bezaly (fl); Torleif Thedéen (vc); Mie Miki (acc); Gothenburg SO. BIS 1449.
Nono: *Variazioni canoniche*; *Varianti*; *No hay caminos, hay que caminar . . . Andrej Tarkowski*; *Incontri*; Mark Kaplan (vn); Basel SO. Col Legno 31822.
Schoeck: *Venus*; James O'Neal (t); Frieder Lang (t); Hedwig Fassbender (ms); Boje Skovhus (br); Lucia Popp (s); Heidelberg Chamber Ch; Basel Boys Choir; Swiss Academic Philharmonic. Musiques Suisse 6112.
Schumann: *Overture, Scherzo, and Finale*; *Fantasy in a for Piano and Orchestra*; *Symphony no. 4*; Gianluca Cascioli (pf); Sinfonieorchester Basel. Novalis 150.

〜

Vonk, Hans
Born 18 June 1942 in Amsterdam, Holland
Died 29 August 2004 in Amsterdam

Vonk, whose father was a violinist in the Concertgebouw Orchestra, attended the University of Amsterdam to study law while taking classes in piano, composition, and conducting at the Amsterdam Conservatory of Music. Music eventually won out, and he went on to study conducting with Hermann Scherchen and Franco Ferrara. His first conducting appointment was with the Netherlands Ballet (1966–69) and, for a time, he was assistant conductor of the Concertgebouw Orchestra. In 1971 he conducted Fortner's opera *Don Perlimplin* at the Netherlands Opera, and from 1973 to 1979 was conductor of the Netherlands RPO. He made his U.S. debut with the San Francisco SO in 1974. He was associate conductor of the Royal PO (1976–79) and musical director of the Netherlands Opera (1976–85). San Diego (Calif.) was the site of his U.S. opera debut (1979), where he led the company in *La Traviata*. The following year he debuted with Stravinsky's *The Rake's Progress* at La Scala. From the time he became chief conductor of the Residentie Orchestra at The Hague (1980–91), he began to make regular appearances with the Dresden Staatskapelle and the Dresden Opera. This led to his appointment as their principal conductor in 1984 and chief conductor in 1985, and thus to his becoming the first individual since the 1930s to be head of both the orchestra and the opera house. He presided at the reopening of the famed Semper Opera House in 1985, and his live recording of *Der Rosenkavalier* issued at that time was lauded both for the vital interpretation and the mastery of the orchestral playing. During his tenure (1985–91), which included several major tours with stops at the Salzburg and Lucerne Festivals, Vonk was often ill at ease with the East German Regime. The orchestra's visit to West Germany in 1989, which happened to coincide with the sudden collapse of the Berlin Wall, was transformed into a celebration of German unity. Vonk returned to work in Holland as principal guest conductor of the Netherlands RPO in 1990 and then embarked on a six-year term as chief conductor of the Cologne RSO (1991–97).

Vonk's term as conductor of the Saint Louis SO (1996–2002) ended sadly when he was obliged to retire due to the onset of ALS (amyotrophic lateral sclerosis), a nerve-wasting disease that led to his early death in 2004. His departure very nearly precipitated the demise of an orchestra that, in the fall of 2001, was close to bankruptcy. Dire financial warnings had been in the air for sometime, although the orchestra could not be faulted artistically. Vonk had maintained and enhanced the performance standard bequeathed by Leonard **Slatkin**'s long tenure. As a deeply committed musician with values absorbed in the great European tradition, he was greatly appreciated and admired by the discriminating, but was not the type of person to man the pumps in time of crisis as **Slatkin** would have been. As neither a populist nor a schmoozer (a PR department's worst nightmare!) he was there simply to do what he did best: conduct the orchestra and give much-admired performances of the core nineteenth-century repertoire. Even there he was thwarted, as the composers closest to his heart, Bruckner and Mahler, were not particularly appreciated by the orchestra's subscribers.

Back in 1996, the orchestra's succession dilemma was whether to follow an act like **Slatkin**'s with a clone or a complete contrast. Either option tends to invite invidious comparison. The orchestra needed to be refreshed by a different approach, and the management needed to return to the core classical repertoire. It would have been hard for Saint Louis to attract a music director from among the international superstars, but the orchestra felt itself to be too good to act as a proving ground for a "young buck." Vonk had conducted the orchestra on three previous occasions, the last as an audition for the job, and had favorably impressed the players. As an experienced and well-respected conductor steeped in the European tradition, he was the search committee's pick, endorsed by the orchestra. Conscientious conductors with modest demeanors are not necessarily appealing to American audiences who sometimes need the antics of a histrionic conductor to focus their attention. Vonk's well-molded, deeply felt performances were never dull but may have looked it! For the majority of the players, though, the qualities that he fostered—spirit, discipline, camaraderie—inspired them to give consistently idiomatic and illuminating performances. They were always willing to provide the colors, textures, and transparency asked of them, and Vonk was very demanding in his stolid, Dutch way. This was not the man to turn to the audience and address it, as **Slatkin** had often done, but he was the man to give terse, honed, and convincing performances of, say, Shostakovich symphonies. Intending to remain audience-friendly, he sought to be more adventurous in his programming and to maintain something of the orchestra's tradition of championing modern American music. He gave the premiere of Richard Wernick's Symphony No. 2 and took Harbison's Symphony No. 1 on tour. He also interspersed significant amounts of French music and Stravinsky into his programs, gave a complete Messiaen program on tour, and even put on the *St. Matthew Passion*—a rare event by a symphony orchestra these days. He was dogged by the downturn in the recording economy, having brought no recording contract with him, and no commercial company was persuaded to take on the orchestra. An SLSO initiative to record performances on its own label, Arch Media, folded after the first few issues proved not to be economically viable. The orchestra's recording of Bruckner's Seventh Symphony is very fine, and one can only lament that a projected complete symphony cycle conducted by Vonk never materialized.

While in Dresden, Vonk and the Staatskapelle recorded a complete Beethoven piano concerto cycle, with Christian Zacharias as soloist, for EMI. On the Capriccio label they recorded discs of Mozart overtures and Tchaikovsky's *The Nutcracker*. On the same label Vonk conducted a complete cycle of the Bruckner symphonies with the Cologne RSO. His guest-conducting roster included the Concertgebouw Orchestra, Oslo PO, London SO, London PO, BBC SO, Philadelphia Orchestra, Cleveland Orchestra, Boston SO, Los Angeles PO, New York PO, Czech PO, and NHK SO in Japan.

Further Reading

"In Memoriam." *Symphony* 55 (November–December 2004): 7.
Koenig, Robert L. "Vonk Has Reputation for Skill, Energy." *St. Louis Post-Dispatch*, 17 January 1995, 6A.
Tommasini, Anthony. "New Saint Louis Conductor Carries on a Tradition." *New York Times*, 6 February 1998, E4.
"Welcoming Vonk." *Symphony* 47, no. 6 (1996): 13.

Selected Recordings

Brahms: *Symphony no. 2*; *Tragic Overture*; Netherlands RSO. Pentatone 5186042.

Bruckner: *Symphony no. 7*; Saint Louis SO. Arch Media 1005.

Diepenbrock: *The Birds: Overture*; *Marsyas: Concert Suite*; *Hymn for Violin and Orchestra*; *Elektra: Symphonic Suite*; *Die Nacht*; *Hymne an die Nacht no. 2*; *Wenige wissen das Geheimnis der Liebe*; *Im grossen Schweigen*; Emmy Verhey (vn); Linda Finnie (ms); Christoph Homberger (t); Robert Holl (b-b); Hague Residentie O. Chandos 10029.

Mozart: *Clarinet Concerto, K 622*; *Sinfonia Concertante, K297b*; Sabine Meyer (basset clarinet); Diethelm Jonas (ob); Sergio Azzolini (fg); Bruno Schneider (cor); Dresdener Staatskapelle. EMI 66949.

Tchaikovsky: *Sleeping Beauty Suite* (exs); *Swan Lake* (exs); *Eugene Onegin: Polonaise*; Bavarian RSO. From Laserlight 15806.

〜

Welser-Möst, Franz
Born 16 August 1960 in Linz, Austria

When Welser-Möst was in his early thirties he was made well aware of the problems that a young and meteorically successful conductor has to face. And face them he did, during a stormy six-year term as principal conductor of the London PO (1990–96)! There he was beset by internal and external political struggles, ill-prepared and insecure musicians, and vituperative criticism from a cabal of London critics out to get him. If ever anyone suffered from premature success, he did. It is clear from the interviews that he gave back then that he likes to talk and has a lot to say (a penchant not appreciated by musicians in rehearsal). Much of what he says is interesting and considered and some of it takes one's breath away! Among his beliefs are that the conductor's role is *primus inter pares* (first among equals); that the discipline of rehearsal is to take care of all the technical issues; and that performances are organisms with lives of their own where musical instinct and intuition take over. He contends that in addition to the Viennese classics, the great Baroque works of Bach and Handel should be a part of the modern orchestra's repertoire, and conductors must understand that the most important thing, more important than phrasing and articulation or concern with authenticity, is the underlying structure: "The way of the composer . . . how it's built and all that." He also speaks perceptively about the Austrian Catholic tradition and Austrian neuroticism and angst, which he sees cropping up musically in unexpected places (Mozart and Johann Strauss, for instance). With regard to Bruckner, he senses an earthy passion and inner conflict that are just as important as the composer's acknowledged godliness. He questions how a thirty-something conductor can be expected to perform on par with the remembered or recorded interpretations of Klemperer, Fürtwangler, or Karajan, to whom he is often unfairly compared. It is important for younger conductors to perform these important works early so that their performances can mature over time.

Welser-Möst, the son of a physician father and a politician mother, showed early musical promise as a chorister and made rapid progress on the violin and, a little later, on the piano. He entered the Linz Musikgymnasium, where he had his first taste of conducting with the school's chorus and orchestra. In 1978 a serious car accident put an end to his instrumental performance ambitions and focused his attention on the possibility of becoming a conductor. He studied with the composer Baluin Sulzer and became principal conductor of the Austrian Youth Orchestra in 1979 after having been a finalist that year in the Herbert von Karajan Conducting Competition in Berlin. He enrolled at the Musikhochschule in Munich, where he studied from 1980 to 1984, but left without graduating. He had made his professional debut with the Vienna CO in 1983. He worked as assistant to **Ozawa** and **Maazel** at the Salzburg Whitsun Festival in 1985 and as Abbado's assistant at the Vienna State Opera (1986–87). Appointments in Lausanne, Winterthur, and Norrköping (1986–91) followed. His big break came when he served as a last-minute substitution for Jesús López-Cobos, conducting an all-Mozart program, including the *Requiem*, with the London PO in 1986. Subsequent guest appearances with this orchestra led to his appointment as principal conductor in 1990. Meanwhile, he had made his first appearance at the Vienna State Opera with Rossini's *L'Italiana in Algeri* (1987) and his U.S. debut with the Saint Louis SO in 1989. He began a successful series of recordings with the London PO, including works by Bartók, Bruckner, Mahler, Mendelssohn, Mozart, Orff, Johann Strauss, and Stravinsky.

After taking a licking in London he left for the relative safety of the Zurich Opera, a refuge run by Alexander Pereira where conductors are assured of adequate rehearsal and a stable cast, chorus, and orchestra. Here he was able to consolidate his technique and broaden his repertoire. As music director from 1995 to 2002 he conducted over twenty new productions, as well as revivals from across the operatic spectrum. He rounded off his term with performances of Wagner's *Ring* cycle (2000–2). Among the guest conductors during this period (who included Nikolaus Harnoncourt, Riccardo Chailly, and Nello Santi) was Christoph von **Dohnanyi**, whose tremendously successful term as conductor of the Cleveland Orchestra was drawing to a close.

In looking for von **Dohnanyi**'s successor, the Cleveland Board was seeking an individual of vision and initiative, with the track record necessary to lead the orchestra into the twenty-first century and maintain its strong musical traditions and excellent performance standards, as well as further enhance its reputation internationally. In Esa-Pekka **Salonen** they thought they had found their man, but he preferred to stay in Los Angeles; so, with von **Dohnanyi**'s imprimatur, the second-choice candidate, Franz Welser-Möst, was engaged on a five-year contract commencing in 2002. News of the appointment caused waves of surprise, doubt, and optimism over the music world! Might the necessary chemistry, achieved in Zurich but so obviously missing from his London years, occur together with the infusion of new blood and a fresh approach? With goodwill on all sides, he received a warm and generous welcome from the Clevelanders. So favorable were first impressions that his initial contract was extended to seven years. The maverick (whom one critic described as "the callow youth with the Byzantine private life") had indeed come a long way to be in charge of one of the world's great orchestras. For sure, he will continue to be his own man, finding his own way with programming choices. Though rooted firmly in the classical tradition, he expands it to include works by Honegger, Schmidt, Martinů, Messiaen, Varèse, and Lutosławski, and he has shown a capable hand at such contemporary works as *Orion* by Saariaho and *Rocks under Water* by Marc-André Dalbavie. He often concludes his programs with the novelty of a waltz or polka by Johann Strauss, music that he performs with consummate skill. A consistent thread of criticism notes that his unassuming, laid-back conducting manner sometimes produces performances lacking an overall sense of rhythmic intensity, inner tension, and sensuous charm.

In recent years he has been a frequent guest conductor with the leading U.S. orchestras (Atlanta, Boston, Chicago, Los Angeles, New York, and Philadelphia) as well as the London SO, Vienna PO, Bavarian RSO, and the Concertgebouw Orchestra in Europe. He has returned to the Vienna State Opera to perform *The Marriage of Figaro*, has appeared at the Deutsche Oper in Berlin (*Clemenza di Tito*), and has conducted *Peter Grimes*, *Cosi fan tutte*, and Lehár's *Die lustige Witwe* for the Glyndebourne Festival. He "rehabilitated" Franz Schmidt's impressive oratorio *Das Buch mit sieben Siegeln*, which he recorded. His recording of the same composer's Symphony no. 4 received a 1996 Gramophone Award. He has also recorded symphonies by Schumann, Kancheli, and Korngold with the London PO.

Further Reading

Clarke, Keith. "Sunny Side Up (Administrators and Conductor Discuss State of Cleveland Orchestra)." *Classical Music* 745 (27 September 2003): 12–13.

Henry, R. Derrick. "Franz Welser-Moest" [sic]. *Musical America* 111, no. 2 (1991): 8–9.

Holland, Bernard. "Conducting a Chemical Experiment." *New York Times*, 20 June 1999, S2, 28.

Johnson, Lawrence A. "An Interview with Franz Welser-Möst." *Fanfare* 22, no. 4 (1999): 52, 57.

Jolly, James. "Youth and Music." *Gramophone* 70 (March 1993): 28–29.

Rosenberg, Donald. "Cleveland Orchestra: Season in Review." *Plain Dealer*, 19 June 2005, J1.

Seckerson, Edward. "The New Man at the LPO." *Gramophone* 68 (November 1990): 925, 928.

Selected Recordings

Bruckner: *Symphony no. 8 in c* (Nowak ed.); Gustav Mahler Youth O. EMI 7243 5 57406 2 5.

Korngold: *Symphony in F#; Die tote Stadt: Glück, das mir verblieb; Einfache Lieder: Schneeglöckchen; Das Ständchen; Liebesbriefchen; Sommer*; Barbara Hendricks, (s); Philadelphia O. EMI 5 86101.

Lehár: *Die lustige Witwe*; Dagmar Schellenberger (*Hanna Glawari*); Rodney Gilfrey (*Danilo*); Rudolf Hartmann (*Baron Mirko Zeta*); Ute Gfrerer (*Valencienne*); Piotr Beczala (*Camille de Rosillon*); Herbert Prikopa (*Njegus*); Zurich Op O and Ch. Arthaus 100 451 DVD.

Mozart: *Mass in c; Requiem*; Felicity Lott (s), Edith Wiens (ms); Laurence Dale (t); Robert Lloyd (b); Willard White (b); Della Jones (ms); Keith Lewis (t); London P Ch; London PO. MSI 75770.

Schmidt: *Das Buch mit sieben Siegeln*; René Pape (b); Stig Fogh Andersen (t); Christiane Oelze (s); Lothar Odinius (t); Alfred Reiter (b); Cornelia Kallisch (a); Friedemann Winklhofer (org); Bavarian R Ch; Bavarian RSO. EMI 85782.

⌒

Wilkins, Christopher (Putnam)

Born 28 May 1957 in Boston, Massachusetts

Wilkins is a conductor destined for the big leagues—maybe. He certainly boasts an impressive pedigree and a sterling track record. After giving up his highly commendable tenure as music director of the San Antonio (Tex.) SO in 2002 without a new appointment, he risked dropping off the radar screen. His reasons for quitting after a ten-year stint were, most likely, sheer exhaustion from the effort of keeping the orchestra afloat and frustration at not being able to fulfill his musical goals; "to be able to concentrate on the artistic experience" was the way he saw his future. Leaving with the title of music director emeritus, he has attempted to attain this goal as artistic director of the Opera Theatre of the Rockies, as resident conductor of the Youth Orchestra of the Americas, and during guest appearances with, among others, the Boston SO and the Los Angeles PO. He accepted the appointment as music director of the Orlando (Fla.) PO, making his debut there in the fall of 2006. During the spring of that year it was announced that he would also become music director of the Akron (Ohio) SO.

What Wilkins achieved in San Antonio was quite remarkable and especially heartening to those wishing to see an indigenous, culturally relevant role for American orchestras. Geographically isolated, the orchestra had existed on a shaky financial basis for many years. A near-bankruptcy in the fall of 1998 was merely the latest crisis and had a restrictive effect on Wilkins's ambitions for extending the scope of the orchestra. What made his tenure so notable was not merely his achievement in raising performance standards, but the way he strove to create relevance and identity within the community. He forged close links with other cultural institutions and planned cooperative endeavors with dance and theater that emphasized the region's southwestern heritage. He received six ASCAP awards for innovative programming and instituted a "Meet the Composer" series with commissions and three-year residencies.

Born into a well-to-do family, Wilkins grew up in Concord (Mass.) and began piano lessons at age five. He took up the oboe at age eight and, while attending the exclusive Milton Academy, took private lessons from Ralph Gomberg at the New England Conservatory of Music. Having attained the first chair of that same institution's youth orchestra, he kept up his oboe playing at Harvard as a member of the Bach Society Orchestra. In fact, it was this orchestra that gave him his start as a conductor—a position he assumed in his junior year without having had any formal training! Graduating in 1978 in Chinese studies but bitten by the conducting bug, he applied himself to music and won a fellowship to study for a year at the Berlin Hochschule der Künste. Back in the U.S. he embarked on graduate studies in conducting with Otto-Werner Mueller at Yale, obtaining a master's degree in 1981. He spent the next year as conductor-in-residence at the State University of New York at Purchase, then, receiving an Exxon/Arts Endowment scholarship, a year with the Oregon SO under James **DePreist**, followed by a three-year apprenticeship as associate to Joseph Silverstein in Utah. Subsequently he served as assistant to Christoph von **Dohnanyi** in Cleveland (1983–86). Colorado Springs (Colo.) SO offered him his first directorship in 1989. A guest appearance in San Antonio in 1990 so impressed the SASO that he was offered the directorship when it became vacant in 1991.

Wilkins's strength has always been thorough preparation and an intellectual grasp of music's structure and balance. What he has had to learn over the years is to respond more freely to its emotive side. In pursuit of rhythmic flexibility he has been involved with dance, aided by his wife, dancer Anne Adair. Indicative of his innovative programming is a release on Warner Brothers Records of a recorded concert featuring cowboy singer Michael Martin Murphey, and a Tex-Mex program for National Public Radio Classics. His list of U.S. guest appearances includes the orchestras of Boston, Chicago, San Francisco, Pittsburgh, Houston, Detroit, Cincinnati, and Indianapolis. Abroad he has appeared in Spain, Germany, Russia, New Zealand, and Latin America.

Further Reading

Burr, Ramiro. "Symphony Enriches Navaira's Classic Tejano." *Austin American-Statesman*, 25 April 1995, E8.

Greenberg, Mike. "Measured Growth: Symphony's Wilkins Keeps Up Steady Beat of Challenge, Accomplishment." *San Antonio Express-News*, 21 February 1999, 1D.

Greenberg, Mike. "State of the Orchestras XV: The San Antonio Symphony." *American Record Guide* 58, no. 2 (1995), 6–11.

Selected Recordings

Amram: *Symphony* "Songs of the Soul"; Berlin RSO. From Naxos 8559420.

Foss: *Elegy for Anne Frank*; Kevin McCutcheon (pf); Berlin RSO. From Naxos 8559438.

Kraft: *Of Ceremonies, Pageants and Celebrations*; Utah SO. From First Edition 44.

A Night at the Symphony; Flash Cadillac; Colorado Springs SO. Flash Cadillac Records (1992).

⌢

Wilkins, Thomas (Adolphus)
Born 10 September 1956 in Norfolk, Virginia

Wilkins was born to a single mother in a housing project in Norfolk (Va.). As a popular, successful, and innovative orchestral conductor, he has to be a poster child for success against the odds and an inspiration to fellow African Americans. He could not avoid this tag, even if he wanted to, for he has devoted much of his energy to promoting the transformative power of music among poorer communities that are generally ignored by "high art" circles. But that is not the whole story, because Wilkins is a dedicated and accomplished musician who, after a long and painstaking apprenticeship, has finally come into his own with his appointment as music director of the Omaha (Nebr.) SO (2005). Now he has the ultimate responsibility for choosing themes, selecting repertoire, and engaging soloists for all the series and special concerts. He is expected to lead the orchestra into a new era.

This inspiring tale is due to the fact that, at age eight, Wilkins attended a children's concert given by the Norfolk SO. Without doubt that single event was pivotal, because he was hooked not just by the power of the music but by a determination to become a conductor. "I learned that my appetite for music was insatiable," he wrote in a *Richmond News-Leader* article in 1991. The year after the concert experience he began taking cello lessons and later played the tuba in high school. His conducting ambitions were not forgotten, however, and he spent two years as assistant conductor of the Shenandoah (Va.) Community SO while an undergraduate at the Shenandoah Conservatory of Music in Winchester (Va.). After graduating with a BME in 1978, he commenced graduate study at the New England Conservatory of Music. He served two years as assistant conductor for the school's Repertory Orchestra before graduating with a master's degree in conducting in 1982. A first appointment took him to Chicago, where he was in charge of orchestral activities at North Park College (1982–86). Additionally, he served as conductor of the NW Indiana YO and assistant conductor of the NW Indiana SO. He supplemented his experience with two church music positions and spent a year as interim music director of the Du Page (Ill.) SO before moving to Tennessee to take up a new teaching post in 1986. During the mid-1980s he assiduously sought out opportunities to develop his skills by attending conducting workshops and institutes sponsored by the American Symphony Orchestra League and the Conductors Guild. At these summer classes he was able to work with, among others, Pierre Boulez, Riccardo Muti, Maurice Abravanel, Harold **Farberman**, and Gunther Schuller.

After two years at the University of Tennessee, Chattanooga, his big break came when he was appointed assistant conductor of the Richmond (Va.) SO in 1989. His impact there was acknowledged when he was elevated to the post of associate conductor two years later. The role of assistant conductor is viewed as a rite of passage that can be tedious and frustrating, includes much dogsbody work, and seldom provides an opportunity to enjoy the limelight.

Duties generally include shadowing the music director, preparing initial run-throughs, and participating in educational outreach, pops concerts, and any other special performances of a less weighty kind. It was clear from the outset, however, that this was an opportunity Wilkins would pursue with vigor. For him the educational mission was key to the orchestra's connection to its community and to building support for its long-term survival. Exploiting ties with the orchestra's musicians, he injected new life into the youth programs at every level. His ability to produce results under tight circumstances together with a personality that could win over youth and adults alike proved major assets. At his next post as resident conductor of the Florida Orchestra in Tampa Bay (1994–2001), an orchestra eager to attract a wider audience by tapping into jazz and pop, Wilkins demonstrated his versatility by, for example, conducting a concert of orchestral arrangements of music by rock icon Frank Zappa. Inevitably, he found a special niche in attending to the needs of minority communities, a role he willingly embraced despite the risk of being pigeonholed, and it led to some of his earliest guest appearances with more prestigious orchestras. In June 1995, we find him at the Dallas (Tex.) SO conducting its African American Festival Concert in a program that included the Piano Concerto by Adolphus Hailstork, one of the most eminent black composers working today, whose music Wilkins has continued to champion.

Wilkins's next move in 2001 was to become resident conductor of the Detroit (Mich.) SO as deputy to Neeme **Järvi**. It was a particularly auspicious appointment as it provided plenty of opportunity to exploit his zeal for musical evangelizing to the minority community, as demonstrated by the annual "Classical Roots" concerts. He led the DSO's gala opening concert in the fall of 2002 with soloists Kathleen Battle and William Butler. Early the next year he and the DSO presented a concert entirely of works by black composers, featuring scores by twenty-year-old student Herman Whitfield III and Detroit native Ozie Cargile. By establishing the DSO's "Emerging African American Artists" program he furthered his quest to bring performance opportunities to other black musicians, especially young composers, including Hannibal Lokumbe, Nkeiru Okoye, and Jonathan Holland. He has also encouraged minority performers through a close association with the Sphinx Organization and Competition, a showcase for emerging African American and Hispanic string players founded by Aaron Dworkin and based in Detroit.

The need to reach out beyond the traditional well-heeled and possibly dwindling middle-class audience by establishing greater relevance within the wider community has been a mantra for survival and growth among symphony orchestras in recent years. No one has been more effective in pursuing that goal than Wilkins. He is a teacher by inclination and brings a dedicated, well-judged approach to presenting children's concerts: "Nothing's more real, more meaningful, than seeing Orchestra Hall filled with beaming young faces . . . so much fun." What may be fun to him would be daunting, if not downright intimidating, to many other young conductors trying to make their way, but it appears that "Tom has a way with kids that helps them focus on the music and the instruments. They become entranced." And with the addition of "KidZone" activities at children's concerts in Detroit, young people are given the opportunity to try out instruments and meet conductor and players close up. This evangelizing is strictly non-patronizing because of Wilkins's belief that "there's nothing inherently elitist about classical music." Such tags as "Classics Unmasked," "Blue Jeans Concerts," "The Beat Goes On," and "Symphonic Storytelling" are simply ways of propagating his faith in the overriding power of music, which ultimately has no sociological or economic boundaries. The "chemistry" of orchestral music-making has the means to unite disparate populations and backgrounds and affect peoples' everyday lives in a way that can be transformative. In Detroit, the orchestra had a second-in-command with the versatility to conduct anything and everything from a formal subscription concert to events in various other settings, and to be an approachable figurehead within the community. With music director Järvi often away, it was understood that Wilkins, with his record of solid achievement, was to be given a good deal of autonomy over choice of repertoire and soloists for his allotted performances. However, when Järvi was incapacitated by a stroke in September of 2001 just before the orchestra was due to leave for a European tour, Wilkins found himself making his subscription concert debut much earlier than planned. And he impressed; the *Detroit News*, waxing almost poetical, claimed: "This is a musician to reckon with and a talent the shadows cannot contain." Particularly impressive was his performance of Rachmaninoff's *Symphonic Dances*, coaxing "an expansive performance that soared, but never pressed." This appearance was no flash in the pan either. The same newspaper reported a year or so later that "he makes a more compelling impression" each time he appears before the orchestra. His reading of the mainstream classics truly enlightens, such as a performance of Beethoven's Fourth Symphony that made one "sit up and blink with a generally undervalued masterpiece." After Järvi announced his resignation, Wilkins's name was unlikely to appear on a short list of successors, even though, at least in one critic's opinion, it deserved a place there. By 2004 his growing reputation was evident, however, in his guest appearances around the country at ever more prestigious locales, not only for African American celebrations, but to conduct regular subscription concerts of mainstream repertoire.

From early in his career Wilkins was perceived as a "no-nonsense conductor—economical and concise in his every movement." He is tall and willowy with a persona at once amiable and authoritative. He is known for focused and stylish performances across a broad swath of repertory, although on one occasion a critic took him to task for being "too hearty." An increasingly common practice at concerts these days is for the conductor to address the audience about the music to be played; Wilkins is blessed with the knack of making brief and pithy comments. Reviewing his return to Richmond as guest conductor in 2004, the *Times-Dispatch* noted the evident maturity that Wilkins's conducting had gained over the ten years since he had been the orchestra's number two. When asked about this, the conductor observed that he was less intimidated by the greatness or traditions of the music and felt more confidence in characterizing it to the extent he felt was appropriate. Another quality noted early on is his flair for imaginative programming. The roster for his first full season in Omaha reflects this. For example, a themed program, "Beyond Our Universe," in February 2007 featured "extra-terrestrial" contributions by Josef Strauss, Michael Daugherty (*UFO*), and Gustav Holst. As well as giving many performances by contemporary African American composers as noted above, he has been a proponent of music by other living composers, among them James MacMillan, Cindy McTee, and Roberto Sierra. He has championed American composers the likes of Bernstein, Copland, Gershwin, and Korngold, and revived such rarities as Morton Gould's *Tap Dance Concerto* and George Antheil's *Jazz Symphony*. His chief bent, nonetheless, is toward the classics (Haydn, Mozart, Beethoven, et al.) where his performances have been noticed as vibrant and creative.

Wilkins cut his conducting teeth on youth orchestras and he continues to return each year to conduct the Summer Performing Arts Camp orchestra at his alma mater in Shenandoah. As a guest conductor Wilkins has appeared with the orchestras of Cleveland, Philadelphia, Indianapolis, Washington, D.C., Dallas, Baltimore, Houston, Buffalo, San Antonio, Oregon, Louisville, Columbus, New Jersey, and Richmond, among others. With his solid track record, he will likely bring top-quality musicianship and a passionate commitment to his new constituency in Omaha, heavily weighted toward educational outreach for all ages and walks of life. Early indications from his 2005 appearances are that his appointment will be an inspired one. He has already staked his claim by demonstrating wit and informality from the podium and by eliciting exciting performances that will endear him to audiences. He will undoubtedly relish leading an orchestra, which, in the much-praised acoustics of the new auditorium at the Holland Performing Arts Center, is poised for progress.

Further Reading

Handy, D. Antoinette. *Black Conductors*, 462–67. Metuchen, N.J.: Scarecrow Press, 1995.

Hassebroek, Ashley. "Maestro's Moment." *Omaha World-Herald*, 16 October 2005, O1B.

O'Neil, L. Peat. "Florida's Symphony in the Key of Z." *Washington Post*, 24 January 1999, G7.

Smith, Whitney. "Conductor Forged a Mission to Popularize Classical Music." *Indianapolis Star*, 8 August 2003, G23.

～

Wolff, Hugh (Macpherson)
Born 21 October 1953 in Neuilly-sur-Seine, France

Wolff's musical education was comparatively late in starting, but such was his innate ability that by the time he took up his first full-time conducting appointment as music director of the New Jersey SO in 1985, he had absorbed a wealth of musical knowledge and experience and had studied with a series of eminent teachers. His musical interests were triggered by his sister's piano practice, and lessons for the twelve-year-old Hugh soon followed. Having caught the bug, he made rapid progress and in high school was taking lessons from renowned pianist Leon Fleisher. Fascinated by Bernstein's televised Young People's Concerts, he ventured into composition and lessons with George Crumb. He entered Harvard with the intention of majoring in sciences, but music soon gained the upper hand and, after studying principally with Leon Kirchner, he graduated magna cum laude with a degree in music composition (1975). During these student years he became thoroughly immersed in the extracurricular musical life of the college. His conducting debut was with a work of his own, and he eventually became conductor of the Harvard Bach Society Orchestra. The following year was spent on a fellowship to the Paris Conservatoire, where he studied composition with Olivier Messiaen and conducting with Charles Bruck, the Hungarian-born protégé of Pierre Monteux. Returning to the U.S., he commenced graduate studies at the Peabody Institute, resuming piano performance studies with Fleisher (MM 1977) and orchestral studies under Frederick Prausnitz (MM 1978). These studies were enhanced by experience conducting a community orchestra in Annapolis and sitting in on rehearsals of the Baltimore SO. He maintained his relationship with Bruck at the Monteux Summer School in Maine. His big break came when he won the audition to become Exxon/Arts

Endowment Conductor with the National SO in Washington, D.C., under Rostropovich (1979–82). In addition, he served as music director of the Northeastern Pennsylvania PO in Scranton from 1981 to 1986. His associa-tion with Rostropovich and the NSO was a particularly happy one and re-sulted in his becoming associate conductor for an additional three years (1982–85). In 1985 he was co-recipient (with Kent **Nagano**) of the Seaver/NEA Conductors Award. The Russian maestro was a generous men-tor not only in giving his associates conducting opportunities with the NSO but also in having them lead concerts when he appeared as cello soloist in Washington and elsewhere. Wolff was deputized for the indisposed Antal Dorati on the NSO's 1979 concert tour and made his London debut with the London PO in 1982 at a concert that included Rostropovich playing Du-tilleux's Cello Concerto. Rostropovich's recommendation was very influen-tial in his obtaining the directorship of the New Jersey SO from a field of two hundred candidates.

The NJSO, "a good community orchestra, hardly more," was not in good shape when Wolff took over in 1985. In its recent past, financial problems had led to a musicians' strike that cancelled the 1980–81 season. The ap-pointment must have seemed, at best, merely a career springboard, provided he could make his mark. He soon began to exhibit traits that were to become hallmarks of his approach: adventurous, imaginative programming and his-torically informed performance styles. His first season justified the most op-timistic expectations, garnering exceptional praise. After three years the or-chestra's operating budget had tripled, reflecting a steady rise in ticket sales. When the NJSO appeared at Carnegie Hall in 1987, the *New York Times* de-scribed its performance of *The Rite of Spring* as "something very much like world-class musicianship." Wolff had shown himself to be not only a skillful conductor but a gifted orchestral trainer as well.

Wolff first became associated with the Saint Paul CO in 1988 as principal conductor in an unusual tripartite arrangement with Christopher Hogwood as music director and John **Adams** as "Creative Chair," and he led it on an American tour that first year. He succeeded to the directorship in 1992 and enjoyed an overall partnership of twelve years. The collaboration was a pos-itive one, reinforced by a demanding recording schedule on contract to the Teldec label, which accrued some twenty albums. The Wolff era was noted for its wide-ranging programming, impeccably tasteful interpretations, and an "effortlessly polished sound." He revelled in the generous rehearsal time and a versatility that could encompass repertoire of some four hundred years. Always an ardent champion of contemporary music (winning two ASCAP awards), he was particularly admired as a classicist, occupying a special niche as a Haydn specialist. During this period, he also served as principal guest conductor of the New Jersey SO (1992–93), artistic director of the American Russian Youth Orchestra, and principal conductor of the Grant Park Music Festival.

From 1997 to 2006 Wolff led the Frankfurt RSO. After a single guest performance in 1993 he was recruited to reestablish the orchestra's classical roots and to institute the kind of wide-ranging repertory that would appeal to both the live and radio audiences. He applied the approach he had developed in Saint Paul to Haydn, Mozart, and Beethoven, influenced by Hogwood's ideas of "historically informed performance," extending it so far as to allow woodwind and brass to experiment with instruments copying eighteenth-century technology. He relished the more central role music takes in German culture and appeared with the orchestra at the Rheingau Festival and the Mozart Festival in Würzburg, as well as on tours to France, Italy, Estonia, and the Far East. One notable event in 2000 was the premiere of Mark-Anthony Turnage's jazz-fusion piece *Scorched*, which incorporated the radio station's jazz band and the John Scofield trio.

Wolff's conducting has always been admired for its precise beat and his lithe, balletic gestures. In commenting on his sense of style, critics have been particularly impressed with the clarity and transparency that mark his interpretations. He is a natural musician who seeks to establish an easy rapport with his players and receives their enthusiasm in return. He conducts without a score whenever possible and invests his performances with "precisely used energy." If he has a fault, it is that his clinical approach sometimes misses out on deep emotion when this is called for. As noted above, he has consistently demonstrated imagination when devising programs, a trait which was first seen in New Jersey, refined in Saint Paul, and further developed in Frankfurt. It is not merely that his programs are wide-ranging and contain a healthy mix of contemporary and traditional repertoire, or that they are often thematic—a New Jersey concert in 1988 was labeled "Music Turns the Century" (the eighteenth in this case) and a whole season in Frankfurt was developed on the theme of "Fate"—but he has developed a concept of significance for works within a program such that "none was an event in isolation—each connected with something heard a short while before, and anticipated something they were to hear soon after."

Wolff's roster of performances by contemporary composers is impressive. He has premiered works by, among others, Stephen Albert, Michael Colgrass, John Corigliano, Aaron Jay Kernis, Tod Machover, and Michael Torke. He has also programmed music by Panufnik, Takemitsu, Jolivet, Harbison, **Adams**, Rautavaara, and Taaffe Zwilich, among more established names. His background in composition and a close working relationship with a number of composers in residence has given him a special insight and real enthusiasm for new music. Equally impressive is his recorded legacy, which spans repertoire from Haydn (First Symphony) to Sebastian Currier (*Microsymph*, 2001) and artists including Garrison Keillor, Jean-Yves Thibaudet, Hilary Hahn, Boris Berezovsky, Dawn Upshaw, Thomas Hampson, and Mstislav Rostropovich. His recordings have appeared on a number of labels, most prominently Teldec, Sony, Decca, and Koch. In addition to his Frankfurt and Minnesota orchestras, he has recorded with the Philharmonia Orchestra, London SO, BBC SO, City of Birmingham SO, and the London Sinfonietta. After the meltdown of the classical recording industry the Frankfurt orchestra has been issuing recordings on its own label, hr-musik. Wolff's disc of three works by Aaron Jay Kernis was nominated for a Grammy, and a recording of the First and Sixth Symphonies by George Antheil and a recording of violin concertos by Samuel Barber and Edgar Meyer with Hilary Hahn as soloist both received the Cannes Classical Award. As a guest conductor he has led all the major North American orchestras and the premiere orchestras in England and France. Elsewhere in Europe he has appeared in Leipzig, Hamburg, Rotterdam, Stockholm, Copenhagen, Prague, and Oslo; he has also performed in Israel and Australia. He has been a frequent visitor to the Aspen, Tanglewood, and Ravinia festivals. His appearances in the opera house have been infrequent, but he directed an admired *The Marriage of Figaro* for New York City Opera in 1986 and has also conducted the Washington and Minnesota Operas. In 2001, Philip Kennicott, writing in the *Washington Post*, described Wolff as having "an anticlimactic middle age filled with accomplishments but no lightning strikes." It is open to speculation as to whether he has fulfilled, or will yet fulfill, his promise. As he himself said back in 1989, "It is one thing to have potential, it's another to be regarded as an artist."

Website
http://www.hughwolff.com/

Further Reading
Barbieri, S. M. "Wolff Moves On." *Strings* 14 (January 2000): 42–43.
Brown, Royal S. "An Interview with Hugh Wolff." *Fanfare* 16, no. 1 (1992): 90.
Marum, Lisa. "Hugh Wolff, Conductor." *Ovation* 7 (July 1986): 42.
Smith, Howard. "Revitalizing the Repertoire." *Gramophone* 69 (July 1991): 20.
Spencer, Peter. "State of the Orchestras XIX: The New Jersey Symphony." *American Record Guide* 59, no. 2 (1996): 6–8.
Wolff, Hugh Macpherson. "Tour de Force." *Symphony* 44, no. 6 (1993): 65–67.

Selected Recordings
Antheil: *Symphony no. 3 "American"*; *Tom Sawyer Overture*; *Hot-Time Dance*; *McKonkey's Ferry Overture*; *Capital of the World: Suite*; Frankfurt RSO. CPO 777 040-2.
Bernstein: *Serenade for Violin and Orchestra "after Plato's Symposium."* McLean: *Elements*; Brian Lewis (vn); London SO. Delos 3357.
Haydn: *Symphonies 85 and 86*; St Paul CO. MSI 2564604512.
Kernis: *Symphony no. 2*; *Musica Celestis*; *Invisible Mosaic III*; City of Birmingham SO. Phoenix USA 160.
Shostakovich: *Piano Concertos 1 and 2*; Gary Bordner (tp); Elisabeth Leonskaja (pf); St. Paul CO. Apex 89092.

⌒

Zander, Benjamin
Born 9 March 1939 in Gerards Cross, Buckinghamshire, England

Zander is someone about whom a whole book should be written and no doubt will be one day. He is an intriguing individual: communicator, empowerer, enabler, and, first and foremost, proselytizer. Although often characterized as a guru who has built up a cult following, he is no charlatan, because music has been his master from an early age and he works entirely in its service. It is easy to tell his biography and list his achievements, but his impact is harder to assess; it is huge and surprising—we do not normally expect orchestral conductors to impress a gathering of four thousand Pizza Hut managers, for example, or Fortune 500 company executives. It is also difficult to assess someone's impact because any single individual is likely to fall short of what they envision for themselves. Like all larger-than-life characters, he is not to everyone's taste, although the fans far outnumber the detractors, and he can claim remarkable success in his stated purpose of bringing music to the masses—to each and every one of us, if he had his way. Although his musical background is solid, he remains somewhat of an outsider and as such enjoys the freedom and resources (his own orchestra) to pursue his own agenda. He was one of the first to reassess and observe Beethoven's controversial metronome markings, which were hitherto considered fallible. His approach to the music of Gustav Mahler, based on the evidence of some piano rolls the composer made, is also idiosyncratic, although not as controversial.

It comes as no surprise to learn that it is for performances of Mahler's music that Zander is best known, and that Mahler is the composer with whom he most closely identifies. Philosophically, he is drawn to the music's universal nature, its inclusivity of expression and appeal—an all-embracing humanity—that takes you "beyond where you've ever been before." What engages him musically is the enormous freedom (emancipation from the tyranny of beat to a flexible pulse) that intensifies the expressivity of line (melody) and asserts the primordially vocal nature of instrumental performance. Mahler's "emotional counterpoint" requires the orchestra to play with the interconnectedness of a chamber music group in order to reveal a complexity and drama found nowhere else. That Zander is able to achieve this degree of freedom with his own orchestra—the Boston PO, which has absorbed his approach for over thirty years—is laudatory; that he can persuade hard-hearted professionals such as the players of London's Philharmonia Orchestra to do the same is remarkable.

Zander believes music has the power to transform lives, to open up what he terms "radiating possibility," transformational thinking that negates the "downward spiral" of disappointed achievement, such limitations as govern most of our lives. (This is the philosophy he expounds in his additional career as a motivational speaker to corporations and other organizations.) His hallmark is the preperformance talk, which can last almost as long as the performance itself. A risk-taker himself, he believes that the barrier to connecting with the "inner spirit" is fear—in particular, the formidableness of music to the "man in the street." To overcome this anxiety, his expositions explain the conventions and engage his audience in the "mysteries" that connect with music's abstract sphere. This approach starkly profiles music's inherent paradox; its endless fascination is at once concrete and esoteric, intellectual and emotional. Most commentators concentrate on the concrete and intellectual, firm ground for pedagogical criticism and analysis, but Zander wades fearlessly into the esoteric and emotional—and he does it unselfconsciously, enthusiastically, and at length. In the process, he both debunks and perpetuates the maestro myth. What other conductor places blank sheets of paper on the players' music stands to invite comments during rehearsals, greets his audience as they enter the auditorium, and promises to refund the price of a ticket to any dissatisfied patron (and carries the bills on his person to back up his offer)? He understands that the power and mystique a conductor wields is a conduit from the composer to the players, and from them to the audience. To achieve this connection, one needs a good deal of faith in one's abilities and an abundance of ego; that they are applied unselfishly and combined with a pedagogical imperative is the key to his particular success. This somewhat patrician attitude helps explain his remarkable achievements with youth orchestras and amateurs over the years. Some professionals, especially critics, find it a little harder to accept. Talking about music "as much as possible" especially rankles with some of them and elicits comments like "Zander's discourse . . . was haughty and condescending," and "the teacherly instincts . . . are interfering with his instincts as an artist." Such criticism is hardly likely to faze someone who, with a mixture of wisdom and naïveté, intends to transform the world by winning over every individual to classical music. In light of all this, one might expect his podium style to be flamboyant à la Bernstein, but in fact it is tightly controlled and focused, using "economic but energy-filled gestures to achieve a level of detail and control which is hugely impressive." *Boston Herald* critic Keith Powers summed up his frustrations neatly when he noted that Zander is "as unobstreperous waving the baton as he is overobstreperous wagging the tongue."

We may begin the Zander story from 1937, when Walter Zander, a Jewish lawyer, scholar, and music-lover, fled Nazi Germany with his wife and three children to live in England. A fourth child, Benjamin, was born near London in 1939. A gifted child in a very talented family, he displayed musical proclivities from an early age and began to compose music when he was nine. Although dismissed as worthless by an eminent, if minor, British composer, this juvenilia was brought to the attention of Benjamin Britten and led to an invitation for the Zander family to spend summers with him at Aldeburgh, his home on the Suffolk coast. As well as receiving encouragement and advice from Britten, Zander received formal instruction from Imogen Holst, who was serving as the composer's assistant at that time (Britten had a habit of taking children under his wing and shunning them later on). At the age of ten he took up the cello, and, after briefly attending one of England's provincial public (i.e., private) schools, he transferred to Saint Paul's School in London, where he took cello lessons from Herbert Withers. At the age of fifteen he came under the aegis of the great Spanish cellist Gaspar Cassado. Zander studied with him in Florence, Siena, and eventually Cologne. Here he attended the conservatory where Cassado was teaching and earned a performance diploma in 1960. During these peripatetic years he played a great deal of chamber music but also, due to a medical condition affecting his fingers, experienced some frustration at cello playing. As a result he decided to return to London to complete his formal education and apply to attend university. In 1961 he graduated from University College London with a degree in English literature, and, incidentally, as the winner of a university-wide essay prize. Meanwhile he had been performing regularly in a trio with clarinetist Thea King and pianist Celia Arieli, and teaching at the Yehudi Menuhin School. A Harkness Commonwealth Fellowship took him to Harvard and Brandeis universities to study literature, and he pursued musical studies with the pianist Leonard Shure in Boston and the Schenker scholar

Ernst Oster in New York. In 1967 he was appointed professor of chamber music, performance, and analysis at the New England Conservatory of Music and has taught there ever since. In addition, he later became artistic director at the associated Walnut Hill High School for the Performing Arts.

Somehow or another (accounts vary) he got into conducting and was appointed first to the conservatory's Youth PO and then to the Civic SO of Boston. He conducted Mahler's music for the first time in 1974: the *Kindertotenlieder* with soloist Jane Struss. Two years later, after twenty-two rehearsals, the Civic Orchestra performed Mahler's Ninth Symphony. So nerve-racking did the board find the whole experience, however, that they fired the conductor for being overambitious, whereupon, so the story goes, the majority of the players upped and formed a new organization specifically as a vehicle for Zander and more of his Mahler; thus, the BPO was born in 1979. As a result of the reputation gained from subsequent performances and recordings by this ensemble, he was invited to debut with the Philharmonia Orchestra in London, conducting Mahler's Sixth Symphony in 1995. He also became a visiting professor at the Royal College of Music (1997). Already well-established as a motivational speaker since 1978, he co-wrote *The Art of Possibility: Transforming Professional and Personal Life* with his wife Rosamund, a therapist and artist. The book expands upon his theories of metamorphosis by applying the practices and metaphors of artistic experience. Frequent visitors to Carnegie Hall, Zander and the BPO returned in 2000 to perform Mahler's huge Eighth Symphony. For the 2003–4 Boston season they embarked on an all-Mahler retrospective, performing almost the composer's entire opus, with just a couple of works left over for the start of the following season. Zander was one of the conductors for the inaugural concerts of the Youth Orchestra of the Americas (2002), and in 2004 he conducted the New England Conservatory of Music's Youth PO in Mahler's Third Symphony, its first performance by a youth orchestra anywhere in the world.

The Boston PO proved the ideal medium for Zander to establish his conducting credentials. What began as an all-volunteer community orchestra became an amalgam of accomplished amateurs, music students, and freelance professionals, a unique arrangement endorsed, with hardly a hiccup, by the Boston Musicians' Association. The early seasons yielded three concerts a year, each preceded by extensive rehearsal. Later, as concerts increased in number, each program was performed at two venues: the conservatory's Jordan Hall and Sanders Theatre on the Harvard campus. In time, as its reputation grew, the orchestra created a signature sound and aura in performances noted for an intensity and commitment that overrode what few technical deficiencies there were. The players gave Zander wholehearted devotion as he experimented with tempi in Beethoven and refined agogic relationships between tempi, pulse, and phrasing, most evident in his Mahler interpretations. The recordings that the orchestra began making in the 1990s caused more than a stir. Leslie Gerber, writing in *Fanfare*, dubbed the performance of *The Rite of Spring* "one of the greatest recordings of the year" (1991) and *Classic CD* called the recording of Beethoven's Ninth Symphony "an essential buy for anyone wanting to discern the real Beethoven."

Under Zander's guidance for more than thirty-five years now, Boston's Youth PO early became one of the finest, if not *the* finest, youth ensembles in America. It tackles formidable repertoire and tours extensively throughout the Americas and beyond. This level of achievement comes from Zander's refusal to set limits on what they can do; Strauss's *Ein Heldenleben*, Mahler's Fourth and Fifth Symphonies, Shostakovich's Fifth Symphony, no problem—and they have the recordings to prove it! Zander's involvement in the founding of the Youth Orchestra of the Americas is a natural extension of his commitment to nourish potential, especially among the young. The dynamic mix of a diverse group of young musicians drawn from an entire hemisphere to make music together proved potent. The orchestra produced a performance of Mahler's First Symphony at its inaugural concert that was typical of Zander's detailed and passionate approach.

At the other end of the spectrum, Zander has established close ties with the players of the Philharmonia Orchestra, where he has been a regular guest conductor since 1995. This relationship is founded on the respect he shows to every individual rather than the more typical regimented approach. Under contract to Telarc, the partnership has embarked on recording cycles of Beethoven's and Mahler's symphonies—this during a period of famine in the recording industry! A distinguishing feature is that each set comes with an extra disc containing the conductor's redoubtable commentary and analysis. Thus far, six of Mahler's and two of Beethoven's nine symphonies have been released.

It might appear from reading the above that Zander is at most a two-composer conductor, but in fact his repertoire is wide-ranging, from Bach to Stravinsky, taking in Schubert, Bruckner, Dvořák, Tchaikovsky, Ives, Vaughan Williams, Joseph Schwantner, and many others on the way. His performances of Mozart are generally thought to be a bit stodgy, partly because he performs with large forces, presumably reluctant to exclude anyone. He recently gave a performance in Boston of Elgar's *The Dream of Gerontius*, the first there for many years. So strongly has Zander's career been centered in Boston that in 1999 the city declared his birthday Benjamin Zander Day. His growing reputation in recent years has led to guest appearances with the St. Petersburg PO, Royal PO, Bournemouth SO, Israel PO, American SO,

Scottish National Orchestra, RTE National SO, and Malaysian PO, as well as the National Youth Orchestras of Australia and New Zealand.

There is a lot more yet to be heard from Benjamin Zander, whose evangelizing zeal shows no sign of flagging. His father (who played under the legendary Artur Nikisch) lived to be ninety-five. A primary influence, he imbued his son with a zest for living, teaching, and compassion, which is standing him in good stead!

Website
http://www.benjaminzander.com

Further Reading

Dyer, Richard. "The Passion of Benjamin Zander." *Boston Globe*, 7 March 1999, N1.
Fox, Sue. "Art of the Possible." *Independent* (London), 28 March 1997, 16.
Fruchter, Rena. "Youth Orchestras on the Go: They Are Professional in All but Name." *Musical America* 109, no. 5 (1989): 26–29.
Oestreich, James R. "The Idiosyncrasies of Boston's Latest Cult Figure." *New York Times*, 16 January 2000, Arts & Leisure 11.
Peacock, Matthew. "Lightning Conductor: Benjamin Zander Is Known for a Dynamic Approach to Concert-Giving." *Classical Music* 726 (4 January 2003): 22–23.
Tuttle, Raymond S. "Zander in Mahlerland." *Fanfare* 27 (March–April 2004): 14–15.
Zander, Rosamund Stone, and Benjamin Zander. *The Art of Possibility*. Boston: Harvard Business School Press, 2000.

Selected Recordings

Beethoven: *Symphonies 5 and 7*; Philharmonia O. Telarc 80471.
Mahler: *Symphony no. 9*; Philharmonia O. Telarc 3CD-80527.
Strauss (R): *Ein Heldenleben*; NEC Youth PO. CPI 3294113.
Stravinsky: *Rite of Spring*; Boston PO. IMP Carlton 6600992.

⌒

Zinman, David
Born 10 July 1936 in New York, New York

Zinman is one of a small number of conductors of his generation who eschew histrionics on the podium in favor of focused gestures conveying affectionate musicality and deep commitment. His career has progressed steadily, and he has gained a reputation en route as an orchestra builder, a quick study, a champion of contemporary—especially American—music, a communicator, a didact, and a rescuer of orchestras under financial stress. In particular, he is credited with raising the standing of the Baltimore SO and the Zurich Tonhalle Orchestra, both of which were previously regarded as second-class provincial orchestras. His performances are often described as "no-nonsense" but this should not be construed in a pejorative sense, as he consistently aims at revealing the heart of the music, even though critics occasionally complain of a lack of passion.

Zinman's musical journey began when he was set to learn the violin. Although he showed talent, the ribbing he received from his peers while carrying a violin case caused him to give up playing altogether between the ages of ten and fourteen. The situation became easier when he attended the High School of Music and Art in New York, which is where he first had the opportunity to conduct. He studied law for a year at City College, but his musical interests got the better of him and he enrolled at Oberlin College, where he spent four years studying violin (1954–58). He attended the Tanglewood Festival, where he pursued conducting under the mentorship of Pierre Monteux. He also won a fellowship to study theory and composition at the University of Minnesota (1960–63). He now values this experience not because he had serious pretensions to become a composer, but for the insight it gives him when preparing scores, especially of contemporary music. His attachment to Monteux grew as he attended the annual Domaine School of Conducting in Hancock (Maine) (1958–62) and he accompanied the Maître to Europe as his assistant (1961–64). At that time Monteux held appointments as conductor of the London SO and the Concertgebouw Orchestra and, as his strength was failing, Zinman was frequently required to step in and take the general rehearsal on the day of the performance. Zinman credits his years in London as being formative to his conducting aspirations—not only the experience of working with the London SO in its heyday but also the opportunity he had to observe the rehearsals and performances of the leading conductors of the day, including Klemperer, Horenstein, Kempe, Giulini, Boult, and Kertész.

Another indisposition, that of the legendary Paul Sacher, led to Zinman's first big break when he conducted a performance with the Netherlands CO at the Holland Festival in 1963. As a result he was invited to conduct a series of concerts with them and, soon after, was appointed co-conductor. He served as principal conductor from 1965 to 1977. At the same time, he was becoming well-known through guest appearances and made his U.S. debut with the Philadelphia Orchestra in 1967. As an up-and-coming conductor looking to consolidate his reputation, he seized an opportunity in Rochester (N.Y.), where, after a brief stint as music advisor, he became music director in 1975. During his eight-year tenure he raised the standard and prestige of the orchestra through recordings by engaging top-flight soloists such as Ashkenazy, Perahia, Perlman, and Harrell. In addition, he inaugurated the orchestra's summer season in Canandaigua (N.Y.). During this period, he also served as chief conductor of the Rotterdam PO (1979–82). This relatively brief term in Holland came to an end when he decided his youngest child should be raised and educated in the U.S.

The move to Baltimore, first as principal guest conductor (1983–85) and then as music director (1985–98), was viewed as a higher profile opportunity to repeat the formula that had worked so successfully in Rochester. The orchestra was fertile ground as it had already achieved some distinction under the sixteen-year tenure of Sergiu Comissiona. From the first, Zinman's commitment was extensive; he conducted the bulk of concerts of a twenty-week subscription series in addition to an innovative summer season. It did not take long for him to make his mark. After a couple of years, the press commented on how the orchestral discipline was tighter and the sound, particularly the strings, had developed an extra bloom. After hearing Zinman and the orchestra in 1988, the *San Francisco Examiner* went so far as to declare, "a major reassessment of the American orchestral hierarchy may be in order." To consolidate and expand the orchestra's standing within and beyond the community Zinman embarked on a number of innovations. In addition to programming an unusually broad repertoire, he signed a contract with NPR for a nationally syndicated concert series with a format that popularized the presentations by including interviews with the soloists and reflections and commentary on the music by Zinman himself. This approach was modeled on the "Saturday Casual Concerts" that he initiated in Baltimore. The "Discovery Series" championing the music of the younger generation of American composers reflected his commitment to contemporary music. Zinman's obvious enthusiasm for this endeavor made the concerts a viable proposition: "It's the most exciting part of my work," he claimed. A CD of music by Berlioz inaugurated a successful series of recordings that culminated in a Grammy award–winning CD featuring the music of Barber and Britten with cellist Yo-Yo Ma, with whom Zinman has had a particularly fruitful collaboration over the years. Other recording achievements include a much-admired version of Rachmaninoff's Third Symphony, a disc of Charles Ives, a Schumann symphony cycle, and impressive recordings of Elgar. Beginning in 1987, he also instituted annual tours within the U.S. and abroad, including the Soviet Union and Far East. While this partnership became one of the great success stories of the U.S. orchestral scene of recent years, it was not without its problems. Quite early on Zinman had to weather a players' strike and then the recession that ate into the orchestra's financial well-being. In addition to having a hectic schedule in Baltimore, Zinman also served as artistic director of the Minnesota Orchestra's Viennese Sommerfest. The extent of Zinman's commitments undermined his health, and he was forced to take an eight-month sabbatical after returning from an East Asian tour in 1994. When he left Baltimore in 1998, he was appointed music director emeritus. However, he severed all ties with the orchestra in 2001 as a controversial protest over what he considered his successor's overly conservative programming, which had dissipated the orchestra's reputation as a champion of new music.

Zinman immediately applied himself to the task of music director of the Aspen Music Festival (Colo.), where his vision and sense of humor allowed him to bring "artistic balance to this community of temperaments." At a celebration of his seventieth birthday and his eight years of service in Colorado in 2006, the "community" threw a riotous party for the diminutive conductor, reflecting the affection in which he is held. The community respects his dedication and appreciates the creation of the American Academy of Conducting, which enables him to immerse himself in music with twenty carefully selected students for nine weeks each year.

Zinman also enjoyed an unprecedented commercial success with his recording of the Symphony No. 3 by the relatively obscure Polish composer Henryk Górecki (on Electra-Nonesuch CD) with Dawn Upshaw and the London Sinfonietta, released in 1993. It has become one of the best-selling classical albums of all time.

Of his tenure as music director of the Tonhalle Orchestra one can say, "Zinman did it again!" Those same qualities that had emerged in Rochester and Baltimore—a broad repertoire, devotion to contemporary music, and historically informed performance style where appropriate—were soon in evidence. Not that he and the orchestra were strangers; he had been a regular guest conductor there since 1983. The right chemistry with the orchestra was soon established, and he encouraged a chamber music style of playing in which the players really communicate with each other. Switzerland's most distinguished orchestra made its presence felt through world tours and an extensive recording roster which now includes complete cycles of Beethoven symphonies and Strauss tone poems as well as, appropriately, a distinguished recording of the music of Honegger. His contract with the orchestra, which initially ran through 2007, was extended to 2010.

Zinman's recording catalog now exceeds one hundred CDs, a number of which have accrued significant distinctions along the way, including five Grammy awards, two Grand Prix du Disques, the Deutsch Schallplattenpreis, and a Gramophone Award. As well as extensive recordings with the Baltimore and Zurich orchestras, Zinman has also made recordings with the Pittsburgh SO, English CO, RSO of Berlin, and Orchestra of St. Luke's, among others. He has appeared as guest conductor with New York PO, Berlin PO, Philharmonia Orchestra, Chicago SO, London SO, Orchestre de Paris, Concertgebouw Orchestra, Royal PO, Los Angeles PO, Cleveland Orchestra, Israel PO, and Leipzig Gewandhaus Orchestra. Regarded as one of the most sensitive of accompanists, he has worked with artists such as Hilary Hahn, Yo-Yo Ma, Sylvia McNair, Hélène Grimaud, and Joshua Bell. In 1995, he was presented with the Ditson Conductor's Award for his propagation of the music of American composers. These include Michael Daugherty, Richard Danielpour, Steven Albert, John **Adams**, Leon Kirchner, and Christopher Rouse. Zinman is a charismatic conductor who uses carefully controlled gestures to display the essence of the music. His performances are free of bombast, sentimentality, and pretension. He reveals new scores with clarity and precision, and he has a "dust 'em off" approach to the classical repertoire, with performances sounding fresh and refined but without mannerism. He keeps his tempi generally brisk, claiming historical authenticity. Among his detractors, lack of emotion and imagination seem to be the most common complaints. They find his approach too cerebral. Zinman is personable, committed, and something of a wit, qualities that make his efforts to engage with the public so successful.

Website
http://www.davidzinman.org

Further Reading

Cowan, Rob. "Setting the Tempo." *Gramophone* 77 (June 1999): 15.

Farach-Colton, Andrew. "'He's a *Seriously Funny Guy.*'" *Gramophone* 81 (May 2004): 24–25.

Loomis, George W. "A Chat with David Zinman in Zurich: Beethoven and Much More." *American Record Guide* 68 (2005): 4–5.

Smith, Cary. "State of the Orchestras XIII: Baltimore Symphony." *American Record Guide* 57, no. 6 (1994): 6.

Whiting, Christopher. "Orderly Conduct: A New Musical Tradition Flowers at the American Academy of Conducting." *Strings* 17 (May–June 2003): 54.

Zagorski, W. "David Zinman: A Word Portrait of a Sound Artist." *Fanfare* 14, no. 5 (1991): 72.

Selected Recordings
Bach (CPE): *Concerto for Flute in A minor; Concerto for Oboe in E♭ major; Concerto for Flute in A major;* Aurèle Nicolet (fl); Heinz Holliger (ob); Netherlands CO. MSI 468191.
Beethoven: *Symphonies 3 and 4;* Zurich Tonhalle O. Arte Nova 59214.
Mendelssohn: *Symphonies 3–5; Midsummer Night's Dream Overture;* Rochester PO. Vox Box 5165.
Strauss (R): *Aus Italien; Macbeth; Ein Heldenleben; Tod und Verklärung; Don Juan; Till Eulenspiegels lustige Streiche; Also sprach Zarathustra; Eine Alpensinfonie; Festliches Präludium; Metamorphosen; Four Last Songs; Oboe Concerto; Sinfonia domestica; Parergon; Don Quixote; Romance in F; Serenade in E♭;* soloists; Tonhalle O. Arte Nova 74321 98495.
Torke: *Green; Purple; Ecstatic Orange; Ash; Bright Blue Music;* Baltimore SO. Ecstatic ER092201.

APPENDIX A

~

List of Conductors

Conductor	DOB	U.S. Birthplace	Non-U.S. Birthplace	Year Naturalized
Adams, John	2/15/47	Boston, Mass.		
Alsop, Marin	10/16/56	Manhattan, N.Y.		
Amado, David	7/26/68	Meriom, Pa.		
Ansbacher, Charles	10/5/42	Cincinnati, Ohio		
Baker, Robert Hart	3/19/54	Bronxville, N.Y.		
Barenboim, Daniel	11/15/42		Buenos Aires, Argentina	
Barra, Donald	8/21/39	Newark, N.J.		
Bay, Peter	3/3/57	Washington, D.C.		
Beck, Crafton	12/18/56	Memphis, Tenn.		
Ben-Dor, Gisèle	4/26/55		Montevideo, Uruguay	2001
Bjaland, Leif	12/12/55	Flint, Mich.		
Blomstedt, Herbert	7/11/27	Springfield, Mass.		
Bond, Victoria	5/6/45	Los Angeles, Calif.		
Botstein, Leon	12/14/46		Zurich, Switzerland	
Brott, Boris	3/14/44		Montreal, Canada	
Brown, Justin	3/2/62		Haywards Heath, England	
Bychkov, Semyon	11/30/52		Leningrad, Soviet Union	1983
Christie, Michael	6/30/74	Buffalo, N.Y.		
Conlon, James	3/18/50	New York City, N.Y.		
Cooper, Grant	4/18/53		Wellington, New Zealand	
Cumming, Edward	8/10/57	Oakland, Calif.		
Davies, Dennis Russell	4/16/44	Toledo, Ohio		
Davis, Andrew	2/2/44		Ashridge, England	
Deal, Karen Lynne	5/7/57	Richmond, Va.		
Delfs, Andreas	8/30/59		Flensburg, Germany	
DePreist, James	11/21/36	Philadelphia, Pa.		
Diemecke, Enrique Arturo	7/9/55		Mexico City, Mexico	
Dohnanyi, Christoph von	9/8/29		Berlin, Germany	

Conductor	DOB	U.S. Birthplace	Non-U.S. Birthplace	Year Naturalized
Eschenbach, Christoph	2/20/49		Breslau, Germany	
Falletta, JoAnn	2/27/54	New York City, N.Y.		
Farberman, Harold	11/11/30	New York City, N.Y.		
Figueroa, Guillermo	4/5/53	Puerto Rico		
Foster, Lawrence	10/23/41	Los Angeles, Calif.		
Freeman, Paul	1/2/36	Richmond, Va.		
Gilbert, Alan	2/23/67	New York City, N.Y.		
Gittleman, Neal	6/29/55		Ancon, Panama	
Graf, Hans	2/15/49		Marchtrenk, Austria	
Hanson, George	1/24/58	Iowa City, Iowa		
Harth-Bedoya, Miguel	5/13/68		Lima, Peru	
Hege, Daniel	9/4/65	Denver, Colo.		
Ioannides, Sarah	4/2/72		Canberra, Australia	
Itkin, David	5/2/57	Portland, Ore.		
Jackson, Isaiah	1/22/45	Richmond, Va.		
Jansons, Mariss	1/14/43		Riga, Latvia	
Järvi, Kristjan	6/13/72		Tallinn, Estonia	
Järvi, Neeme	6/7/47		Tallinn, Estonia	1984
Järvi, Paavo	12/30/62		Tallinn, Estonia	
Jean, Kenneth	10/25/52	New York City, N.Y.		
Kahane, Jeffrey	9/12/56	Los Angeles, Calif.		
Kalmar, Carlos	2/26/58		Montevideo, Uruguay	
Kreizberg, Yakov	10/24/59		Leningrad, Soviet Union	
Lane, Louis	12/25/23	Eagle Pass, Tex.		
Levine, James	6/23/43	Cincinnati, Ohio		
Levine, Joel	6/26/48	Lakewood, N.J.		
Ling, Jahja	10/25/51		Jakarta, Indonesia	
Litton, Andrew	5/16/59	New York City, N.Y.		
Llewellyn, Grant	12/29/60		Tenby, Wales	
Lockhart, Keith	11/7/59	Poughkeepsie, N.Y.		
Lockington, David	10/11/56		Dartford, England	1997
Loebel, David	3/7/50	Cleveland, Ohio		
Maazel, Lorin	3/6/30		Paris, France	
Macal, Zdenek	1/8/36		Brno, Czechoslovakia	1986
Masur, Kurt	7/18/27		Brieg, Silesia, GDR	
Mechetti, Fabio	8/27/57		São Paulo, Brazil	
Mester, Jorge	4/10/35		Mexico City, Mexico	
Nagano, Kent	11/22/51	Berkeley, Calif.		
Nelson, John	12/6/41		San José, Costa Rica	
Oue, Eiji	10/3/56		Hiroshima, Japan	
Ozawa, Seiji	9/1/35		Fenytien, China	
Perick, Christof	10/23/46		Hamburg, Germany	
Preu, Eckart	8/24/69		Erfurt, GDR	
Previn, André	4/6/29		Berlin, Germany	
Prieto, Carlos Miguel	11/14/65		Mexico City, Mexico	
Rachleff, Larry	2/25/55	New London, Conn.		
Reischl, Bridget-Michaele	8/13/63	Lakewood, Calif.		
Richman, Lucas	1/31/64	Los Angeles, Calif.		
Robertson, David	7/19/58	Santa Monica, Calif.		

Conductor	DOB	U.S. Birthplace	Non-U.S. Birthplace	Year Naturalized
Runnicles, Donald	11/15/64		Edinburgh, Scotland	
Salonen, Esa-Pekka	6/30/58		Helsinki, Finland	
Sanderling, Stefan	2/8/64		East Berlin, GDR	
Sawallisch, Wolfgang	8/26/23		Munich, Germany	
Schermerhorn, Kenneth	11/20/29	Schenectady, N.Y.		
Schwarz, Gerard	8/19/47	Weehawken, N.J.		
Seaman, Christopher	3/7/42		Faversham, England	
Segal, Uriel	3/7/44		Jerusalem, Israel	
Sheffer, Jonathan	10/19/53	New York City, N.Y.		
Shimada, Toshiyuki	12/23/51		Tokyo, Japan	
Slatkin, Leonard	9/1/44	Los Angeles, Calif.		
Sloane, Steven	7/19/58	Los Angeles, Calif.		
Smith, Mark Russell	6/4/62	Phoenix, Ariz.		
Solzhenitsyn, Ignat	9/23/72		Moscow, Soviet Union	1985
Spano, Robert	5/7/61	Conneaup, Ohio		
St. Clair, Carl	6/5/52	Hochheim, Tex.		
Stern, Michael	12/12/59	New York City, N.Y.		
Summers, Patrick	8/14/63	Washington, Ind.		
Tchivzhel, Edvard	1/29/44		Leningrad, Soviet Union	1999
Temirkanov, Yuri	12/10/38		Nal'chik, Soviet Union	
Thomas, Michael Tilson	12/21/44	Los Angeles, Calif.		
Vänskä, Osmo	2/28/53		Sääminki, Finland	
Venzago, Mario	7/1/48		Zurich, Switzerland	
Vonk, Hans	6/18/942		Amsterdam, Holland	
Welser-Möst, Franz	8/16/60		Linz, Austria	
Wilkins, Christopher	5/28/57	Boston, Mass.		
Wilkins, Thomas	9/10/56	Norfolk, Va.		
Wolff, Hugh	10/21/53		Neuilly-sur-Seine, France	
Zander, Benjamin	3/9/39		Gerards Cross, England	
Zinman, David	7/10/36	New York City, N.Y.		

APPENDIX B

~

List of Orchestras

Tiers are established based on approximate budget size, according to the American Symphony Orchestra League's list of member institutions (published in *Symphony* magazine, January 2006). Tier 1 includes all orchestras whose budgets exceed $14,750,000. Tier 2 includes orchestras whose budgets lie between $5,550,000 and $14,750,000. Tier 3 includes orchestras whose budgets lie between $2,800,000 and $5,550,000.

An asterisk (*) denotes orchestras where the top position is not musical director (MD) but principal conductor. In addition to musical and artistic responsibilities such as planning the season, inviting guest conductors and soloists, and auditioning new players, musical directors usually have administrative, outreach, and fund-raising commitments. Principal conductors tend to concentrate on the artistic responsibilities. The top music position at the Pittsburgh SO has the title artistic advisor (**).

† For these orchestras, the musical director position is currently vacant; a musical director search is in progress.

†† These orchestras are self-governing cooperatives that only employ guest conductors.

Orchestra	Tier	Current MD	Past MD
Alabama Symphony Orchestra	2	Justin Brown 2006–	
American Symphony Orchestra	3	Leon Botstein 1992–	
Arkansas Symphony Orchestra	3	David Itkin 1993–	
Atlanta Symphony Orchestra	1	Robert Spano 2001–	Brott (1971)
Austin Symphony Orchestra	3	Peter Bay 1998–	
Baltimore Symphony Orchestra	1	Marin Alsop 2007–	Temirkanov (1999–2006)
			Zinman (1985–98)
Boston Symphony Orchestra	1	James Levine 2004–	Ozawa (1973–2002)
Buffalo Philharmonic Orchestra	2	JoAnn Falletta 1999–	Bychkov (1985–89)
			Thomas (1971–79)
Chamber Orchestra of Philadelphia	3	Ignat Solzhenitsyn 2004–	
Charlotte Symphony	2	Christof Perick 2001–	
Chicago Symphony Orchestra	1	†	Barenboim (1991–2006)
Cincinnati Symphony Orchestra	1	Paavo Järvi 2001–	
Cleveland Orchestra	1	Franz Welser-Möst 2002–	Maazel (1972–82)
			Dohnanyi (1984–2002)
Colorado Symphony Orchestra	2	Jeffrey Kahane 2005–	Alsop (1993–2004)
Dallas Symphony Orchestra	1	Jaap van Zweden 2008–	Litton (1994–2006)
			Lane (1975–77, acting)
Dayton Philharmonic Orchestra	3	Neal Gittleman 1995–	Jackson (1987–93)
Detroit Symphony Orchestra	1	†	N Järvi (1990–2005)
Florida Orchestra	2	Stefan Sanderling 2003–	Ling (1988–2002)
Florida West Coast Symphony	3	Leif Bjaland 1997–	
Fort Wayne Philharmonic Orchestra	3	Edvard Tchivzhel 1993–2008	
Fort Worth Symphony Orchestra	2	Miguel Harth-Bedoya 2000–	
Grand Rapids Symphony	2	David Lockington 1999–	Bychkov (1980–85)
Grant Park Orchestra and Chorus	3	Carlos Kalmar* 2000–	Wolff
			Slatkin
			Zinman
			Macal
Hartford Symphony Orchestra	3	Edward Cumming 2001–	
Honolulu Symphony Orchestra	2	Andreas Delfs* 2007–	
Houston Symphony	1	Hans Graf 2001–	Eschenbach (1988–99)
			Previn (1967–69)
Indianapolis Symphony Orchestra	1	Mario Venzago 2002–	Nelson (1976–87)
Jacksonville Symphony Orchestra	2	Fabio Mechetti 1999–	
Kansas City Symphony	2	Michael Stern 2005–	Mester (1973–79)
Knoxville Symphony Orchestra	3	Lucas Richman 2003–	
Long Beach Symphony Orchestra	3	Enrique Arturo 2001–	Falletta (1989–2000)
		Diemecke	
Los Angeles Chamber Orchestra	3	Jeffrey Kahane 1997–	Perick (1991–94)
			Schwarz (1977–85)
Los Angeles Philharmonic	1	Esa-Pekka Salonen 1992–2009	Previn (1985–89)
Louisiana Philharmonic Orchestra	3	Carlos Miguel Prieto 2006–	
Louisville Orchestra	2	Jorge Mester 1967–79, 2006–	Segal (1998–2004)
Memphis Symphony Orchestra	3	David Loebel 1999–	
Milwaukee Symphony Orchestra	1	Andreas Delfs 1997–2009	Macal (1986–95)
			Schermerhorn (1968–80)
Minnesota Orchestra	1	Osmo Vänskä 2003–	Oue (1995–2002)
Naples Philharmonic	2	Jorge Mester 2004–	Seaman (1993–2004)

Orchestra	Tier	Current MD	Past MD
Nashville Symphony	2	†	Schermerhorn (1983–2005)
National Symphony Orchestra	1	Leonard Slatkin 1996–	
New Jersey Symphony Orchestra	1	Neeme Järvi 2005–	Macal (1993–2002) Wolff (1985–91) Schermerhorn (1963–68)
New Mexico Symphony Orchestra	3	Guillermo Figueroa 2001–	Lockington (1995–2000)
New York Philharmonic	1	Lorin Maazel 2002–9	Masur (1991–2002)
North Carolina Symphony	2	Grant Llewellyn 2004–	
Oklahoma City Philharmonic	3	Joel Levine 1988–	
Omaha Symphony	3	Thomas Wilkins 2005–	
Orchestra of St. Luke's	3	Donald Runnicles* 2001–	
Oregon Symphony	1	Carlos Kalmar 2003–	DePreist (1980–2003)
Orpheus Chamber Orchestra	2	††	
Pacific Symphony	2	Carl St. Clair 1990–	
Philadelphia Orchestra	1	Christoph 2003– Eschenbach	Sawallisch (1993–2003)
Phoenix Symphony	2	Michael Christie 2005–	
Pittsburgh Symphony Orchestra	1	Sir Andrew Davis** 2005–	Jansons (1997–2004) Maazel (1988–96) Previn (1976–84)
Portland Symphony Orchestra	3	Robert A. Moody 2008–	Shimada (1986–2006)
Puerto Rico Symphony Orchestra	3	Guillermo Figueroa 2001–7	
Rhode Island Philharmonic	3	Larry Rachleff 1996–	
Richmond Symphony	3	Mark Russell Smith 1999–	
Rochester Philharmonic Orchestra	2	Christopher Seaman 1998–	Zinman (1974–85)
Saint Louis Symphony Orchestra	1	David Robertson 2005–	Vonk (1996–2002) Slatkin (1979–96)
Saint Paul Chamber Orchestra	1	††	Delfs (2001–4) Wolff (1992–2000) Davies (1972–80)
San Antonio Symphony	2	Larry Rachleff 2004–8	C. Wilkins (1991–2000)
San Diego Symphony	2	Jahja Ling 2004–	
San Francisco Symphony	1	Michael Tilson 1995– Thomas	Blomstedt (1985–95) Ozawa (1969–76)
Seattle Symphony	1	Gerard Schwarz 1985–	
Spokane Symphony Orchestra	3	Eckart Preu 2004–	Mechetti (1993–2004)
Syracuse Symphony Orchestra	2	Daniel Hege 1999–	Mechetti (1993–99)
Toledo Symphony	2	Stefan Sanderling* 2003–	
Tucson Symphony Orchestra	3	George Hanson 1996–	
Tulsa Symphony Orchestra	2	†	Jean (1997–2000)
Utah Symphony & Opera	1	Keith Lockhart 1998–	
Virginia Symphony	3	JoAnn Falletta 1991–	
West Virginia Symphony Orchestra	3	Grant Cooper 2001–	

Index

Note: Bold page numbers refer to the conductor's entry.

Akiyama, Kazuyoshi, 191
Akron Symphony Orchestra, 132, 152, 284
Akron School of Music, 152
Akron Youth Symphony Orchestra, 152
Alabama Symphony Orchestra, 15, 33, 104, 156, 170
Albert, Stephen, 142, 292; works of, 303
Algarve Symphony Orchestra, 16
All-Soviet Conducting Competition, 260, 264
Aller, Eleanor, 238
Allesandro, Raffaele d': Piano Concerto No. 3, 276; Symphony No. 1, 276
Allison, John, 38
Alsop, Marin, xiii, xiv, **2–5**, 25
Altenburg Opera, 195
Amado, David, **5–6**
American Academy of Arts and Letters, 234
American Academy of Conducting (Aspen), xii, 302, 325
American Ballet Theatre, 235, 224
American Brass Quintet, 227
American Classical Music Hall of Fame, 241
American Composers Orchestra, 49, 73, 172, 244
American Conductors Program, 15, 20
American National Orchestral Association Award, 42
American Record Guide, 12, 38, 51, 77, 84, 92, 161, 163, 168, 173, 177, 181, 184, 185, 187, 191, 220, 235, 265, 269, 275, 285, 293, 303
American Russian Youth Orchestra, 28, 292
American Symphony Orchestra, 3, 28, 29,79, 106, 172, 195, 227, 298
American Symphony Orchestra League (now League of American Orchestras), xvii, 39, 63, 78, 82,

102, 152; Conducting Workshop, 157; Conductors Guild, xii, 82, 201, 286; Helen M. Thompson Award, 39, 91; Summer Institute, 13
American Russian Young Artists Orchestra, 121, 195
American-Soviet Youth Orchestra, 201
Amram, David, works of, 224; Symphony, 285
Amsterdam Conservatory of Music, 277
Ancerl, Karel, 53
Anchorage (Alaska) Festival of Music, 46
Anchorage Symphony Orchestra, 93, 97, 157, 248
Anderson, Colin, 121
Anderson, Leroy, works of, 154
Anderson, Marian, 64
Andrew Wolf Chamber Music Award, 125
Anhaltisches Theater (Dessau), 127
Ann Arbor Symphony Orchestra, 252
Annapolis Symphony Orchestra, 15, 18, 58, 103
Annenberg School of Communications, 64
Ansbacher, Charles, **6–7**
Antheil, George, works of, 270; *Capital of the World: Suite*, 294; *Hot-Time Dance*, 294; *A Jazz Symphony*, 188, 289; *McKonkey's Ferry Overture*, 294; Piano Concerto No. 1, 188; Piano Concerto No. 2, 188; Symphony No. 1, 293; Symphony No. 3, 294; Symphony No. 6, 293; *Tom Sawyer Overture*, 294
Anthony, Michael, 186, 187
Anton Bruckner Prize, 24
Antonio Pedrotti International Competition for Orchestra Conductors, 203
Apone, Carl, 26
Arasimowicz, George, works of, 184

Brown, Steven, 124
Bruch, Max, works of, 44; *Schön Ellen*,
97; *Schwedische Tänze*, 97; *Serenade
for Strings*, 97; Symphony No. 2, 176
Bruck, Charles, 254, 290
Bruckner Conservatory (Linz), 95
Bruckner, Anton, works of, 23, 50, 70,
141, 222, 276, 278, 279, 281, 298;
Symphony No. 2, 74; Symphony No.
3, 75, 180; Symphony No. 4, 216;
Symphony No. 6, 72; Symphony No.
7, 131, 279, 280; Symphony No. 8,
51, 283
Brückner-Rüggeberg, Wilhelm, 75, 193
Bruno Walter Memorial Scholarship, 6,
60, 79, 102, 144
Buchau, S. von, 212
Budapest Symphony Orchestra, 200
Buenos Aires Philharmonia, 99
Buenos Aires Philharmonic of the
Teatro Colon, 67
Buffalo Philharmonic Orchestra, 35, 36,
47–48, 79, 81, 93, 94, 158, 170, 173,
175, 187, 267, 270
Bunkamura Orchard Hall Award, 91
Burgin, Richard, 224
Burkhard, Willy, works of, 276
Burr, Ramiro, 285
Burton, Tim, 215
Burton, William Westbrook, 34
Busch, Fritz, 54
Bush, George W., 66
Busoni, Ferrucio, works of, 178
Butler, William, 287
Butterly, Nigel, works of, 106
Butterworth, George: *2 English Idylls*,
150; *A Shropshire Lad*, 150; *Banks of
Green Willow*, 150
Bychkov, Semyon, xx, **35–38**, 79, 128

Cabrillo Music Festival, 1, 3, 25, 49
Cage, John, 22, 51; works of, 213, 266,
269

Caldwell, Michael, 230
Caldwell, Sarah, 132, 178
Calgary Philharmonic Orchestra, 94,
96, 150, 158, 200
Callas, Maria, 42
Cambiata Soloists, 236
Cambridge University, 33, 53, 149, 210;
Bach Society, 8; King's College, 52,
53, 231; Purcell Society, 149
Camerata Salzburg, 126
Campbell, K., 93
Campbell, R. M., 230
Canadian Brass, 31
Canadian Opera Company, 32
Canterbury Cathedral Choir School,
231
Cape Town Symphony Orchestra, 175
Caramoor Festival, 183
Carbon, John, works of, 5
Cargile, Ozie, works of, 287
Carl Nielsen Prize, 24
Carlson, David, *Quantumsymphony*, 21
Carlton College, 16
Carnegie Hall, 35, 36, 78, 79, 80, 83,
101, 111, 122, 129, 144, 147, 177,
182, 184, 208, 222, 224, 225, 239,
271, 291, 297
Carnegie Opera Theater (Cincinnati),
16
Carnegie-Mellon University, 152
Carpenter, Clinton, 82
Carter, Elliott, works of, 23, 136, 215,
224: Concerto for Violin, 34;
Holiday Overture, 226; *Lauds*, 34;
Piano Concerto, 224, 226;
Symphony No. 1, 224, 226
Caruso, Enrico, 258
Carvalho, Eleazer de, 82
Casals Festival Orchestra, 227
Casals Festival (Puerto Rico), 172
Cassado, Gaspar, 296
Cassilly, Richard, 182
Castiglioni, Niccolo, 213

Krauss, Clemens, 220
Krefeld-Mönchengladbach Opera, 129
Kreizberg, Yakov, xx, **128–131**
Krenek, Ernst, works of, 33, 130
Krips, Josef, 79
Kubelik, Raphael, 35, 134, 183
Kunzel, Erich, 16, 153
Kupferberg, Herbert, 12, 38, 51, 168
Kupferman, Meyer, works of, 28, 89;
    Concerto for 2 Clarinets, 90; *Icon
    Symphony*, 90
Kurka, Robert, works of, 127; *Julius
    Caesar*, 128; *Music for Orchestra*,
    128; *Serenade for Small Orchestra*,
    128; Symphony No. 2, 128
Kwak, Sung, 79

La Salle Quartet, 133
La Scala (Milan), 43, 56, 120, 144, 159,
    179, 209, 277
Lackmeyer, Steve, 138
Lademan, Ezra, works of, 176
LaGuardia High School of Music and
    Art and Performing Arts (NYC). *See*
    High School of Music and Arts
Lahti Symphony Orchestra, 34, 272, 273
Lake Erie Opera Theater, 154
Lake Forest Symphony Orchestra, 104
Lakehead Symphony Orchestra, 30
Lakehead University, 30
Landesmusikschule (Breslau), 166
Landessinfonieorchester Gotha, 196
Landestheater (Halle), 166
Landowski, Marcel, *Galina*, 185
Lane, Chester, 185
Lane, Louis, **131–132**
Larsen, Catherine, 202
Larsen, Libby, works of, 124, 142
Las Vegas Philharmonic Orchestra, 104
Laurel de Oro a la Calidad, 67
Lauridsen, Morten, works of, 150
Lausanne Chamber Orchestra, 40, 85,
    175

Lausanne Opera, 244
Law, Andrew, works of, 226
Lawrence Symphony Orchestra, 203
Lawrence University Conservatory of
    Music, 203, 204
Le, Khoa Van, *Symphonic Ode to
    Vietnam, 1975*, 47
League of American Orchestras. *See*
    American Symphony Orchestra
    League
Lear, Evelyn, 182
LeBaron, Anne, works of, 172
Lebrecht, Norman, xiv, xvi, xxi, 108
Leeds Conductors' Competition, 149
Leem, Jinny, 193
Lees, Benjamin, *Passacaglia*, 66
Leese, Michael, *Music for harp,
    percussion and strings*, 206
Lehár, Franz: *Der Rastelbinder*, 96
Die lustige Witwe, 99, 282, 283
Leifs, Jon, Symphony No. 1, 273
Leinsdorf, Erich, 129
Leipzig City Theater, 166
Leipzig Conservatory, 167
Leipzig Gewandhaus Orchestra, 24, 95,
    130, 141, 167, 168, 276, 303
Leister, Karl, 272
Lemba, Artur, works of, 115
Lener Quartet, 170
Leningrad Conservatory, 36, 107, 115,
    260. *See also* St. Petersburg
    Conservatory
Leningrad Phiharmonic Orchestra. *See*
    St. Petersburg Philharmonic
    Orchestra
Leningrad School for Talented
    Children, 264
Leningrad Symphony Orchestra. *See* St.
    Petersburg Symphony Orchestra
Leonard Bernstein Conducting
    Fellowship, 3
Leoncavallo, Ruggero, *I Pagliacci*, 42,
    61, 86

~

About the Authors

Roderick L. Sharpe was born near Nottingham, England, and graduated from the Royal Academy of Music in London, having been a cello student of Muriel Taylor. He worked as a music teacher and freelance cellist; he was director of ensembles for the City of Sheffield Instrumental Music Service and a founding member of the Cavendish Ensemble. During the 1980s he collaborated extensively with the eminent Anglo-Hungarian violin teacher Kato Havas. From 1983 to 1987 he was music director of the Oxford Sinfonia CO and conductor of the International Festival Orchestra of Oxford.

He obtained an MM degree in orchestral conducting from Drake University, where he studied under John Canarina. During this time he was conductor of the Des Moines Community Orchestra and guest conductor of the Southeast Iowa SO.

A back injury resulted in the decision to embark on a new career path as a librarian and he received an MLS from the University of Iowa. He spent ten years as access services librarian at Western Illinois University before becoming music librarian in 2006. His research interests focus on the role of orchestral concert-giving in the twenty-first century, and he maintains a website devoted to the Austrian tenor Julius Patzak.

Jeanne Koekkoek Stierman is a professor and reference librarian at Western Illinois University in Macomb, Illinois. She graduated from Dordt College in 1984, earning her BA in accounting and business administration. In 1986 she was awarded an MBA and in 1987 completed an MLA, both from the

University of Iowa. Jeanne was public services librarian for business and economics at Ithaca College in New York from 1987 to 1990, before joining the WIU faculty in 1991. Her musical training includes piano, timpani, and voice. She studied piano under Goldie De Jong, Dr. Noel Magee, Dr. Garrett Allman, Brent Assink, and Joan Crull, and plays regularly for church services. Jeanne studied voice with Dr. Gary Warmink and sang soprano in the Dordt College Concert Choir for four years under the direction of Mr. Dale Grotenhuis. She continues to do solo work and sing in the Chancel Choir at her church.